W9-BBC-872

Throw
fire

Throw fire

by Fr. John Fuellenbach, SVD

June 10, 1998
Manila

First Edition, 1997
Second Revised Edition, 1998
Reprinted, 1999
Fourth Printing, 2000
Fifth Printing, 2001
Sixth Printing, 2002
Seventh Printing, 2003
Eight Printing, 2004

The National Library of the Philippines CIP Data

Recommended entry:

Fuellenbach, John.
   Throw Fire / John Fuellenbach - Manila
Logos Pub., c1998
   347 p. ; 23 cm

   1. Christian life I. Title

BV4495 248.4 2004 PO41000444
ISBN 971-510-116-X

The Society of the Divine Word (SVD) is an international missionary congregation of priests and brothers serving in more than fifty countries all over the world. Through the Logos Publications, the SVD in the Philippines aims to foster the apostolate of the printed word in the biblical, theological, catechetical and pastoral fields in order to promote the inculturation of the Christian faith into the Filipino way of life. The opinions expressed by the author do not necessarily reflect those of the SVD community.

Copyright © 1998 Society of the Divine Word
Published by LOGOS Publications, Inc.
All Rights Reserved
Printed in the Philippines

ISBN: 971-510-116-X

Cover artwork by: Paul Schaefer

Contents

Foreword to the Second Edition

Since the first edition sold out within six month, we decided to publish a new edition rather than reprint the first one. In this way some necessary editing could be done. At the end of the reflections a number of questions were rephrased and new stories were included while others were replaced. Furthermore, two more chapters were added: one on the *Holy Sprit* and, as a conclusion to the book, the *Our Father*.

A special word of thanks goes to Fr. John Donaghey SVD, who with great dedication and skill read through the whole text, made the necessary corrections and did the final editing.

Since we are celebrating the Year of the Holy Spirit, I pray that *the Spirit's fire enkindle* the hearts of those who read this book.

Rome, Pentecost 1998

Preface

"I have come to throw fire on the earth and how much I desire to see it burning" *(Lk 12:49).* This is called Jesus' view of reality and the understanding of his mission. This book is about the vision, which Jesus expressed with his two most authentic words: ABBA and *Kingdom of God.*

Over the last 25 years I have given the content of this book to various groups of people, but mostly to priests, religious and lay-people who took part in renewal or pastoral programs, often called theological updating. Most of the people had a vast missionary or pastoral experience. Many had lost their enthusiasm for the Kingdom because of fatigue, overwork, or disappointments in their ministry. They were worn out; in short, the fire had been extinguished and was no longer enkindling their zeal.

It all started with an experience when I was the director of our International Renewal Center in Nemi near Rome. We had an excellent updating program based on a vast variety of topics related to the different fields of theology. But soon I came to realize that the participants' greatest need was to be *recaptured* by the vision of Jesus. That alone would fill them with a renewed sense of joy and purpose. It had the power to convince them again that their commitment to God's Kingdom was their best choice, even if at the time of the renewal they felt weary and far from their original zeal and enthusiasm. The question was how to set them on fire once again.

The book is an attempt to present the message of Jesus in order to rekindle the fire in those who have been disciples of Jesus for many years. But also, it wants to reach those who are unsure of what a commitment to Jesus' vision involves in our time.

Most of the contents of this book are also found in the two other books I wrote: *Proclaiming His Kingdom* and the *Kingdom of God, Jesus' Message for today*. But the difference is that in this book, I had to make the text more spiritual and pastoral so that it would help people in their struggle for a renewed commitment to the Lord. Therefore, the stories in the text and the reflections at the end of each chapter aim to challenge the reader to a personal stand on the issues discussed. This approach, as I used in the course had proven helpful in different places: Bombay, Manila, Bangkok, South Africa, Quito, Rome, Germany, France, Ireland, Canada, and the USA. Those who responded most enthusiastically were people who often claimed that they, for the first time, understood what Jesus was all about.

The first four chapters deal with Jesus' vision of who God really is. The foundational reality of our Christian faith is: the God who loves us unconditionally, who forgives us always and opens to us a future full of hope, is always with us no matter at what point we are in our lives. This should always be the starting point for our self-understanding and the understanding of our mission. This God-image is the newness of Jesus' message. When the disciple shares this vision of Jesus, he/she will be compelled to make this vision the basis of his/her mission as well.

The remaining chapters of the book describe what this vision means for the disciple and how the message has to be preached and communicated today. In other words, the book speaks about discipleship, the call to follow the Lord. Those who dare to follow will go out to *"throw fire"* as the master did. They will tell people who God is and what he has in store for them and the whole of creation. The book wants to rekindle the enthusiasm that drove the first disciples, just as St. Paul describes his own vocation:

I, who am less than the least of all God's holy people, have been entrusted with this special grace, of proclaiming to the nations the unfathomable treasure of Christ and of throwing light on the inner workings of the mystery kept hidden through all the ages in God, the Creator of everything (Ep 3:8-9).

All I hope and pray for is that these pages may inspire those who read them with the fire that Jesus came to throw into this world (Lk 12:49) and which he so ardently wanted to see burning.

Acknowledgment

The content of this book grew out of study, reflection and prayer, but foremost out of many encounters with people deeply committed to Christ and his mission. They were my most valuable source of inspiration. I cannot list them all here, but to them I owe a word of thanks and acknowledgment.

Special thanks, however, go to Sister Christel Daun, S.Sp.S., who more than any one else worked with me to bring the book to completion. Her constant search for stories and her hard work to make the reflections after each chapter challenging are a real asset to the book. Besides all the manuscript checking and rechecking that she did she was also the person who constantly encouraged me to finish the work and to make it available to a broader readership.

I dedicate this book to those who have supported me with their prayer, their constant interest in my work and the suffering they perceive as their mission. They know whom I mean. Their contribution not only makes the message reach the minds and hearts of the readers but, through the strength of the Holy Spirit, also sets them on fire with the vision of Jesus.

Rome, Pentecost 1997

Fr. John Fuellenbach , SVD

Chapter One

Called to Follow Jesus who Revealed God as Abba

Let me start with a simple question: What does it mean to be a Christian? There is an innate tendency in human beings to summarize and to synthesize everything, to put it in a nutshell. A painter wants to portray all he sees and imagines in one single painting, the masterpiece of his life. Poets dream and labor for the one poem that would contain all they feel deep in their being and try to express this truth in such a way that everyone might comprehend it immediately.

Is there a phrase in the Gospels that equally contains everything that Jesus came to communicate? There is indeed one phrase that occurs frequently in the utterances of Jesus. It is the simple demand: FOLLOW ME.

These two words contain in a nutshell what God wants of us, and what we should regard as the ultimate obligation we have towards God in this life. The phrase appears twenty times in the Gospels. Therefore, we have to conclude that to be a Christian means to follow the Lord.

Discipleship: a call to follow the Lord "who walked this earth".

The Council told us that the following and imitation of Christ is the determining occupation and pattern of life for all Christians, and with regards to religious the Council says:

> *Since the fundamental norm of the religious life is a following of Christ as proposed by the gospel, such is to be regarded by all communities as their supreme law (Perfectae Caritatis 2).*

In other words, the Council is stating here that the pattern to be followed and the standard by which everything must be measured is *the Jesus who walked this earth*. We are called to follow the Jesus who lived our life and who suffered our death. His actions, his behavior and his attitudes are the pattern to be followed by everyone who calls himself/herself a disciple of Jesus.

Following the Jesus *who walked this earth* not only in theory but also in practice will give us the needed answer to three important questions: Who am I as a Christian? Who are we as Church community? Who is Jesus really? There is actually no other adequate way to answer these.

Latin American theologians in particular have pointed out that most Christologies deal in length with the incarnation of Christ and develop their Christology from there; others put all the stress on the death and resurrection of Christ and unfold their Christology from there. What is missing - so the argument goes - is a theology of the Jesus who walked over this earth, his adult activities. In their own words: if one reads the common Christologies one gets the impression that Jesus was born and died but he apparently never lived. It is not as if these theologians do not deal with Jesus' public ministry; it is rather that they see and evaluate it only from its beginning and from its end point. The Liberation theologians, too, are not so naive as to presume that we can reach the Jesus "who walked this earth" directly through the Gospels, as if these were historical records about the life of Jesus.

Not only Liberation theologians but also contemporary biblical scholars in general, when studying the Gospels, accord first rate importance to the ministry of Jesus. It is interesting that for centuries, Catholic Christology did not deal very extensively with Jesus' adult activities but focused its attention on his birth and death. Elizabeth Johnson remarks concerning this observation: "If you doubt this, just think of the traditional mysteries of the Rosary, where meditation skips from the joyful to the sorrowful mysteries without lingering over what happened in between" (E. Johnson, *Consider Jesus*, p.50).

The underlying motivation of such attention to the earthly ministry of Jesus is this - if God became a human being, then it is very important to see what kind of human being God became. What matters are Jesus' concrete actions. They embody the way God envisages our way of discipleship in this world today. The stress is therefore on doing what Jesus did and behaving as he behaved if we have to understand this man at all. The use of discipleship imagery is associated with the attempt to stress on the active practice of following Jesus - orthopraxy - vis-a-vis orthodoxy as the more adequate method of coming to an understanding of who Jesus is (P. A. Schoelles, *"Liberation Theology and Discipleship"*, p. 50).

The claim is, there is no other way to know Christ and to understand oneself as a disciple of his than to follow him.

> Every attempt to know Christ, to understand him is therefore always a journey, a following. It is only by following and imitating him that we know whom we are dealing with. Following Christ is not just a subsequent application of the Church's Christology to our life: the practice of following Christ is itself a central part of Christology, if we do not wish to identify the logic of this Christology and of Christianity in general with the purely contemplative logos of the Greek (J. B. Metz, *Followers of Christ*, p. 39).

Or in the words of Jon Sobrino:

> The positive assertion that I wish to make here is that the following of Jesus is both the concrete embodiment of Christian life as well as that which makes it possible for Christians to know Jesus precisely as the Son. Looking at the concrete lifestyle of Jesus, we must first consider the special relationship between orthodoxy and orthopraxis ... Jesus did not disdain orthodoxy. The problem he faced in life was not that of choosing between orthodoxy and heresy, but that of choosing between an abstract orthodoxy and a concrete orthodoxy. For Jesus it was impossible to concretize his orthodoxy simply by pondering orthodoxy intellectually. It could only be concretized through a concrete praxis (J. Sobrino, *Christology at the Crossroad*, pp.389-390).

If we look back at the history of our Christian faith, we can detect that most often it was discipleship language and imagery that saved theology from an exaggerated concern for abstract truth or an almost exclusive identification of Christian convictions with adherence to intellectual or propositional formulae. Already in the early writings of the Christian martyrs, the emphasis was on the practical living of faith over a more intellectualized understanding of it. It was the model of the historical Jesus who encouraged them and gave meaning to their martyrdom. The Reformers once again refer to discipleship in their concern to emphasize the concrete living of the Gospel over a preoccupation with speculative theology.

> So going back to the historical Jesus does not mean wanting to know more about him, but wanting to know him better. Knowing Christ - and not just knowing more about him - is something we achieve not intellectually, but in doing. We know him to the extent that we understand what he did through experience, and by assimilating this and making it ours, we come to be more fully in tune with his cause and his person, which complement one another. We believe that what Jesus did is what provides access to the whole of him, what enables us to shed light on him, understanding better, and judge the importance of other aspects that go to make up the whole: isolated incidents from his life, his teaching, his inner disposition, his fate and what we might call his personality. The best setting for really knowing Jesus is simply carrying out what he did, following him. (P. Casaldaliga and J. M. Vigil, *Political Holiness*, p. 65).

Individual Identity: Who am I as a Christian?

Discipleship as seen in the Gospels means literally walking in Jesus' footsteps. It is a symbol by which I can focus on and understand myself as a Christian. It gives me an identity. It tells me who I am and what I am striving for in this life. According to discipleship imagery, this basic identity is constructed in terms of being called by Jesus and following him, living in companionship with him and sharing in his mission of serving the inauguration of the Kingdom (Mk 1:16-20; Mt 9:9; Lk 5:27-28; Mt 8:20ff.; Lk 9:57-62).This is seen as a response to a call for which one may not be prepared. It is the Lord who calls and he invites not on the basis of skills or merits but on the basis of his love for me.

Discipleship emphasizes our granting the first place over all other loyalties, claims and commitments to Jesus (Mt 8:21-22; Jn 15:15,18; Mk 10:21ff.), and more often than not involves suffering (Mt 10:38,16:24; Lk 14:27).

In the light of the *image crisis* of the Church today, Avery Dulles proposes a new conception of the Church which he calls *Community of Disciples*. Behind this image we find again an expression of the newly discovered realization that the basic vocation of any Christian is first and foremost to follow the Lord as he walked on this earth. The emphasis here is on following the Lord rather than following the Church, on being constantly on the road rather than having already reached the goal. The Church must be seen as the community of those who have made it their life's profession to follow the Lord and as such to build a community called Church (A. Dulles, *A Church to Believe In*, pp. 1-18).

Community identity: Who are we as Church Community?

Discipleship does not only provide a foundation for the subjective self-understanding of the individual Christian in the Church community, but it also furnishes an objective identification for Christians and their Churches. By supplying their primary "identity-image," discipleship refers Christians to their fundamental chart of meaning and the ultimate basis of their standards of judgement. In addition, we can see that in the history of the Church, the return to discipleship as an identity-image has been a powerful tool for urging reform within the Church. This aspect is essential for the "revival of Church life."

Metz uses discipleship as a reforming image for the life of the Church, relying on the identity-instilling capacity of the imagery of following Jesus to call the Church back to its origins and authentic life and mission.

> The church... cannot solve the crisis of its historical identity and its societal legitimation in a purely interpretative or hermeneutical manner, but only by practical identification. The problem of its identity is fundamentally a theory-praxis problem. That praxis whose intelligible and identity-securing power cannot be replaced by interpretation is called discipleship. The church's crisis

is due to a deficit in discipleship and to difficulties in adapting to Jesus (J. B. Metz, "For a RenewedChurch before a New Council: A Concept in Four Theses", p. 139).

The most salient sentence in this quotation is the last one concerning the crisis in the Church today. As early as 1968 the German Bishops' Conference, assessing the situation of the Church in Germany and looking for an appropriate response to the then emerging faith crisis in the country, proposed a solution that echoed the words of J. B. Metz: "The way out of the situation in which we find ourselves today can only be once again a way into fellowship with Jesus the Lord." Today, almost thirty years, later the crisis has heightened, and the response proposed at that time seems to be even more urgent now: "the way out ... can only be a way into following the Jesus who walked this earth."

The bishops, looking at their Churches, found it necessary to stress the following 'signposts' to discipleship: *the obedience of the cross, poverty, freedom and joy* - attitudes and behaviors that counted so high in Jesus' own life. The bishops then confess, that their Churches portray, a 'religion of prosperity' rather than a 'religion of the cross'; a 'rich Church' rather than a Church in solidarity with the poor and weak; a Church anxiously holding back from the risk of the freedom of the Gospel rather than going on the offensive; and finally a Church which looked anxiously inward rather than radiating the joy of the redeemed. They felt the urgent need to return to the root of our commitment, the Jesus who walked the earth and died for a vision that the world today needs very badly.

Who is Jesus really?

Biographical notes

Jesus' public life was very brief: one year or maybe two and a half. Moses led his people for forty years; Buddha taught for forty-five years after his enlightenment and Muhammed for about twenty years. Jesus' ministry, in comparison, was a light flashing momentarily but brilliantly like a meteor in the night sky. Who was this Jesus of Nazareth? (*identity*) What was central to his proclamation and teaching? (*message)* What was his purpose? What did he himself hope to accomplish? (*mission)*

Historically we can establish only the following facts: he was born around the year 7 or 6 B.C. and grew up in Nazareth in Galilee, a town of around 200 to 2000 people. He probably became a woodworker (*tekton* in

Greek). As such he worked on such things as doors, door frames, roof beams, furniture, cabinets, boxes, even yokes and ploughs. This also determined his social standing. As such he

> was at the lower end of the peasant class, more marginalized than a peasant who still owned a small piece of land. We should not think of *a tekton* as being a step up from a subsistence farmer; rather, a *tekton* belonged to a family that had lost its land (M.J. Borg, *Meeting Jesus*, p. 26).

In his late twenties, Jesus left his profession and his hometown and became a follower of John the Baptist. From this we can surmise that he had had a religious experience that had changed his whole life. The relationship to John was important for Jesus as the Gospel stories indicate. But he later separated himself from John and became an itinerant preacher. He was likely able to read and write Aramaic and Hebrew and might also have known some Greek. He showed remarkable verbal gifts as his parables and debating skills reveal. In facing the prospect of being put aside like his mentor John the Baptist, Jesus revealed great courage in holding on to his vision no matter what it would cost. He was a remarkable healer:

> more healing stories are told about him than about anybody else in the Jewish tradition. He attracted a following, including people who left their previous life behind, and any sketch of Jesus with a claim to historical credibility must account for this fact. There must have been something quite compelling about him. He also attracted enemies, especially among the rich and powerful (M. J. Borg, *Meeting Jesus*, p. 31).

He was put to death by the powerful elite and died by crucifixion around 30 A.D.

The vision of Jesus: "I came to throw fire on this earth"

What was it that Jesus communicated so powerfully that people felt as if they had been under a spell and left everything to follow this man from Nazareth? Jesus himself expressed his mission in these words:

> *I came to throw fire on this earth and how much I desire to see it burning (Lk 12:49).*

> *Do you suppose that I was sent to bring peace on earth? No, I tell you, but rather division (12:51).*

> *The Kingdom of God does not consist in spoken words but in power (DYNAMIS) (1 Cor 4:20).*

By vision we mean something to live for, to suffer for, to work for and ultimately to die for; something one cannot keep to oneself; something one is so caught up with that one has to communicate it, let it out, spread it.

Where there is no vision the people perish (Proverbs).

What is this FIRE, this DYNAMITE Jesus came to throw into this world and with which he himself was apparently burning? Both words are symbols. What do they stand for? What does it mean to say, "Jesus' message is fire and dynamite?" What did Jesus want to say with the symbol of fire? This much is sure, fire and dynamite indicate something dangerous, revolutionary, not leaving things as they are. Jesus' message is not just an idea, not even a grand idea which one can store with many other ideas without it affecting any change in one's life. On the contrary, his vision aims at transformation. It has a revolutionary thrust as the phrase that follows in 12:52 indicates, *"I did not come to bring peace but division."* Jesus is saying: "Do not think that I came to leave you in peace, no, I came to disturb, to upset and to change things. The world will never be the same after I have thrown my fire on it."

Jesus - a man "on fire" with the Spirit

We could say that, in line with other great religious figures, Jesus was a man of the Spirit, a charismatic figure. The term 'charismatic' means a person who is in touch with the power of the Spirit and who becomes a channel for this same power to enter the world of ordinary experience. People were amazed at him; they were astonished by his teaching. He was seen as one of the great in Israel: Elijah or John the Baptist. As a man of the Spirit, Jesus had an intense relationship with the world of the Spirit, with that other reality, sometimes spoken of as the sacred, or the holy, or the other world, or simply as God. This relationship was the source of his power and teaching, his freedom, courage, and compassion. It was the driving force behind his mission to the culture and society of his day. In the words of M. J. Borg:

> The most crucial fact about Jesus was that he was a "spirit person," a "mediator of the sacred," one of those persons in human history to whom the Spirit was an experiential reality (*Meeting Jesus*, pp. 31-32).

Luke records this Spirit-experience of Jesus in his Gospel quite dramatically in the "inaugural address" of Jesus' ministry which we find in 4:16-21: *The Spirit of the Lord is upon me.* At the center of Jesus' life was a profound and continuous relationship with the Spirit of God.

All four Gospels, but particularly Luke, testify to Jesus as being a man of the Spirit. From the very beginning he is uniquely a man of the Spirit, even by origin, so that he is "holy, the Son of God" (Lk 1:35). While John the Baptist is "filled with the Holy Spirit" (Lk 1:15), Jesus is "conceived by the Holy Spirit" (Lk 1:35). In his baptism by John, Jesus receives a special bestowal of the Holy Spirit to such a degree that John characterizes Jesus as "the baptizer with the Holy Spirit" (Jn 1:33). In his public life Jesus "is driven by the Holy Spirit" (Mk 1:12); he prays in the Holy Spirit (Lk 5:16, 6:12); he "overflows with joy in the Holy Spirit" (Lk 10:21); he drives out demons by the "power of the Holy Spirit" (Mt 12:28); he heals the sick through "the power that is in him" (Lk 5:17). How strong this power *that goes out from him* can be is shown in the story of the woman who touched his cloak from behind (Lk 8:43-48; Mk 5:25-34).

In his three-fold pattern of salvation history, Luke portrays the relationship of Jesus and the Spirit in the following way: In his first stage, Jesus is the *creation of the Spirit* (Lk 1:35). At the Jordan (second stage) Jesus becomes the uniquely anointed *Man of the Spirit* (3:22). In the third stage, his exaltation, Jesus becomes the *Lord of the Spirit* and *Baptizer of the Spirit* (Acts 2:23). The same three-epoch pattern is also found in Mark and Matthew. As in Luke, Jesus is the *creation of the Spirit*, the *unique bearer of the Spirit* and the *future dispenser of the Spirit* (James D.G. Dunn, "Spirit and Kingdom", *The Expository Times* 32 (1970-71) 38-39).

The way Jesus called his disciples revealed an almost irresistible power flowing from him. Though it was relatively common within Judaism for a teacher to have devoted students, the phenomenon of discipleship as presented in the Gospels is different and rather uncommon; it involves an uprooting and a close following. The stories of the call of the disciples describe with compact vividness the imperative of Jesus' call, the immediacy of the disciples' response, and the radical break from their previous lives. When Jesus called Peter and Andrew he just said to them, *"Come with me, and I will teach you to catch people." At once they left their nets and went with him"* (Mk 1:17-18). When he called the two brothers James and John the text simply says: *"As soon as Jesus saw them, he called them; they left their father Zebedee in the boat with the hired men and went with Jesus"* (19-20).

Jesus - a social prophet: "Compassion I want not sacrifice!"

Besides being a *Spirit person*, one of those figures in human history with an exceptional awareness of the reality of God, Jesus was a *social prophet* similar to the prophets of ancient Israel. As such, he criticized the elite (economic, political and religious) of his time, was an advocate of an alternative social vision and was often in conflict with the authorities.

Being a social prophet has something to do with having a different social vision. While the dominant social vision of Judaism was centered on holiness, the alternative vision of Jesus was centered on compassion. It was Jesus' image of God which led him into constant conflict with his opponents. We can only realize how radical Jesus' message and vision were if we appreciate this dimension of Jesus' emphasis on compassion. For him, compassion was not just a quality of God; it was a social alternative. He directly and repeatedly challenged the dominant social vision of his time and advocated instead what has been called *politics of compassion.* What should rule the life of a community was not holiness, which means separation and withdrawal leading to marginalization and oppression, but 'compassion which calls for creating a community that is inclusive and tears down what separates and creates division among the people. More will be said about these two social visions later.

Jesus - the teacher of Wisdom: "unconventional and alternative"

Besides his being a *Spirit person* and a *social prophet,* Jesus was a *teacher of wisdom* who regularly used the classic form of wisdom speech (parables and memorable short sayings known as aphorisms) to teach a subversive and alternative wisdom. All scholars agree that whatever we can say about the pre-Easter Jesus, one thing is certain: he was a teacher of wisdom; he was a *sage.* When we distinguish between conventional wisdom and subversive or alternative wisdom, we group Jesus with the sages who did not teach conventional but rather alternative wisdom (Lao-tzu, Buddha or Socrates). Jesus' wisdom questioned and undermined conventional wisdom and spoke of another way, another path.

How did Jesus present this wisdom? As a teacher, Jesus frequently made use of literary forms, especially aphorisms and parables. Aphorisms are short, memorable sayings, great 'short liners.' There are about 200 aphorisms in the Gospels used by Jesus which challenge the listener or reader to reflect, to pause, to think and to see things in a radically new way. Here are a few: "You cannot serve two masters.", "If a blind person leads another blind person, will they not both fall into a ditch?" "Leave the dead to bury the dead." These sayings appeal to the imagination, to the inner place where our images of reality and life are born.

Jesus was also a great story teller of parables and short stories. His aim was to invite his listeners to see something they might otherwise overlook. Aphorisms, short stories and parables are invitations to a different way of seeing, to creating different images for shaping our understanding of reality. He was indeed a special story teller-

> People in an African village purchased a television set. For weeks all of the children and all of the adults gathered around the set, watching the programs morning, afternoon, and night. Then after a couple of months, the set was turned off and never used again. A visitor to the village asked the chief, "Why do you no longer watch television?" "We have decided to listen to the storytellers," he replied. "Doesn't the television know more stories?" the visitor asked. "Yes," the chief replied, "but the storyteller knows me."

That is the *how* of Jesus' teaching. It is a wisdom that is a far cry from conventional wisdom. But what is the content, the *what* of his teaching?

> Jesus used these invitational and provocative forms of speech - aphorisms and parables - to subvert conventional ways of seeing and living, and to invite his hearers to an alternative way of life. As a teacher of wisdom, Jesus was not primarily a teacher of information (what to believe) or morals (how to behave), but a teacher of a way or a path of transformation. A way of transformation from what to what? From a life in the world of conventional wisdom to a life centered in God (M. J. Borg, *Meeting Jesus,* p. 75).

We cannot go into details here concerning the meaning of conventional wisdom. But generally, it can be said that conventional wisdom is the dominant consciousness of any culture. It is the most taken-for-granted understanding of the way things are and the way to live. It is "what everybody knows" - the world that everybody is socialized into through the process of growing up in family and society.

What is of interest here is the corresponding image of God. In conventional wisdom God is primarily presented as lawgiver and judge. God is seen as both the source and the enforcer of the law, and therefore, the one who legitimates the religious form of conventional wisdom. God becomes the one whom we must satisfy, the one whose requirements must be met. Jesus subverted that world of conventional wisdom and offered alternatives. First he demolished the old so that the new could appear clearly.

Like most sages he spoke of two ways; a wise and a foolish way; the way to life and the way to death; a narrow way and a broad way, 'enter through the narrow gate, for wide is the gate and easy the way that leads to destruction.'

Here Jesus reversed the normal order and undermined conventional wisdom. He directly questioned and even attacked the central values of his social world's conventional wisdom: family, wealth, honor, purity and religiosity. Things that were sanctified by tradition and whose importance was part of the taken-for-granted world. For example, "Let the dead bury the dead." "Who is my mother and who are my brothers and sisters?" "Don't call anyone Father on earth." "Sell everything you have...You cannot serve God and mammon. It is easier for a camel to go through the eye of a needle than for a rich man to enter the Kingdom...only if you become like a child can you enter the Kingdom." All these sayings question conventional wisdom.

Jesus - the movement founder

Lastly Jesus should be regarded as a *movement founder* who created a Jewish renewal movement that challenged and shattered the social boundaries of his day, a movement that eventually became the early Christian Church.

These four traits ultimately come down to two: "Jesus was *a spirit-filled mystic* and *social prophet.* Not only was he a witness to the reality of the Spirit as an element of experience, but also that his passionate involvement in the culture of his own time - social world - connected two realities which Christians have frequently separated." The two realities - Spirit and Prophet - have to be maintained in one's understanding and appropriation of all the other New Testament titles for Jesus. They are to communicate the same Spirit-experience to Christians and empower and guide Jesus' disciples in acting within their culture and social world (P. Knitter, *Jesus and the other Names,* p. 93).

The Good News Jesus is "on fire with": the God-experience of Jesus

But what was it that drove this man, that burned in him, that gave him an identity, that defined his mission and that he had to communicate to others? To sum it up, we could say it was his *personal experience of who God really is.* Jesus experienced God as one who was coming as *unconditional love,* who was entering human history in a way and to a degree not known by the prophets. This God he named *"ABBA."* The word belongs to the language of childhood and the home, a diminutive of endearment, which was also used by adults for their own fathers. For the Jewish mind, ABBA was THE word that could express most adequately the most intimate and personal relationship anyone could think of without denying that there were other ways as well. By using this word, Jesus revealed the heart of his relationship with God: a simple trust and confidence, with which a little child comes to a father whom he knows, loves and trusts. Jesus, therefore, spoke with God as a child speaks with his father — simply, intimately, securely. The word ABBA encompasses the whole message and claim of Jesus:

> The simple name "Father", then, carries with it the whole revolution in the concept of God which is linked to the message and especially to the destiny of Jesus Christ: Immanuel, the God of faithful nearness in the deepest, most binding, and truly unconditional sense, in the sense of incarnation, his identification with sons and daughters in life and death and to all eternity, God not merely in the height of his heavenly but also in the depth of his earthly course (J.M. Lochman, *The Lord's Prayer*, p. 20).

This experience of God as ABBA, which Jesus realized and which determined his whole life, is the real core of the Kingdom message. God was coming now in him in a definite way to bring all of humankind into that union and communion of life with Him that he had promised to accomplish at the end of time. And this end-time was breaking in now not in judgement but in unimaginable love and forgiveness.

Regarding the difficulties with exclusive language when speaking about God in the context of Jesus' use of the word ABBA, the following has to be said. The word *Abba* connotes an intimacy in the relationship between Jesus and God as well as God's compassion and suffering for the sake of overcoming evil and offering true liberation. *Abba* stands for a liberating message, doing away with any discrimination and oppression including that against women. Jesus' experience of God as ABBA cannot be used to prove that God is male. God has no gender and Abba is one powerful symbol for God, but it cannot be claimed as being exclusive of feminine qualities. As a matter of fact, Jesus used more symbols and analogies than this one when talking about God. If we take the Gospel tradition as a whole, we see a variety of terms used by Jesus when he spoke about God. He did not restrict himself exclusively to the term father. It is worth noting the observations of women theologians who tell us:

> To select this one metaphor and grant it sole rights does not follow the pattern of Jesus' speech but is governed by other considerations, most likely a subtle endorsement of the priority of the father in social arrangements...

> Jesus' Abba is not a patriarchal figure who can be used to legitimate systems of oppression, including patriarchal rule but a God of the oppressed, a God of community and celebration. Everyone related to the one Abba stands in a relation of mutuality with one another. In the words of the Matthean Jesus: *You are not to be called rabbi, for you have one teacher, and you are all*

brothers and sisters. Call no man father on earth, you have one Father, who is in heaven. Neither be called masters, for you have one master, the Christ. Whoever is greatest among you shall be your servant; whoever exalts oneself will be humbled and whoever humbles oneself will be exalted (Mt 23:8-12).

Jesus' Abba signifies a compassionate, liberating God who is grossly distorted when made into a symbol and supporter of patriarchal rule. The difficulty with the appeal to Jesus' use of father to restrict other options in naming towards God thus becomes apparent. It presses speech that was pluriform, subtle and subversive into an exclusive, literal, and patriarchal mold, and simply does not do justice to the evidence at hand. It also does not take account of the effective history of the father symbol in Christianity, which grew and hardened and fixed in alliance with patriarchal rule, thus imprisoning rather than releasing the good news it was originally intended to convey. Both the fluidity of Jesus' own language and the intent of the paternal metaphor itself in his hands allow and indeed call for other ways of Christian speaking about God in addition to the language of father (E. Johnson, *She Who Is*, pp. 81-82).

A serious analysis of "Father" as used by Jesus should make it clear that any patriarchal understanding of "Father" was always a serious misunderstanding. The Father of Jesus Christ is a wholly non-patriarchal Father. The best proof is the parable of the Prodigal Son, where the father behaves in a totally non-patriarchal and previously unknown manner. Lochman explains:

We have only to note the figure of the father in the story. Against all prevailing laws and customs he does not stand in his son's way but lets him go, even though it is a highly risky and misconceived freedom that the younger son chooses. And when the prodigal returns crushed, the father does not count up and expect repayment but runs to meet him. The father runs: an unheard-of action in the patriarchal code. But this unheard-of feature in the father's attitude characterizes the New Testament concept. It cuts right across all pagan and pseudo-Christian ideas of God (*The Lord's Prayer*, p. 21).

In order to understand the "father symbol" that Jesus used for God we must remind ourselves constantly that Jesus preserved this *Father-child* relationship first of all for himself alone. Nobody can call God ABBA except Jesus. Only he can call God in this way because only he knows who God is and what this word "ABBA" as a symbol for God contains. *Nobody knows the Father except the Son and to whom the Son will reveal him (Jn 14:2).*

It is therefore not possible to call God Father separated from the person of Jesus himself. Doing so would block the way to God as mystery of life and as the way to truth. To call God Father can only be done by those to whom Jesus has revealed the meaning of the word and whom he has empowered to use it (Lk 11:1). The key to God as Father is Jesus, since he alone can say: *He who sees (knows) me sees (knows) the Father*. It is the identification that Jesus makes with the Father that will reveal to us that God is Father in the way Jesus demonstrated it through his union with him. To experience God as Father is linked to the experience one has of Jesus. Jesus becomes so to speak the "filter", the "bridge" that can lead from the concrete experience with earthly fathers, an experience that may need purification, clarification and in some cases even de-toxication, before God can be addressed and experienced as a kind and loving Father.

From here we can understand why Jesus forbade his disciples to call anyone Father here on earth (Mt 23:9). No earthly Father can vouch for what the word Father for God really means except Jesus himself. Jesus put an end to what was so dominant in the structures of patriarchal societies with regards to father figures, namely, POWER. The new family of Jesus no longer knows the word father except when it refers to the one who is in heaven and whom Jesus came to reveal: a God who is a caring and kind father, someone in whom we can place our unconditional trust.

With this, Jesus put an end to the patriarchal systems on this one point: God did not come to "rule it over", to exercise power and force but "to serve and to give his life way so that we may have life and have it in abundance (Jn 10:10). In the words of Lohfink:

> Power and rule belong only to God who the disciples may address as *Abba*. If there no longer exists for them the kind and caring fathers of the past, but only the one Father in heaven, then it is all the more true that the authoritarian fathers exercising power have gone out of existence. It would be paradoxical to leave tender fathers behind and then find authoritarian fathers in the circle of disciples. It was precisely for this reason that Jesus mentioned no fathers in Mark 10:30. The disciples will find everything again in the new family of God, brothers and sisters, mothers and children: but they will find fathers no longer. Patriarchal domination is no longer permissible in the new family. But only motherliness, fraternity and childlikeness before God as Father (*Jesus and Community*, p. 49).

Psychologists have helped us to understand the role the father symbol plays in the life of every human being positively as well as negatively, in the life of every human being. The word father as the archetype of the human soul signifies in general a living space, a principle that enables life, makes existence possible, annuls everything that constantly threatens life and keeps the chaotic and demonic powers in check. That is the reason why father represents order in contrast to chaos, authority which creates a space to live, obedience because from experience it knows the ways one has to walk if one wants to find life. It is important to realize that this symbol not only facilitates life, but affirms it, nurtures it, rejoices in it and loves it dearly The very last dimension is the most endangered.

We have to admit exactly that these positive qualities of the father symbol created again and again a threat to life rather than a space for living, absolute power instead of authority, absolute dependence and unfreedom instead of obedience. Such a negative development of the father symbol is a real possibility in every patriarchal structure, a possibility demonstrated, over and over again in the course of history, so far as to completely invert its original meaning.

The abuse of the father symbol as *power* prevents so many people from perceiving and naming God "father". The personal father experience often excludes that which the symbol wishes to express: to be accepted, affirmed, loved and protected. This is the reason why people hesitate to use the father symbol for God (Cf. Jaschke, *Gott Vater?... pp.125-170).*

Psychologists and anthropologists have made us aware of the role the father figure plays as the "proto-symbol" of human existence. However helpful this might be to modern people to understand the difficulties they may find in addressing God as father, this will not solve their problems as long as the name Father for God is seen as a purely human application of the earthly father symbol transferred to God.

In the modern controversy concerning wether we should keep on praying to God as Father or not, we should keep in mind that the biblical use of Father for God is in no way to be understood as a Christianized version of some of the ancient world's patriarchal gods nor a divinized version of the Greco-Roman *pater-familias.* The Father name for God is rooted not in human initiative but in God's own decision to reveal Himself to His people in this way. It is God's choice and not just a human crafting of poetic language to be altered at will. It is not the "name" *we* supply, but one which has been established through God's self-revelation. The God revealed under this name is a loving and a compassionate God who stands over against the possible abuses of power found in the Greco-Roman society and often in that society's *pater familias.* Most assuredly God the "Father" as revealed ultimately in Jesus Christ transcends in loving contradiction our own contemporary society's examples of authority's abuse or the poor or irresponsible (male) parenting.

This image of God that Jesus revealed with the symbol ABBA finds its expression in a personalized way most adequately in the following three statements which form the foundation of our Christian faith:

God always loves me unconditionally

No matter how I feel, who I am, what I have done, how sinful I may imagine myself to be, how far I am from God, how messed up my life may be, there is one sure reality I can count on: God loves me personally, is concerned for what is best for me, and he will never give me up as a hopeless case because he loves me. I can neither reduce this love nor increase it. I can only graciously accept it and find in it the fulfillment of my life, my identity and my joy.

> Don't you understand! God is running after you day and night as though he has nothing to do but simply to occupy himself with you (Catherine of Siena).

The same thought was expressed by a thirteen year old boy:

> Young people wanted to know the exact answer. They went to the city center with their microphones and tape recorders and at the railway station they interviewed the passers-by asking them, "What do you think God is like?" In answer to such a question people most of the time become rather embarrassed or evasive. Some began to utter platitudes. But there was a thirteen year old boy who simply said, "I imagine God is a person who has managed to create four and a half billion or more people and loves each one as if he or she were his only child."

Many find it hard to accept such a statement about God's love for them. They are not sure if God can love them without conditions. They feel rather guilty when thinking of God and definitely unworthy of such a love. After they would have amended their lives through good deeds and penance then God might love them. They think they have to make themselves first worthy of such a love. The problem is not God's love for me but whether or not I let this love into my life and let it change my life. God's love is always there but am I willing to respond to this love? Does my answer find its expression in the great commandment where I am asked to love God with all my heart, with all my soul and with all my strength? (Mk 12:28-34)

The first thing I will realize and see clearly, after having passed into the world beyond death, will be the immensity of God's love for me. How he "knitted me together in my mother's womb" (Ps 139); how he cared for me and loved me in a thousand ways all my life long, in every detail and in every second of my life. This realization will fill me with an immense amazement, joy and overwhelming peace. But my second realization when looking at my life in the light of this love will be: how far did I respond to this love? Did I let it into my life? Did it guide my actions and behavior or was it of no consequence to me? Did I remain indifferent? It is before this love of God for me that I stand judged. God does not have to judge my life but I will judge myself in the face of this unbelievable love. It is here that I will see clearly what needs to be amended and straightened out. I will have to enter a process of growth in order to outgrow my lack of love in the past and make up for the damage this lack of love has caused in my life with regards to God, my fellow human beings and myself.

Full happiness with God is only possible if I respond to this stupendous love of God with an equivalent love as the great commandment asks. If that is not accomplished in death I will still have to grow into such a love-response no matter how long and how painful the process may be. One thing I know— I will reach the goal, the ultimate union with God, since God's love is accompanying me even now in this very painful processes of growth.

God always forgives me

God will never give us up: the constancy of his love depends on what he is and not on what I am or on how I behave.

> *For I know well the plans I have in mind for you, says the Lord, plans for your welfare not for your woe. Plans to give you a future full of hope. When you look for me, you will find me. Yes, when you seek me with all your heart, you will find me with you," says the Lord, "and I will change your lot" (Jer 29:11-14).*

No matter how I may have messed up my life, how unchristian, how indifferent my life has been, with what indifference I have behaved towards this love, God always forgives me. Even more, he offers me a future full of hope that exceeds all expectations and dreams I might ever have entertained for myself. For God there is never a "too late," therefore, I have not missed anything yet. Remember: if I really believe in God's constant forgiveness then I must also hold to the truth that the best years of my life are still ahead of me and not behind me. At every moment God offers me "a future full of hope."

> *I forget what is behind me and stretch myself out to what is in front of me (Phil 3:13).*

Sad to say, there are scores of people who find it difficult to believe in such a forgiving God. They cannot accept a God who gives them a second chance. Karl Barth called this God the "therefore god" who allows no margin for error, no second chance. This God we must replace with a "nevertheless god" whose forgiveness is always there for us. The best image of such a "nevertheless god" is the father in the Prodigal Son story who receives us always without any questions asked. Age, barrenness and repeated failures are no obstacles for such a God, as Scripture testifies more than once and human experience shows:

> Let me tell you about a teenager whom we will call Tom. Getting on the train, he was very nervous and excited and you will soon see why. He sat opposite a middle-aged man that he had never met before, but he felt he should tell him his story.
>
> He told him that he had just been released from reformatory school, where he had spent three years for robbery and other crimes. He realized how wrong he had been and he just wanted a second chance to go straight and to show that he was sorry. He felt so sorry for letting his family down, and he hoped that they would forgive him. They had never visited him or written to him during the three years but he did realize that neither of his parents could write and that they were too poor to be able to come to the reformatory which was a long distance from their home. He wanted so much to be able to go home but he wanted to make sure that he was welcome. He wrote to his parents and asked them to give him a sign. His home was just beside the railway track and they had an old apple tree at the end of the garden. If they wanted him back, all they had to do was to put a white ribbon on the apple tree. If he was not welcome home, they were to put nothing on the tree and he would just pass on to some town where he knew nobody and no-one knew him.
>
> As the train was close to home, he was so nervous that he could not look and he asked his new found friend to look for him. After a while, the man caught Tom by the shoulder with joy on his face and said, "Just take a look!" Tom looked and saw the old apple tree and it was wearing not just one white ribbon but a whole host of ribbons. Tears ran down Tom's face and the bitterness and anger of the years washed away. The other man said later, "I felt that I had witnessed a miracle" (F. Barron, *Short and Sweet,* p. 63).

How forgiveness of sins leads to the restoration of a person's full life we find in the story of the paralytic in Mk 2:1-11:

> *When Jesus returned to Capernaum after some days, it became known that he was at home. Many gathered together so that there was no longer room for them, not even around the door, and he preached the word to them. They came bringing to him a paralytic carried by four men. Unable to get near Jesus because of the crowd, they opened up the roof above him. After they had broken through, they let down the mat on which the paralytic was lying.*
>
> *When Jesus saw their faith, he said to the paralytic, "Child, your* sins are forgiven." Now some of the scribes were sitting there asking themselves, "Why does this man speak that way? He is blaspheming. Who but God alone can forgive sins?"

Jesus immediately knew in his mind what they were thinking to themselves, so he said, "Why are you thinking such things in your hearts? Which is easier, to say to the paralytic, 'Your sins are forgiven,' or to say, 'Rise, pick up your mat and walk'? But that you may know that the Son of Man has authority to forgive sins on earth"-- he said to the paralytic, "I say to you, rise, pick up your mat, and go home."

He rose, picked up his mat at once, and went away in the sight of everyone. They were all astounded and glorified God, saying, "We have never seen anything like this."

The story reveals Jesus' remarkable capacity to discover how people behave and operate. When looking at the man, Jesus understood right away that what he needed most was reconciliation with God and the realization that God loved him and had forgiven him all his sins. Jesus perceived that he could heal this man only if he was willing first to receive and accept God's forgiveness and assurance of his love. The stretcher on which he was lying was not just something that supported him in his sickness. As Jesus saw it, the man was more than just physically sick. He seemed to use his sickness, the hurts in his life, his resentments and anger about his sickness as a stretcher to rest on, to arouse pity and draw attention. To heal him from that ailment needed a more profound touch because he seemingly did not want to get healed on that level. Jesus consequently said to him first, "Your sins are forgiven." With this the deepest root of his sickness was removed. But after the cure Jesus added a surprising remark: "Pick up your stretcher and walk." Why should he do that? Why forget all about the past enfleshed in this stretcher? Jesus told the man, "Your past is forgiven and healed. You now can carry your past (symbolized in the stretcher) on your shoulders. Never again use the past with your failures, your faults, your hurts, your misconduct and your self-pity as a 'stretcher' again to carry you. Since you are forgiven and your wounds are healed, never again allow the past to become the stretcher to lay on once again. Walk as a free person and carry your past as forgiven, never allowing it to paralyze you again."

Stretch Out Your Hand!
(Mark 3)

In the Gospel
Jesus initiated the cure,
told the man to
"Come here"
and performed magical surgery on
his shriveled hand

so its fingers unfolded into flesh.
Perhaps the man wasn't grateful.
The Healer had snatched away his excuse
for the random pities and coins of others.
Now his hand couldn't remain unemployed;
would be expected to find work.
You're never completely grateful for being cured.
Knowing your impairments snag you kindness,
put you in the spotlight
so others cringe at their fully functional selves.
It's a kind of power.
So you pray with ambivalence
for your own healing,
half frightened at the compassion God may feel
for whatever is withered in you,
half frightened at how you'll handle
being whole again.
(*Schnapp, RSM*)

When we are forgiven, our faults, sins and hurts can no longer be used as an alibi. We have to take our past courageously on our own shoulders, knowing we are forgiven. We can move once again into freedom and joy. The past cannot paralyze us anymore. Our forgiven sins will now serve as signs of what God has done to us. We are to get up, walk, be free and live because we are meant for this.

We can always begin anew and live in the present moment. The problem is that we often allow our past to say: "You know it all; you have seen it all, be realistic; the future will just be another repetition of the past. Try to survive as best as you can." With such an attitude in mind we will to once again allow the past to paralyze us and become the stretcher which we allow to carry us.

It is hard to live in the present. The past and the future keep harassing us. The past with guilt and the future with worries. There are so many things in the past that make us feel uneasy, regretful, angry and hurt. In addition, guilt is often a very strong advocate that says: "You ought to have done something other than you did; you ought to have said something other than you said." These oughts keep us feeling guilty about the past and prevent us from being fully present to the moment. And there are the worries of the future: what if? What if I have to go back to the same place and people? How can I change? What if I become sick? Lose my position? What if the bishop transfers me? What if war breaks out?

The real enemies of our lives are the "oughts" and the "ifs." They pull us backward into the unalterable past and forward into the unpredictable future. But real life takes place in the here and now. God is the God of the present. Jesus came to wipe away the burden of the past and the worries of the future. He wants us to discover God right where we are.

In the Gospel according to Luke we read the following:

But Peter said, 'Man I do not know what you are talking about.' At that moment, while he was still speaking, a cock crew; and the Lord turned and looked straight at Peter....and Peter went outside and wept bitterly.

I had a fairly good relationship with the Lord. I would ask him for things, converse with him, thank him.
But always I had this uncomfortable feeling that he wanted me to look into his eyes... And I would not. I would talk, but look away when I sensed he was looking at me.
I always looked away. And I knew why. I was afraid. I thought I should find a demand there: there would be something he wanted from me.
One day I finally summoned up courage and looked! There was no accusation. There was no demand. The eyes just said, 'I love you.' I looked long into those eyes. I looked searchingly. Still, the only message was, 'I love you!'
And I walked out and, like Peter, I wept. (A. De Mello, The Song of the Bird, pp. 144-145)

But we have to remind ourselves constantly that if the past has been forgiven, it does not mean that the effects of my sins are already healed. If I have lived a totally indifferent or self-centered life, caring only for my personal interests, seeking only my own fortune and pleasures, not caring for anyone except myself, I will not be able to overcome such tendencies with one stroke. Deeply ingrained habits will not go away over night. I need healing even if God has forgiven me my sins. I have to let God's forgiving love penetrate my past and heal it; and this means on my part that I have to cooperate with this love through discipline and sincere efforts to overcome the craving of the past and to let myself be gradually cured. What gives me the strength to discipline myself is precisely the realization of this forgiving love that is present in and available to me as I try to overcome the past and stretch myself out to a new future full of hope. The following story might illustrate this point more clearly:

Some year ago a young man at the University in Rome approached me with the request if I would be willing to become his spiritual director. But he warned me frankly that it would not be easy because he had tried a few others before. After some hesitation I agreed. He was around thirty years of age. What had happened? He had entered a church in Rome out of curiosity and since it was empty and cool he set down and looked at the big crucifix hanging in the middle of the aisle.

Suddenly he was shaken to his bones because he realized that the crucified Christ was looking at him with such intense love and tenderness that he burst into tears. His whole life appeared to him in an entirely new light. Theologically we would say he had just experienced one of those great conversions like Paul did on his way to Damascus. He knew instantly that he could never again be the same person.

His first reaction was immense joy and inner peace. Then he saw his whole life clearly before his eyes and felt extremely ashamed. He never had cared about God or Christ. He had experienced it all: sex, drugs, violence - a life of total self-centeredness and utter indifference to any one under the sun. Now Christ had forgiven him and shown him such an intense love which he had never experienced before or known of.

He immediately wanted to change radically and become a priest or religious. But I discouraged him from such an endeavor and told him that he first had to integrate this vision into his life and that his past must be healed before he could even consider such a choice. This would definitely demand a lot of discipline and hard work on his side. He was ready.

As the weeks passed and the new vision wore out its initial splendor and brightness, his past life moved in on him with full force. The only thing I could do was to stay with him and remind him constantly of the vision he had seen: to stay with it, to return to it again and again and not to let go of it. Only from this vision could he draw the strength, courage and discipline needed to overcome the grave sins of the past and be healed. It was a long struggle but in the end he managed it brilliantly.

When we dare to believe that we are never alone but that God is always with us, always cares for us, and always speaks to us, we can gradually detach ourselves from the voices that make us feel guilty or anxious and allow ourselves to dwell on the present moment. Only in this way will we gradually overcome our distrust in God, our fear, our worries and discover that God has only one desire at heart: to give us his love and life.

However, only he who admits his sins and faults without any excuses can really receive God's unconditional forgiveness. We all have our difficulties to admit that our sinfulness and rebellion are at the heart of the problems of our own life as well as of society at large. We are much more comfortable discussing imperfections, weaknesses, mistakes, and errors in judgment. These terms are socially acceptable, and almost everyone identifies with them. But an outright acknowledgment of guilt before God and men, a 100-percent acceptance of responsibility for wrong-doing, runs against the grain. Yet this kind of honesty is the first step for receiving God's pardon and forgiveness.

The story is told that one day Frederick the Great, King of Prussia, visited a prison and talked with each of the inmates. There were endless tales of innocence, of misunderstood motives, and of exploitation. Finally the king stopped at the cell of a convict who remained silent. "Well," remarked Frederick, "I suppose you are an innocent victim too?" "No, sir, I'm not," replied the man. "I'm guilty and deserve my punishment." Turning to the warden, the king said, "Here, release this rascal before he corrupts all these fine innocent people in here!"

God is always "present with me"

There are many names given to Yahweh in the Bible, but the most adequate seems to be *EMMANUEL,* which means *GOD - WITH - US.* Yahweh is a God who belongs to us, who cares for us and who loves to be among us.

And they heard the sound of the Lord God walking in the garden in the cool of the day, and the man and his wife hid themselves from the presence of the LORD God among the trees of the garden (Gen 3:8).

What does this TO BE WITH really mean? The one word that might most adequately express the true nature of EMMANUEL God in his relationship to us human creatures is *COMPASSION.*

The Lord, the Lord, a compassionate and gracious God, slow to anger and rich in kindness and fidelity (Ex 34:7).

In the Hebrew language the word is "rahamin." The word is taken from the word "womb of a woman." Thus the word "compassionate" bears the connotation of "wombishness," loving the way a mother loves the child of her womb, nourishing, giving life. It is a very feminine and motherly term and denotes the ability to suffer with, to enter deeply into a situation, to be filled with empathy, as if one is experiencing the situation personally and not as an observer. The word really means to be able to share the suffering and pain of others and also to experience their joy and happiness as if it were all happening to me. The word, as applied to God, is comprehensible only to those who know, with all the fibers of their being, in total self-surrender and with passion the meaning of unconditional love (cf. E. Johnson, *Consider Jesus,* p.117).

Such compassion does not remain merely passive, on the level of feelings; it asks for a physical response in the sense that compassion for another is felt in the center of one's body. It is a love which calls for concrete action. It is a feeling often expected of Yahweh who has mother-love (Is 49:15; Jer 31:20) or father-love (Ps 103:13; Is 63:15-16) for Israel. It is this "womb-love" of Yahweh which leads to forgiveness for his wayward children.

Can a woman forget her baby and not love the child she bore? Even if a mother should forget her child, I will never forget you. I have written your name on the palms of my hands (Is 49:14-16).

Compassion is therefore not a bending towards the underprivileged from a privileged position, it is not reaching out from on high to those who failed to make it in the upward drive. On the contrary, it is a moving directly to those people and places where suffering is visible and most tangible so as to build a home there without ever leaving again.

What is so unexpected and disturbing in God's compassionate love in Jesus is that it is characterized by a downward pull. Through his whole life and mission, Jesus reveals the limitlessness of God's compassionate love for his creatures in accepting absolute powerlessness. The true mystery of our God is not that he takes away our pain and our suffering but that he first wants to share it with us. Only when he has tasted it, experienced it, can it be changed; only then can new life come forth. The God of Jesus is not an all-powerful God but a compassionate God. The real news in Jesus' message is that God is not a distant God, unmoved by our misery and pain but a God who is 'with us,' who is moved by our pain and misery, who participates in the fullness of our sin-permeated human condition, a God who is 'our God.'

A little girl was sent to the store with specific instructions from her mother to come straight home when she had bought everything. She was more than two hours coming home, much to the distress of her anxious mother. "Where have you been?" scolded the mother.

"I'm sorry, Mommy. I know I am late, but Jane broke her doll and I had to stop and help her fix it."

"And how could you help her fix that broken doll?"

In her precious, childlike manner the girl responded. "I really couldn't, but I sat down with her and helped her cry."

The nature and behavior of God towards his creature does not guarantee that we will never have to suffer or that we are "insured" against every eventuality, or that we will never die. It simply tells us that God will always be there, that we can count on his presence at all times. The problem is that our image of God is too far removed from the image that Jesus gave us.

Many people imagine God as all powerful, far removed from all earthly concerns. He is just 'up there'. If we are in deep trouble and all seems to crumble under our feet, when suffering and hurt seem to question even God's very existence, then we cry out to him like this: "You are all powerful; you claim to love me and care about me. If this is so, where are you? Please, come and rescue me; help me! Open a window and stretch out your mighty arm and pull me out of all the misery and hurt I experience right now. Do something about it!" These are the cries we hear in so many psalms.

God's answer in such a situation will be something like this: "I cannot reach you from on high; my mighty arm is too short. But trust me. I really do love you and, therefore, I will surely do something that fits your situation. I will come down into your life, into your misery and anguish. Just pull up a chair for me and I will be there to share your anguish, taste your misery and I weep with you. I will console you, help you, comfort you, heal you, show you a way out. I will be your guide. I will be with you as your friend. But you will have to understand something very important: I cannot live your life and make everything pleasant for you, free of pain and suffering. That I cannot do. You must live your life and to live means to encounter anguish, pain, suffering, many worries and real problems and ultimately death. This you share with every creature on earth. The difference is: I will always be there with you and in particular when you feel lonely, dejected and hurt."

Even if I go through the deepest darkness,
I will not be afraid, Lord, for you are with me (Ps 23:4).

Reflection: Set on Fire by Jesus.

When the Holy Spirit came on the fearful apostles gathered in the upper room with Mary, there appeared tongues of fire. Thus disciples of Jesus are people on fire sent to set fire to the world just as the Master who said: "*I have come to set the earth on fire, and how I wish it were already blazing.*" *(Lk 12:49).* As disciples of Jesus we should be burning torches that not only are on fire, but also set on fire everyone who comes in contact with us. Is this really the case? If we are indeed torches then the fire that burns in us should also transform us and our surroundings. Do we notice this effect on the environment in which we live and work?

Only in as far as God is a burning flame in us can we communicate our experience of the Abba of Jesus to others. Do we share the sentiment of Jeremiah who exclaimed:

Your message is like fire burning deep within me (Jer 20:9).?

This was exactly what was driving Jesus when he began his public ministry in the synagogue of his own village and reading the passage from the book of Isaiah (Lk 4 and Is 61). He was convinced that the Spirit was sending him not first to the scribes and the Pharisees, nor to the wealthy and the ruling class or the seats of power and learning, but to the lowly the sick and the poor; the oppressed and the suffering; all those who had no voice, could not fulfill the Law and felt lost, seemingly excluded from God and caught up in prisons of guilt.

Jesus was determined to reveal a God to them who was understanding, forgiving and loving. The God Jesus reveals to us is Yahweh, who wants to be near to us.

YAHWEH - I AM THERE

I am there - when you are alone
I am there - when you are full of consternation
I am there - when they reject you and cast you out
I am there - when you cannot see any progress
I am there - when you despair and are saddened
I am there - when you are anxious and afraid
I am there - when no one likes you
I am there - when there seems to be a wall between
               you and your friend
I am there - when you worry and cannot sleep
I am there - when someone hurts you
I am there - when you are in grave danger
I am there - when you are sick and need help
I am there - when you cannot bear your sorrow alone
I am there - when your world falls apart
I am there - when you need love and are ready to confide
I am there - when you are suffering great pain
I am there - when no one listens to you any more
I am there - when you can no longer stand upright from exhaustion
I am there - when you have a bad conscience
I am there - when you call on me
I am there - when you die

I am there - like an angel who protects you in great needs
I am there - like the sun that gives you warmth and joy
I am there - like a father who makes you feel secure
I am there - like a mother who feels with you
I am there - like a heart that is always with you
I am there - like an eye that always sees you
I am there - like an arm that supports you
I am there - like a cloud that envelops you with love
I am there - like a hand that shows the right way
I am there - like a light that inspires you well
I am there - like a voice that tells you

That I shall be with you always.

QUESTION: Which "I am there" statement describes best my experience of God?

Only in as far as we are fascinated by this Jesus who entered into placed forbidden by the Law, who ate with sinners and tax collectors, who touches and healed lepers and enters into close relationships with people in pain and with women, can we make a difference to the world around us. Coming closer to this fire will burn away our wrong concepts of God, our false hopes for this life and our illusions about ourselves. Gradually we will become people who know who their God is and not just what has been said about him.

A famous actor was invited to a function where he was asked to recite for the pleasure of the guests. Having recited a few common verses, he asked if there was anything in particular they wanted to hear. After a moment or two, an old pastor asked to hear Psalm 23, "The Lord is my Shepherd". The actor paused for a moment and then said, "I will, but on one condition - that you will recite it also, after I have finished."
The pastor was taken by surprise. "I'm hardly a public speaker, but if you wish, I shall recite too."
The actor began quite impressively. His voice was trained and his intonation was perfect. The audience was spellbound and when he finished, there was great applause from the guests. Now it was the old pastor's turn to recite the same psalm. His voice was not remarkable, his tone was not faultless, but when he finished, there was not a dry eye in the room.
The actor rose and his voice quivered as he said, "Ladies and gentlemen, I reached your eyes and your ears; he has reached your hearts. The difference is this: I know the Psalm but he knows the Shepherd." (C. Arcodia, Stories for Sharing, p. 71)

QUESTION: How well do I know the Shepherd of the Psalm? When in my life has this knowledge been very significant for me?

The Gospel tell us of Jesus moved by compassion and in this way revealing the heart of his ABBA, the one whose 'stomach turns over' at the sight of crushed and abandoned people. In all the chaos of division, hatred, fear and anger in Israel Jesus appeared as a man of compassion leaving no doubt that this was the message that burned like fire within him. In doing so, he has invited us to meet the God of Compassion and become more and more like him:

It was a bitter cold evening in northern Virginia many years ago. The old man's beard was glazed by winter's frost while he waited for a ride across the river. The wait seemed endless. His body became numb and stiff from the frigid north wind.

He heard the faint, steady rhythm of approaching hooves galloping along the frozen path. Anxiously, he watched as several horsemen rounded the bend. He let the first one pass by without an effort to get his attention. Then another passed by, and another. Finally, the last rider neared the spot where the old man sat like a snow statue. As this one drew near, the old man caught the rider's eye and said, "Sir, would you mind giving an old man a ride to the other side? There doesn't appear to be a passageway by foot."

Reigning his horse, the rider replied, "Sure thing. Hop aboard." Seeing the old man was unable to lift his half-frozen body from the ground, the horseman dismounted and helped the old man onto the horse. The horseman took the old man not just across the river, but to his destination, which was just a few miles away. As they neared the tiny, but cozy cottage, the horseman's curiosity caused him to enquire, "Sir, I noticed that you let several other riders pass by without making an effort to secure a ride. I'm curious why, on such a bitter winter night, you would wait and ask the last rider. What if I had refused and left you there?"

The old man lowered himself slowly down from the horse, looked the rider straight in the eyes and replied, "I've been around here for quite some time. I reckon I know people pretty good." The old-timer continued, "I looked into the eyes of the other riders and immediately saw there was no concern for my situation. It would have been useless even to ask them for a ride. But when I looked into your eyes, kindness and compassion were evident. I knew, then and there, that your gentle spirit would welcome the opportunity to give me assistance in my time of need."

Those heartwarming comments touched the horseman deeply, "I'm most grateful for what you have said," he told the old man. "May I never get too busy in my own affairs that I fail to respond to the needs of others with kindness and compassion."(B. Cavanaugh, Fresh Packets of Sowers's Seeds, pp 43-43).

QUESTION: What moments of true compassion - received and given - can I recall in my life?

Chapter Two

The Gracious God in the Bible and our God Image

Does the Bible support the God image that Jesus came to throw like fire into this world? Where in scripture does Jesus concretely reveal the gracious God? What actions and words of his demonstrate a loving, forgiving and compassionate God?

Jesus' image of God

Jesus saw reality very differently from the way we see it. He had the vivid sensation that reality was ultimately gracious and compassionate. He expressed this in poetic imagery as in Matthew 6:26-33 *"Look at the birds in the sky and the lilies in the field... Your Father in heaven cares for them all....."* For Jesus, nature was filled with God's glory, cosmic generosity and profound care. He revealed his image of God not in abstract terms or theological definitions but in parables and symbolic actions. The most vivid ones are probably found in Luke chapter 15. A. Greeley once remarked, "If we would have nothing of what Jesus said and did, except the three stories of Luke 15 - the Prodigal Son, the Lost Sheep and the Lost Coin - we would still have the essence of his message."

Others have singled out the following three parables that demonstrate most clearly the image of God that Jesus came to reveal: the Parable of the Unmerciful Servant or the Parable of the Merciful Master (Mt 18:21-35), the Parable of the Prodigal Son or the Parable of the Unbelievably Merciful Father (Lk 15:11-32), the Labourers in the Vineyard or the Parable of the Good Employer (Mt 20:1-16).

What is the outstanding message of these parables? They reveal the true image of God that Jesus came to communicate to us: a God whose basis for dealing with us is unbelievable, compassionate love. The behavior in all three parables is different from what a reasonable human being would normally demonstrate. This is precisely the point Jesus wants to make in these parables: God is someone who acts out of love and not out of rationality or even common sense. Like any true lover God behaves foolishly because his motive in dealing with us is love alone. This is the Good News of God's Kingdom to which Jesus wants us to be converted and in which we are called to believe.

The theological message in all these parables is the same. They show the incomprehensible goodness and kindness of God towards all human beings fully visible when the Kingdom has come in its glory. Yet even now, a new order is starting, which is not based on distributive justice but on God's goodness and kindness. Justice is subordinated to this kindness and compassion of God. We should never doubt God's forgiving love:

> Once a very bad man died and went before the judgment throne. Before him stood Abraham, David, Peter and Luke. A chilly silence hung heavy in the room as an unseen voice began to read the details of the man's life. There was nothing good that was recorded. When the voice concluded, Abraham spoke.
>
> "Men like you cannot enter the heavenly kingdom. You must leave."
> "Father Abraham," the man cried, "I do not defend myself. I have no choice but to ask for mercy. Certainly you understand. Though you lied to save your own life, saying your wife was your sister, by the grace and mercy of God you became a blessing to all nations."
>
> David interrupted, "Abraham has spoken correctly. You have committed evil and heinous crimes. You do not belong in the kingdom of light."
>
> The man faced the great king and cried, "Son of Jesse, it is true. I am a wicked man. Yet I dare ask you for forgiveness. You slept with Uriah's wife and later, to cover your sin, arranged his death. I ask only forgiveness as you have known it."
>
> Peter as next to speak. "Unlike David, you have shown no love to God. By your acid tongue and your vile temper you have wounded the Son of God."
> "I should be silent," the man muttered. "The only way I have used the blessed name of Jesus is in anger. Still, Simon, son of Jonah, I plead for grace. Though you walked by his side and listened to words from his own lips, you slept when he needed you in the garden, and you denied him three times in his night of greatest need."
>
> Then Luke the Evangelist spoke. "You must leave. You have not been found worthy of the kingdom of God."
>
> The man's head bowed sadly for a moment before a spark lit his face. "My life has been recorded correctly," the man began slowly. "I am guilty as charged. Yet I know there is a place for me in the blessed kingdom. Abraham, David, and Peter will plead my cause because they know of the weakness of man and the mercy of God. You, blessed physician, will open the gates to me because you have written of God's great love for the likes of me. Do you not recognize me? I am the lost sheep that the Good Shepherd carried home; I am your younger, prodigal brother." And the gates opened, and Luke embraced the sinner (White).

In the Parable of the Labourers in the Vineyard, Jesus is demonstrating that all human beings stand in need of God's kindness and compassion which will, if the person responds to it, undoubtedly be extended to each one at the end, when the Kingdom comes in its fullness. But even more, the parable reveals the true nature of God: *God longs for us.* He goes out to the market places again and again at any hour of the day to look for us and to invite us into his Kingdom, his house, with the sole purpose of letting us participate in his own life! The fact that God goes out at any hour of the day implies that he does not favor the fit and eager ones who are ready in the early morning hours to be hired, but he invites the less efficient and weaker ones just the same. The real lesson of the parable is: We cannot merit God's Kingdom, we can only follow his invitation to come and be his beloved children.

The ultimate question in the parable is: How does one enter the Kingdom? The answer we receive is: It is not by merit but by accepting an invitation. Grace in the parable is symbolized by the need of the landowner for more workers. The need seems to be urgent because he goes out several times. Grace is depicted here in a way that God seems to be moved to a response by our needs. The inner nature of God is revealed: he has to respond to our needs. God has desired us into being, we are desirable to him; we are desired by God. So he goes out to seek us and to invite us into his Kingdom, into his intimacy, into his house, for the ultimate purpose of sharing his own life. And he does so again and again!

With this parable Jesus justifies his going out to the sinners and outcasts. For this reason Jesus seeks out the marginalized. Their behavior does not merit anything, but their need is particularly great, and he is responding to their need. They win God's favor not through their merits but through their needs. It seems that our need creates God's need to reach out to us whether we recognize it or not. The invitation to enter the vineyard comes from God's goodness and compassion because the very essence of compassion is to respond to need. In order to reveal the true nature of God, Jesus had to show the Father's burning concern for those most in need of his grace and help. The parable tells us that human standards of judgement have no place in God's infinite need to show compassion (Keating, *The Kingdom* ..., pp.70-74).

Jesus' image of God questions the whole idea of merit and reward which is so much at the core of conventional wisdom. To speak of God as gracious or being womb-like in his compassion is worlds removed from imaging God as the lawgiver and judge enforcing demands and rules. Such a God-image directly undermines the world of conventional wisdom. For Jesus the notion that we have to meet God's requirements here on earth if we want to enjoy eternal life seemed too foreign or, at least, not central. What then was Jesus' alternative way that would lead to life?

The narrow way he proposed has two closely related dimensions. First, God is a gracious and womb-like God in his dealings with his people rather than an enforcer of requirements, boundaries and divisions. Second, the narrow way is an invitation that leads away from conventional wisdom to a life that is more centered on God. It is a way of life that is concerned with a deep relationship with the Spirit, not with duties and rewards. It is a way that leads to an experience of God as compassionate love and a state in which one is 'put on fire' with the Spirit in the way Jesus himself had experienced this Spirit. The road less travelled is a life centered on the Spirit of God (Borg, *Meeting Jesus*, pp 85-88).

In short, a true disciple of Jesus is first someone who is burning with the same Spirit that drove the master, who has had a deep experience of God and who wants to share this experience with others. Secondly, he or she is a person whose principle for action is compassion, a virtue by which he/she not only suffers passively with people but also stands up for justice and the creation of a society that is based on compassion and not on competition, perfection and profit.

> The idea that everything in this world has to be perfect went against the understanding and experience of the disciples. So the Master phrased it in a way they could comprehend more easily, "God weaves perfect patterns with the threads of our lives," he said, "even making use of our sins. The reason why you do not see this is because you are looking at the underside of the carpet." Or more succinctly, "What for some people is only a glittering stone, the jeweler recognizes as a diamond" (de Mello).

Such was the vision that determined Jesus' whole life. For this vision he lived, suffered and ultimately died. It has been called the 'agapeic vision' of the New Testament. With this vision Jesus offended the just of his time. Jesus' proclamation of God as unconditional love was always upsetting. It upset all standards in so far as he saw salvation not coming from what human beings would do but from the acceptance of a "God who comes to love us first."

Objections to this image

Is Jesus' God image as presented above not too one-sided? Is there not also an image of God which we find so frequently in the Old Testament: the God of judgement, who punishes and stirs up fear and does not let us get away with anything? The God who is incomprehensible and whose actions seem at times so utterly strange and even hostile towards human beings? Does this image of God completely disappear in Jesus' teaching?

The gracious and loving God-image of Jesus does not take God's transcendence away. God remains for Jesus the transcendent, the incomprehensible, the one who, at times, hides his face. Jesus shared the experience of many who encountered the God of Israel. This God appeared at times to be so alien, so incomprehensible, so unapproachable and even impenetrable (Job 9:32). This aspect is most vividly expressed in the psalms of lament where the person feels abandoned and rejected by God and cries for help or even accuses God of being so remote and seemingly totally insensitive to the needs of human beings.

The Old Testament gives two interpretations of this God who is seemingly hiding. First it is explained as punishment or as an expression of God's anger with his people. This is the usual and common explanation known to all religions. Sickness, personal misfortunes, natural disasters and wars are seen as punishment for sins committed. Many psalms describe the irritation and pain God's hiddenness causes.

The second explanation found in the Old Testament, unique and most important, argues as follows: God's hiding his face is a way of describing metaphorically and perhaps humanly speaking what it felt like to experience God's abandonment, wrath, inscrutable withdrawal, or failure to respond. It was Israel's way of saying "I don't know"- the answer to questions about the way God did something or did not do anything, why enemies and harmful forces had the opportunity to hurt and to destroy. God's ways remain incomprehensible, he cannot be measured by any human standards (cf. Sobrino, *Jesus the Liberator,* p. 138).

Jesus knew this *hidden God*, the incomprehensible one. The God of Job and Jeremiah (Jer 20:7-9), the God of silence, the God he experienced on the cross who caused him to cry out: *"Why have you forsaken me?"* Jesus progressively integrated this image of God into his life experience as well. But even in the darkest hour of his life, he did not give up his absolute trust in God. For Jesus, God is all goodness and love, someone to whom he relates with trust and confidence

Brueggemann gives the following interpretation of how to understand the God of the Old Testament who deals out vengeance and yet shows constantly compassion as well.

There are two texts in the Old Testament which disclose the struggle in the heart of God. In the flood narrative, the beginning in Gen 6:5-7 has God resolve to take vengeance on "his" wayward creation. But note that God makes the resolve not in anger, but in *grief and sorrow*. The flood narrative spins out the troubled tale. But by 8:12 something decisive has happened. Nothing is changed in the imagination of humankind, which is still evil. What has happened is a change wrought in the heart of God, who will no longer take vengeance. The move in God's heart from 6:5-7 to 8:21 suggests that instead of humankind suffering, God takes the suffering as "his" own. God resolves to turn the grief in on "himself" rather than to rage against "his" creation. God bears the *vengeance* of God in order that "his" creation can have compassion.

The same "turn" is more visible in Hos 11:1-9. Verses 1-7 are a conventional statement of God's anger and punishment. But in vv. 8-9, God has internalized the rage, turned the anger so that "his" own "heart quakes." God resolves not to take vengeance on Israel, but to contain in within "his" own person. In this profound moment, God breaks with his habits of heaven and earth. God presents "himself" in a radical graciousness. "He is God and not man." This God is also a God unlike any other gods (Ps 82). Such graciousness is not easy, in heaven or on earth. It is not simply or obviously gained. It is gained only by God's acceptance and internalization of the vengeance which gets outwardly expressed, now, only as compassion. Unmitigated compassion is possible only because God hears the pain of vengeance in "his" own person (*Praying the Psalms*, pp. 76-77).

The reality of God, continually emerging as Old Testament theology develops, is like that of a mother and the children she has carried in her womb and nurtured. There's no punishing them and certainly no destroying them. God is in love with us and can't act any other way but to forgive and live with the suffering children's cause. "Overstep the line, that's it!" God doesn't threaten that way. Seventy times seventy, in other words, perfectly and without measure. God is the first to forgive like that. Imagine, God saying quite righteously: "I'm so furious I could wring your neck!" But don't forget to add the conclusion: "But what can I do? You're like the beloved child I bore in my womb. I can't destroy you, for I am God and your Father."

Here's a story that can help us understand this point.

Recently I saw a TV program about a young man who had brutally raped and murdered a girl. He was scheduled for execution the next day. It showed two separate interviews. First, the father of the murdered girl was asked how he felt about the pending execution of the man who had murdered his daughter, an only child. He was extremely bitter and poured out his hatred. All he wanted was to see this "misfit and big mistake of God burning in hell for ever because there could never be a pardon for such a monster if there was any God in heaven." He was going to enjoy watching that life terminated and consigned to hell.

Then the camera shifted to the second interview, the mother of the young murderer. A simple woman, she was totally ashamed about what her son had done. Sobbing and with tear-filled eyes she said: "My son deserves his punishment, he did something horrible. I never expected anyone to forgive him. How much I cried and suffered with the family of that poor girl. If only I could do something for them. But my son - whatever he did - is not a monster. He was always a good boy. I know God will forgive him. He's my son, how can I stop loving him?" Then she broke down in tears and had to be carried away.

I imagine God is like this mother, but with a difference - in loving that young man even more than his mother ever could. Knowing that terrible crime cannot be undone, God's "womb-like love" will suffer even more than the parents of the murdered girl. But there is no cutting off this young man from the divine love. He was created out of love and for love. Our God is like a mother who could say to her criminal child: "I'm so outraged at what you did, I could kill you and you'd deserve it, but I can't do it, because I love you."

On the cross Jesus identifies himself with all of us and represents us before the Father. He takes upon himself the "outrage" that God feels because of our behavior and in love and fidelity he overcomes God's justified anger. On the cross God has taken humankind's suffering as his own. God takes on the grief himself rather than raging against his creation. As Brueggemann states it above: God bears the vengeance of God in order that his creation can have compassion. On the cross Jesus is revealed as the incomprehensible compassion of God which cannot destroy but must forgive, must give life again because he is driven by his womb-like love. This is the unfathomable mystery of God: the almighty, the absolute Lord wants to save through love. And true love is defenseless, but this defenselessness is stronger than all other powers in the world.

Jesus expressed this God-image in the Aramaic word "*ABBA*" which, translated, means 'dearest father'. This God-image is the key to unlocking the secret of his life; it is the standard of his life and world-view; it is the ultimate foundation of his relationship with God and his fellow human beings; it is the vantage-point from which he relates the present time to the end-time. His vision of God's Kingdom is like a magnifying lens that gives us an enlarged picture of the whole world as he saw it and as we must see it. For this vision Jesus lived, worked, suffered and died.

Only if we become sensitive, only if we attune ourselves to such a God, will we be able to see his presence in our life and world today. What we need is a feel for the *defenselessness of God's love.*

> Whoever wants to experience God today must let himself be guided into a dimension in God's being that was already there all the time but comes forcefully into the foreground today: the defenselessness of God' love. God is so inconspicuous, so defenseless in our violent time, that he disappears. He vanishes - so to speak - from our sight. We are no longer in touch with him. Most people live in a way as if God does not exist at all. They have no need for him. God has simply vanished from their thinking and planning. He is not only missed but he is just not there any more (Bours, "Die wehrlose Liebe, p. 69).

This is the mystery of our God: he has decided to deal with us only with love, a womb-love which can never destroy the child of his "womb." The terrible thing is that his free creature can attack him, offend him, deny him, ignore him, hate him and persecute anyone who believes in him. God has no power to defend himself; he cannot force himself upon us; he is defenseless love.

There are two kinds of attack on God's love: first, outright persecution, hate and outrage shown against him and those who serve and proclaim him; second, total indifference and inattention by those who do not want to acknowledge God as their personal God and moral norm.

Our Image of God

The foundational reality of our faith

This image of God that Jesus revealed to us is the essence of our faith. His perception of reality as gracious and caring is the presupposition for all Christian life. Without it we cannot live the Gospel demands. Our being disciples of Jesus means a life lived in complete response to the love of God for us. According to St John, love does not mean that we love God but that he has loved us first (1 Jn 4:10). Only in the light of such a God can we see and commit ourselves to the ultimate goal in life as *"Loving God with all our heart and all our mind and with all our strength and our neighbor as ourselves"* (Mt 22:35-40). This is the vision that should determine our behavior and our way of life. Knowing this, we cannot help but be filled with joy, a deep joy in God, and then radiate this joy to others.

What kind of God image you have and hold on to might be easily discovered in the answer you give to the following question: which of the following two statements would you agree?

> Fear not, trust in God, and God will see that none of the things you fear will happen to you.

> Fear not, trust in God, the things that you are afraid of are quite likely to happen to you, but they are nothing to be afraid of because God is right there with you.

Only the second sentence is true religion. The first one is an illusion. Our God does not come into our lives to free us from all our problems and worries but to be with us and to help us find a solution or to bear with us that which cannot be solved. Of course, we would prefer that God deftly and decisively pluck us out of our problems. But God has always answered our urgent requests for help in the same way as he answered Moses when he asked, "Who am I that I should go to Pharaoh and lead the Israelites out of Egypt?" God's answer was short and to the point: *"Don't worry, I will be with you"* (Ex 3:12).That however, does not exclude the fact that God does hear our prayers and may also enter our life miraculously here and there in order to help us in our difficulties, cares and problems. But these occasions will remain exceptions not the rule.

> The enjoyment of God should be the supreme end of spiritual technique; and it is in that enjoyment of God that we feel not only saved in the Evangelical sense, but safe: we are conscious of belonging to God, and hence are never alone; and to the degree we have these two, hostile feelings disappear... In that relationship Nature seems friendly and homely; even the vast spaces instead of eliciting a sense of terror speak of the infinite love; and the nearer beauty becomes the garment with which the Almighty clothes Himself (Barry, *Paying Attention to God*, p. 16).

Others have expressed the same reality in a different language. They refer to it as the 'experience of mystery', a touch by the 'inexhaustible depth' within us or the 'person's self-experience' at its deepest. These experiences are seen as the starting point for any faith journey (Gallagher, *Where is your God?*, pp. 13-21).

One of the most difficult pastoral tasks today is to develop techniques and practices that will help people to have such a foundational experience and to discover once again the mystery that surrounds us. The question in all renewal is: does the mystery of God touch people on the level of their deep personal experience? Anyone who has conducted renewals knows that the real struggle in such courses is how to reach the hunger and wonder at the core of each person. How can one reach the heart where the Spirit dwells?

Particularly in our time, when traditional expressions of faith are eroding or disappearing, and pronouncements of faith are supplanted by natural explanations, only a personal God-experience can lead us, individually and as faith community, out of this ever deepening crisis. Years ago K. Rahner remarked that "the Christian of the future will be a mystic, one who has experienced God, or he/she will be nothing at all."

Genuine mysticism is a deep, personal rootedness in God, a perception of things from the inside. It seeks to bring the divine fire that burns within us to our contemporaries, and indeed to the whole world (Arnold, "Through Darkness to Light", p 19). All spiritual writers seem to agree that to be a Christian in the future means to have made a God-experience and to convey such an experience to other people. But first we have to be convinced that the fire burning within us can overcome the darkness of uncertainties which we do not like to bear.

> The student Tokusan used to come to the teacher in the evenings to talk and to listen. One night it was very late before he was finished asking questions. "Why don't you go to bed now?" the teacher asked. Tokusan bowed and lifted the screen to go outside. "But it is very dark out there, " the student said. "Here, take this candle," the teacher suggested. But when Tokusan reached for the candle the teacher leaned forward and blew it out.

With our eyes on the cross

With our eyes on the cross
our hearts ready to be broken,
our minds eager for challenge and change,
and our souls enriched by the nearness of God,
are we willing to go out into the dark,
into the unknown
holding the candle of Christ's love?

Only then can we hope to build the Kingdom -
on earth as in heaven.

Jesus had a genuine in-depth experience in mind when he revealed God to us as "Abba." This is the foundation for a way of life which lets God become more and more the core relationship and the touchstone for all other relationships. Only when we believe in such a God and experience such a God will we be able to reform our lives in line with what true discipleship demands of us and what the Kingdom of God calls for.

Spiritual authors have pointed out that this conversion is the most crucial one we have to make in our life: a conversion from the brain to the heart. What that means can best be explained with the following story:

> When I was just ordained, I met a Sister who had been working for forty years in a leper colony. She was known to be a very joyful and lively person, and so I asked her, "How is it that you are such a joyful and inspiring person in spite of all the hard and often frustrating work you have to do continuously?" She answered, "Well, Father, it took twenty-five years of religious life before I suddenly realized that God truly loved me. That experience changed my whole life. From that day on I became a different person. And only if you had known me before could you appreciate what a different person I have become."

True conversion, then, would mean that I let the theoretical knowledge that God loves me travel from my head to my heart and that I start living in response to this love which I experience with growing intensity as the ultimate source of my being. His love for me has to become more and more the only motive for all my prayer, work and action. Then my life will begin to be a response to that incomprehensible love for me. But most of us are afraid of God and avoid the risk of getting too close. We restrict ourselves to a "fairly good relationship" but we don't want to get totally drawn into him because then I may lose the control over my life.

> The Master said: "As your perception is, so will your action be. The thing to change is not your action but your outlook." "What must I do to change it?" the disciple asked. "Merely understand that your present way of looking is defective" (de Mello).

If I let this God-image into my life to determine my actions and behavior, *joy* should become the basic mood of my being. The double-parable of the Treasure in the Field and the Costly Pearl (Mt 13:44-46) is regarded by many exegetes as the key to unlock all the other parables. The stress in this parable is the phrase "*full of joy.*" Something the farmer could have never dreamt of happens to him: he finds a treasure that will change his whole life. This fills him with tremendous joy and the actions that follow the discovery are only consequences to what has happened to him so unexpectedly. The problem with us is that we think we have already found the treasure and forget that we might find it now for the first time and let ourselves be overwhelmed by it so that we "cry tears of joy" just like people we see on television who have won a great prize. Their first reaction is boundless joy and excitement before they even see the prize they have just won.

Joy is essential to spiritual life. Joy is the experience of knowing that we are unconditionally loved and that nothing - sickness, failure, emotional distress, oppression, war or even death - can take that love away. Joy is not the same as happiness. We can be unhappy about many things, but joy can still be there, because it comes from the knowledge of God's love for us.

Joy is the result of our choice. I have a choice in the way I respond to the circumstances of my life. Though I have no control over them, I have a choice in how I react to them. The external circumstances may be the same but the choice of response can be completely different. Some people become bitter and even malicious as they grow old. Others grow old graciously and joyfully. That does not mean that the life of those who have become bitter was harder than the life of those who have become joyful. It means that different choices were made, inner choices, choices of the heart.

Rabbi Schmelke and his brother came to the maggid to ask for advice: "Our sages once said something that does not give us any peace, because we do not understand its true meaning. He proposes that a person should thank and praise God for all the misfortunes that have befallen him in the same way as he would thank God for all the good things that happened in his life and which fill him with deep happiness. Please tell us how we should understand this message."

The maggid replied, "Go to the Torah School where you will find Sussja. He is the one smoking a pipe and he will explain the meaning to you. They did as they were told and approached Sussja with the same question. He only laughed at them and said. "You really came to the right person! You need to look for someone else and not ask me because no misfortune has happened to me throughout my whole life." However, they knew very well that Rabbi Sussja's life had been one long sequence of misfortunes and suffering from the day of his birth to the present moment. That very instant they understood what it means to accept suffering with love and not to become bitter. (Hoffsümmer)

It is important to be aware that at every moment of our life we have an opportunity to choose joy and we can learn to develop our capacity to do so. If I spend a few moments at the end of the day and decide to remember this day as a day to be grateful for - whatever may have happened - I increase my heart's capacity to choose joy. And as our hearts become more joyful, we will become, without any special effort, a source of joy for others. Just as sadness begets sadness, so does joy beget joy (Nouwen, *Here and Now...*, pp. 14-15).

Ultimately, it is a matter of attitude. As someone remarked correctly: The longer I live, the more I realize the impact of attitude on life. Attitude, to me, is more important than facts. It is more important than the past, than education, than money, than circumstances, than failures, than successes, than what other people think or say or do. It is more important than appearance, giftedness, or skill. It will make or break a company, a church, a home. The remarkable thing is we have a choice every day regarding the attitude we will embrace for that day. We cannot change our past — we cannot change the fact that people will act in a certain way. We cannot change the inevitable. The only thing we can do is play on the one string we have, and that is our attitude — I am convinced that life is ten percent what happens to me and ninety percent how I react to it. And so it is with you — we are in charge of our Attitudes (Swindoll).

False God-images and false spiritualities: What to do about them?

There is a close link between our God-image and our spirituality. One depends on the other. If one is wrong the other is definitely affected. A false God-image leads easily to a false spirituality and vice versa.

Our false images of God and how to redeem them

In each of us there is an image or picture of reality, whether conscious or not, which more than anything else shapes the way we live. Reality may be imaged as indifferent, as hostile, as something one has to protect oneself against or as a judge who has to be appeased. The result is a constant search for security on all levels of life. Such a view is accompanied by a corresponding God-image. The common misconceptions of God are well known. Some of them are: the God out there, the watchmaker God who couldn't care less about his creation, a God who slides into the Big Bully and, even worse, becomes the Torturer God, vengeful or punitive. He is seen as planning the downfall for each as punishment for our wrongdoings (cf. Gallagher, *Free to Believe, pp. 51-60)*. One more common image is the God who-Didn't-Give-What-I-Asked. He is the God who fails to live up to our expectations or to co-operate with our plans. This is the God whom others call the "manipulated god", the God to whom people prayed so hard but who never gave them what they were asking for. Therefore, we often hear the complaint, "What good is such a God who never answers my prayers?" It is so difficult for many people to accept the fact that a God who loves all and respects the freedom of each human being, will not be manipulated, neither by prayers nor by good works.

The most damaging image of all is a God who is perceived as someone who is angry, out to "get me", "always snooping around looking for sinners." He is a God who needs to be appeased. When thinking of him I feel guilty and worthless.

Some people carry around with them an image of God that is in fact superstitious. It is the image of the punishing puppet-master who has to be humored and pacified in case he might pull the wrong string. Others picture him as a distant, inaccessible authority figure who is totally out of tune with the friendship held out to us in Christ. A surprising number of people look on God as a kind of clock-maker - a God of explanation for the universe but a God irrelevant to ordinary life. There are even those who only know him as a God of the gaps. He has no compelling existence until favors are needed or trouble strikes. (*Pastoral Letter of the Irish Bishops to mark the International Year of Youth in 1985*)

These images are the demons that Jesus came to expel. The erroneous images that many of us have about God are mind-boggling and sad. Most of these images originated in childhood and are not easily wiped out by doctrine learned later about a God of love. Even many years of Christian life do not guarantee that we have changed our image of God to the image that Jesus came to convey to us.

Probably the damage can only be undone by some positive contrary experiences. The first thing we have to do is to examine our own image of God. In our "brain-bag" we may have stored a fairly true biblical image of God, but the God who guides our lives, to whom we pray and to whom we entrust ourselves daily, often has a totally different face. The result of such an examination may be painful.

For years I have been conducting a seminar at the university called *My true God-Image*. The experience I have made with the participating students from all over the world has shown me how difficult it is for many to even find out what God-image is ruling and directing their lives. It has taught me how difficult it is for many to grow out of a false image and to embrace the image of God that Jesus came to reveal to us. Even religious and priests carry with them wrong, unconscious demonic and unhealthy images of God and are formed by these images.

He/she who is cruel against and hard on him/herself has an equally cruel and rigid God-image or vice versa. My God-image uses up most of my psychic energy. It is the most hidden center of my human existence and proves to be the most dangerous partner if it is wrong. Because of this, the God-image has an enormous effect on the health or sickness of our human subconscious. A mature, healthy God-image has a beneficial influence on our whole being. From a neurotic and weird God-image flow unhealthy powers which cause psychic instability and rigidity in our relationship to reality. Our life can only become truly genuine if we have the right God-image.

When trying to change our wrong God-image and become free of the enslavement of false gods, three things can be very helpful.

First, we need to inform ourselves about the true image of God as it is presented in the Bible. It needs real study and interest in the Word of God. Many Christians don't really know the Bible and the Teaching of the Church.

Secondly, we must trust our own experience and self-reflection. We must search our life and find the God who loves us and has shown his love through the thousand shapes this love has taken over the years of our lives through persons, events and direct God experiences. It needs an attentive heart and mind to discover God's love in our lives.

Thirdly, we need some good companions who can guide us and with whom we can share our life experiences. Their sharing will help us to see God in their lives and to discover more easily the finger of God in our own lives and the love that has accompanied us from the moment of our birth.

Another way of becoming conscious of God's love for me is through a prayer called the *Prayer of Reminiscence*. It is a prayer that aims at helping us to become perceptive of God's presence in our lives as a God who loves us unconditionally, who forgives us always and who surrounds us always with a womb-like love.

If we search our lives we can and will find numerous occasions where God has shown us, in many different ways, his love and concern. We should always keep in mind what Gandhi once said, "God always reveals himself to us in some concrete shape." To discover him in my life I have to seek out these "concrete shapes" through which he revealed himself to me.

I can start from the present and move backward as far as I can in remembering my earliest days of childhood, or I can begin with my childhood and move forward to the present time. In relation to this, there are four main areas to consider:

Persons: God does not deal with us directly, but most of the time he reveals himself through other persons such as our mother, our father, or people who have really shaped our lives. They have done much for us and their influence in our lives has affected our present state. If I search my life I will be surprised to realize how many people there are to whom I owe almost everything I am.

As a seminarian I did some pastoral work with prison-inmates who were 16 to 18 years old. They all told me the story of their lives and why they had ended up where they were. This had two effects on me. First, I realized that it was not virtue on my part that I had not ended up like them, but most probably, it was only because I had lacked the opportunities to go wrong. If I had been born into their life-situation and surroundings, I might have behaved in the same way they did. Secondly, I became grateful for all the people who had raised me, shaped me, and who gave me a true example of a Christian life.

Joys: There are thousands of small joys in our lives which we have experienced frequently but most of the time taken for granted. If I am convinced of God's love for me, I will discover his love even behind the smallest things. As Bernanos says, "There is not the smallest incident in our lives behind which we cannot discover his providence."

Special moments of grace: In each person's life there are moments of intense experiences when we feel particularly graced. Every person will have at least a few 'peak experiences' when he or she feels God's presence almost physically. It could be a moment when we have been protected from great danger - or an intense experience of God's loving presence.

One incident that happened during my childhood convinced me that God had a particular interest in me.

After the war, there was much abandoned ammunition left scattered in the fields around my home village. One day I found a hand-grenade. Not knowing what it was I looked for some tools to get at the core of the matter! Strangely enough, no tool could be found. My mother, who generally never bothered much about what we village children were playing, suddenly became interested in why I so urgently wanted a hammer. Going back with me to the group of expectant playmates, she discovered to her horror what I had wanted to do with the hammer, had I found one.

I am sure everyone has similar experiences. The question is how we look at them.

Important days in our life: Graduation-day, or entrance into religious life, or first or final profession, ordination, a birthday, a jubilee. These are days when one can be more aware of God's choice, of his guidance and goodness.

Prayer of remembrance can easily be supported by Scripture texts, such as Psalms 103 or 145.

Bless Yahweh, my soul, bless his holy name, all that is in me! Bless Yahweh, my soul, and remember all his kindness: in forgiving all your offenses, in curing all your diseases, in redeeming your life from the pit, in crowning you with love and tenderness, in filling your years with prosperity, in renewing your youth like an eagle's (Ps 103:1-5).

I sing your praises, God my King, I bless your name for ever and ever, blessing you day after day, and praising your name for ever and ever (Ps 145:1).

The Magnificat or other canticles of Scripture could be used as well. They should lead us into a prayer of "day-dreaming", marveling about all God has done for us. On special days we should spend some time in such prayer and end the day with a joyful, thankful attitude, knowing more deeply how good and kind the Lord has been to us through each and every day of our lives (cf. Fuellenbach, *"Prayer of Reminiscence"* in *Proclaiming his Kingdom*, pp 93-102). If we do this more or less regularly we might discover to our great surprise and joy the basic pattern and the guiding hand of God in our life. From the Sufi masters comes this story:

Once upon a time - among an ancient people - an only child of a family of threadmakers was orphaned. Wandering nomad weavers took the boy into their tribe for awhile but, for lack of means, eventually had to sell him as an apprentice to a family of shipbuilders. In their situation, the shipbuilders trained him to make masts. Mastmaking was a good trade, in very great demand in this sailing town.

The young man liked the work; but years later, while on a business voyage for the mastmakers, this same young man - once an abandoned weaver and now a satisfied mastmaker - was shipwrecked on a primitive island.

And in this place the people lived in wait for the fulfillment of a promise that God would some day send a foreigner who would help them save their religious treasures from ruin by the hostile environment. All other foreigners were to be rejected.

"Are you the one for whom we wait? Are you the one who will save our religious treasure?" they asked.

At that very moment the young man understood both his past and his future. He took the memory of his experience as a spinner of thread and made rope; he took the memory of his experience as weaver and made cloth; he took the memory of his experience as a mastmaker and made long, strong poles. And out of all these memories, he fashioned the vision of a tent which saved the values of that people (Chittister).

The greatest sin of our life is probably our stunning insensibility or constant inattention to the million proofs of God's kindness and love which reach us through persons, circumstances and special signs of care and love like the protection and liberation from all kinds of danger or harm. The prayer of reminiscence, frequently practiced, could help us to become for the first time seriously conscious of and alert to the God Jesus came to disclose to us.

To proclaim and to witness to such a God-image that Jesus came to throw like fire into this world is not always easy. Whenever I explain this

God-image to people in seminars, workshops and lectures it turns out to be a real challenge for all concerned. There are moments I have to ask the Lord to prove me right. Some years ago I gave a workshop on the Kingdom of God in South Africa. While explaining the vision of Jesus concerning his image of God, I was made aware that many of my participants had dreadful experiences behind them which made it almost impossible for them to accept such a God-image in a situation of violence and discrimination, which was the reality in South Africa at that time. Feeling their pain and apprehension I pleaded with God for a sign that would confirm I was right with my message. God did give me a sign but he let me wait for it until the end of the course. On the last evening one of the participants asked me to accompany her home because her grandmother wanted by all means to see me. The young lady had shared with her every evening the lectures I had given and now the grandmother wanted to see me personally. With reluctance I finally agreed and we went to Soweto. When we arrived I was introduced to a lady whom they called Mama Zibi.

She was at least 100 years old. She could still remember the war with England. All her life she had been a simple African servant. But one thing she knew very well was the Bible. Every day she read it and she knew many passages by heart. When I met her she was very sick. She could die at any time. Both her legs had been amputated because of diabetes. The message of my talks had delighted her. She looked at me with an alert expression and said in the most gentle way, "Father John, thank you for coming to see me. I just wanted to let you know the secret of the Holy Book as I have come to understand it in my long life. It is the message you have conveyed so beautifully to my little niece during this week. Yes, Father John, you are right. All that counts is love, only love can redeem the world. Yes, God loves us unconditionally; he forgives us always and he is always with us. That is the experience of my life. He has always shown me his care, he has never left me alone, and he was always on my side to strengthen me and to give me joy and courage, no matter how difficult my life had been." I was really moved. God was giving me the sign I had asked for. Here was a woman who had experienced all the humiliations a black woman in South Africa could experience. So many tragedies and so much suffering had been part of her life! Her husband had been shot, her two sons had lost their lives in riots, she had been sick all her life and had tried to eke out a living by doing all kinds of jobs. But there was no bitterness, no resentment in her at all. Her face was one of the most peaceful faces I have ever seen. All she wanted me to know was the secret of the Bible: love is the only thing that matters in the whole universe.

The real content of Jesus' message consists in his image of God: God loves every human being with unconditional love. He is good; he constantly forgives and he is always with us in our daily life with all its ups and downs.

Conversion to the message of Jesus therefore means, first of all, a conversion to the image of God that Jesus revealed to us. How far I have become a true Christian depends ultimately on how deeply I have been transformed by this God-image and how far I live according to this God-image. This may be my ultimate conversion which I have to undergo again and again for the rest of my life.

The change from a *life-denying* to a *life-affirming* spirituality

Life-denying spirituality

A world-negating spirituality, deeply rooted in the Christian tradition itself, goes together with a negative God-image. A rather negative attitude towards earthly realities, *a life-denying* mentality, penetrated the whole of our Christian faith right from the beginning. Where did this come from? Two reasons are normally mentioned by scholars: first *the near-expectation* of the parousia in the early Church; second the adaptation of the Christian faith to the *dualism* of Greek philosophy.

The early Christians were convinced that the Lord would be coming soon, therefore, why should they bother about this world? His coming would mean the present world would be restored anew. There was no reason, no meaning in getting involved in the present age that was fading away fast. The order of the day was: stay ready, do what ever is asked of you, make sure you are awake when the Lord comes! Even marriage was seen as too bothersome since the end was near.

Unfortunately this *near-expectation* led to a "blindness towards God's creation." The beauty of creation, so much praised and appreciated in the Old Testament got clouded, to say the least. What counted was the life to come and the question was: how can I get out of this world as fast as possible to be with the Lord in eternal life?

Judaism, our parent in the faith, does not know this kind of asceticism that says no to the world and to life before death. On the contrary, it knows a real passion for life here and now and shows no eagerness to get out of this world fast. One only has to read the Psalms of Lament to realize how much pleading for this life, rather than the life to come, is the center of the praying person. For a Jew, the enjoyment of the things in this world will lead the person to the joy in the Lord. Any withdrawal or any kind of asceticism is justified only if it leads me back to nature in order to be led once again to the encounter with the God of life.

The second reason for a world-denying spirituality in the Christian tradition was the adaptation to *Greek dualism*. Instead of returning to the roots from which Christianity comes - Judaism - and with it to a life-affirming spirituality after the near-expectation faded away, Christianity turned to the Greek philosophy of dualism.

Here God is absolutely transcendent and in no way involved in this messy world. The world is looked upon as a mistake that was never intended. This view is contrary to what the Bible has to say about creation, namely, that the world is God's creation brought into existence out of love with the desire to lead all its creatures to the fullness of God's own life. Although we have to admit that Jewish apocalyptics held a rather negative world view, as we will see later, they never held on to a metaphysical dualism. For them the world in all its sinfulness and submission to evil powers and principalities was still God's creation.

Through the encounter with this aspect of Greek culture, the Church became the Church of the ascetics. Creation did not really play an important role any more in the Christian tradition. What counted was *redemption*. The dominant question was: how do we get out of this corrupt world ruled by the effects of original sin and the powers of evil?

There were, of course, many voices in the history of the Church that protested against such a spirituality but the Church was never able to rid herself fully of this world-denying mentality of dualism. The way back to God had primarily to start with *the way of negation and purification* followed by *the way of enlightenment,* leading finally to *the way of unification.* The bodily existence of the person does not enter into this unity with God. Unity with the divine happens outside of the bodily sphere and outside of space and time. Neither do fellow human being, nor the social and the political realm enter into this union.

The material world is seen as a hindrance to be overcome through negation and all kinds of ascetic practices. The aim is to get through this world fast. There emerged a kind of death-wish spirituality that wanted to shut out anything related to this world and its pleasures in life. Particularly in religious life, this kind of Christian spirituality was widely fostered and advocated.

Excesses of this spirituality have always been fought in the tradition of the Church, but it is safe to say there is still a great need in the Church today to exorcize this evil spirit of a negative spirituality in order to bring back life, spontaneity and joy in the Lord. God is the "lover of life." He wants to see his creatures alive and full of joy and not burdened with a spirituality that lives out of the fear of a punishing God and declares the way to God as something to be attained through mortification and denial alone.

One can still hear good, dedicated Christians say: "I feel really good; I enjoy life so much but at times that worries me. I ask myself, is this really Christian and what does God think of such an attitude?" According to the Old and the New Testament God's will for us is undoubtedly that we should be well and that we should enjoy life. God wants people who are fully alive physically, psychologically and spiritually.

To the objections that this rather negative spirituality produced, after all, thousands of saints, one would have to reply that it was their experience of God's infinite love and the radical response to this love that made them saints in spite of the dominant world-denying spirituality they lived.

Life-affirming spirituality

Contrary to such negative spirituality which still lingers on, there is a great need for a life-affirming spirituality. We must rediscover the *God of Life* who created everything out of love and wants all things to be fully alive (Wis 11: 24-26). In Deuteronomy 30:15f we find a text which is a kind of summary of the Old and New Testament statements about God. God tells us here, *"I put before you life and death today, choose life so that you will live."* The life meant here is not life after death but life in this world. Sure, the option for life in this text means an *option for God*, because God is the ultimate source of life. God is a God of the living and he wants all creatures to live and enjoy life.

Jesus' message portrays the same zest for life. The Kingdom he proclaims is God's intention with creation aiming at bringing all human beings to the fullness of life not only in the life to come but in this world, in the here and now as well. The Gospel of John reveals the same attitude in Jesus: *"I came that they will have life and will have it in full"* (Jn 10:10). Jesus himself enjoyed life and this is shown particularly in his sitting at table with all kinds of people. He seemingly relished these meals so much that his opponents called him a glutton and a drunkard (Lk 7:34).

Summary: the God in whom I believe

The God of our faith reveals himself under two aspects: on the one hand, he is a loving God but, on the other hand, he always remains the incomprehensible God. We have to live with both aspects.

The loving God

In view of all that has been said so far, the *"credo"* of a disciple of Jesus could be summarized in these words:

"I believe in the God of life who loves me at each moment without any conditions whatsoever, and who wants to see me alive and well. I believe in the God, who always forgives me and opens to me a future full of life and hope. I believe in the God who is with me every second of my life to help me, heal me, console me, strengthen me, suffer with me and be my best friend. I believe in the God who knows only love and compassion; who is a "lover of life" and who begs me to "choose life." In this faith I find joy and peace in the present life and hope for the life to come."

Some of us believe that God is All-Power and can do all, and that God is All-Wisdom and knows how to do all. But that God is All-Love and wants to do all, here we restrain ourselves. And this ignorance hinders most of God's lovers as I see it (Julian of Norwich).

The incomprehensible God

However, there is a second aspect to our God experience which we cannot overlook. At times it may even push our faith in a compassionate God to its utter limits.

The experience of a loving, forgiving and compassionate God will never take away the reality of an incomprehensible and hidden God: the God of Job and the God Jesus had to experience on the cross. God will always remain the transcendent God, the one we cannot understand. There are events and realities in life which seemingly contradict all that we have said about the God of Jesus. There is so much suffering of the innocent, such incomprehensible violence, so much pain, so much evil in this world - and God is so silent. If he really cared, where was his care in Rwanda, in Bosnia, in the gulags of the Stalin era?, or where is it in the refugee camps of today? Where was and is he in all of this? Isn't it too easy to say that he was right there and suffered with these people? But why did he not interfere? Why was he so silent, so hidden? Are those not right, who say God died in the holocaust of the Nazis and in the killing fields of Cambodia, Liberia and Guatemala?

Ultimately, we have no answers to these questions or accusations. We must not pretend either that we know God or that we can speak for him. Our compassionate love for God must include the admission that we also suffer under our God who does not answer to so many and, often so unbearable questions that surface in us when we look at our world and its innumerable problems.

To bear such agony in the face of senseless suffering and not to give up hope but to go on believing in a loving and compassionate God will demand of us to hold on to, to bear with, to put up with, to ultimately suffer such a God.

Since the days of Abraham, this kind of faith was part of Israel's heritage: a strong and unshakeable faith, no matter how incomprehensible, cruel or wrathful God might have appeared. The following story illustrates such faith:

During the time of the inquisition in Spain a famous Rabbi escaped execution by taking flight in a small boat with his wife and children. While they were at sea a terrible storm broke. The children were thrown overboard and drowned. The boat itself was smashed against the rock of a little island and the Rabbi and his wife were thrown onto the land. At that very moment a bolt of lightning killed the wife. Only the Rabbi survived the ordeal naked, bruised and totally exhausted. In that state he crawled to his knees, raised his hands to God and said:

"God of Israel, I fled to this terrible place because I yearned to serve you undisturbedly. I wanted to fulfill your commandments and to sanctify your Holy Name. You, however, have done everything to stop me from believing in you.

If you think you will succeed in diverting me from my way, I will tell you now, God of my fathers, you shall never succeed! You may beat me, you may take away from me the most precious and most valuable things I possess in this world, you may torture me to death - I shall always believe in you, I shall always love you - no matter how you treat me.

These are my last words, you wrathful God: You will not succeed! You did everything to kill my belief in you and make me despair. But I will die as I have lived with a firm faith in you. I will hold on to my fathers' unwavering faith: "Listen Israel, the eternal is our God, the unique and the only God!"

This is the challenge of our faith: to find enthusiasm, joy and deep peace in the knowledge that God loves, forgives and is compassionate with us, while at the same time holding on to this God and suffer under this God who leaves so many burning question unanswered and renders us "defenseless in the sight of our foes."

Reflection: *Who is my God?*

Jesus communicated his image of God through parables which turn many of our treasured concepts and views upside down. The following parables can especially be considered the heart of his message:

Parable of the Lost Sheep	Lk 15:1-7
Parable of the Unbelievably Merciful Father	Lk 15:11-35
Laborers in the Vineyard	Mt 20:1-16

In all parables, but especially in these, Jesus reveals what he considers to be essential in the image of the Father, namely his tremendous joy in forgiving. The father of the prodigal son experienced an enormous joy when he embraced his lost and returned son and clothed him with his love as with a festive garment.

> Love proves its genuineness in fidelity,
> but it reaches its completion in forgiveness.
> (*Werner Bergengrün*)

How hard it is for us to imagine the unimaginable gratuitous love of God and his invitation to enter the Kingdom gratuitously! We 'create' God again and again according to our image and likeness and find it so hard to imagine otherwise.

There was once a lady who scrimped and saved for years in order to take an ocean cruise. At long last, she had saved enough money to pay for her ticket. However, there was not much money left for luxuries. She nevertheless decided to go. "For I will take along a large supply of cheese and cracker biscuits," she thought, "and eat them in my cabin. That way it won't cost as much."
This is just what she did. She went on the cruise and had a fine time. At mealtimes, when the other passengers went to the dining room, she went to her cabin and ate her cheese and crackers. She consoled herself with the knowledge that she had saved just enough money for one dinner. On her last night aboard she was going to splurge and have a gourmet meal!
The last night finally arrived, and she dressed in her best clothes. Finally, she was to eat with the other passengers in the dining room. With great anticipation, she ordered the most delicious meal. "Oh," she said, "the sacrifice was worthwhile."
At the end of the meal, she called the waiter and asked for her bill. The waiter looked at her in great surprise. "Madam," he said, "didn't you know that all of your meals were included in the price of your ticket?" (Arcodia)

QUESTION: What is my response to a God who acts out of pure love, who operates from the heart and ignores all standards of common sense and rationality? Which elements in my image of God object to this and which confirm such a view of God?

The prophet Zephenia portrays God as someone who looks at us with love and delight and rejoices in our being present to him:

> Yahweh, your God, is in your midst, a mighty savior; He will rejoice over you with gladness, and renew you in his love. He will sing joyfully because of you, as one sings at festivals (3:17-18)

Can we imagine God dancing for joy because of us? Do we have the courage to bathe in the warmth of his love unabashed?

In Genesis chapter 16 Hagar, after being abused by Sarah is filled with such desperation that she runs away from her mistress into the desert. There Yahweh appears to her and promises to answer her prayers. This inspires Hagar to call the Lord "God who sees," and she cries out in joy, "I have seen the one who sees me" (cf. Gen 16:13-14). For us, who might not always bear a pain similar to that of Hagar, God is also "One who sees me." And this seeing means looking at us with eyes of love not seeking to find faults, so as to pounce on us at any moment.

We might say that, actually, it is not so hard for God to love us more than we love ourselves. Most of us really do not love ourselves that much. We need constant affirmation from others and even 'self-strokes' to make up for a healthy self-love. It would be so much better to realize how much God's loving gaze is really upon us.

But even if I have a beautiful and inspiring image of God, the question still remains: does it determine my actions and behavior? The score of false God-images is limitless and each one of us has his or her own. We reveal these images in the way we live and relate. Karl Rahner once said, "The way we know, love, treasure the things presented to us is the way we know and love God." We could also say, "Tell me how you experience God and who he is for you, and I will tell you how you relate to and value your own self, your fellow human beings and the environment around you."

QUESTION: What image of God do I communicate through my actions, attitudes and behavior? Is it a God to be aware of, to be feared or a God of compassion and love?

If I am really concerned with becoming a joyful disciple of the Lord I must rid myself of false God-images which enslave and keep me down and get in touch again and again with the God of the scriptures and keep on **revising my God-image.**

QUESTION: **How seriously do I want to discover the God of Jesus in Scripture and theology? Do I ever reflect on my own experience of God? Am I willing to share my God-experience with others and listen to theirs?**

Story: *The God of the Lake*

The story is about a little boy - of about ten - growing up in an orphanage. One night in the large dormitory he wakes up in the dark but knows that the dawn can't be far away. It is summer-time and there is a lake in the grounds of the orphanage.

He feels a great urge to see the dawn at the lake side but the rules are rigid: on no account should any child get up before the bell and it is strictly forbidden to leave the dormitory until the proper time. But he decides to risk it. He dresses quickly and creeps out, holding his shoes in his hands so as not to wake the others. Then there is a long corridor: he does not want his eyes to be caught by the disapproving glances of the figures on the walls.

He comes to the lake and waits in darkness for the dawn; sure enough, the drama of day begins, and the colors change from orange to red to bright sun. He watches all this reflected in the water of the lake, absorbed by the sheer beauty of it. Then suddenly he remembers the time. They will be up by now. He will be missed. He will be in trouble. So he gets up to return and speaks his last words to the lake: "I'll go back now. Thank you. I don't care if I'm punished. Because I know something now - I know that the God of the lake is greater than the God of the orphanage (*Gallagher)*

Chapter Three

God's Vision for Creation: Kingdom of God

Exegetes will agree that there are at least two authentic Jesus words to be found in the Gospels: Kingdom of God and its personified reality which he called ABBA. Abba is the word Jesus used to express his intimate relationship with God whom he experienced as unconditional love. As we have already seen, with the term Kingdom of God, Jesus expressed the whole of reality and of what is to be done with it. Kingdom of God is that final state of creation where God's being Abba will be the all embracing and determining factor. All reality will be fully permeated by this love and fully respond to it. It is that state of creation which Scripture calls New Heaven and New Earth. Both realities, Kingdom and Father, though distinct and not simply interchangeable, complement each other. The Kingdom explains God's being Abba and the Fatherhood of God provides a basis for and an explanation of the Kingdom. Everything Jesus said and did was said and done in the light of the Kingdom of God that was coming with him and through him.

> The reign of God is the key. Jesus without it is a disincarnated person - a person without a body. Jesus separated from it is a theological construct that does not correspond to the reality. Jesus only loosely connected with it is a phantom that preoccupies the doctrinal interest of the religious authorities but haunts the hearts of people in the street. Jesus without the reign of God is an incomplete Jesus. Jesus whose life and mission are not shaped by it is not the way, the truth, and the life (John 14:6), to use that profound expression in John's Gospel. Jesus is the way because his is the way of God's reign. Jesus is the truth because his is the truth revealed by it. Jesus is the life because his is the life empowered by it (Song, Jesus & the Reign of God, pp 8-9).

The two terms Abba and Kingdom of God embrace Jesus' vision, the vision for which he lived, suffered and died.

God's intention - his plan for the world

Jesus' vision has something to do with the ultimate meaning of every human being, the fulfillment of the deepest aspiration of every human heart, the plan God has for all of creation. It has something to do with what Saint Augustine expressed in this way: "Restless is our heart, O God, until it rests in you." Or, in the words of M. Gandhi: "Man's ultimate aim is the realization of God. I live and move and have my being in pursuit of this goal."

The deepest desire of every human heart is complete union with God, a union which includes union with all of God's family and harmony with the universe. It embraces God, all human beings and the world and nature as well. To the vexing question that has haunted millions of people, "Why did God create the universe and human beings?" there is a simple answer that could be phrased as follows: God, the Triune One said, "We enjoy life so much that we want to share it with other beings whom we will create for that purpose." God created us with the sole purpose of bringing us to share his own life with him. But it is not only we humans that will participate in his life; it is the whole universe that God's love wants to lead into the fullness of life because God is "a lover of life."

Yes, you love all that exists, you hold nothing of what you have made in abhor-rence, for had you hated anything, you would not have formed it. And how, had you not willed it, could a thing persist, how be con-served if not called forth by you? You spare all things because all things are yours, LORD, LOVER OF LIFE, you whose imperishable spirit is in all (Wis 11:24-26).

This plan of God to let us share in his own life was unknown in its full content up to the coming of Christ and has to be seen as a comprehensive inclusion embracing all human beings and the whole of creation.

Unknown:

This mystery, as it is now revealed in the Spirit to his holy apostles and prophets, was unknown to humanity in previous generations... I, who am less than the least of all God's holy people, have been entrusted with this special grace, of proclaiming to the gentiles the unfathomable treasure of Christ and of throwing light on the inner workings of the mystery kept hidden through all the ages in God, the Creator of everything (Eph 3:3-11).

The message which was a mystery hidden for generation and centuries and has been revealed to his holy people (Col 1:26).

Even the angels long to catch a glimpse of these things (1 Pet 1:12).

For all human beings:

God wants everyone to be saved and reach the full knowledge of the truth (1 Tim 2:4).
You see, God's grace has been revealed to save the whole human race (Tit 2:11).

For the whole of creation:

For God so much loved the world that he sent his only Son so that everyone who believes in him may not perish but have eternal life. For God sent his Son into the world not to judge the world, but so that through him the world might be saved (Jn 3:16-17).

The whole of creation is waiting with eagerness for the children of God to be revealed. It was not for its own purpose that creation had frustration imposed on it, but for the purpose of him who imposed it - with the intention that the whole creation itself might be freed from its slavery to corruption and brought into the same glorious freedom as the children of God. We are well aware that the whole of creation, until this time, has been groaning in labor pains (Rom 8:19-22).

This plan of God which is ultimately revealed in Jesus finds different expressions in Scripture and theology:

	Plan
	Intention
	Salvific Will
	New Creation: New Heaven
	and Earth
Mysterium	Redemption
Salutis	Salvation
	Transformation
	Transcreation
	Kingdom of God

Jesus himself chose the phrase Kingdom of God while theologians prefer to speak about salvation as the all embracing word of the Bible. The Kingdom is therefore the plan God had in mind for the whole of creation when he decided to create everything.

Kingdom as belonging to this world

There is a danger of seeing the Kingdom as a totally transcendent, other-worldly reality that lies beyond this one as if it had nothing to do with the "labyrinth of this world." Such a view could be called the "trampoline effect". Whenever life begins to become oppressive and troublesome, a person just leaps into the air with a bold kick and soars relieved and unencumbered into so-called eternal fields.

Jesus did not envision the Kingdom that he preached as something that belonged totally and exclusively to the world to come. His Kingdom-vision leaves room for interpreting it as belonging to this world as well as for proclaiming a future that cannot be deduced from the circumstances of present history. The future, as the Bible understands it, is something qualitatively new. It lies beyond human planning and capability, something we can only allow to be given to us. While this symbol takes the world and human effort in history seriously, it does not surrender openness to a transcendent future in the fullness of God. Only God can ultimately guarantee the fulfilment of human-kind's deepest aspirations.

> Our engagement in this struggle (to make the kingdom hope come true) can be without illusions because we know by faith that no human program by itself will bring in the eschaton. Our engagement can also be without ultimate despair, because we believe that, no matter how great our self-created horror becomes, God is faithful to his promise and he will bring the kingdom which has already drawn near to us in his Son (Viviano, The Kingdom of God, pp. 28-29).

The correct interpretation of the Kingdom symbol will show that its content does not signify something that is purely spiritual or outside this world.

> It is a total, global and structural transfiguration and revolution of the reality of human beings; it is the cosmos purified of all evils and full of the reality of God. The Kingdom is not to be in another world but is the old world transformed into a new one (Boff, Jesus Christ Liberator, p. 56).

Here the Kingdom is viewed as the consummation of history, the final fulfillment of humankind's social destiny, the accomplishment of God's own intentionality for the whole of creation. Therefore, we always have to be on guard not to view- the Kingdom as a utopia that is situated only on the horizon of history. The Kingdom is a present reality at the heart of history. Thus, Elliott proclaims:

> The Kingdom is not some kind of extra-terrestrial entity that will be superimposed on this world. Nor is it a process of spiri-tual or internal change that leaves the outer realities looking much the same. It is the liberation of the world we live in, know, touch, smell, suffer, from all that corrupts and destroys it (Praying the Kingdom, p. 1).

The Kingdom of God is incarnated in history, in human society and in the world. Although it is not purely and simply identical with the world, it is "identifiable" in the world. We could also say that the Kingdom shows itself in society and is encountered in society, but this society is not the Kingdom.

> To discover the theme of the Reign of God is to discover the full dimension of the inevitable historical character of Christianity. Our God is a god of history, has entered into history, has a purpose and a plan for history, and has shown these to us in Jesus. God's plan is the Reign of God. The Reign is the dream, the utopia God cherishes for history, God's overall design for the world, the arcane mystery hidden for centuries and now revealed fully in Jesus (Casaldáliga, Political Holiness, p.82).

This seems to have been the Kingdom message Jesus came to proclaim. It is a vision of God, the world, humankind and creation as a whole as well as of each individual human person. It is the most grandiose vision that the world has ever known. For this vision Jesus lived, labored, suffered and died. This is the vision he entrusted to his disciples: "As the Father has sent me, so I send you" (Jn 20:21).

Two conceptions of God's plan with creation

The plan of God for creation has been conceived in different ways. The two best known are the following. The first one sees salvation primarily as a rescue operation from this sinful and evil world whereby the good ones are selected and taken into the New Heaven and the New Earth. This view corresponds well with the one which sees the Kingdom as a totally transcendent reality, something not related to this world. Just like the man in the following story who saw no connection at all between this world and the next:

> There was a man whose one consuming passion was to go to heaven. Finally, he died and did go there. An angel took him by the hand and showed him the beautiful sights, the majestic mountains, lovely flowers, gorgeous sunsets, little children playing in the streets. He exclaimed, "Isn't heaven wonderful?" But the angel said, "This isn't heaven; this is the world in which you lived but which you never saw (Wharton).

The second one sees God's plan of salvation more holistically as including all of creation. It means a transformation of all reality rather than a selective process.

Individualistic view of salvation

The plan of God for creation is here primarily conceived as totally otherworldly and transcendent with no connection to this present world and its social dimensions. We could describe such a view in this way: God created human beings with the intention of leading them here on earth to their final destiny which we usually call heaven. The individual human being, however, must prove himself or herself worthy of such calling. For this reason he or she is put into this world which is sin-permeated, corrupt and therefore, dangerous. This world resembles a huge testing-ground created to provide for human beings the perfect occasion where he or she can gain or lose his or her eternal salvation. If the person stands the test, God will reward him or her with eternal life. In terms of gnostic and mystery religions, the gods are busy trying to populate Olympus with a few selected souls who have been rescued from the tumultuous sea of matter and human history. The individual is regarded as a self-contained unit, a Robinson Crusoe, to whom God's call is addressed as to someone on an island, whose salvation takes place exclusively in terms of a relationship with God. What is overlooked is the fact that no individual exists in isolation. It is not possible to speak of salvation without reference to the world of which one is part.

Such a picture is, of course, accompanied by a corresponding spirituality concerned only with the salvation of one's own soul. In such a view, salvation is easily conceived of as being totally individual and deprived of any connection to one's fellow human beings, to this world and its destiny. History with its constant flow of people and cultures has no meaning. Human achievements on this earth have no connection with the world to come. They will all disappear with the arrival of New Heaven and New Earth. Not a trace of them will be found in the new creation. This world does not matter at all. It is totally unimportant whether one is rich or poor, sick or healthy, of high esteem or low caste. The only thing that counts is that I will stand the test and get to heaven, no matter what else I or we accomplish here on earth.

Such a view reveals a decidedly pessimistic view of historical change; history and its corrupted institutions will only get worse. Only the in-breaking of the future Kingdom will be able to change the world. The structures of the fallen world cannot be transformed this side of the second coming of the Lord. The emphasis must be placed on the transcendence of God who will intervene at the end of history to bring about the hoped for, dramatic reversal of events, by destroying what is and creating a lasting and perfect world. Historical existence as we know it does not really matter since the powers which transform it come at history's end and not before. In this interim period, the community of faith experiences God's Kingdom "personally, inwardly, spiritually and vertically."

God's transcendence is preserved without dilution. He is "the heavenly Father" who reigns now from his "heavenly Kingdom" in the hearts of his disciples. The mission of the community of disciples is not to bring about structural changes in the prevailing sociology of conflict. Their mission is to work for spiritual change and not to attempt to usurp God's work on his future day. Christians should not forget that the most important result of being saved is not a change in the structures of society and the practice of justice, but rather the persuasion of others to become followers of Jesus so that they too may be eternally saved. But is such a conception of God's plan correct?

Universal view of salvation

Taking into consideration what Vatican II had to say concerning human history and the salvation of people of other religious traditions and belief, we will find in Scripture images of the 'World to Come' which allow a different interpretation. Here God's plan for the world is perceived not in terms of total destruction but in terms of transformation or transcreation aiming at the salvation of all.

The New Heaven and New Earth are understood as being this world transformed, renewed, cleansed and made new. It is this old, sin-permeated, corrupt world, a world in which there is so much hatred, egoism, oppression, despair and suffering, that will be the object of trans-formation. It will become something totally new. Our world is the arena where God's ultimate plan for creation unfolds. The 'Kingdom of God' happens here, in the midst of human affairs. It is meant for this world here and now. It has happened already in our presence although the fulfillment is still to come.

Since the most general characteristic of human existence is being in the world, and the primary mode for human interaction is relationship, salvation for each person cannot be a deliverance from creaturehood or an escape from bodily existence. The resurrection of the body is an integral part of biblical hope. The world is not evil "per se," and therefore, not a realm from which a person must escape in order to find true life. There must be a total transformation of nature if we ourselves are to be transformed. This view can be found in Paul's writing once again: "The whole of creation groans with pain and awaits its transformation" (Rom 8:19-25).

If we accept this view of God's plan for creation, our whole understanding of salvation will change. Being saved does not mean being taken out of this world and being transferred to another place. Being saved means remaining part of the whole of creation that has been transformed into the New Heaven and the New Earth. I will be saved because creation as a whole will be saved. My salvation is imbedded in the salvation of all human beings. Because my brothers and sisters will be saved, I will be saved since I am one with them. Strictly speaking, we cannot talk about individual salvation since we are tied with a thousand strings to each other and to creation as a whole. The salvation offered to us in Jesus Christ is universal in scope. God wants all people to be saved (1 Tim 2:4).

Thich Nhat Hanh, the Vietnamese poet and Buddhist monk, describes our being part of the total global reality in his poem "Please Call Me by My True Names":

> I am the child in Uganda, all skin and bones,
>   my legs as thin as bamboo sticks,
> and I am the arms merchant, selling deadly
>   weapons to Uganda.
>
> I am the 12-year-old girl, refugee
>   on a small boat,
> who throws herself into the ocean after
>   being raped by a sea pirate,
> and I am the pirate, my heart not yet capable
> of seeing and loving.
>
> I am a member of the politburo, with
>   plenty of power in my hand,
> and I am the man who has to pay his
>   "debt of blood" to my people,
> dying slowly in a forced labor camp.
>
> My joy is like spring, so warm it makes
>   flowers bloom in all walks of life.
> My pain is like a river of tears, so full it
>   fills up the four oceans.
>
> Please call me by my true names,
> so I can hear all my cries and my laughs
>   at once,
> so I can see that my joy and pain are one.
>
> Please call me by my true names,
>   so I can wake up,

and so the door of my heart can be left open,
the door of compassion. (Thich Nhat Hanh)

How one single good deed, no matter how small and insignificant it may have been, could have had a saving effect on the most desperate souls, is imaginatively demonstrated by the following story of Dostojewski:

Once upon a time there lived a mean old woman. Throughout her whole life she had never done a single good deed. When she died the devil came, picked her up and threw her into the fiery sea. Her guardian angel stood by in sadness regarding himself a failure. As his last resort he went to God saying, "I will never be happy again in all eternity because I lost the woman you entrusted to me. Is there nothing that could still be done to save her?" The Lord replied, "If you find a single good deed - no matter how insignificant - that woman has done during her life, I will save her." The guardian angel searched all the books of her life and all he could find was that a long time ago she had pulled a green onion out of her vegetable patch and had thrown it at a poor beggar woman just to get rid of her. The angel returned to God and told him what he had found. God replied, "Though it is not much, take that very same onion and hold it out to her in the fiery sea so that she can grasp it and you may pull her out."

The angel went on his way and held out the onion to her crying, "Come, catch hold and I will pull you out." The woman followed the angel's instruction and the angel began pulling her out of the fire. Just as she was being lifted above the flames, the other inhabitants of hell, seeing her escape, began grabbing hold of her so that they too would be released. When the old woman realized what was happening and in keeping with her wicked ways, she started kicking them and shouted: "I am to be pulled out, not you! It's my onion, not yours!" The moment she said this, the onion split in two and the old woman fell back into the fiery sea. The angel went away and wept.

When referring to redemption and salvation, the Bible always includes the whole earth when referring to redemption and salvation. There exists an essential unity between human beings and nature, a reality which we have come to see again much better today. The earth is not merely an indifferent theater in which a person carries out his or her daily tasks but it is here where we become human beings and together forge the destiny of the whole of creation. There is an inseparable unity between human person and nature. The earth took part in the sin of humanity, therefore, it will also share in God's final redemption. The transformation of one demands the transformation of the other. If the world will not be transformed, we ourselves cannot be transformed either. The Kingdom aims at the transformation of all human reality including the whole of nature. Animals, plants, inorganic nature are all destined to participate in the New Earth and the New Heaven. The final consummation of the Kingdom will have cosmic dimensions. God's final intervention is seen as a new creation of the sin-cursed creation of old: "Behold, I create a New Heaven and a New Earth" (Is 65:17; 66:22).

> *The wolf lives with the lamb, the panther lies down with the kid, calf and lion cub feed together with a little boy to lead them. The cow and the bear make friends, their young lie down together. The lion eats straw like the ox. The infant plays over the cobra's hole; into the viper's lair the young child puts his hand. They do not hurt, no harm, on all my holy mountain, for the country is filled with the knowledge of Yahweh as the waters swell the sea (Is 11:6-9).*

The most important implication is the realization that it is this sin-permeated and corrupted world - a world in which there is so much hatred, egoism, oppression and hopelessness - which is the object of transformation into the New Heaven and the New Earth. This world is the arena where God's ultimate plan for creation unfolds. The Kingdom of God happens here, in the midst of our human affairs. It is meant for this world here and now, although its future fulfillment is still to come.

> *The seventh angel sounded his trumpet, and there were loud voices in heaven, which said: "The kingdom of the world has become the kingdom of the Lord and of his Christ, and he will reign for ever and ever" (Rev 11:15).*

Our work and efforts to change this world into God's design will appear in full glory when the Kingdom comes in glory:

> After we have obeyed the Lord, and in his Spirit nurtured on earth the values of human dignity, broth-erhood and freedom, and indeed all the good fruits of our nature and enterprise, we will find them again but free of stain, burnished and transfigured. This will be so when Christ hands over to the Father a kingdom eternal and universal: "a kingdom of truth and life, of holiness and grace, of justice, love and peace." On this earth the kingdom is already present in mystery. When the Lord returns, it will be brought into full flower (G S 39).

There is a power for God in the world, an energy at work in the deepest forces of nature and the human heart. To believe in God, to believe in the resurrection and the Kingdom is to believe that this power for God is stronger than the power for evil - and will prevail! And our faith in Jesus and in the Kingdom will release this power.

A PRAYER TO THE GOD OF SURPRISES

O God, how you surprise me
with your KINGDOM!
Attack
when the sun has turned the lake to flame
and the wind is music on the trees.
Ambush me
in the quiet beyond words
I have with my neighbor.
Spring at me
from the enthusiasm of a "born again."
Vanquish me
in the courage of the weak.
Take me by surprise
in the wrinkled smile
of the lady with the floppy hat.
But be warned.
I will be on my guard
resisting the Kingdom
yet welcoming defeat
in your love, O vulnerable God,
storming my defensive heart
by your love and compassion.
(Adapted from John Shea)

Reflection: The Kingdom is God's Dream for Creation

The Kingdom of God in Jesus' proclamation is not a territory, a structure or system; in short, not an institution, nor is it a homogeneous or uniform regime. In Jesus' vision of the Kingdom, people find fulfillment in God, in the company of one another and in union and harmony with the whole universe. The challenge of Mark 1:15 "The time is fulfilled and the Kingdom of God has come near; repent and believe in the Good News." implies that if our minds accept the Gospel, and if our hearts internalize the message and values of Jesus, God's Kingdom will quicken in our wounded and damaged world. In other words, the whole cosmos will be purified of all evils and filled with the reality of God. Then we can pray with great ease -

O Great Spirit
Whose voice I hear in the winds,
and whose breath gives life to all the world,
hear me! I am small and weak,
I need your strength and wisdom

Let me walk in beauty, and make my eyes
ever behold the red and purple sunset.

Make my hands respect
the things you have made
and my ears sharp to hear your voice.

Make me wise
so that I may understand the things
you have taught my people.

Let me hear the lessons
you have hidden in every leaf and rock

I seek strength, not to be greater than my brother,
but to fight my greatest enemy - myself.

Make me always ready to come to you
with clean hands and straight eyes.

So when life fades, as the fading sunset,
my spirit may come to you without shame.

(Traditional Native American Prayer)

We accept that the Kingdom of God is manifest when changes occur
for the better in relationships that involve human beings, the world and God.
These changes are the transfiguration of life and the entire creation; they
are the epiphanies of the Kingdom in the harsh realities of our world. To
see these epiphanies and to rejoice in them is the continuous challenge for
each Christian who is open to the Spirit of Jesus and the message of the in-
breaking Kingdom.

QUESTION: If the correct Christian view of salvation contains three basic elements: (1) union and communion with God; (2) union and communion with all my fellow human beings; (3) a transformed cosmos, how does this concept of salvation determine my way of being a Christian?

God's desire is to save all human beings. His design for his creation includes every creature in heaven and on earth. Each individual person is part of this universal design. If God looks at me with all the affection and intense love with which he called me into existence, he could not look at me without seeing in me and through me all my brothers and sisters also. Standing before him I always represent to him the whole of humanity. He sees in me all my brothers and sisters as well. Only when all have really become my true brothers and sisters will God's Kingdom have fully arrived.

The old rabbi once asked his disciples how they could tell when the night ended and the day was on its way back. "Could it be," asked one student, "when you see an animal in the distance and know whether it's a sheep or a dog?"

"No," replied the rabbi.

"Could it be," another asked, "when you look at a tree in the distance and can tell whether it is a fig tree or a peach tree?"

"No," said the rabbi.

"Well then, when is it?" his pupils demanded to know.

"It is when you can look at the face of any man or woman and see that he is your brother or she is your sister. Because if you cannot do this, then no matter what time it is, it is still night." (Hoffsümmer)

QUESTION: How far is my spirituality still geared to the individualistic view of salvation? Can I identify with the cosmic view? If yes why? If no why not?

Christian spirituality is rooted in the incarnation and so considerations of social factors must come into it. A spirituality for us today will have something to say about the unjust distribution of wealth, about the destruction of the environment, about oppression and abuse in all its forms. And we cannot remain mere spectators, but have to realize that 'in our age the road to holiness passes through the world of action' (Dag Hammarskjold).

QUESTION: Do I see myself and my daily work as directly related to the Kingdom? How conscious am I that my work for justice, peace and liberation will determine the way the new creation will look as it is stated in the above quoted text of Gaudium and Spes 39?

In all our efforts for a more just and peaceful world determined by the values of the Kingdom, we need to remember this:

There are always two worlds. The world as it operates is power; the world as it should be is love. The secret of Kingdom life is how can I live in both - simultaneously. The world as it is will always be built on power, ego and success. Yet we also must keep our eyes intently on the world as it should be - what Jesus calls the Reign of God. Power apart from love leads to brutality; love that does not engage with power is mere sentimentality (Rohr, Jesus' Plan, p.41).

Our greatest temptation might very well lie in the desire to increase our power while starving our ability to love.

Story: When Power and Love got separated

In the beginning of time it was like this. Power and Love were born twins. Their mother was Wisdom and their father Courage. The twins were inseparable. Wherever they went, they spread life in fullness. Where there was division and war, they mediated and brought peace between warring parties and people. They justly distributed the goods of this earth. Power and Love were one in mind and heart. Wherever they found a place in the homes of people, everything changed for the better. In this way they wandered all over the world.

One day Envy crossed their path. He looked most attractive and magnificent. His garment glistened in the sun and his jewellery sparkled in the light. "I always see you walk in the shadow of Love," Envy said to Power. "You can't get anywhere that way. Come join me! In my company you'll get bigger and stronger. You shall see: People will bow and kiss your hands and feet; they will flatter you and do you homage; they will sell you their souls just to possess you."

Power was blinded with this vision. He thought for a while and then said to Love, "Envy is right. Let's part for some time. If we walk separately, we can each develop and grow independently. Neither of us will depend on the other or have to worry about the other. I'll become an apprentice with Envy. Maybe we'll meet again some day."

Before Love could answer, Power and Envy disappeared around the nearest corner. Love still caught a glimpse of Envy letting Power walk ahead. Love just stood by the side of the road, totally powerless, and wept. Cut off from Power, she felt weak and without strength. She realized that alone there was little chance for survival. Like a dark shadow, Fear crept over her soul, she was afraid of getting lost, of being hurt or misunderstood.

Power, in the meantime, felt free, liberated. Envy did not bother him, because he always remained a step behind and let Power go ahead. Power started realizing that in this way he was growing and growing. But with growth came a certain coldness. He enjoyed it when people humbled themselves before him or gave all they possessed just to join him. Power mounted a big throne and had himself carried high above the heads of people. He enjoyed being cheered and applauded. Soon Power had completely forgotten Love. He surrounded himself with arms and soldiers. He robbed people of their peace and made them leave their homes. Only those willing to sell their souls were tolerated in his presence and allowed to feel secure. Power was always followed by Envy.

The world slowly changed. Wars among peoples became more barbarous, and Love was too powerless to prevent these conflicts. People no longer recognized Love but mistook her for egoism or weakness. She no longer had the strength to keep evil within limits. Greed and indifference grew. Nature was being plundered and trampled down. Darkness and cold settled over the earth. People and animals began to suffer from the cold. They became sick and died in loneliness.

Finally Love decided to go looking for Power despite the long journey. One day they met at a crossroad. Power came forward in all his might and splendour. In front and behind he was protected by heavily armed bodyguards. Power looked sinister, covered in a thick, black coat, his face almost invisible and chest completely covered with decorations of honor. On his left and right, servants carried placards with all his titles so that people would fall on their knees in awe.

Love mustered all her courage and wisdom, which she had inherited from her parents and stood in the path of Power. "You look sad," Love began and looked Power straight in the eyes. "Your eyes are dark. Before you were radiant and beautiful." "Get out of my way," shouted Power, "I do not know you."

"Don't you remember," countered Love, "how we walked all over this earth together? You wore a light coat; you were able to dance and skip; together we ran to meet people, and everyone opened their doors to us. We were able to create peace, and all shared what they possessed. We were both powerful — without arms. You didn't need protection, and Envy did not follow your steps. Let's go through this world together once again. Send all these fellows back where they came from, because they keep you from me and people. I, too, need you, because without you I am weak and helpless. Without you I have little credibility. People laugh at me, hurt and abuse me."

While Love was saying all this, Power started warming up. And because Power too was a child of Wisdom and Courage, he began thawing out and got smaller and smaller until he was the same height as Love. At that moment the dark coat slid off his shoulders and the decorations shattered into pieces on the road. The bodyguards hit the ground like dead men, and the titles all blew away in the wind.

Before they realized it, Power and Love were looking at one another. They broke into laughter and hugged. When Power's companion, Envy, saw that, he made tracks, and the shadow of Fear left Love. Since then, Power and Love walk together again over this earth. They have grown strong, the two. Should you meet them, call me, so that I can also walk with them (Bruners).

Chapter Four

Our Call: To be "set on fire" and to "throw fire"

What is a vocation?

The question that might arise in the context of a universal view of salvation is this, if all can be saved and most probably will be saved, what is the meaning and the importance of a particular vocation? The pattern of any vocation appears most explicitly in the call of Moses.

In Exodus 3:7-9 God appears for the first time to Moses. This story is central to the Bible and provides us with the first self-identification of God. Here the true essence of God is revealed as we are shown who God will be in the history of humankind:

> *I have seen the miserable state of my people in Egypt. I have heard their cry to be free of their slave-drivers. Yes, I am well aware of their suffering. I mean to deliver them out of the hand of their oppressors (Ex 3:7-9).*

Yahweh is a God who *SEES - HEARS - IS CONSCIOUS OF* human oppression, misery and suffering. Our God is neither blind nor deaf nor unaffected by what people have to go through. Since God is the "lover of life" he suffers wherever he sees life diminished or taken away. He always sides with those whose life is threatened or endangered, who are denied their basic right to life, be it through other people, social structures or natural causes.

In Exodus we are told that God has decided to do something about the misery, the oppression and the suffering of the world. The text says: "I have decided to DO something." What is it that he is going to do? *"I will liberate my people from their misery and oppression and I will set them free."*

But here the puzzle starts. If God is determined to set oppressed people free, to do something about the misery and the suffering in this world, why does he not do so? Look into the world; if ever there was oppression and misery, then we definitely have it today. Why does God not enter into it effectively? Why does he not do something?

Now comes the description of the startling process, the inconceivable way in which God has decided to pursue and to accomplish his aim.

> *I send you to Pharaoh to bring the sons of Israel, my people, out of Egypt (3:10).*

God chooses people as his representatives to "do the work FOR him". In order to accomplish his promise God chose Moses, one of the oppressed, to be his agent of liberation.

That is not fair, you might say. But here is the mystery: God will not nor can he directly intervene in this world. He needs people who are willing to give him their "flesh and bones," their bodies, their talents and gifts through which he then will make himself present in the human situation. He needs people in order to do what he wants done for the people and for the world as a whole. Whenever God calls a person, he asks, "Are you willing to give me your body, your capacity to serve, to love, to care, to organize and to connect, in short, all your gifts so that through them I can be present in the world and can accomplish my plans? I have no body, so I need yours to be present in history and in the midst of concrete human reality."

The reaction of those God calls is the same every time. They are afraid, they are scared once they realize what such a call entails. Moses objects four times by insisting, "I cannot do that; I am unfit; I have a speech impediment as you know; I have a thick tongue, why don't you take my brother Aaron, who is much better and more capable of fulfilling such a task?" But God's answer is: "I want you - not your brother. If I had wanted him I would have asked him. I just want you!"

MOSES

Come.
     When?
Now. This Way. I will guide you.
     Wait! Not so fast.
Hurry. You. I said you.
     Who am I?
Certainly I will be with thee.
     Is nothing, then, what it is? I had rather the rod had stayed a rod and not become a serpent.
Come. Quickly. While the blast of my breath opens the sea.
     Stop. I'm thirsty.
Drink water from the rock.
     But the rock moves on before us.
Go with it and drink.
     I'm tired. Can't you stop for a while?
You have already tarried too long.
     But if I am to follow you I must know your name.
I will be that I will be.

You have set the mountain on fire.
Come. Climb.
  I will be lost in the terror of your cloud.
You are stiff-necked and of a stiff-necked people.
  YOUR people, Lord.
Indubitably.
  Your wrath waxes hot, I burn.
Thus to become great.
  Show me, then, thy glory.
No one may see my face and live. But I will cover you with my hand while I
pass by.
  My people turn away and cry because the skin of my face shines.
Did you not expect this?
  I cannot enter the tent of the congregation while your cloud covers it and
your glory fills the tabernacle. Look. It moves before us again. Can you not
stay still?
Come. Follow.
  But this river is death. The waters are dark and deep.
Swim.
  Now I will see your face? Where are you taking me now?
Up the mountain with me before I die.
But death
bursts into light.
  The death is
what it will be.
  These men: they want to keep us here in three tabernacles. But the cloud
moves. The water springs from a rock that journeys on.
You are contained in me.
  But how can we contain you in ark or tabernacle or...
You cannot.
  Where, then?
In your heart. Come.
  Still?
I will be with thee.
  Who am I?
You are that I will be. Come.

(Madeleine L'Engle)

To stress it again, all vocation stories in the Bible follow the same
pattern. God chooses the person he wants; the one chosen feels inadequate
or unworthy to respond to this call and is afraid; God in turn assures the
person of his presence and constant help. If the person chosen says "yes,"
a deep joy and peace will enter into his/her life.

The only reassurance the reluctant Moses gets is: "I WILL BE WITH YOU. Do not be afraid! It is not you who are asked to do the work, no, I ask you only to let me do through you what I wish to do. I will be with you and see you through it all. Just trust me, have confidence in me. I need you, your cooperation and help, but let me determine the work you have to do and you worry about the how." God, who had put so much effort into saving the child Moses from the death threat of Pharaoh by engaging a whole team of women, would not let him down now that Moses was old enough to become the leader of his people.

This phrase, "I will be with you," will be the leitmotif throughout God's redeeming actions in history: it is addressed to national leaders such as Joshua (Jos 1:9) and the Judges (Gideon, Judg 6:16) to kings (Solomon and David, 1Kgs 1:37), to prophets (Jer 1:8) to Jesus (Acts 10:38), and finally to the disciples of Jesus (Mt 28:20).

God needs people through whom he can reach other people. God loves all human beings unconditionally but he chooses some to reach others. In calling me, God asks me whether I am willing to help him reach others so that all will be saved. My vocation is an invitation from God to help him radiate his saving love into the world so that it may reach all. The following story might illustrate the point:

> Past the seeker on the prayer rug, came the cripple and the beggar and the beaten. And seeing them, the Holy One went down, down into deep prayer and cried: "Great God! How is it that a loving Creator can see such things and yet do nothing about them?" And out of the long, long silence, God said, "I did do something about them. I made you" (J. Chittister, *Winds of Change*, p. 144).

What faith this demands in our daily living may be shown in the following story:

A little fellow in the ghetto was teased by one who said, "If God loves you, why doesn't he take care of you? Why doesn't God tell someone to bring you shoes and a warm coat and better food?" The little lad thought for a moment then with tears starting in his eyes, said, "I guess He does tell somebody, but somebody forgets."

The beauty of a vocation is that my human life, my human actions become the carriers of God's saving actions. There is a deeper dimension which God has woven into my life, not because of any merit on my part but just because he chose me out of love, because he wanted me. Why he called me will remain a mystery forever. Anyone who asks this question "why me?" will only get the answer God had already given to the chosen people in the Old Testament: "I did not choose you because you were more virtuous, more gifted, more suited. No, I chose you because I loved you." This means I am someone; I have a place in God's plan; I am important for God's great design for creation; I am a partner; my life counts.

> Our ordinary lives are given an extraordinary significance when we accept that our lives are about something much larger, our pain is a participation in the redemptive suffering of God, our creativity is the very passion of God for the world. No longer do we need to self-evaluate, self-congratulate or self-doubt - our place in the cosmos is assured. I do not need to be the whole play or even understand the full script. It is enough to know that I have been chosen to be one actor on the stage. I need only play my part as well as I can (R. Rohr, *Jesus' Plan*, p.125).

It is not easy at times to hold on to this divine dimension in our lives. How does a life of one chosen by God differ from any other life in this world? Outwardly one may see no difference. It is God's choosing. He adds the "extra" and will make it work in spite of my messing it up - at times even hopelessly. Remember the old saying "God can write straight on crooked lines." God's fidelity prevails over all our failures and unfaithfulness. The Jacob story in the Bible is a beautiful illustration of how God stays with the one he has chosen. Esau, the brother of Jacob in the story is actually the nicer person, more likable, more gentle, but God had taken a fancy to Jacob and chose him for his purpose. In the night when Jacob encountered the angel and had to wrestle with him, he received a new name, he was called ISRAEL instead of Jacob which literally means: "God prevails, God proves to be stronger." God's fidelity to the one he has chosen proves to be stronger than all the evasive maneuvering of Jacob.

If God chooses someone he will stay with this person no matter how unfaithful the person may turn out to be. If something is obvious about God in the Bible it is his faithfulness to us and, in particular, to those whom he has called to help him accomplish his purposes. If I refuse, God will not stop loving me but he might have to use others to reach me.

Called to "throw fire"

In Mark 3:13-15 we find the basic and most significant elements that pertain to discipleship as Jesus understood it: *(1) I chose you; (2) to be with me; (3) to be sent out.*

Discipleship is first of all a gift (The *origin* of discipleship)

No one can become a disciple unless it is given to him or her (Jn 6:65). *"You did not choose me, but I chose you and appointed you"* (Jn 15:16). The call is from eternity even before the one called consciously realizes it. The repeated references to "being called from your mother's womb" stresses this point. Isaiah would say, *"the Lord called me from the womb of my mother and gave me a name"* (Is 49:1). And to Jeremiah the Lord proclaims, *"Before I formed you in the womb of your mother I knew you, and before you were born I consecrated you"* (Jer 1:5). In Psalm 139 we read, *"For you formed me and you knitted me together in my mother's womb"* (Ps 139: 13-15). In the New Testament Paul will say, *"He had set me apart before I was born"* (Gal 1:15). Of John the Baptist it is said, *"He will be filled with the Holy Spirit even from his mother's womb"* (Lk 1:15). This womb-choice by God is spelt out concretely in the external call addressed to the disciple.

At times it is worth meditating on how we received our vocation or particular calling in order to understand that it is a concrete realization of God's unconditional love for us. But why did he choose me? There is no answer except the one already given in the Old Testament: 'I did not choose you because you were more virtuous or pious, more handsome or beautiful, no, I chose you because I loved you.'

> *If Yahweh set his heart on you and chose you, it was not because you outnumbered other peoples...It was for love of you (Deut 7:7-8).*

This concrete bringing about of our call in space and time often involves many people who are chosen on their part to make sure that our vocation will be realized. We see a beautiful example of this in the story of Moses. A whole group of women were called to make sure that Moses would become what God had destined him to be: the leader of his people. Who were these persons who made it possible for Moses to become God's chosen servant? There was a whole network of women who ensured that Moses would live to fulfill the plans of Yahweh.

Shiprah and Puah, the Hebrew midwives in Egypt. God-fearing women and mothers themselves. They defied Pharaoh's orders to kill all male babies born to Hebrew women, enabling the Jews to increase in number. They might have delivered Moses (Ex 1:15-22). Though they were slaves, they stood unafraid before the king and his court.

Moses's mother defied the Pharaoh and nurtured her infant son for a few months. When he was three months old she hid him in the basket and placed him in the Nile.

Pharaoh's daughter. She rescued Moses from his basket in the Nile and raised him in the royal household until he was an adult (Ex 2:2-10). She is a symbol of one in authority taking an initiative to supersede an unjust law.

Miriam, the sister of Moses; who *"stood at a distance to see what would happen to him."* When Pharaoh's daughter noticed the basket and found the baby, Miriam stepped out of her hiding place, asserted herself by offering to find a nurse for the baby and went to get her mother.

When reflecting on our own vocation we should not forget the network of people involved in bringing it about. In order to appreciate more profoundly one's call to discipleship it is helpful to ask oneself now and then: who were the persons with whom God surrounded me to ensure my being selected right from *my mother's womb.*

Called to be with him (The *vertical* aspect of discipleship)

The essence of being a disciple is biblically expressed in the phrase *to be with him.* Discipleship was well known in Israel. Rabbis had their disciples whom they trained, but the following chart shows the main differences between the two:

Jesus - Disciples	**Rabbi - Disciples**
1. Jesus himself chooses his disciples (Jn 15:16; Mk 3:13; Lk 9:59 etc.).	1. The disciples choose their respective rabbis.
2. Jesus binds his disciples to his own person (Mk 3:14).	2. The disciples are committed to the Torah.
3. The community of life with Jesus is an end in itself (Mt 10:24-25).	3. Discipleship is only a step towards becoming an ordained rabbi oneself ("semikah").
4. Jesus sends his disciples to proclaim the Kingdom (Lk 9:60; Mk 3:14).	4. The duty of the disciple is to learn the Law and the Traditions and become an expert in interpreting them.

5. Jesus calls any and everyone to become his disciple (Mk 1:16-20; 2:14; Lk 6:15).	5. The choice of the disciples is based on differences in grade and rank.
6. Jesus needs no ordination to be a rabbi; he is simply named rabbi (Mk 9:5; 14:45).	6. One acquires the title rabbi by ordination.
7. Jesus has not studied under any rabbi (Jn 7:15).	7. Rabbis have become so by learning from another rabbi.
8. Jesus exhorts his disciples to humility and service (Mt 23:5-12).	8. Rabbis teach their disciples to acquire rank and excellence.
9. The disciples in turn do not form their own disciples (Mt 5:19; Mk 6:30).	9. After their training the disciples in turn form other disciples (cf. School of Rabbi so and so).

The specific element to note is the self-understanding that Jesus exhibited in his relationship with his disciples. Jesus demands a total self-commitment and surrender which breaks all other ties. Discipleship does not mean learning a trade, becoming a professional, pursuing an academic career, graduating from a university or famous school. Not at all. Being a disciple means sharing in a fundamental experience made and communicated by the master. It means being caught up in the vision of the master, being on fire with the fire of the master. In the Gospel of Thomas we find Jesus saying, "He who is near me, is near the fire to be consumed by it" (G.Th. 86). Here the identification is so complete that the great divide between God and the disciple is obliterated to the point that now only the Lord remains (cf. R.J. Raja, "Follow me - Discipleship in the Synoptic Gospels", pp. 513-533).

> Abbot Lot came to Abbot Joseph and said: Father, according as I am able, I keep my little rule, and my little fast, my prayer, my meditation and contemplative silence; and according as I am able I strive to cleanse my heart of thoughts: now what more should I do? The elder rose in reply and stretched out his hand to heaven, and his fingers became like ten lamps of fire. He said: Why not be totally changed into fire?

It ultimately means the disciple has become like the master. A disciple is a person who has had the same fundamental experience that Jesus had and which we regarded above as the foundational reality of our faith: God loves every human person with an unconditional, compassionate love; he forgives us always; he is always with us. A disciple is someone who starts living his daily life out of this experience and who sees his/her witness to this experience as taking part in Jesus' own mission. Only if we stay with the Lord and experience his intimacy and love for us always, can we be sent out on a mission.

Called to be sent out (The *horizontal* aspect of discipleship)

The disciples are not merely companions of Jesus, they become co-workers, they are sent out. Their mission consists in proclaiming and witnessing to the vision that drove Jesus: God is "Abba", and the Kingdom has arrived. The disciples are not to convey a doctrine but a personal experience in what they proclaim. The disciples are driven by one deep desire: to draw others into the experience they themselves have had.

Ultimately, to be called by God means to be drawn into God's own plan, into the mission of his Son in order to be sent and to become a co-worker with God for the salvation-transformation of the world into God's final design. "To be called, to be with him" means to be holy, consecrated, set apart. God gives the person called a share in his design, in his eternal plan. That person belongs in a special way to God. He/she already enjoys an intimacy with God that God, intends every person on this earth to enjoy.

Therefore the correct understanding of 'being sent' should not lead us to look at the community of those chosen in purely functional terms. This community itself is a sacramental anticipation of God's final plan for the whole of humanity. It is the celebration of the final achievement of God's plan of salvation in the here and now that gives meaning and joy to the mission entrusted to those invited to share in God's own mission for the world.

But this union and intimate communion with the Lord, this sharing in God's design for all humanity is nevertheless done with a purpose: to be sent out, to engage actively in God's mission, to become 'fishers of people' (Mk 1:17). Mission is, therefore, the ultimate aim of all calling in life. Being called does not mean taking up any special place of honor or being treated with reverence and awe. It simply means being sent. Every Christian is called to mission on the basis of the sacrament of baptism. Baptism is neither a passport to heaven nor a ticket for entry into eternal life; it is primarily a call to mission. Most people will find eternal life without being baptized. The privilege of being a Christian consists in having been called to participate in a special way in the mission of Christ in saving all human beings.

The story is told of Gordan Maxwell, missionary in India, that when he asked a Hindu scholar to teach him the language, the Hindu replied: "No Sahib, I will not teach you my language. You would make me a Christian."Gordan Maxwell replied, "You misunderstood me. I am simply asking you to teach me your language.? Again the Hindu responded. "No, Sahib, I will not teach you. No man can live with you and not become a Christian."

The biblical name for the person called by God is 'servant.' The prototype of such a calling is Moses. The highest name Moses was awarded for by God was My Servant Moses. In the Acts of the Apostles we find a beautiful description of the life of Moses (7:20-47). There are three periods of forty years each, which characterize his life-span of 120 years. For forty years God lets him grow up at the court of Pharaoh in order to prepare him well for his task in the service of Yahweh. For forty years Moses lives in the desert where he gets to know Yahweh intimately and is schooled in the ways of the Lord. Moses is introduced into the plan of God for Israel and is told of the role he will have to play in bringing about the initiation of this plan. Lastly, in the third period of his life Moses becomes God's servant to his people. This is the highest honor he could ever be awarded. God trusts in him and he becomes an intimate with God, a friend of God.

> *With my servant Moses I speak face to face, plainly and not in riddles, and he sees the form of the Lord (Num 12:6-8).*

> *I shall do what you have asked, because you enjoy my favor and because I know you by name (Ex 33:17).*

> *Whenever Moses went into the presence of the Lord to speak with him, he took the veil off until he came out (Ex 34:32-35).*

Jesus took up this theme of being a servant of Yahweh in many ways. He felt sent to bring about God's plan for creation and regarded this as a service. He understood his whole life as a being sent to serve and not to be served, and he expected the same from his disciples whom he commissioned to continue his mission (Jn 20:21). Greatness among them would mean serving one another and not being served (Mk 10:43-45). The most outstanding example Jesus gave to illustrate his view of service is his symbolic action of washing his disciples' feet (Jn 13:1-15).

Being on a Journey

If the word of Jesus *'follow me'* contains in a nutshell what God wants of each one of us, it is obvious that discipleship is a life-time occupation. It is not something I can claim as having reached already; I am always on the road towards it. In the words of St. Paul: *"Don't think that I have reached it yet, no! But one thing I do: forgetting what lies behind and straining forward to what lies ahead of me"* (Phil 3:13-14). Discipleship in the Judeo-Christian tradition is seen as a journey. That means, it is a goal towards which we travel and not something we have already realized. Our faith begins with Abraham and Sarah who trusted God, left their homeland and went on a "journey" to a new land. Abraham became the model for every disciple of the Lord, a pilgrim on a journey trusting in the Lord to lead him home. The Church, too, is often described as the "pilgrim Church."

Another description for a disciple is "one who is on the way" or "one who is on the road." The Jewish word 'Torah' comes from the word 'to throw'. When the nomadic tribes would lose their way in a desert sandstorm and would not know which way to move to get out of the storm, they would put a spear in the hand of their leader and spin him around several times while incantations, songs and prayers were recited by the whole tribe. At a particular moment the leader would let go of the spear. The whole tribe would then "walk" in the direction which the spear indicated. For them "the throw" became "the way to life" which God himself had pointed out. To gain life meant to walk in the direction indicated by the Torah.

Jesus continued this tradition. He was a journeying prophet, an itinerant preacher, constantly on the road. He had no place to lay his head and rest. Luke as well as Mark portray the whole life of Jesus as a way from Galilee to Jerusalem. The discipleship vocabulary in the Gospels occurs always in the context of going behind, walking after or following Jesus. The first name ever given to the disciples after Easter was the 'followers of the way.' We, in the footsteps of the first disciples, should see ourselves as being constantly on the way as well. We are, therefore, always on the way to becoming disciples, never already being disciples.

But there are still a constantly nagging questions that will not go away: who on earth can live discipleship the way Jesus demanded it? Is it not just impossible? These were the same questions and objections formulated by some cardinals at Pope Innocent III's court, when St. Francis tried to obtain approval for his rule asking to live the way Jesus had lived. The cardinals argued: "Living in such a way as the Lord Jesus lived when he walked this earth is a thing untried and too hard for human strength."

We may perhaps be allowed to think that the cardinals, in voicing this objection, were subconsciously expressing their own reason for not observing the Gospel more strictly. The Bishop of Sabina deflated the objection by a simple observation:

"This poor man is in fact asking us to approve the pattern of Gospel-life. Let us be careful not to make the Gospel of Christ a stumbling-block. For if anyone says that in the observance of Gospel perfection there is contained anything that is untried, or contrary to reason, or impossible to observe, he would clearly seem to contradict Christ himself, the author of the Gospel." (J. Wijngaards, *Experiencing Jesus*, pp. 91-92)

The vision for which Jesus lived and died will always be a challenge to anyone who wants to commit him/herself in discipleship to him. It is not difficult to demonstrate how such a Jesus was not only difficult for his own time and soon caused scandal, but also has precisely the same effect on the culture today.

Anyone who shows such freedom as he did in inexorably enquiring behind dominant interests for the sake of the well-being of all and acts accordingly will at least be irritating, even today. Indeed such a person will be irritating particularly today, especially if it is maintained that Jesus reveals that last claim of God in a way which is 'utterly inconspicuous and ordinary, human and historical.' To raise such claims to truth and universality is generally regarded as crazy and outdated, at the latest in the context of the *de facto* popularity of religions, ideologies and world-views - though people tend to ignore the fact that the same claim is made for the technological and economic rationality which has largely broken through everywhere and is taken for granted (N. Mette, "The Difficult Jesus: Problems of Discipleship", p. 21).

Reflection: *What Kind of Disciple am I?*

The Lord Yahweh has given me a disciple's tongue.
So that I may know how to reply to the wearied
he provides me with speech.
Each morning he wakes me to hear,
to listen like a disciple.
The Lord Yahweh has opened my ear. (Is 50:4)

To the question of the first Christians who asked Jesus, *"Where do you live?"* Jesus responded with an invitation, *"Come and see."* ... and the process of discipleship began. His final word to them was his command to *"go* and *make* disciples of all the nations." Through their response to his invitation and his teaching, the disciples were slowly transformed into apostles, witnesses and ministers. They learned to see that their vocation to discipleship was always meant for the service of others.

The Lord Yahweh has given me a disciple's tongue.
So that I may know how to reply to the wearied
he provides me with speech.

The call to discipleship always remains *"Come and see"* and is always evolutionary. Christ will ask us again and again to go a step further and no one knows to what lengths he will call us. Bonhoeffer's word is one to grapple with: "When Christ calls a man to follow him, he bids him come and die." No wonder we hesitate like many before us have done. Growth in discipleship is to be sought, prayed for, struggled for. Jesus keeps asking, *What about you, do you want to go away too?"* (Jn 6:86).

To be a disciple is to walk on water... and yet we may reach the moment when with Paul we can say, *"neither death nor life...nothing still to come, not any power...can ever come between us and the love of God made visible in Christ Jesus our Lord"* (Rom 8:38).

Discipleship costs. When Jesus commanded his disciples to feed the multitude saying, *"Give them something to eat yourselves,"* he implied that they, too, were to be broken, distributed and eaten - just like Jesus when he gave himself at the Last Supper and continues to give himself in the Eucharist. In this process of self-giving, the disciple becomes more and more like the master and begins to realize his or her vocation of being "another Christ."

Story: *Are You Jesus?*

Several years ago a group of salesmen from Milwaukee went to a regional sales convention in Chicago. They assured their wives that they would be home in plenty of time for dinner. But with one thing and another the meeting ran overtime so the men had to race to the station, tickets in hand. As they barraged through the terminal, one man inadvertently kicked over a table supporting a basket of apples. Without stopping they all reached the train and boarded it with a sigh of relief. All but one. He paused, and experienced a twinge of compunction for the boy whose apple stand had been overturned. He waved goodbye to his companions and returned to the terminal. He was glad he did. The ten-year-old boy was blind.

The salesman gathered up the apples and noticed that several of them were bruised. He reached into his wallet and said to the boy, "Here, please take these ten dollars for the damage we did. I hope it didn't spoil your day." As he started to walk away the bewildered boy called after him, "Are you Jesus?" (Adapted from: W.J. Bausch, *Storytelling,* pp 177-178)

QUESTION: How sensitive and alert am I in my daily life to my mission to be a disciple of Jesus?

From my "mother's womb" God surrounded me with persons who through their life, their love, their effort and their sacrifice have led me to where I am now. They have helped me grow in my vocation as a disciple of Jesus. Besides such persons, there are numerous incidents in my life which have shown me the guiding finger of God. If I search my life story with an attentive heart and mind, I will discover these.

QUESTION: Who were the persons in my vocation story whom God called to make his dream for me come true? Recall some according to their importance? List a few happenings in your life that make you realize that God had something special in mind for you.

God needs us to continue the mission of his Son, and the Holy Spirit seeks tirelessly for another body in which to prolong the incarnation. In the fullest sense of the word Jesus can say "I have no hands but yours." Accordingly, the farewell message of the risen One is, *"As the Father has sent me, so I send you"* (Jn 20:21).

I will give all I have to you but...

You asked for my hands
that you might use them for your purpose.
I gave them for a moment, then withdrew them
for the work was hard.

You asked for my mouth
to speak out against injustice.
I gave you a whisper that I might not be accused.

You asked for my eyes
to see the pain of poverty.
I closed them for I did not want to see.

You asked for my life
that you might work through me.
I gave a small part

that I might not get too involved.
Lord, forgive my calculated efforts to serve you
only when it is convenient for me to do so,
only in those places where it is safe to do so,
and only with those who make it easy to do so.

Lord, forgive me,
renew me,
send me out
as a usable instrument
that I might take seriously
the meaning of your cross.

(Seremane , *Bread of Tomorrow*, p.76)

Imagine how differently we might live our lives if each day when we awaken we envisioned ourselves as an instrument of God. We would know each day that we were not alone. Cardinal Newman voices his basic conviction of his personal mission in this way:

God has created me to do Him some definite service. He has committed some work to me which he has not committed to another. **I have my mission** - I never may know it in this life, but I shall be told it in the next. Somehow I am necessary for His purposes, as necessary in my place as an Archangel in his - if I fail, He can raise another, as He could make the stones children of Abraham. Yet I have a part in this great work; I am a link in a chain, a bond of connection between persons. He has not created me for naught. I shall do good, I shall do His work; I shall be an angel of peace, a preacher of truth in my own place, while not intending it, if I do but keep His commandments and serve Him in my calling (Breemen, *Let All God's Glory Through*, p. 47).

QUESTION: What does it mean to me that God chose me from my mother's womb to be part of his eternal plan to bring salvation to all my brothers and sisters? Does this thought fill me with gratitude and joy - or am I afraid of the consequences?

Story: *A Tree tells its Story*

"When I was still small, I did not see anything. But when I grew taller and looked at myself, I began to notice the difference. I was small, gnarled and knotty, a little bent and deformed and my roots clung tightly to the rock. However, the other trees that I could see were sturdy: mighty beech trees with giant tops, tall, slender fir trees and mountain maples in their glorious golden autumn foliage. You should know that my place is a rock face. I grow on a narrow ledge having dug my roots into the little soil that is there, clinging desperately to the cracks in the rock.

I always wanted to be tall and beautiful, letting the wind play with my branches, the rain caress my leaves and the sun dry them gently. But I remained rather small; the wind blew mercilessly through my branches when it roared across the rock face. The sun warmed me only until midday before disappearing behind the rock face to shine only on the lovely trees in the valley and on the slope of the opposite hill.

Why was I made to grow in this place? The little soil that was there on the ledge did not give me enough strength to grow tall, nor did it allow all my beauty to unfold. I was discontented with my destiny. Why did I have to be and become like this?

One beautiful spring morning, when the scent of the earth in the valley rose up to my heights, the thrush began to greet the morning with its song and the first rays of the sun kissed my leaves, a wonderful feeling took hold of me and warmed my whole being. What a wonderful view I enjoyed! No other tree could see as far into the valley as I could, and the rock face at my back protected me from the icy cold that came down from the glacier above.

From this day on I began to reflect, and it became ever clearer to me: I am something special just the way that I am. What is special about me is my crooked trunk, my gnarled roots and my short, stubby but strong branches. I fit into the place where I am and I am worth something. All I need to do is to open my eyes and look at myself properly. The other trees, the pine trees on the opposite slope and the beech trees in the valley all have their own beauty and stand in their proper place. But I too have my own place, and the narrow rock face is the place where I belong. Why did it take me so long to realize this? (Hoffsümmer)

QUESTION: How do I thank God for who I am and for the mission given to me in God's plan of saving all my brothers and sisters?

When reading the post-resurrection appearances of Jesus in the Gospel of John one will find it astonishing that members of the Twelve who saw the risen Jesus in Jerusalem, were sent out by him (Jn 20:21), and received the Holy Spirit also reverted to fishing in Galilee (Jn 21:1-8). Could it be that moving from belief in the risen Jesus to action based on that belief is not something that we can take for granted? The disciples were far from being successful in the trade of fishing which they knew so well, but Jesus reversed human incapacity and brought about a great catch. The Beloved disciple who believed first in the risen Jesus, now once again was him who recognizes the Lord. The others recognize him finally in the breaking of the bread on the sea shore.

Disciple of Jesus

Disciple of Jesus, weary and silent,
aware, in the darkness of challenges
failed and longings unfulfilled,
remembering the passion that sent you forth,
young and bright, and fired with hope.

Disciple of Jesus, weary and silent,
world unchanged, its darkness still deep,
dreams dispelled and visions blurred,
How is it now with you?

Trailing behind me the sparkle and fire
of early passion,
bruised and tender from love's long thrust.
Now is the finest, greatest moment
and now the ultimate death.

For I, Disciple of Jesus,
to stand before my God,
weary, silent, and all alone,
claiming only, "I was there" (Gateley)

Chapter Five

"To remain on fire:"
The Gospels as Handbooks of Discipleship

If following the Lord is our essential vocation, some questions arise: How do we get in touch with the Lord? How can we remain in a life-giving relationship with the Lord? Where do we find Jesus and how can we keep his God-image alive in us? How can we stay on fire with his vision?

The answers may vary. Many people today do not ask any more: who was this Jesus of Nazareth? Instead they will ask: Where can I find this Jesus who made such a stir? Are there still persons, are there still communities that can convey this Jesus to me, make him alive for me, put me in touch with him? They are looking for a community of disciples that has kept the fire of the master burning. But what about us, his disciples, how do we keep in touch with the master? Where do we find his words, his deeds, his healing and liberating actions?

The first answer is: by turning to the Gospels. The Gospels are best described as *'handbooks of discipleship.'* They contain the Jesus experience; they still *glow with his fire* enshrined particularly in his parables. They witness vividly to his infinite love and compassion. In them we see Jesus the *teacher* who succeeded in enshrining his message with amazing clarity in the haunting and unforgettable poetry we call parables. In them we can still hear Jesus the *prophet* lashing out in indignation and anger at all forms of discrimination that kept people separated from one another in the name of Yahweh. In these handbooks we find the Jesus whose movement has been called *table fellowship movement* because of his habit of sitting at table with all kinds of people but especially with the outcasts and sinners. We feel the indignation and outrage such behavior caused among the righteous. Eating and drinking with the outcasts would make one unclean and unholy. But Jesus used these practices to show how he understood his mission and the Kingdom he came to bring. God was gathering all people into the great banquet of the end-time. What counted was not *holiness and purity,* which had ousted more than half of the people from the Covenant, but *justice and compassion* that would bring them back into the Covenant once again.

These handbooks want to teach us in different ways how we can become and remain true disciples of the master. They are written for those who want to follow the Lord and are asking for a guide. Each handbook differs from the other and each sees discipleship from a different angle and with a specific emphasis. What really accounts for the differences is the situation in which each was written and the kind of people to whom each was addressed.

The Handbook of Mark

The claim has been made that Mark's Gospel should be seen as an *initiation* book written to introduce those soon to be baptized into the fellowship of Jesus. The whole Gospel - so the argument goes - was written to be read straight through in one sitting during the Easter vigil, and then to be followed at dawn by the baptism of the catechumens. Whether this theory is true or not, the Gospel's main concern is certainly those who want to follow the Lord.

The vocation accounts in this Gospel have a pragmatic character. They have to be seen in the light of the Kingdom of God that Jesus proclaimed as having arrived with him. The disciples were called to become *fishers of people* in the company of Jesus. The intention of Jesus was not to make them his servants but to call them co-workers and co-servants in God's plan of salvation for his chosen people then, now, and in the future for all human beings. The disciples were called to share in the mission of Jesus that aimed at universal salvation, and to be part of an apostolic community.

The handbook of Mark is composed of two parts which are almost equal in length. What concludes the first and opens the second is a question concerning the person of Jesus: *Who do you say I am?* (Mk 8:29) and Peter's answer: *You are the Christ!* (29) From here onwards the second part of the disciples' training begins. We could call the first part *the journey through Galilee* (Mk 1:16-8:21) and the second part *the way to Jerusalem* (8:27-10:45) having its end in Jerusalem itself (11:1-15:39).

The first part: the journey through Galilee

The first part of being a disciple in Mark's handbook could also be called the springtime of the disciples' vocation, the time with the master in Galilee. It is exciting, fulfilling and rewarding to be with him. The disciples become important, they bathe in the success of the master, they are honored and considered lucky. There is great coming and going; they don't even have time to eat; their expectations are lofty. But they still have a long way to go before they really become his disciples.

This *way in Galilee* comes to an end with two healings of blind people. Both stories are found only in Mark. The first takes place at Bethsaida before Peter's confession (Mk 8:22-26) and the second is that of the blind beggar Bartimaeus at Jericho (Mk 10:46-52) when Jesus is determined to go to Jerusalem to face his final destiny, the cross.

Mark describes true discipleship in the passage 8:27-10:45 and introduces this section with the healing of a man who is blind (8:22-26). Somewhat surprisingly, the healing has to be done in two stages. The first attempt is seemingly not enough to restore the sight of the man. At the end of this whole section on discipleship, Mark again presents a healing of a blind man called Bartimaeus (10:46-52). Here the healing is an instant success. Bartimaeus' sight is completely restored and, after throwing off his possessions, he follows Jesus *on the way* to Jerusalem.

It is obvious that Mark purposely uses the 'progressive' healing of the blind man as an introduction to Peter's confession that Jesus is the Messiah. Peter, however by proclaiming Jesus as Messiah, has only perceived half of the story and is not yet able to see clearly all its implications. He realizes in his confession that Jesus is the only way to salvation, but he is not yet ready to go with him *on the way* to Jerusalem. Therefore, he only understands half of the story; his sight is only half restored. The full vision of who Jesus is will be revealed only in the cross and resurrection.

Recognition of Jesus' messiah-ship is not sufficient if one does not also accept the scandal of the cross (8:31-32). The two elements should not be separated from each other; their union constitutes the pivot of Mark's gospel (J. Dupont, *"Blind Bartimaeus"*, p.224).

These two healings are beautiful illustrations of what has to happen to the disciples of Jesus before they can really recognize who Jesus is. The first cure not only demonstrates the blindness of the disciples but also points to what Jesus will do *on the way*: he will grant sight to them. The second, the cure of the blind Bartimaeus, makes it very clear that the disciples, even though they are following Jesus *on the way*, still lack sight.

Mark sees Bartimaeus as representing any disciple who reaches full perception. As long as Bartimaeus cannot see the way, he cannot walk along it. All he can do is to sit at the wayside (10:46). The contrast before and after the healing is obvious: At the beginning Bartimaeus is *blind - seated - on the side of the road (10:46);* at the end he is *sighted - follows - on the way* (10:52). Only after his cure through Jesus' touch can he follow Jesus *on the way*.

It is an obvious truth that no one can walk a way without sight but it is especially true of *Jesus' way*: whoever does not see Jesus cannot follow him, and whoever does not follow him cannot see him. Mark seems to say that of all the followers of Jesus only the beggar from Jericho is no longer blind but sees. From this point on we must also understand the risen Lord's instruction to the disciples, given to them by the angel: *'He is going - tracing the way - before you to Galilee, there you will see him'* (Mk 16:7).

The second part: the way to Jerusalem

After the confession of Peter, the time had come for the disciples to enter into a new phase of being followers of Jesus. In this second phase they were to follow the master down to Jerusalem with the prospect of being crucified with him. In Galilee, the place of his public life, Jesus was in total control. He was the active one: he called disciples, he healed the people and they responded to him; he cast out demons and battled with his opponents. In Jerusalem, the place of his passion, Jesus played the passive part: *he is handed over*. The Gospels use the phrase *"he was handed over"* twenty-two times. The basic meaning of this phrase is that in the life of Jesus there came a moment when he was no longer the active subject, fully in control of all his actions, but had become the object on which others acted. Jesus moved from being active to being passive, from the role of subject to that of object and from working in freedom to waiting for what others decided and accepting what others did.

To introduce his disciples to this way of being disciples, Jesus posed a crucial question: *Who do people say I am?* The disciples, like a bunch of kids, were eager to give an answer: John the Baptist, Elijah, or one of the prophets. The real question, however, was: *Who do you, my disciples, say I am?*

Peter, being the spokesman of them all, gave the answer: *You are the Christ!* Jesus, taken by surprise, realized that they had gotten it right. Admittedly, Peter gave an answer he could not have produced by his own insight. (According to Matthew *"It was not flesh and blood that revealed this to Peter but the Father in heaven"* 16:17) Now the time had come for Jesus to lead them into the mystery of his suffering and to prepare them for what was to come. They would have to make a decision whether or not they wanted to remain or, better, become his true disciples.

The way of the master would not go up and up and up. There was a bend in the road that led down to the cross, to Jerusalem. Would they be willing to go with the master on that stretch of the way as well? Peter, as their leader, gave the initial answer: NO!

Peter took Jesus aside and started to remonstrate with him (to put him straight, to tell him to drop this nonsense) (Mk 8:33).

Peter who gives the right answer to the question of who Jesus is, now took the initiative to tell Jesus what, according to his opinion, being the Messiah meant. Anything but - for God's sake - suffering and violent death. He steps in front of the Lord and tells him so: I have been following you up to now, I walked behind you faithfully, but now I ask you to follow me, and let me indicate the way.

Jesus' answer is very harsh and uncompromising: Devil, get out of my way! If you want to be a follower of mine you'd better *"Get behind me!"* Do not tell me which way to go! Get your feet into my footprints, Peter! From now on Jesus talks constantly about his cross and his death:

He was telling them, 'The Son of Man will be delivered into the hands of men; they will put him to death; and three days after he has been put to death, he will rise again.' But they did not understand what he said and were afraid to ask him (Mk 9:31-32).

It is not only Peter who cannot accept the thought of a suffering and rejected Messiah. Here, after the second announcement of his suffering and death, the only thing the disciples can do is to get into an argument about who of them should be regarded the greatest among them (9:34).

Once more taking the Twelve aside he began to tell them what was going to happen to him. Now we are going up to Jerusalem, and the Son of Man is about to be handed over to the chief priests and the scribes. They will condemn him to death and will hand him over to the pagans, who will mock him and spit at him and scourge him and put him to death; and after three days he will rise again (Mk 10:32-34).

Again the reaction of the disciples is strange. They seem not to comprehend at all what Jesus is talking about. They are still preoccupied with future places of honor and importance. John and James ask Jesus for the first places in the glorious Kingdom to come. The rest of them get indignant revealing in fact that they had harbored the same thoughts (Mk 10:33-41).

For the Son of Man himself did not come to be served but to serve, and to give his life as a ransom for many (Mk 10:45).

Jesus' definition of discipleship according to Mark includes the willingness to go with the master up to Jerusalem, to suffer and be rejected.

If anyone wants to be a follower of mine, let him renounce himself and take up his cross and follow me (Mk 8:34).

As we saw, Mark frames his catechesis on discipleship with two healing miracles in which Jesus heals a blind man. The first time the healing does not succeed immediately, while the second healing, that of the blind Bartimaeus, is an instant success. Here the essential elements of true discipleship become obvious: Bartimaeus *throws off his mantle* meaning, he leaves all security behind. The mantle was the only possession the poor people normally had and the beggar's mantle entitled him to receive alms. This reminds the reader of the call of the first disciples (1:18;20) who *abandoned everything and followed Jesus.* After Bartimaeus has committed himself totally to the Lord he *goes after him on the road to Jerusalem.* Now it becomes clear what being a disciple means for Mark: *to go after the Master - to deny oneself - to take up one's cross.*

Jesus' disciples failed miserably in their first attempt to be disciples of the master and to follow him *on the way to Jerusalem.* They all deserted him and ran away. *"A young man who followed him had nothing on but a linen cloth. They got hold of him, but he left the cloth in their hands and ran away naked"* (Mk 14:50-52).

Knowing that "being naked" in Scripture means having lost one's dignity, Mark tells us here that the disciples, like our first parents, lost everything on the night they abandoned their master. They had stopped being his "followers."

Handbook written for the Roman community

It is still generally accepted that the Gospel of Mark was written in Rome around 65 AD during or shortly after the persecution that had struck this community unexpectedly. (Some, however, hold that the Gospel was written in Roman-occupied Syria.)

This community in Rome was well established and consisted of people as socially prominent as members of the imperial court. Among its founders they could list Peter as the most renowned. They had been living as 'disciples of Jesus' for some time. But now something unforeseen had happened: persecution had come unexpectedly. Many had been killed, driven out and lost all they had. The question was: does being a disciple of Jesus mean to be subjected to all this and even to losing one's life?

Mark addresses this crisis situation and writes his handbook of discipleship, his Gospel for this specific group. His handbook is designed to answer the crucial question about the relationship between suffering and discipleship. The central place in his handbook is given to the apostle Peter, one of the group's most prominent founders. Mark presents Peter as an example of how he and all the other disciples had to undergo a very painful conversion before they were ready to follow the master, if necessary, down to Jerusalem. Taking Peter as an example, Mark shows the Roman community that accepting the cross is vital to discipleship, and could mean readiness to lay down one's life.

Peter and all the other disciples had failed, but this was not the end. They, the Romans, could go back just as the disciples were taken back by the Lord after Easter. Mark is saying: "Look at your founder, Peter! How difficult it was for him to come to grips with the master's sense of obligation to go to Jerusalem and be crucified. Take Peter as your example and learn from him what being a disciple means." Peter's attempt to avoid the cross will always be a temptation for everyone when faced with a similar situation. But there is no way around it.

If any want to become my followers, let them deny themselves and take up their cross and follow me (8:34).

It was important that Jesus said: THEIR cross and not MY cross. The cross or the "cup" that the Father has allotted to each one of us according to his will and our own capacity will always differ from that of other persons. But whenever we want to follow the Lord we have to reckon seriously with the possibility of encountering the cross. It means that being disciples of Jesus might become an obstacle for our daily life, or might go against our inclinations and wishes. In these moments the "cross" will appear and we are asked to carry THIS, OUR CROSS as Jesus carried his.

The following illustration might show what this daily cross could consist of. We know from history that the one to be crucified had only to carry the horizontal crossbar. The vertical pole was already firmly in place and remained there to be used again and again. The condemned person was nailed to the crossbar, then lifted up and fixed to the vertical pole. Figuratively speaking, we could say the crossbar that we have to carry day in and day out is made up of our own character and habits, our temperament and inconsistencies, our ailments and suffering. The 'vertical pole' could be described as the milieu we find ourselves in, the circumstances of our lives that we cannot change or the difficult people we have to face or live with. These are all things that are firmly fixed on my road and which I can neither change nor remove. Where these two parts of the cross meet and "cross" each other is the place where my daily "crucifixion" will take place, where I am to "drink the cup the Father has assigned to me." In the handbook of Mark the disciple receives only one assurance: that he will not be left alone. *I will go ahead of you. Do not be afraid* (Mk 16:7). There shall be nothing the disciple will have to experience that the master has not experienced before him. The Lord is always going ahead of us.

Whenever the disciples find themselves in difficulties and the cross weighs heavily, they are encouraged to recall the springtime of their vocation, the time of their Galilee with the Lord when they had seen and experienced the power of God's Kingdom already present. It is on such occasions that the master will tell them: *"Go back to your Galilee, there you will see me!"*

The Handbook of Matthew

The key to the Gospel of Matthew is found in Mt 28:16-20. Jesus sent his disciples on a world mission. They were sent to go to all nations - in contrast to their first mission which was to the lost sheep of Israel alone (Mt 10) - to make them disciples through baptism while conveying to them the message Jesus had taught them. Jesus himself was going to accompany them; he was always going to be with them until the end of time.

Matthew wrote his handbook for a community of disciples who lived in the midst of Israel of old. Many of the new disciples had been law-observing Jews who wanted to maintain the bond between the Old Covenant and the New Dispensation, brought about by the death and resurrection of Jesus. But soon they experienced a growing hostility from their fellow Jews. This happened in spite of their deep conviction that Jesus had not done away with the Law and the prophets:

> *Do not think that I have come to do away with the Law of Moses and the teaching of the Prophets. I have not come to do away with them, but to make their teaching come true. Remember this! As long as heaven and earth last, the least point of the smallest detail of the Law will not be done away with (Mt 5:17-18).*

The disciples' effort to keep as much of the Law as their commitment to Christ would permit was not enough for their opponents. Their main adversaries became the Pharisees who regarded the new interpretation of the Law given by Jesus as blasphemous. So the disciples had to constantly be on guard not to fall prey to the interpretation of the Pharisees once again. Matthew clarifies this by showing that the Pharisees had always been the real opponents of Jesus. Could a disciple expect anything different from what had happened to the master? He has to expect to be thrown out of his family and home because he has chosen another family, the family of those who believe that in Jesus the true Covenant has been established. The disciples of Jesus form a new family no longer based on blood relationships but solely on their being disciples of Jesus. As Matthew indicates in 12:47-50 the disciple will find new mothers, brothers and sisters in the Christian community which exceeds that of any community related by blood.

> *While he was still speaking to the crowds, his mother and his brothers were standing outside, waiting to speak to him. Someone told him, "Look, your mother and your brothers are standing outside, wanting to speak to you." But to the one who had told him this, Jesus replied, "Who is my mother, and who are my brothers?" And pointing to his disciples, he said, "Here are my mother and my brothers! For whoever does the will of my Father in heaven is my brother and sister and mother."*

This scene is regarded as being a pivotal point in Matthew's Gospel, *the symbolic middle of the Gospel*. Jesus turns the whole bloodline family system upside down, even at the risk of slighting his mother. For Jesus, blood is not the determining factor that makes family; it is trust, union and commitment. And with this he redefines family for a kinship-based culture. This is extremely daring and even scandalous in a culture where kinship takes precedence over everything else. But Jesus takes this risk of opposing conventional wisdom by redefining the family in terms of a universal family of love. With this he broke the addiction to false patriotism, loyalty and nationalism that have brought so much hatred and war into this world (R. Rohr, *Jesus' Plan for a New World*, pp. 23-24).

For Matthew, one can only be and remain a disciple of Jesus by being rooted firmly in the community of disciples. Only the community can provide the atmosphere, the concern, the mutual love and the experience of Christ risen and alive that will enable the disciple to live true discipleship. Outside the community one cannot live discipleship fully. Medieval wisdom offers the following story:

> The abbot of a monastery was asked by visitors, how it was possible that all the monks, despite their varied origins, talents and education could live together in unity. Instead of presenting a theoretical discourse he answered by using an image: Imagine a wheel with its rim, its spokes and its hub. The rim is the wall that holds everything together but only externally. However, from this periphery

of the wheel the spokes converge to the middle and are held together by the hub. We are the spokes, the diverse individuals in the community. Jesus Christ is the hub. He gives life to us all. He holds us together.

The visitors became pensive, they had understood something very important, but the abbot continued: the more the spokes approach the center, the closer they come to each other.

Matthew shows this need for a community clearly in the way he presents the Sermon on the Mount, which for him is the New Rule and the New Law for the disciples. This "Magna Carta" of Christian behavior is to be understood as the new way of life for those who want to follow the master. But Matthew also makes it clear that the Sermon on the Mount presupposes the existence of a community of those already committed to the Lord, one in which the demands of the Sermon are practiced and lived. The community provides the necessary support for the individual, who cannot live these virtues except as a member of a Christian community, we might even say a church. All the hard sayings in the Sermon on the Mount are meant to remind us that we cannot live without the support and trust of others. Without a community one cannot live discipleship fully.

Another feature of Jesus' ministry that Matthew emphasized strongly, and which expresses his idea of discipleship, is Jesus' custom of sitting at table with his followers who represent all kinds of people but who always include the outcasts of society. Some scholars hold that the movement Jesus initiated could best be summarized as a "table community movement." They base the validity of this phrase on the undeniable fact that one of Jesus' basic feats was his frequent sharing of a meal with the poor, the hungry, and the outcasts who made up the majority of his followers. What marks the community of Jesus' disciples is therefore the continuous practice of "sitting at table," remembering that Jesus would remain with them in this celebration until the day he would come again to fulfill it (Mt 26:29).

The banqueting idea finds its most spectacular expression in the multiplication of the bread at the end of Jesus' public ministry (Mt 15:29-39). The mountain fellowship from which the Gentiles were excluded is offered to them at the end in Matthew 28:16-20. "The banquet on the mountain is a sign to the gentiles that the time of their inclusion is near" (H. Hendrickx, *A Key to the Gospel of Matthew*, p 11).

One more aspect in the Gospel of Matthew needs attention: the authority of the community. It is the community which decides who can become, and under what conditions one can remain a member of the community of the disciples. The community can *excommunicate* members whose life and conduct do not comply with the community's standards (Mt 18:15-18). It can set up conditions under which one can participate in the table fellowship expressed most visibly in the eucharistic celebration (Mt 22:11-13).

The Handbook of Luke

In the Gospel of Luke, a disciple is one who has received the master's Spirit and who is on fire with the master's vision. Jesus - as we have seen - came to throw fire on this earth and all he wants is to see it burning (Lk 12:49). This fire is bestowed on the disciples at Pentecost when they receive the Spirit who comes down on them *"like tongues of fire and fills them"* (Acts 2:3-4). As the *Spirit of the Lord* anointed Jesus *"to preach the Good News to the poor"* (Lk 4:18-19), so the disciples received the same Spirit and were commissioned to preach the Good News of the Kingdom to the poor. As Jesus saw himself compelled to proclaim the Kingdom to every village and town (Lk 4:43), so they (apostles, the seventy, the unknown disciple) are under the command to go and proclaim the arrival of the Kingdom (Lk 9:1-6, 9:60, 10:1-16). The place to which the disciples have to bring the Good News is not any more the "villages and towns of Galilee" but the whole world.

Luke seems to have taken his cue for describing discipleship from the Old Testament story of Elisha and Elijah. He presents this story as a paradigm of true discipleship.

Here are the main points:

1. The prophet throws his cloak over Elisha and the latter has no choice but to follow the call.

So Elijah went from there and found Elisha son of Shaphat. He was plowing with twelve yoke of oxen, and he himself was driving the twelfth pair. Elijah went up to him and threw his cloak around him. Elisha then left his oxen and ran after Elijah. "Let me kiss my father and mother good-bye," he said, "and then I will come with you." "Go back," Elijah replied. "What have I done to you?" So Elisha left him and went back. He took his yoke of oxen and slaughtered them. He burned the plowing equipment to cook the meat and gave it to the people, and they ate. Then he set out to follow Elijah and became his attendant (1 Kgs 19:19-21).

2. Elisha becomes such an ardent follower of his master that he will not leave him.

Three times he responds:

When the LORD was about to take Elijah up to heaven in a whirlwind, Elijah and Elisha were on their way from Gilgal. Elijah said to Elisha, "Stay here; the LORD has sent me to Bethel." But Elisha said, "As surely as the LORD lives and as you live, I will not leave you." So they went down to Bethel. The company of the prophets at Bethel came out to Elisha and asked, "Do you know that the LORD is going to take your master from you today?" "Yes, I know," Elisha replied, "but do not speak of it." Then Elijah said to him, "Stay here, Elisha; the LORD has sent me to Jericho." And he replied, "As surely as the LORD lives and as you live, I will not leave you." So they went to Jericho. The company of the prophets at Jericho went up to Elisha and asked him, "Do you know that the LORD is going to take your master from you today?" "Yes, I know," he replied, "but do not speak of it." Then Elijah said to him, "Stay here; the LORD has sent me to the Jordan." And he replied, "As surely as the LORD lives and as you live, I will not leave you" (2 Kgs 2:1-6).

3. Elisha's only request is a share in the spirit of his master:

*Elijah said to Elisha, "Tell me, what can I do for you before I am taken from you?" **"Let me inherit a double portion of your spirit,"** Elisha replied. "You have asked a difficult thing," Elijah said, "yet if you see me when I am taken from you, it will be yours — otherwise not." As they were walking along and talking together, suddenly a chariot of fire and horses of fire appeared and separated the two of them, and Elijah went up to heaven in a whirlwind (2 Kgs 2:10-11).*

4. What makes Elisha a true disciple of his master is the recognized possession of the spirit.

*He picked up the cloak that had fallen from Elijah and went back and stood on the bank of the Jordan. Then he took the cloak that had fallen from him and struck the water with it. "Where now is the LORD, the God of Elijah?" he asked. When he struck the water, it divided to the right and to the left, and he crossed over. The company of the prophets from Jericho, who were watching, said, **"The spirit of Elijah is resting on Elisha."** And they went to meet him and bowed to the ground before him (2 Kgs 2:14-15).*

These points in Luke's Gospel

Concerning discipleship in the New Testament, the Gospel of Luke seems to have taken up most of the story of Elisha.

1. Jesus is the one who chooses, who throws his cloak over the disciples, and they have no chance to go home and say goodbye.

He said to another man, "Follow me." But the man replied, "Lord, first let me go and bury my father." Jesus said to him, "Let the dead bury their own dead, but you go and proclaim the kingdom of God."

Still another said, "I will follow you, Lord; but first let me go back and say good-bye to my family." Jesus replied, "No one who puts his hand to the plow and looks back is fit for service in the kingdom of God" (Lk 9:57-62).

2. A true disciple will follow the master wherever he goes:

As they were walking along the road, a man said to him, "I will follow you wherever you go." Jesus replied, "Foxes have holes and birds of the air have nests, but the Son of Man has no place to lay his head" (Lk 9:57).

Simon Peter answered him, "Lord, to whom shall we go? You have the words of eternal life" (Jn 6:68).

3. The disciples will inherit the master's spirit who will remain with them and will be the sign that they are his disciples.

On one occasion, while he was eating with them, he gave them this command: "Do not leave Jerusalem, but wait for the gift my Father promised, which you have heard me speak about. For John baptized with water, but in a few days you will be baptized with the Holy Spirit" (Acts 1:4-5).

As it was for Elisha, so for the disciples, the fact that they will see the master go up to heaven is the sign that they will receive his spirit.

But you will receive power when the Holy Spirit comes on you; and you will be my witnesses in Jerusalem, and in all Judea and Samaria, and to the ends of the earth." After he said this, he was taken up before their very eyes, and a cloud hid him from their sight. They were looking intently up into the sky as he was going, when suddenly two men dressed in white stood beside them. "Men of Galilee," they said, "why do you stand here looking into the sky? This same Jesus, who has been taken from you into heaven, will come back in the same way you have seen him go into heaven" (Acts 1:8-14).

Once again, in conclusion we can say: To be a disciple for Luke means to have received the master's spirit, to have been set on fire with the vision of Jesus who came to throw fire on this earth (Lk 12:49). This "fire" is finally given to them on the day of Pentecost. It is worth noticing that according to Luke the fire of the Spirit is given to them while they are *all joined together constantly in prayer.*

> *Then they returned to Jerusalem from the hill called the Mount of Olives, a Sabbath day's walk from the city. When they arrived, they went upstairs to the room where they were staying..They all joined together constantly in prayer, along with the women and Mary the mother of Jesus, and with his brothers (Acts 1:8-14). When the day of Pentecost came, they were all together in one place. Suddenly a sound like the blowing of a violent wind came from heaven and filled the whole house where they were sitting. They saw what seemed to be tongues of fire that separated and came to rest on each of them. All of them were filled with the Holy Spirit and began to speak in other tongues as the Spirit enabled them (Acts 2:1-4).*

In the power of the Spirit the disciples will truly be his messengers until the end of the world. The reception of the Holy Spirit is ultimately meant for mission. Luke records in Acts an episode after the ascension which illustrates this point beautifully.

> *Men of Galilee, why do you stand looking up towards heaven? This Jesus who has been taken up from you into heaven will come in the same way as you saw him going into heaven (Acts 1:11).*

Luke is telling the disciples: now is the time for mission; you have work to do, go and don't worry about that Jesus. He will come in due time. Your work is cut out for you: you have to carry on his work and his mission. Also in Luke, being a disciple, basically means being on mission. That this mission is a participation in the mission of Jesus will be made clear to the disciples through the power of the Spirit of the master who will work through them.

> *You will receive power when the Holy Spirit has come upon you; and you will be my witnesses in Jerusalem, in all of Judea and Samaria, and to the ends of the earth (Acts 1:8).*

In Luke's Gospel there are other important aspects of being a disciple of Jesus. For example, the ideal disciple is the one *who believes* like Mary (Lk 1:45), who *"keeps all these things pondering them in his or her heart"* (Lk 2:19; 2:51). One who not only *follows* Jesus as in Mark and Matthew but who *leaves everything* and follows Jesus (Lk 5:11). One who like Levi has *left everything and rose and followed him* (Lk 5:28). One who is willing to leave even *his wife* because of the wholehearted and all-exclusive love that Jesus would demand of his disciple. The path of love is too narrow; there is no place for two there (Lk 18:22-30). It is important to realize what is important for Luke. In the first place it *is the act of following Jesus;* all renunciation is subordinate to that. It is the enthusiasm, the fire with which the disciple commits him/herself that counts. The freedom from all bonds is freedom for the Kingdom, for Jesus and his mission, for service to Jesus' poor.

The radicalism which such a commitment demands is its logical consequence. This radical commitment to follow is ultimately a commitment to a person, to Jesus. It is he with whom and for whom the disciple is willing to bear all deprivations and sufferings.

Only the person of Jesus makes the costly commitment to discipleship a yoke easy to bear. What is impossible for human beings is possible for God (Lk 18:27 par) who is the one who calls into discipleship. What makes discipleship ultimately possible is the *fire*, the *spirit of the master* which the disciples will receive and who will remain with them. It should not be overlooked that a disciple is not to imitate exactly what the master has done but to let him\herself be guided by the master's spirit who will tell them what has to be done in the different circumstances and situations where they have to witness to Jesus' vision.

A young man was apprenticed to a Master artist who produced the most beautiful stained glass windows anywhere. The apprentice could not approach the Master's genius, so he borrowed his Master's tools, thinking that was the answer. After several weeks, the young man said to his teacher, "I'm not doing any better with your tools than I did with mine." The teacher replied, "It's not the tools of the Master you need but *the spirit of the Master*."

The Handbook of John

The Gospel of John is even more concerned with discipleship than the other Gospels. It arose from a community of equals whose being Christians flowed directly from their individual relationship with Jesus and from the mutual service of love.

To be a disciple of Jesus according to John, the beloved disciple, means to have grown into deep friendship and intimacy with the master. It consists in an intimate relationship with Jesus which is the end point of a long process. In this handbook, the first words that Jesus speaks are a question addressed to the two of his disciples whom the Baptist had directed to Jesus.

The next day John was standing there again with two of his disciples, when he saw Jesus walking by. "There is the Lamb of God!" he said. The two disciples heard him say this and went with Jesus. Jesus turned around, saw them following him, and asked. "What are you looking for?" They asked, "Where do you live, Rabbi?" "Come and see," he answered. And so they went with him and saw where he lived, and spent the rest of that day with him (Jn 1:35-39).

It is Jesus who very pointedly asks the question and who gives the answer to the disciples' request. He names their deep desire and at the same time offers the answer to the request saying: come and stay with me and you will find what you are looking for.

Discipleship begins with this "staying with the master." Thus the process of becoming a disciple is initiated. But the disciple has to grow from mere outer acquaintance to genuine friendship; from being "with the Lord" to being "in the Lord." John uses the analogy of the vine to convey this idea of intimacy and dependence of the disciple on the Lord (Jn 15:4-5,11). This "abide in" is what Mark means by "to be with" and Paul by "in Christ." When the master has taken up his abode in the disciple, then discipleship is accomplished. *Indwelling is the endpoint of discipleship*. One has truly become a disciple of Jesus when the master has taken his abode in the person, when he lives in him/her, when the person has become totally absorbed by the master. The most important aspect of discipleship in John is this "being with." The disciple is taken into Jesus' own mission; he has become a partner - so to speak - in the great mission of Jesus.

> I saw that all compassion, exercised in love,
> is a mark of Christ's indwelling.
> *(Julian of Norwich)*

According to John, the mission of Jesus is twofold. Its first purpose is to manifest God's unconditional and compassionate love for humankind.

> To reveal God is the heart of Jesus mission, for John's Gospel, the key to understanding all that Jesus says and does (D. Senior, *The Passion of Jesus in the Gospel of John*, p. 16).

The revelation of God's true name and love is the reason why the Father sent his only Son into the world (Jn 17:26). The disciple must come to realize and experience this intense love of God in his own life as Jesus, the master, did. He must be burning with the same love revealed to him through his friendship with the master.

The second purpose of Jesus' mission is to save the world by sharing God's own love and life with all men and women who will welcome him in faith:

> *For God so loved the world that he gave his only Son, that, whoever believes in him should not parish but have eternal life. For God sent his Son into the world not to condemn the world but that the world might be saved through him (3:16-17).*

And in the Good Shepherd story Jesus says: *"I came that they may have life and have it abundantly"* (10:10). A disciple is someone who believes that God has revealed his infinite love for us in Jesus, the Son of God and who demonstrates this love of God for all by loving his brothers and sisters as Jesus loved them.

> *And this is his commandment, that we should believe in the name of his Son Jesus Christ and love one another, just as he has commanded us* (1 Jn 3:23).

This is why the disciple can carry on Jesus' mission because he has become part of this mission, a mission the Father had given to His Son. Jesus in turn extends this mission to his friends. This mission they will take up after they have received the master's Spirit. This Spirit was released when Jesus was glorified in his death on the cross. John describes the death of the crucified Jesus in the words: *and bowing his head he handed over the Spirit* (Jn 19:30), indicating that "the last breath of Jesus is the first moment of the outpouring of the Spirit."

When the risen Lord appears on Easter morning to his disciples he bestows on them his greatest gift: the Holy Spirit. As in the creation story where the "ruah Eloim" is breathed into Adam to make him a living creature so the risen Christ breathes on his disciples and fills them with the new life he has gained for them through his death and resurrection.

> *"Peace be with you. As the Father has sent me, so I am sending you."* *When he had said this he breathed on them and said to them, "Receive the Holy Spirit"* (Jn 20:21-22).

As in the handbook of Luke so also in John we must say: it is the Holy Spirit who makes men and women around Jesus into disciples of the master, and who empowers them to carry on his mission. Their mission like that of Jesus is to *"give life in abundance"* (Jn 10:10). They can do that because, as the Spirit *"descended on Jesus and remained with him"* (Jn 1:32-33), so the same Spirit which Jesus let *descend on them* by *breathing* it into them will remain with the disciples. In the power of this Spirit they will stay in communion with the Father and the Son and will carry on the Son's mission in all its aspects until he comes again.

The Father's concern for our living in his Son and his Son living in us can be illustrated in the following dialogue:

I: I rent my house cheaply to others.

God: I don't want to rent, I want to buy.

I: I don't know if I will sell my house, but you may enter and look at it.

God: Yes, I would like to see it.

I: I can give you one room or two.

God: Yes, I like these rooms, I'll take both of them. Perhaps some day, you will decide to give me more. I can wait.

I: I would like to give you more, but it is a little difficult. I need some space for myself.

God: I know that, but I can wait. I am beginning to like this house.

I: Hm...Maybe I could give you one more room. After all, I don't need so much for myself.

God: Thank you, I"ll take this too. I like this house.

I: I would like to give you the whole house, but I am not sure.

God   Think about it. I would not put you out into the street. Your house would be my house and my Son would live here. And you would have more space than before.

I: I do not understand what you mean.

God: I know but I cannot explain it to you. You will have to discover it for yourself, and this will happen only if you give me your whole house.

I: That is a little risky.

God: Yes, but try to experience it with me.

I: I don't know, I don't know...I will think about it and then tell you.

God: I can wait, but I really like this house.

What assurance will the disciples have once the master is gone? How will he, the master, be with them when it is their turn to carry on his work here on earth? Once again we can say: in John's Gospel as in Luke's it is the presence of the Holy Spirit that will make Christ and the Father present to the disciples. *"I and the Father will come and take up our abode in you through the power of the Holy Spirit"* (Jn 14:15-23). Here also the endpoint of being a disciple, after having been chosen and been drawn into God's own mission is to *be sent out* to carry on the world-transforming task that will bring all creatures into God's ultimate design: participation in the life of the Triune God.

Women and Discipleship in the Four Handbooks

There is still an important question we have to deal with: Jesus grew up and proclaimed his message of the Kingdom in a male dominated culture and society. His twelve apostles were men and so were the 72 disciples he sent out. The word *disciple* is never applied to a woman in the Gospels. The question therefore is: how do women fare in the company of Jesus? Are they equal to men when it comes to being disciples?

In the Gospel account of Mark, Matthew and Luke women who followed Jesus appear at the end of their Gospels (Mk 14:40-41; Mt 27:55-56; Lk 23:49; 23:55; 24:10). In John's Gospel the women are near the cross without any reference being made that they had followed Jesus (19:25). The news that women did follow Jesus is therefore found in the synoptic Gospels but not in John. Mark and Matthew speak of women following Jesus from Galilee only in the closing stages of their narratives describing the events of the passion.

Presupposing the cultural and sociological prejudice against women in the time of Jesus, it seems that as long as the male disciples are around Jesus, the women in his company are ignored. But once the male disciples have left Jesus and betrayed him (Mk 14:50; Mt 26:56), the women appear. Only then is it said of them that they followed Jesus already in Galilee and went with him to Jerusalem to become the witnesses of his crucifixion and resurrection.

The reason is obvious: Women are only introduced when the men were not there anymore. If the men would have followed Jesus faithfully to the cross as the women did, the women would most probably never have been mentioned. In the words of Clara Ricci:

> The redactors, being unable to cite the witness of the male disciples because they had fled, are forced to refer to the women who stayed. At this point they state who these women are: women welcomed by Jesus and who had been with him since the time in Galilee; they thereby provide a testimony to their fidelity at this serious and dramatic time when the male disciples abandoned him (*Mary Magdalene*, p. 26).

In Mark and Matthew we find, therefore, a great silence about the women in the public life of Jesus who followed him right from the beginning of his ministry in Galilee. The exception, however, is Luke in his summary account early in the Gospel 8:1-3:

> Soon afterward Jesus went through cities and villages, proclaiming and bringing the good news of the Kingdom of God. The twelve were with him, as well as some women who had been cured of evil spirits and infirmities: Mary, called Magdalene, from whom seven demons had gone out, and Johanna, the wife of Herod's steward Chuza, and Susanna, and many other, who provided for him out of their resources.

This text has long been a puzzle and, most often, either ignored by exegetes or dealt with lightly. Clara Ricci, after a thorough investigation of the passage, draws the following conclusion:

The particular news this little passage provides is the information that a group of women followed Jesus constantly on his travels since the beginning of this public activity in the Land of Galilee. A circle of women: Mary Magdalene, Johanna, Susanna and many others; they set out with him, leaving home, family, relations, their village, their everyday life, and stayed with him listening, speaking, traveling, offering goods and services, living with him, in short, and in the end followed him to the cross, where they, the only faithful witnesses, were to see him die (*Mary Magdalene*, p. 53).

This trace disappears in the continuing story of the Gospel. Considering the status of women in his time, what Jesus did was absolutely revolutionary. Quite obviously, Jesus wanted the restricted and privileged circle that lived with him as he went from village to village to include a group of women.

We should not forget that the Gospel stories about women have come down to us through the eyes and hands of men who lived in a male dominated culture and society. Some of these restrictions, imposed by culture on women, were, for example, the following: A worship service could not be conducted unless at least ten men were present no matter how many women attended it; the testimony of a woman had no value in court; the Torah could not be taught to women. In the Talmud we read: "The words of the Torah will be destroyed in the fire sooner than be taught to women."

The ideal man was the Rabbi, the "wise student" whose first and primary purpose was to spend as much of his life as possible in Torah study, prayer and fulfilment of the mitzvot which he was helping to reveal. The Jewish wife and mother was forbidden by the male-interpreted Torah those very activities like Torah studies and public worship that gave worth to men's lives. Women were under considerable pressure to bear many children but especially boys. The ideal of womanhood was to support and reproduce as many ideal men as possible.

In the context of such a cultural background, we can assume that the Gospel writers *re-edited* many stories in favor of a male perspective. But a careful study of passages which indeed deal with women as disciples of Jesus can be very rewarding. The ways in which women approached Jesus and Jesus approached women reveal certain striking features.

When dealing with women, Jesus clearly reveals his aversion to discrimination which we called earlier "Jesus' allergy." He challenges any social and religious restrictions that intend to exclude women, while they break taboos and risk the fury of the crowds or the irritation and reproach of the disciples. The Syro-Phoenician woman even tries to teach Jesus a lesson and extends his horizon (Mk 7:24-39). The menstruating woman, fully aware how outrageous her action is, which she can only perform in secret by approaching him from the back, nevertheless dares to touch Jesus (Mk 5:25-34). The Syro-Phoenician and the Samaritan woman are outsiders because of their race, and yet Jesus engages in conversation with them. He ignores the strict Sabbath rules when he heals the bent woman and praises Mary of Bethany for having stepped out of her proper role as a housewife (Lk 10:38-42). While the women in these stories 'forget their place' without making any apology for doing so, Jesus accepts and even supports them publicly.

Thus for the women in these stories discipleship means courageously taking the initiative: they touch his garment, they offer a drink to the stranger at the well and when the "sinner" in the Gospel of Luke intrudes at a meal, she performs an act the host had forgotten or overlooked. When women disciples give, they give generously to the extent of extravagance as we see in the example of the widow at the Temple treasury (Mk 12:41-44) and the woman who pours out the precious ointment (Mk 14:1-9).

Besides the many similarities in the Gospels concerning women in the company of Jesus, there are also different emphases.

Mark, in his Gospel, presents us with a number of women named and unnamed. Four of them are put in especially exemplary narrative roles: the hemorrhaging woman (Mk 5:24ff), the syro-Phoenician woman (7:24ff), the poor widow at the treasury (12:41ff), and the woman who anoints Jesus in Bethany (14:3ff). These women are portrayed as "bold and faithful, self-denying and serving". They are presented by Mark as outstanding models of faith for missionaries and their audience, both Christians and non-Christians (Swartley, *The Role of Women in Mark's Gospel*, pp. 16-22).

However, women disciples in Mark's Gospel come into full view in the context of the abandonment of Jesus by those who had *followed* him in Galilee but were not ready to go with him to Jerusalem. It was the women who *went with him on the road to Jerusalem*.

There were also women looking on from afar, among whom were Mary Magdalene and Mary the mother of James the Younger and of Joses, and Salome who, when he was in Galilee, followed him and served him; and also many other women who came up with him to Jerusalem (15:40-41).

This text is all the more remarkable when we remember how important the phrase *"following Jesus"* is for Mark's handbook. These women, listed by name, had been his disciples already in Galilee when the first male disciples had been called. But in contrast to the male disciples they were ready to follow Jesus to Jerusalem, and they accompanied him in his Passion while on the night of his arrest all the male disciples *deserted him and fled* (14:50). These women were disciples in the fullest sense. They, and not the Twelve or any of the other disciples, were witnesses of the death (15:37), the burial (15:47) and the resurrection (16:6) of Jesus.

MESSENGERS

It suddenly strikes me
with overwhelming force:

It was women
who were first to spread the message of
Easter -
the unheard of!

It was women
who rushed to the disciples,
who breathless and bewildered,
passed on the greatest message of all:

He is alive!

Think -
if women had kept silence
in the churches!
(Märta Wilhemson, Sweden)

The phrase *and they served him* (15:41) needs our attention as well. The women who follow Jesus on his way to the cross exemplify - so to speak - the other aspect of discipleship: to *serve and not to be served* (10:45). The verb *diakonein* is sparingly used in the New Testament and only four times in Mark. It is never used of the male disciples but only of angels, Jesus and women. Of the angels who served Jesus in the desert: *and the angels waited on him* (1:13); of Jesus himself who *came to serve and not to be served* (10:45) and of the women who *served him*.

First, it is Peter's mother in law who, after being healed by Jesus, got up and *began to serve them* (1:31). The second instance when women *serve Jesus* is when they stand beneath the cross as quoted above(15:41).

It is striking that the two groups who specifically 'serve' Jesus himself, the angels and the women, appear at the two great moments of crisis at the beginning and end of his public life, and so frame it. This together with the rarity of *diakonein* in the Gospel as a whole, reinforces the impression that more than ordinary concerns are involved (Dines, *"Not to be served, but to serve"*, p. 441).

Mark's statements that "women from afar were watching Jesus' death" (15:41) and "their flight from the tomb saying nothing to anyone" (16:8) are often seen as proof that the women were also fallible disciples. Such an interpretation is not necessarily negative: "women from afar watching" means they came *from afar* and the "not telling anyone" means not telling *anyone else* besides the disciples and Peter in which case the comment is like Jesus' command in 1:44.

Even more than Mark, **Matthew** restricts the term 'disciples' to the twelve, a reflection of his audience's concept of Jewish leadership. However, women play a significant role in the genealogy of Jesus, among the members of the crowds that follow him, in the passion narrative and among those of all nations who are made disciples.

In **Luke** women are prominent. He portrays a God who put himself into women's hands:

his mother wrapped him in diapers (2:7); women served him and showed him hospitality in their homes (8:1-3; 10:42); at a banquet an unknown woman washed and anointed his feet (7:1f);as he stumbled towards his execution women cried over him and accompanied him (23:38); and finally it was women who wanted to anoint his tortured body and who received the resurrection message (23:55; 24:1-10) (Gubler, "Luke's Portrait of Mary", p. 23).

Women in Luke are equal to the male disciples and at times even called prior to their male partners. Elizabeth and Mary illustrate that women receive the Holy Spirit (Lk 1-2). They discern the action of God in what is happening to them (Visitation) and are among the faithful at Pentecost (Acts 1:12-2:4). In the story of the sisters Mary and Martha (Lk 10:38-42) Jesus does not exalt the service of the word above that of the table; he only tries to shift Martha's focus from her self-pity and preoccupations to the one who is the source of all we do, whether in service at table or in the service of the word. That Jesus did not undervalue the *service at table* is obvious because he himself understood his role as *one who serves at table* (Lk 22:24-27).

In spite of all his references to women and their restored dignity through Jesus, Luke does not stress the role of women in active ministry beyond the faith response to the word and the performance of charitable services.

It is **John** who portrays most clearly the discipleship of equals, as he does not restrict any material to the apostles or the twelve alone. This indicates that his Gospel grew out of a community of Christian equals whose lives were grounded in their relationship with Jesus and flowed out into a life of mutual service of love. The five women portrayed in John's Gospel can rightfully be considered models of discipleship.

Mary, who opens the public ministry of her son, is also present under the cross where she ceases to be merely the mother of Jesus and becomes as well the mother of the new community of believers, the new creation.

The *woman of Samaria* meets Jesus as a weary traveler who asks her for a drink. In return she becomes a missionary to whom Jesus reveals his true identity. He does so because she overcomes all social barriers and any initial feeling of inferiority to enter into dialogue with him. It is the person who attracts and fascinates her more than the argument.

Towards the end of the Gospel of John we encounter *Mary and Martha* who also take the initiative in seeking Jesus' help and are willing to grow in their faith. Martha's confession that Jesus is 'the Messiah and Son of God' (Jn 11:25-27) could be compared with the confession of Peter in the other Gospels. Her belief in Jesus, contrary to that of Peter, is made perfect through the manifestation of his glory (Jn 11:39). Mary, in anointing Jesus with precious ointment, demonstrates the cost and total commitment of discipleship, and thereby prefigures Jesus' washing of the disciples' feet and in a way preparing his body for burial (Jn 12: 23-36). There is no instance of any of these women reproving Jesus as Peter did at the first indication of suffering.

Mary of Magdala completes the circle of women as she establishes the resurrection (Jn 20: 1f, 11-18) in a process of coming to full faith rather than as an automatic reaction. She has first to face the empty tomb and tell Peter and the beloved disciple about it. Then, despite their initial disbelief, she continues to search for Jesus. When he addresses her by name, she immediately recognizes him, but has to enter into a different relationship. She is not to cling but to go and proclaim: 'I have seen the Lord.' (Cf. Janet and John Gaden, *"Women and Discipleship in the New Testament"*, pp 113-123).

A CREED

I believe in God,
who created women and
men in God's image,
who created the world
and entrusted to men and
women the care of the earth.

I believe in Jesus,
Child of God
chosen by God
born of the woman Mary
who listened to women
and loved them
who stayed in their homes
and talked with them
about the Kingdom of God
who called women to
be his disciples and accepted
their generous support.

I believe in Jesus, who talked
about theology to a woman
at a well and for the first time
revealed his identity to this
woman, who inspired her to
proclaim this great news
in her town.

I believe in Jesus ,
who was anointed by a woman
in the house of Simon,

who reprimanded the
male guests who despised her.

I believe in Jesus,
who said that her deed will be
remembered -as service
to the Messiah.

I believe in Jesus,
who acted fearlessly
and without human respect,
who rejected the blood
taboo of ancient peoples
by curing the woman who
dared to touch him.

I believe in Jesus,
who spoke of God
as a woman
who searches for the lost coin
who in her efforts to clean
her house searches for what
has been lost.

I believe in Jesus,
who spoke of pregnancy and
birth with deep respect
not as punishment - but
as a revolutionary event
as a metaphor for
transformation as being
born from pain into joy.

I believe in Jesus,
who described himself
as a mother hen gathering
her young under her wings.

I believe in Jesus,
who appeared first to
Mary Magdalene and gave her
the burning message:
GO AND PROCLAIM...

I believe in the wholeness
of the redeemer,
in whom there is neither Jew
nor Greek
slave nor free person
neither man nor woman;
because we are all one in
the mystery of salvation.

I believe in the Holy Spirit
who moves over the waters
of creation and the earth.

I believe in the Holy Spirit
the feminine spirit of God
who gave life to us like a hen
who bore us
and covered us
under her wings.
(Knippenkötter)

Mary the Mother of Jesus

Among all the women disciples mentioned in the Gospels and the Acts, Mary, the mother of Jesus, takes on a central role, especially in Luke. In the Acts, Mary appears for the last time in the midst of the early Christian community awaiting the Spirit in prayer (Acts 1:14). This community has an egalitarian vision as it no longer considers itself a community based on age, sex, or social status (cf. Ga 3:28) (cf. *"Luke's Portrait of Mary,"* pp 19-24).

The same Spirit who is being poured out on the disciples at Pentecost, was poured out on the young woman in the Galilean village of Nazareth about thirty years earlier. As it was with the call of the other women in the Gospels who meet Jesus in the ordinary circumstances of their daily lives, so it is with Mary engaged to a carpenter. In this Mary makes history: from now on God's revelation no longer occurs in the priestly cult (see Zachariah), but in the daily events that rank so very low on society's value scale. This young woman questions the angel, just as the woman at the well and the Syro-Phoenician woman question Jesus. Once convinced of God's saving plans and the great deeds God intends to do for his people, Mary, like the other women in the Gospels, cannot help but go out and proclaim. The 'power of the Most High' that overshadows Mary creates something new and sets something in motion. Mary allows herself to be touched and moved by 'the power of the Most High' to enable God to be the life and breath of all people.

Mary is a woman captured and seized by the Spirit of God, because of God's love for the world which Jesus continues to make manifest in his proclamation and making present of the Kingdom. God is no longer sought in the clouds but "in the flesh", in a birth and in a grave.

Mary who kept all the things told to her about her son in her heart to ponder and reflect on, trying to understand their meaning, becomes a model believer whose faith journey involves a difficult and painful learning process on the long road of discipleship. In the oppressive situation of her time regarding women, Mary found the way to Jesus' new world, the Kingdom he came to bring, and in faith bore the hardship of her life. She believed and lived the words of her song of praise that God has lifted up the poor (Fuellenbach, "Mary as the Model of True Discipleship in *"Proclaiming His Kingdom*, pp. 203-210).

Reflection: *Keeping alive Jesus' Dynamism*

The four Gospels put before our eyes concrete 'role models' of how to understand and live discipleship. Each Gospel presents discipleship from a different perspective.

Mark outlines what he regards as the essential elements of true discipleship with these *words: to go after the master - to put oneself second - to take up one's cross* .

His Gospel is the 'story of the passion with an elaborate introduction' written with the certainty of the resurrection. In the passion of Jesus the fidelity of the Son to the Father comes to the fore, while in the resurrection the faithfulness of the Father is emphasized. Blessed Edith Stein (+ 1942) came to the Catholic faith through the mystery of the cross. The occasion was the death of her professor who died in World War I. The condolence visit with his widow became a turning point in her life: "It was my first encounter with the cross and with the divine strength it conveys to those who carry it. It was the moment in which my unbelief collapsed and Christ radiated: Christ in the mystery of the cross." This experience shaped her life so much that when she became a Carmelite she chose the name Sister Teresa Blessed by the Cross.

But as the story of the blind Bartimaeus (Mk 10:46-52) shows, we need healing before we can see and follow the Lord *on the way* to Jerusalem.

QUESTION: What do I have still to *throw off* and from what *blindness* does the Lord have to heal me, before I am ready to follow him on his journey to Jerusalem?

Matthew claims that we can only be and remain disciples of Jesus *by joining the community of disciples*. Only the community can provide the atmosphere, the concern, the mutual love and the experience of Christ risen and alive that will enable the disciple to live true discipleship. *Outside the community one cannot live discipleship.*

To be a disciple it is not enough to do theology; it is not enough to do good. To be disciples we must *"do the Gospel together."* We witness as a community of disciples in a world where people suffer from isolation and exclusion. Matthew seems to speak especially to those who favor team ministry.

Story: *Close to the Fire*

Someone came to Jesus and asked him, "Is there no way one can be a follower of yours without belonging to your group of disciples? I would love to follow you, in other words, I would like to be a Christian, but preferably without being part of this so-called community of followers or the Church and all the rest of it...!? Jesus looked at him intently and replied, "Listen, I will tell you a story:

Once upon a time there were a few men who sat down to have a good chat. When night fell and darkness was all around them, they gathered pieces of wood, piled them up and lit a fire. There they huddled together, warmed by the fire while its glow lit up their faces. However, there was one among them, who no longer wished to be part of the circle. He preferred to be by himself. So he took one of the burning logs from the common fire and sat alone, at a considerable distance from the others. The burning wood gave him warmth and light, but soon the fire died down and the lonely man felt the cold and darkness of the night. He came back to his senses, took the burnt down piece of wood and carried it back to the blazing fire, where it caught the flames and began to burn once more. The man joined the group sitting around the fire. His cold bones warmed up again and the blazing flames lit up his face."
And Jesus added, "Those who belong to me, live close to the fire. Yes, indeed, I have come to light a great fire on this earth - and how I long to see it burn brightly."

QUESTION: **What does this story tell me about the way I remain on fire with the vision of Jesus? How do I deal with the frailty and the shortcomings of the community of disciples to which I belong?**

Luke sees the disciple as one who has *received the master's spirit*, who has been set on fire with the vision of Jesus (Lk 12:49), and he stresses that this *baptism with fire* only occurs "when the disciples are at prayer."

In the power of the Spirit the disciples will truly be Christ's messengers until the end of the world. All their skills and talents will not help them if they do not know how to kindle the fire and keep it burning.

Once upon a time there was a young man. And this young man ardently longed to be a blacksmith. So he learned all the necessary techniques of the trade. How to hold the tongs How to lift the sledge. How to smite the anvil. Even how to blow the glowing fire with the bellows.

Having finished his apprenticeship, he was chosen to be employed at the smithy of the Royal Palace. However, his new found delight soon came to an end when he discovered that all his skills and knowledge in handling the tools were of no avail, for he had failed to learn how to kindle a spark.

QUESTION: In what ways do I keep my fire burning, do I kindle the spark? How do I nurture my original enthusiasm?

John places *"staying with the master"* at the beginning of every discipleship. The process of becoming a disciple is initiated in this way. But the disciple has to *grow from mere outer acquaintance to sincere friendship; from "being with" the Lord to "being in" the Lord.* When the master has taken up his abode in the disciple, then discipleship is accomplished. *Indwelling is the endpoint of discipleship.* One has truly become a disciple of Jesus when the master lives in the disciple, when the disciple has become so absorbed by the master that "he who hears him hears the master."

QUESTION: How far is following the Lord really priority number one in my life? What does the reality of God's indwelling in me mean to me? Does it affect the way I look at and treat my fellow human beings and the whole of God's creation?

Breaking Loose

Afraid of the people in the street,
they locked themselves in,
no communication,
doors closed,
windows shuttered,
a piece of paper in the opening of their hearth.

We might think
that this was because
they had not received the Holy Spirit.
But they had received the Spirit
already fifty days before.
The Gospel tells
that on the evening
of the first day of the week
- after his death and resurrection -
Jesus had come
and he had given them the Holy Spirit,
breathing over them
the breath of the new creation,
just as his Father had done
so many million years before
over those first human beings -
Adam and Eve.

The Spirit was there;
the Spirit did not work;
it did not live because they were afraid.
They were afraid
of the people in the street;
they were afraid
of the world around them;
they were afraid
of themselves,
full of that Spirit.
Now at **Pentecost**,
that Spirit in them
could no longer be contained
within the limits of their fear.
Now the Spirit suddenly, in thunder and lightning,
in multiple flames, burst loose in their hearts
and above their heads.

It was a fire
that did not come from outside them alone;
it was a fire that came from within them too.
It was a fire that made them finally move.

> Some day, after we have mastered the winds, the tides,
> and gravity, we will harness for God the energies of love;
> and then, for the second time in the history of the world
> man will have discovered fire! (Teilhard de Chardin)

As Christians we believe in the doctrine of original sin and a heritage of sinfulness, which more often than not obscures our judgement. We cannot take it for granted that the present state of affairs, in which women are confined to certain roles and functions in Church and society, is God's explicit will and command. Moreover, if the "Jesus Movement" is indeed a prophetic movement, it ought at all times speak to us and the whole world about another order of human affairs, more responsive to God's intent and call that has come to us in the message and reality of the Kingdom.

QUESTION: What is my vision of mutuality in discipleship? How do I envisage a Church in which the gifts of ALL are welcomed?

A PSALM OF PARTNERSHIP IN MINISTRY

We are partners in the mystery of redemption,
partners in the mystery of reconciliation,
partners in the misery of the world's population,
partners in the way of the cross.

We are partners in the ministry
of service,
partners in the ministry of
justice and peace,
partners in the liturgy
of church and life,
partners in healing and hope.

Together we reach out
to touch the untouchables.
Together we move out
to teach the untaught.
Together we stand up
to preach right practice.
Together we practice
what we preach.

Ours is the gift of good
company on days when
there's nobody else
there beside us.

Ours is the gift of affirming
the ways of the God who
is working within us.

Blessed is the partnership
rooted in love that spills over,
spreads over, covers over everything
negative and uninspiring.

Blessed is the fellowship
partnership shares with its circle of friends
and supporters.
God of relationship,
bless this relationship,
strengthen this partnership,
deepen this fellowship;
let it be a symbol of Your mode of Being
and sign of Your own non-competitive ways.

God of Companionship,
may we be supportive,
may we be effective,
bringing to life all the best in each other,
so that we may help others
see good in themselves.

Thank You, O God,
for the gift
and the grace
of partnership
in the mystery
of living.

Chapter Six

"The Kingdom of God "in your reach"

Jesus was not a systematic theologian and, therefore, did not define the Kingdom of God in abstract terms but expressed its content in parables, similes and symbolic actions among which his eating and drinking with outcasts was the most striking. With this practice he wanted to indicate that God was coming to create fellowship first of all with the marginalized. Since he understood his mission initially as *gathering and restoring the people of Israel,* his heart went out to the marginalized and *lost sheep of the people of Israel. To them he felt sent* (cf. Mt 15:24). His message was to be understood as *"Good News for the poor."* (Mt 11:5) They were the first 'addressees' and were regarded as the ones with a better sense for grasping the message, since their situation offered a better background for the understanding of the Kingdom. They were the ones who had the least hope of sharing in the Kingdom when it would come. Jesus, in gathering first the lost and forgotten before all the others, revealed God's final intention for humanity: to call all people into a communion of brothers and sisters in union with the Triune God in a new, transformed world. Scholars have tried to summarize the message of the Kingdom by pointing to its most outstanding characteristics. Some of them will be taken up in the subsequent chapters. The first characteristic is expressed in Jesus' announcement that the Kingdom has arrived with him.

The Kingdom of God is "at hand"

The phrase that best summarizes Jesus' mission is found in Mark 1:14-15:

The time is fulfilled and the Kingdom of God is at hand; repent and believe in the good news.

Mark indicates here that with Jesus the time of waiting has come to an end and the Kingdom has broken into history. The "TIME IS FULFILLED" means, the measure of time assigned by God for the fulfillment of the promise of the Kingdom has been filled up. Behind this conviction lies the Jewish view that history is not simply an endless repetition of the same cycles but under God's guidance is moving forward towards a goal. The time has become really full, not "almost" or "nearly" full. The unsurpassable future of God has begun. The time *before the Kingdom is* finished and the *time of the Kingdom* has begun - the Kingdom has entered human history. Jesus' words and actions initiate God's dynamic activity which aims at completing the work of salvation in a transformed universe.

Luke provides us with his summary of the central message of Jesus in the first sermon of Jesus in his home town (Lk 4:14-21). The fundamental meaning of the two passages is the same. Luke, instead of using the phrase "Kingdom of God," (as in Mark) presents its reality by means of the symbol of the Jubilee release which brings final salvation. Jesus quotes a passage from Isaiah which is an affirmation of Israel's hope, the promise of God's liberating and reconciling future.

The most important statement in this section of Luke is: *"Today this Scripture has been fulfilled in your hearing"* (Lk 4:21). The question is, what would have come to the mind of a listener who heard Jesus speak these words? What did he mean by saying "the Kingdom of God is here, is present, has arrived?" What did people expect to happen when God would finally come and fulfill the promises made to Israel through the prophets? They knew four basic consecutive stages would take place once the Kingdom had come.

First, all the bad people and all unjust men and women will be judged and disappear from the earth. Yahweh will then lead his people into their final glory for everyone to see.

Secondly, from the glorified Israel the Kingdom was to spread to all the nations (cf. Is 2:1-6). Then all the peoples of the earth will be blessed through Israel and will participate in the creation of the New Heaven and the New Earth.

Thirdly, with the blessing of all the nations the transformation of nature will take place (cf. Is 25:7; 11:6-11). The whole universe will be overtaken by the final Kingdom: animals, plants and even inorganic matter will be transformed. A new world will appear without any trace of violence or death, a universe totally at peace.

Fourthly, all the dead, who lived before the coming of the Messiah, will rise to take their place in the New Heaven and the New Earth (cf. Is 26:19). God's Kingdom in glory will affect the whole universe from beginning to end.

But how could Jesus say that all this was happening now "in your very hearing?" People asked him: where is the Kingdom you proclaim as having come? We don't see the things promised happening in our midst. The crooks are still with us; the oppressors are still doing their evil work; we are as miserable as ever; nothing has changed or is changing. How can you say: the time is fulfilled and the Kingdom is here? Demonstrate its presence; show its transforming power! We could ask the same questions still today: where is the Kingdom? Where is its world-transforming power? Can it be convincingly stated that God's Kingdom has arrived? Has the world changed since Jesus came? Commenting on Mark 8:29, where St. Peter confesses that Jesus is the Messiah, Martin Buber wrote:

> According to my faith it is not the case that the Messiah has appeared in a definite moment of history but his appearance can only mark the end of history. In the perspective of my faith, the redemption of the world did not happen nineteen centuries ago. On the contrary, we still live in an unredeemed world.

Is not Buber's observation correct? What then does it mean to say the Kingdom of God has arrived in our midst?

This question has been answered in different ways. The famous exegete Rudolf Bultmann explained the presence of the Kingdom as follows. He uses the example of a train that is pulling into a station. The passengers are waiting and the moment they see the train coming they get ready, grab their luggage and give goodbye kisses. What puts them into action is the incoming train even though the train has not yet reached the platform. Or another example of his: the nearness of the Kingdom is like an approaching rain cloud already pouring down rain in the distance. People who see it coming get themselves ready although the rain has not yet arrived. As the incoming train and the coming rain determine people's actions when they see them so does the coming Kingdom challenge people to act now. For him the Kingdom is very near, we can see it already but still the train has not yet reached the platform of the station and we are not yet wet from the rain that is approaching fast. Is this the way we should explain the nearness of the Kingdom when Jesus said: "the Kingdom has arrived, is here?"

Most scholars today would not agree with this explanation. Rather, correcting the metaphor, the train has already arrived and the rain is actually falling, we are getting wet! Jesus does not announce the nearness of the Kingdom nor does he merely heighten the expectation. His mission is to bring people into the actual relationship with God which the coming Kingdom promises. The Kingdom is the final act of salvation, the final decisive intervention of God on behalf of his people. This cannot be stressed enough. But how can we demonstrate its presence already?

The Kingdom of God

The kingdom of God is inside you. - Jesus
   God's kingdom is where the king is and he is in you and in me
- not tied to buildings of wood or stone
- not tied to names or titles
- not tied to times and plans
- not tied to language and expressions
- not tied to our abilities and inabilities
   tied only to the possibility of living in you and me as Lord of life.

   Are we in the kingdom or is the kingdom in us?
   Are we tied to a visible kingdom?
   Even if we talk of the kingdom
   but don't carry it in us we will be talking in the wind.

      It is never more important
      to DO something for God
      than it is to BE in God. *(U. Schaffer)*

Jesus himself was constantly pressed to respond to the question about the "already" and "not yet". What was his answer?

How to explain the "already and not yet"

Jesus explained the tension between the present beginnings and the final coming of the Kingdom in analogies, parables and stories. The best of them may be the Parable of the Mustard Seed and the full-grown mustard shrub (Mk 4:30-32). In this parable the Kingdom is compared to the tiny seed and the full-grown mustard shrub. For Jesus the Kingdom is present now like a little seed which contains and guarantees the future full-grown shrub. Surely, the seed itself is not the full-grown shrub but without the seed there will be no mature bush. So it is with the Kingdom. It is fully present in the form of a seed and therefore its final coming is guaranteed. Because of its presence now, we can be absolutely confident of its final coming in glory. The following story explains this point beautifully:

Once in his dream, a young man entered a shop. Behind the counter he saw an angel willing to serve him. Hastily he asked him, "What do you sell here, Sir?" The angel replied with great friendliness: "Everything you would like." "In that case," the young man replied, "I would like to have the following: an end to all the wars in the world, better living and working conditions for the marginalized, the elimination of all the slums, work for the unemployed and a deeper community spirit and more love in the Church and...and..." At that moment the angel interrupted him; "Excuse me, please, you misunderstood - we do not sell the fruits, we only sell the seeds."

Jesus explained the tension of the "already" and "not yet" by introducing a distinction between the presence of the Kingdom that had come with him then and is present now, and its future fulfillment that was and is still to come. What people of his time considered as ONE EVENT - the decisive intervention of God in history - Jesus split into two related but separate events. He did this by bringing the beginning of the eschatological time into the "now" and postponing its fulfillment into the future yet to come. He created an "in-between time," a time-span located between his first and his second coming. In this way he formulated the classic problem of the "ALREADY" and the "NOT YET."

The relationship between the *already* and the *not yet* is vividly explained through this story:

I used to ask students in the Philippines in their examinations to explain the tension that exists between the 'already' and the 'not yet.' One student gave the following explanation: there is a tasty little fish in the ocean that is usually dried in the sun and then served for breakfast, fried in a strong mixture of herbs and vinegar. When the fish is being fried, a strong smell fills the whole house. In the seminary this fried fish was served twice a week for breakfast. The seminarian, referring to this custom wrote: "The 'already and the not yet' can easily be explained through this fish we get for breakfast. When we are still sitting in church during our morning service we can already smell the fish we have not yet eaten. So it is with the Kingdom, we can already smell its presence although we have not yet 'tasted' its fullness. Just as the smell of the fish is not yet the actual fish, yet it is of the fish so we already have something of the Kingdom now, its foretaste in the form of a smell, without being able to claim having tasted it.

Jesus manifests the dynamic presence of the Kingdom in history not only in words, but particularly in his wonder-working activity. His demon-exorcisms, for example, demonstrate that God is penetrating the present and establishing his Kingdom here and now. One often quoted passage that clearly indicates that God is inaugurating a new era of history is Matthew 12:28: *"If it is by the Spirit of God that I drive out demons, then the Kingdom of God has come upon you."* Other sayings of a similar tone include Luke 10:18, where Jesus sees Satan falling from heaven like lightning, or Matthew 11:12 which speaks about the Kingdom "that exercises its force" since the day of John the Baptist. These passages indicate that something is happening now. God is entering the present age in a totally new way to bring to fulfillment the promises made to the prophets. Against the often voiced objection that the Kingdom cannot be present in the world now because Jesus himself said *"My Kingdom is not of this world,"* J. Moltmann has this to say:

> The people who would like to see it as belonging to the next world always point to Jesus saying that 'my Kingdom is not of this world' (Jn 18:36). But in so doing they are overlooking the fact that this is a statement about the origin of the kingdom, not its place. Of course it is not 'of' this world in the sense of coming from it. It comes from God. If it didn't come from God, it couldn't heal this sick world. But in and through Jesus it is in the midst of this world, and when Jesus said these words the kingdom of God in person was standing in front of Rome's imperial governor, Pontius Pilate (J. Moltmann, *Jesus Christ for Today's World*, p.20).

Other Scripture passages place the accent on Jesus' common practice of table fellowship and interpret his festive "eating and drinking" as an already present celebration of the banquet of the Kingdom understood as an "active anticipation of banqueting in the fully consummated Kingdom of God." Jesus saw the actualization of this historically present Kingdom in the coming of the gentiles who will sit at table with Abraham, Isaac and Jacob (cf. Mt 8:11).

The fact that the Kingdom of God is a present reality has never been denied in theological writings. But most of the time this "being present" has been so qualified that the future and not the present of the Kingdom seem to be the primary concern, as G. Lohfink puts it:

> In order to be fair to Jesus' message and praxis, one must, more than anything else, hammer out the PRESENCE of the BASILEIA that Jesus himself maintained. That God would establish his kingly rule in the future was believed by everyone in Israel during Jesus' time. Generally speaking, people lived in the end-time hope. Jesus' unmistakable uniqueness lay in the fact that with frightening awareness he could speak of fulfillment: The Kingdom of God is here and now. And he not only said it, but fulfilled it in messianic praxis (G. Lohfink, *"The Exegetical Predicament.."*, p. 104).

According to Lohfink it is not enough to say that the Kingdom is present in the person of Jesus, or in his signs, or proleptically, in an anticipatory way. He is afraid that such expressions push the Kingdom off into the future once again. As an "exegetical probe" for the presence of the Kingdom now, Lohfink discusses the parables of the Costly Pearl and Treasure in the Field (cf. Mt 13:44-46), or as he called them, "The time of the Kingdom present." He writes:

This adventure does not happen in the sometime of a future yet to come, or a vague everywhere-and-nowhere somewhere, but where Jesus is and where Jesus gathers Israel together. The Kingdom of God is found and acquired here and now. The treasure and the pearl are not proleptically, anticipatorily, and dynamically acquired, but really acquired. The parable does not say that the Kingdom of God is like a merchant who acquires a costly pearl which he only temporarily has in his possession (G. Lohfink, *"The Exegetical Predicament.."*, p. 106).

The presence of God's Kingdom is so overwhelming that those who recognize it will drop any activity and will do everything to enter it. Ordinary rules are broken and subversion of conventional morality is inevitable if what is final and transcendent has become available within one's experience. Was Jesus not too harsh when he told the young man - who wanted to go home and first bury his father before committing himself totally - to "let the dead bury their dead?" What difference would a week or two have made for that total commitment the young man was willing to make? Did he not have an obligation and a holy duty first to take care of his father? Or what kind of morality does Jesus seemingly promote in the Parable of the Unfaithful Steward, who cheats his master out of property (Lk 16:1-8)? Such behavior and suggested actions by Jesus remain totally incomprehensible and even offensive unless one sees them in the light of what is happening in the present moment: God's Kingdom is breaking into the world right now and is in the very reach of everyone who wants it.

That availability of the Kingdom right now becomes an occasion greater than any other, an opportunity in comparison with which any wealth or status is only of instrumental worth. Everything else is there to be disposed of in the attempt to squeeze through the narrow gate (Mt 7:13-14; Lk 13:23-24) or to capitalize on the talents one has been given (Mt 25:14-30; Lk 19:11-27). Commenting on the *leaven* of the Kingdom Chilton remarks:

> The Kingdom is so ordinary that it proves that everything is extraordinary. Just as the line between the usual and the unusual disappear in the light of the Kingdom, so the local awareness of the hidden incursion point forward to its thorough leavening of the whole experience. The presence of the Kingdom is so thorough that Jesus sees it as permeating what can be seen and felt, and as by no means standing apart from experience, as if in an ideal realm (*Pure Kingdom*, p. 71).

A saying found in the Gospel of Thomas puts the presence of the Kingdom even more into focus:

If those who lead you say to you "see, the kingdom is in heaven," then the birds of heaven will precede you. If they say to you "it is in the sea," then the fish will precede you. But the kingdom is within you and outside you.

But the next question will be: if the Kingdom is so all-pervasively present, how can we concretely experience its presence now? Where do we find it in our midst? In what form does it appear here on earth now?

God slipped in

God slipped into the brothel
when no one was looking
and sat among the ladies
who were drinking coffee
and smoking reefers.
The jokes were loud and raucous,
the language harsh and strong,
until Debbie broke down and cried,
because a client refused to take her,
and threw her out with a curse,
useless, even for sex.
Then a hand reached out and held her.
A voice murmured, "We love you,"
and in the silence, between the sobs,
I knew that God had slipped in,
sitting amongst the ladies,
in silent and painful compassion (Gateley).

If God's plan is to lead all human beings into union with him and with each other, we can confidently say: Wherever in our midst the following things happen, God's Kingdom makes itself felt.

- wherever injured people forgive those who have injured them;
- wherever love and care for one another overcome fear of one another;
- wherever the hungry are fed, the thirsty given a cup of water, the naked clothed, the homeless housed and prisoners are visited (cf. Mt 25:31-46);
- wherever, in other words, there exists a community that is inclusive in principle, there the Kingdom of God is present; there God is bringing about the Kingdom.

Wherever life is enhanced or broken life restored, wherever we find joy and true happiness, wherever people build community with vital life-giving relationships, there the Kingdom has taken root.

Did I See You?

Did I see You, God?
On the Broadway,
where dirty garbage and broken glass
is kicked about and
scattered around the greasy sidewalk,
I thought I smelled God.

In the bar,
with music shrieking,
air thick with tobacco haze, and
the stink of stale beer,
I thought I heard God.

In the brothel,
with its despairing waits
joyless jokes,
distorted sex and verbal violence,
I thought I touched God.

In the soup kitchen,
where sick and lonely people
shuffled in line for
plastic plates and orange juice.
I thought I saw God.

God, God,
Oh, did I really see you, God?
Where did I see you, God?
(Gateley)

Wherever life is celebrated and God's ultimate goal of leading all human beings into the great community of brothers and sisters in union with him is promoted, there we can 'smell and touch' the Kingdom as having arrived already in our midst. As long as in the middle of all the ethnic atrocities and cruel wars there are persons like Felicitas, a Hutu woman who saved the lives of Tutsi refugees and in doing so gave her life, we know that the Kingdom is present in this world:

Miss Felicitas, a Rwandese Hutu, about 60 years old, was an Auxiliary of the Apostolate in Gisenyi. She and her companions welcomed Tutsi refugees into their house. Knowing she was in danger, her brother, a colonel in the army, asked her by phone to leave and escape the inevitable death. The letter she wrote in reply reads:

Dearest Brother, Thank you for wanting to help me. To save my life I would have to abandon the 43 persons I am in charge of. I choose to die with them. Pray for us that we may reach God's house. Say good-bye to our old mother and to our brother. I shall pray for you when I am with the Lord. Be of good health. Thank you very much for thinking of me.

Your sister, Felicitas Niyiteggeka.

And if God saves us, as we hope, we shall see each other tomorrow.

On the 21st of April the militia came to take all of them to the cemetery by lorry. At that moment, Felicitas said to her sisters: "The time has come for us to give witness. Let us go!" As they climbed into the lorry they sang and prayed. They arrived at the cemetery where a common grave was already dug. Fearing the colonel, the killers tried to save her. One of them said to her: "You there, are you not afraid to die?" As the victims were esteemed by the soldiers they used guns to kill them (instead of piercing their throats with bamboo sticks). Having killed 30 of them, the killers tried once more to save her. "No! I have no reason to live any more because you have killed all my sisters." Felicitas was the 31st to die. Six other auxiliaries were killed with her. When her brother arrived, she had already been thrown naked into the common grave. He had the grave dug up. Clothes were found for her. Then he buried his sister and said, "You chose to die. Pray for us."

God's Kingdom is experienced in the present moment in companionship with Jesus. Where the sick are healed and the lost are found, where people who are despised are accepted and the poor discover their own dignity, where people who are rigid and fossilized come alive again, and old, tired lives become young and fruitful once again - there the Kingdom of God begins. It begins as a seed which is already implanted in this life, so it can be experienced. Being a seed, it is also the object of hope, but a hope firmly founded on experience and remembrance: the seed wants to grow, the one who has been found wants to return home; those who have been healed want to rise from the dead; and people liberated from some compulsion want to live in the country of freedom (J. Moltmann, *Jesus*, p.19).

The presence of God's Kingdom is to be seen and experienced not only on the personal, internal level but in the concrete situation of public life as well.

Concrete instances of liberation make the Kingdom of God present in history. Where we find real growth in justice, where oppression is defeated and freedom is granted, there the Kingdom is present. Any partial and limited instances of historical liberation on the socio-economic-political level are to be seen as "real mediations" and "anticipatory concretizations" of the eschatological Kingdom. Wherever liberation movements begin to realize equality, participation, fellowship and communion, there the Kingdom of God breaks into history... Whenever bonds of fellowship, of harmony, of participation and of respect for the inviolable dignity of every person are created, then the Kingdom of God has begun to dawn. Whenever social structures have been imposed on society that hinder persons from exploiting others, that do away with the relationship of master and slave, that favor fair dealing, then the Kingdom of God is beginning to burst forth like the dawn (L. Boff, *The Lord's Prayer*, pp 61-62).

The real issue is: am I able to notice the Kingdom's presence? Am I able to smell it? God does not need us so much to bring about the Kingdom as to notice its presence in our midst. We must school ourselves to pay attention to our experience of reality. If we are touched by the Kingdom, we will be able to discern its presence in our daily experiences, we will be able to see its presence and to point it out and to witness to its presence in the midst of people's lives. How difficult this can be is illustrated by the following story:

The idea that everything in this world is perfect was more than the disciples could accept. So the Master put it in concepts that were more within their grasp. "God weaves perfect designs with the threads of our lives" he said, "even with our sins. The reason why we can't see this is we're looking at the reverse side of the tapestry."
And more succinctly, "What some people take for a shiny stone, the jeweler recognizes as a diamond." (A. de Mello, *One Minute Nonsense*, p. 29)

As Christians we are called to "sniff out" God's Kingdom, to sense it and to celebrate its presence here and now. The presence of God's Kingdom will be missed if there are no people to notice it and witness to it. Our "staying with the Lord" as disciples is absolutely essential for remaining in tune with the Kingdom. Without celebrating its presence in the liturgy, worship, prayer and songs it is not possible to stay in touch with the reality of the Kingdom. But ultimately our actions and our behavior are the touchstone for our contact. We can only discover and discern the presence of God's Kingdom on earth if we in practice attune our actions to the great goal that God aims at with his Kingdom already present (W. A. Barry, *Paying Attention to God*, p. 77ff.)

Since Jesus made the Kingdom concretely present through his actions and his behavior we, as his disciples, will show its presence now by acting and behaving in the way he did. In doing what Jesus did we will make God's Kingdom present in this world and visible to all those who are attuned to God's plan of salvation.

Sobrino raises a warning note that we should not forget that the world in which we live gives more witness to the all pervasive presence of the anti-kingdom than to the Kingdom already present. He distinguishes between the mediator of the Kingdom (Jesus Christ) and what is mediated: the Kingdom of God itself which he calls in this connection: *mediation.* For him the Kingdom of God has come on the level of the mediator and we do not need to wait for another one. But the Kingdom has not yet fully come on the level of the reality of mediation: the world as a whole is not yet conformed to the heart of God.

> It is good to proclaim the definitive appearance of the mediator; this should be done in liturgies and doctrines and experiences above all in personal faith and following Jesus, but none of this should make precisely those who believe in a God "of the Kingdom" forget the tragic reality of history or hasten to intone triumphal canticles just because believers know and await a happy ending. They should never forget the anti-kingdom (*Jesus the Liberator*, p. 109).

Sobrino does not want to kill our joy in the Kingdom. He simply wants to remind us that to proclaim and celebrate the Kingdom in hymns and songs is good but we should not take this as the ultimate test of its presence now. It is in the concrete active struggle against the forces that contradict the Kingdom where we will experience that God's Kingdom has already entered this world.

Reflection: *The Kingdom of God is Here*

As disciples of Jesus we are called to be constantly attuned to the Kingdom in order to sense its presence around us. However, the cares and worries of our daily life cause us easily to forget that God's Kingdom is constantly within our reach. How "insensitive" we can be at times to the reality of the Kingdom around us is illustrated by the following story:

> A sailing ship had been at sea for months and months. She was now miles out from the coast of Brazil and had been there for weeks. There was no wind; the ship had hardly moved. Rations were gone, and then the people on board finished their drinking water. In the morning the crew could scrape some dew from the sails, but that was all.

The situation was desperate. Then one morning the lookout saw another ship - bigger, better equipped, and making some progress. At the shouts of the lookout, the captain immediately started signaling to the other ship, "Please, send us some water, we are dying with thirst." The other ship signaled, "Lower your buckets right where you are!" The distressed captain couldn't believe his eyes, and again he signaled, "Please, send us fresh water, we are dying of thirst!" He got the same return message. Those messages went on for quite some time, until the captain - in utter despair - lowered buckets into the ocean. And he drew up sparkling fresh water!

The ship was off the coast of Brazil, where the gigantic Amazon River pushes fresh water into the Atlantic Ocean for miles and miles (William Herr, as quoted in J. Donders, *Charged with the Spirit,* pp 19-20).

QUESTION: **What efforts do I make to see in myself, in my community and in the world around me God's Kingdom coming alive?**

Name a few signs of the Kingdom already present in today's world. Name persons who make the Kingdom transparent.

We will continue to ask the question - What can I do for God's Kingdom, I, just one person? And the answer is simple. Each of us can effect some change in the small corner of the globe where we find ourselves. I may not be convinced that I can do much, but each of the apostles would have said and felt the same. How different is the attitude of the little girl in the following story:

Years ago, after a magnificent cathedral had been built, a gentleman stood outside admiring it. Standing beside him was a little girl about six or seven years old.
"Mister," queried the little one, "do you like that church?"
"Yes my dear, I think it is quite lovely."
"Well, Mister, I'm glad you like it because I helped to build it."
"You? You helped to build it?" was the astonished enquiry.
The child nodded.
"But," went on the gentleman, "you are only a little girl. How did you help to build it?"
"My daddy is a bricklayer," came the reply, "and he worked on the church ever since it began, and every single day I brought him his lunch." (Frank Barron, *Short and Sweet,* p. 41)

QUESTION: Where in my environment could I make an impact, bring about a change that would be a sign of the Kingdom already present?

Each day can be a day for God and we all have a part to play in the coming of God's Kingdom on earth. I need to offer it a chance to come through me. What role do I play then? We know that the Kingdom is basically a future event, but we can find in ourselves and in the world some seeds of the Kingdom, some signs of the Kingdom, some partial realization of the Kingdom. The Spirit of God is at work in the midst of all the falsehood and cruelty like the leaven in the dough. If we make a real effort at *"sniffing out the Kingdom,"* we will find the values of the Kingdom in the hearts of those who really believe in it and hope for it. It is true, we do not build God's Kingdom. That is God's task. We discover it when we

- live as brothers and sisters with the intention of not excluding anyone from our community, and become a community in union with the community of the Trinity;
- become aware of God's action in our daily lives and witness to it;
- prayerfully try to read the signs of the times; and
- try to attune our actions to the one action of God and become God's co-creators.

God needs people who take the time to notice his action in the world. This might at first discourage us, because we would like to see the fullness of the Kingdom right away in our own life as well as in all public affairs. We would like to be involved in structural changes and see positive results for all our efforts, but it is important to remember that Jesus did not and does not primarily call individuals who are ready, who are perfect instruments and who will automatically bring about peace and harmony. No, we are weak and sinful instruments and like the apostles, we are anything but ready - at best - we are willing. We are not very different from Nathaniel, the prejudiced one, from Simon, the Zealot, who thought redemption required military and political force, or Andrew, the cynic, who lacked a sense of risk when asked to feed the crowd with five loaves and two fishes. And yet, they were the chosen instruments, the disciples to whom Jesus entrusted his work of salvation.

A PRAYER OF ARCHBISHOP OSCAR ROMERO

It helps now and then to step back and take the long view.
The Kingdom is not only beyond our efforts,
   It is even beyond our vision.

We accomplish in our lifetime
only a tiny fraction of the magnificent enterprise of God's work.
Nothing we do is complete, which is another way of saying
   that the Kingdom always lies beyond us.

No statement says all that could be said.
No prayer fully expresses our faith.
No confession brings perfection.
No pastoral visit brings wholeness.
No program accomplishes the Church's mission.
No set of goals and objectives includes everything.

This is what we are about:
We plant the seeds that one day will grow.
We water the seeds already planted,
   knowing that they hold future promise.

We lay foundations that will need further development.
We provide yeast that produces effects, far beyond our capabilities.

We cannot do everything, and there is a sense of liberation in realizing that.
This enables us to do something and do it very well.

It may be incomplete, but it is a beginning, a step along the way,
an opportunity for the Lord's grace to enter and do the rest.

We may never see the end results,
but there is a difference between the master builder and the worker.
  We are workers, not master builders,
  ministers, not messiahs.
   We are prophets of a future not our own. Amen.

Chapter Seven

The Anti-Kingdom of Evil

God's eschatological Kingdom which is permeating history in the coming of Jesus does not remain unopposed. There are hostile forces that want to destroy it. Apocalyptic literature focuses on these hostile forces and gives shape and content to them.

The literary style of apocalyptic writings

The prophets held that God's creation had been invaded by evil forces and that people everywhere were constantly exposed to its awesome power. Evil was experienced as a fact and seen as contrary to God's original design and will. People expected that when the Messiah came he would free creation from all evil and put an end to its power and even its existence.

In the later writings of the Old Testament we find a type of literature called apocalyptic writings which focused in particular on the evil in the world and in creation as a whole. These writers had experienced evil so strongly that they were almost paralyzed by its all-pervasive presence and its immense power over everything. The world, human history and society are so afflicted and permeated by evil that no future other than total annihilation seems possible. There is absolutely no hope left for this creation, since it is just too corrupt to be salvaged by God's intervention at the end of time. The only hope is a totally new creation without any connection or relation to the world as it exists now.

These writers, however, wrote their books primarily not in order to proclaim doom but first of all to "console." They wanted to offer consolation and strength to those in the world who had not yet fallen prey to evil but felt its onslaught, being oppressed and persecuted by it. The style used by these writers belongs to the so-called "apocalyptic genre" of literature. Through visions and images they tried to assure the faithful that God had not forgotten them. On the contrary, they were precious to him. God is still the Lord of history and he will soon come to put an end to such abominable evil. He will come and rescue his people and destroy evil once and for all.

By analyzing the past, these authors tried to discover a definite plan in history in order to be able to see when and how it would end. Since the world was totally corrupt, there was no way that things could get better in the future. Things could only get worse. The nearer the end was approaching, the worse things would get. The end of history could only be imagined as a total catastrophe: the world would go up in flames and definitely cease to exist. Only then could the New Heaven and the New Earth arise as a totally new creation, and those who had not fallen prey to the evil one would belong to it.

While the apocalyptic writers intended to console and to strengthen the just in this troubled world, their visions and predictions in dreams and symbolic language cannot be taken literally. To do so would be to miss their message and distort the beauty of such powerful language meant to console and to strengthen. Since the apocalyptic writers do not tell us anything about the actual end of this world, we cannot conclude from their literary style that the world is becoming worse or that the end is near.

How did Jesus look at evil?

Did Jesus share the vision and world-view portrayed by the apocalyptic writers? The answer is yes and no. Jesus was by no means naive in his perception of the state of humanity in his time. He revealed a remarkable sensitivity to the all-pervasive presence of evil in human affairs, be they private or public. He certainly saw the beauty of creation (cf. Mt 6:25-36) and the goodness of human beings, because they are God's children, but he could not be deceived when faced with evil in its life-denying and destructive force. Confronted by evil, be it individual, social or cosmic, Jesus assumed an uncompromising attitude which aimed at its total destruction.

In the time of Jesus, disease and mental illness were not merely seen as evil that had to be eliminated, but as slavery from which people needed to be liberated. The New Testament shared this world-view; it even radicalized and transformed it. It radicalized it by compressing all the different malevolent forces into the one term, the EVIL ONE, thereby giving this 'figure' a universal dimension.

Judaism knew individual demons. Jesus, however, stressed the unity of them all in Satan. The evil at work is not just the isolated actions of individual devils but something that permeates everything. This state of affairs is the first thing the Kingdom of God, as it is preached by Jesus, immediately reveals: the world is in deep trouble and not a place where the Kingdom of God is present. The Kingdom that Jesus brings into such a world carries with it a spirit of conflict. Mark 1:16-3:12 portrays very pointedly the power struggle between Jesus and the evil one, between the Son of God and the demons. Jesus' entire mission is directed towards the ousting of the demonic powers. These powers know well the mission of Jesus and that the end has come for their power. Therefore the pointed question always asked when Jesus encounters these forces, is *"Have you come to destroy us?"* (Mk 1:24)

This undoubtedly reveals Jesus' universal purpose: He came to destroy not individual protagonists of the powers of darkness, but the kingdom of evil itself (cf. Lk 10:18). Jesus' whole public life can be seen as a confrontation and battle with Satan. It begins with the temptation story (cf. Lk 4:1-13) and intensifies throughout his ministry. The climax is the hour of his passion (cf. Jn 12:31, 13:2).

Throughout the entire New Testament *this age* is viewed as an age in which Satan has been permitted by the sovereign purpose of God to exercise a tragic sway over humankind (cf. Lk 13:16, 22:31). In the theology of John and Paul, Christ is seen as the one *"who came to reduce to impotence him who holds the rule of death, the devil, and to destroy his works"* (1 Jn 3:8), or in Paul's words *"to replace the reign of Satan with that of the Father"* (1Cor 15:24-28; Col 1:13ff.). Jesus' ministry can only be fully understood against the backdrop of two opposing kingdoms: The Kingdom of God and the kingdom of evil, or in the words of E. Ladd:

> It is indeed impossible to interpret the New Testament teaching about the Kingdom of God except against the background of a great spiritual struggle . . . The Kingdom is God's dynamic power, and it must come because there are real spiritual enemies which oppose it, both human and superhuman. The coming of God's Kingdom means the invasion of the power of Satan and the overthrow of his kingdom. ... The coming of the Kingdom in Jesus must be interpreted in terms of a great struggle between mighty spiritual powers (E. Ladd, *The Presence of the Future*, p. 154).

In his exorcisms, Jesus revealed how deeply human beings can be caught and held prisoners by the powers of evil. But even more important is that in driving out demons, Jesus demonstrated the real purpose of God's Kingdom, namely to overthrow all evil powers under which people suffer and to set a definite end to them. One of the most vivid illustrations of this fact is found in the story of the *Gerasene Demoniac* (cf. Mk 5:1-20).

For the first time Jesus enters a gentile environment. He immediately encounters resistance in the form of a demonically possessed person, a 'man with an unclean spirit' living among the tombs. Jesus finds himself in a land of demons and of the dead. The non-Israelite nature of the surrounding is further stressed by the presence of the pigs. The descriptions fit the power of the demons in the pagan surroundings and the heartless treatment of the demonic being chained by his follow-human beings for a period of time.

The man is totally in the power of evil. He lives among the tombs and on the mountain far away from human habitation either by preference or by forcible segregation imposed on him by 'normal' people. He himself has lost all human bearings: he is 'crying out - yelling and shrieking' unable to speak, 'bruising himself', filled with self-destruction and hatred.

They came to the other side of the sea, to the territory of the Gerasenes. When he got out of the boat, at once a man from the tombs who had an unclean spirit met him. The man had been dwelling among the tombs, and no one could restrain him any longer, even with a chain. In fact, he had frequently been bound with shackles and chains, but the chains had been pulled apart by him and the shackles smashed, and no one was strong enough to subdue him. Night and day among the tombs and on the hillsides he was always crying out and bruising himself with stones. Catching sight of Jesus from a distance, he ran up and prostrated himself before him, crying out in a loud voice, "What have you to do with me, Jesus, Son of the Most High God? I adjure you by God, do not torment me!" (He had been saying to him, "Unclean spirit, come out of the man!") He asked him, "What is your name?" He replied, "Legion is my name. There are many of us." And he pleaded earnestly with him not to drive them away from that territory.

Now a large herd of swine was feeding there on the hillside. And they pleaded with him, "Send us into the swine. Let us enter them." And he let them, and the unclean spirits came out and entered the swine. The herd of about two thousand rushed down a steep bank into the sea, where they were drowned. The swineherds ran away and reported the incident in the town and throughout the countryside. And people came out to see what had happened. As they approached Jesus, they caught sight of the man who had been possessed by Legion, sitting there clothed and in his right mind. And they were seized with fear. Those who witnessed the incident explained to them what had happened to the possessed man and to the swine. Then they began to beg him to leave their district.

As he was getting into the boat, the man who had been possessed pleaded to remain with him. But he would not permit him but told him instead, "Go home to your family and announce to them all that the Lord in his pity has done for you." Then the man went off and began to proclaim in the Decapolis what Jesus had done for him; and all were amazed.

In analyzing the story several points can be highlighted.

First, the situation of the man is described as one of absolute hopelessness. The effects of being possessed are portrayed in the violent anti-social and self-destructive behavior of the person. He lives in the abode of the dead. He has been cast out from the community which had attempted to bind him. He has become an outsider, excluded from the community and from all human communication. No one dares to live with him; no one talks to him; no one loves him. He is like a dead man since he is exiled, cut off, and despised.

Secondly, the mission of Jesus is clearly demonstrated as setting free and leading the person back to full authenticity and dignity. This liberation is not a peaceful surrender of Satan. The evil forces fight vigorously to maintain control over the person. The actual "driving out" involves violent convulsions of the possessed person (cf. Mk 1:24-26, 9:20-26). Jesus is the one who "crosses over" to this man, who communicates with him, who feels deep compassion and cares about him. He restores his human dignity; he integrates him once again into the life of the community. In this the true mission of Jesus is revealed. The man *"whom no one had the strength to subdue"* (Mk 5:4) is found by his countrymen *"seated, clothed and in his right mind"* (Mk 5:15). Now since he can communicate again, Jesus sends him back to those who have excluded him from the community. The non-person has been made a person again. He is now sent to proclaim to his countrymen, *"How much the Lord has done for you and how he has had compassion on you"* (Mk 5:19).

Thirdly, the story reveals the Kingdom as a power that deprives evil of any place in the world. Not even in swine will it find a place to stay. The coming Kingdom means the end of all evil. The presence of the Kingdom of God is seen as a dynamic force overthrowing the kingdom of evil and liberating the present age by restoring human beings to their true authenticity and dignity.

The evil powers today

The approaching year 2000 will give rise to strong millennial thinking. Prophets of doom will spread their message of a world coming to an end and of imminent catastrophes everywhere. What should a disciple of Jesus think about this? What stand should he/she take? The world may look bad but to maintain that its end is near because of corruption and sin is based on an unwarranted assumption. The world has always been corrupt and sin-permeated. But God did not create a world only to allow it to be destroyed by evil. The apocalyptic preachers see evil as being so interwoven into the fabric of the world that the latter cannot be freed from it any more. When God comes to judge the world - and according to these writers he will come soon - the present world will have to be destroyed as well, since evil can seemingly not be extracted from it without destroying the world in the process. The only way out is a totally new creation without any connection to the old.

If this is so, it seems God failed in his first attempt to create a world that was destined to share in his own life. His plan failed and the anti-kingdom won. All God can do is to begin a salvage operation and save what can still be saved - a few souls that finally make it. Apocalyptic preachers always talk about the few who will be saved while most will be lost. But that is not the message Jesus brought, since he came not to condemn the world but to save it (cf. Jn 3:17). And at times the evil can be a source for the good as the following story illustrates:

> One day the master said, "You are not ready to 'fight' evil until you are able to see the good it does."
> This left the disciples in considerable confusion which the master made no attempt to clear.
> The following day he offered them this prayer that was found scrawled on a piece of wrapping paper in the Ravensbruck Concentration Camp:
> "Lord, remember not only the men and women of good will but all those of ill-will. Do not only remember the suffering they have subjected us to. Remember the fruits we brought forth thanks to this suffering - our comradeship, our loyalty, our humility, our courage and generosity, the greatness of heart that all of this inspired. And when they come to judgement, let all these fruits we have borne be their reward and their forgiveness (A. De Mello, *One Minute Nonsense*, p. 289).

Based on Jesus' own way of encountering evil forces, we hold that God will accomplish his plan no matter how sin-permeated the world may look and actually be. He will not abandon creation and let it be destroyed by evil because creation is something precious to him and it is good, which means it is destined for life and not for death. The goodness of creation is guaranteed by God himself who created it and values it. Furthermore, through the incarnation of his Son, the goodness of creation is once again affirmed and in the resurrection of Jesus it has already been transformed into the new so that it can finally participate in God's own life.

The Kingdom Jesus came to proclaim confirms that the world is good and that God will set it free from all that has corrupted it. God will not let this world end up in the hands of the anti-kingdom that wants to destroy it, and in so doing, frustrate God's original plan. The anti-kingdom, for all its power and seductive skills, will not be able to destroy the deepest aspirations and hopes of humankind and lead it to despair. The Kingdom that Jesus came to bring is the Good News that God's intention for creation will be accomplished and that justice and love will win in spite of all the forces in this present world that lead us to believe the opposite.

Though the Kingdom of God has entered a world that is dominated and ruled by the anti-kingdom, its final aim is to overcome this all-pervasive power. God's Kingdom and the anti-kingdom are mutually exclusive. There is no alternative to the anti-kingdom. It will be destroyed and definitely cast out of creation. Enslavement to the evil one is not the final destiny of humanity. People can be liberated from it. Jesus engages in the struggle against the evil powers and will overcome them. As the Kingdom of God is invading this world, which is under the sway of the evil one, it will be engaged in a struggle that can at times be very intense and not without casualties.

The anti-kingdom is not just the absence or the not-yet of the Kingdom but its formal contradiction. The Kingdom of God is not being built from a *tabula rasa* but in opposition to the anti-kingdom. The in-breaking Kingdom stands therefore in *combative relation* to the anti-kingdom. They are not merely mutually exclusive; they fight against each other. Building the Kingdom implies, by necessity, actively struggling against the anti-kingdom. If the latter does not fight back, this means that the former has not truly been built (something to be always borne in mind when outlining and trying to understand the mission of the Church) (J. Sobrino, *Jesus The Liberator*, p. 95).

With the coming of Christ the "cosmic conflict" is unleashed and there will be no peace until it is over. The place in which we live is hotly contested territory. The Kingdom of God has really entered the world, so it has become an object that can and will be attacked since the evil powers will not let themselves be overthrown so easily. There will be defeat as well as victory. Individual battles are sometimes won and sometimes lost, but the war has been won.

As disciples of Jesus, we should never underestimate the power of evil in the world but our mission is to be not stunted by its power. On the contrary, we are to announce its defeat. Both powers are at work in the world and the conflict is neither evident to the naked eye nor audible to the human ear. One must be attuned to God's Kingdom in order to discern its presence. We need a "bifocal" vision. Eyeglasses are bifocal-focal when a lens has two portions, one for near and one for far vision. To see the Kingdom with bifocal-focal glasses is to see both the OLD AGE and God's invading NEW AGE. Here lies the crucial difference: the difference between single vision by which one sees one level only, and bifocal-focal vision by which one is given the grace and the power to see the two levels simultaneously. Faith gives us this added vision. It is not that we do not see the un-redeemedness of the world, that is, the forces of dehumanization and oppression which cause our world to appear so unredeemed and at times so God-forsaken. Being attuned to the Kingdom enables us to see deeper, to go beyond the appearances of outer reality and to discover the real powers that guide history, the power of evil and the power of the Kingdom already present.

We can pray with conviction: *The earth is full of the goodness of the Lord* (Ps 33), but we cannot deny the evil that we see all around us. There are those who speak seriously about the power of Satan, but tend to mean a personal devil who picks off individuals, one by one. And there are others who are totally embarrassed by such language or prefer not to mention sin at all - social or personal. Both views seem naive. Not only are we faced with evil acts of culpable individuals but also with evil structures. This world is marked by exploited populations, massive poverty, sectarian violence, North-South polarization, racism, millions of refugees, obscene consumerism, maldistribution of wealth and the devastation of the earth's natural resources. In many parts of the world people are involved in bloody civil war and unrest. Our cities are divided between the poor and the rich. There is growing violence. Families are disintegrating and individuals find it difficult to retain their moral integrity and self-worth.

However, a truthful recognition of the pervasiveness of evil should not lead to despair but rather to hope and the affirmation of the words of Jesus announcing the defeat of evil, *"I have seen Satan fall"* (Lk 10:18-19). Even in the worst times of human history, people have upheld hope in the midst of excruciating suffering. Etty Hillesum, a young Jewish woman who died at Auschwitz in November 1943 at the age of twenty-nine, wrote a few months earlier from a detention camp in the Netherlands:

> *I often walk with a spring in my step along the barbed wire and then time and again it soars straight from my heart - I can't help it, that's just the way it is, like some elementary force - the feeling that life is glorious and magnificent, and that one day we shall be building a whole new world. Against every new outrage and every fresh horror we shall put up one more piece of love and goodness, drawing strength from within ourselves. We may suffer, but we must not succumb. And if we should survive unhurt in body and soul, but above all in soul without bitterness and without hatred, then we shall have a right to a say after the war* (Etty Hillesum, *An Interrupted Life*, p. 247).

A disciple should be able to see both the power of evil and, even more markedly, the power of God's Kingdom already operative in the midst of this world. However, the reality of the anti-Kingdom has to be established methodically and systematically. Persecution of those who are mediating the coming of the Kingdom is effective proof of the anti-kingdom. The persecution, in turn, becomes the criterion of whether the Kingdom is actually being built or not (*Jesus the Liberator*, p. 126).

We are called to do two things: to denounce and to unmask the anti-kingdom and to proclaim and witness to the Kingdom of God. The Good

News of the Kingdom is that the final victory is assured. Because of that, evil can be defeated even now in our daily life. Evil's power is already broken. Our mission is to point first and foremost to the power of the Kingdom as it is overcoming and defeating the anti-kingdom right in the midst of this world, at this very moment, through the commitment of those who in Jesus' name are fighting against the evil forces. Our proclamation of the Kingdom is a liberating message. It aims at setting people free from whatever may bind them to the powers of evil so as to give life and to bring joy.

This transforming power of God's final intervention now breaking into the world does not only set us *free from* evil influences but empowers us to a *freedom for*, moving us, so to speak, into positive action. Schillebeeckx describes this experience of the Kingdom now as an experience of the freedom we have received from Christ through the power of the Holy Sprit:

> *The freedom to accept* that, despite sin and guilt, we are accepted by God;
> *The freedom to be able* to live in this earthly world without ultimate despair about our existence;
> *The freedom to commit ourselves* disinterestedly for others in the confidence that such dedication is ultimately of decisive significance (Mt 25);
> *The freedom to accept experiences* of peace, joy and communication and to understand them as manifestations, however fragmentary, of the saving presence of the living God;
> *The freedom to join in* the struggle for economic, social and political justice;
> *The freedom to be free from oneself* in order to be free for others, free to do good to others.

For Christians, all these experiences are a specifically Christian experience of faith in the God who discloses himself in Jesus Christ as the sacred mystery of all-embracing love. They are the experiences of salvation offered by God. Christian redemption is indeed liberation from sin. But liberation from sin also has a cultural context. In our time, the Christian understanding of sin also includes the recognition of systematic disruptions of communication like sexism, racism and fascism, anti-Semitism, hostility and arrogance. The Christian love which is the basis of community, therefore, includes the necessity of recognizing the need for a deep involvement in the present-day work of political, cultural and social emancipation (cf. Schillebeeckx, *Church: The human Story of God*, pp. 130-133).

Evil may be strong and, at times, it may look as if its victory is assured but it cannot win the ultimate battle. We should heed the words of K. Barth who remarked about the forces of evil:

"They may rattle the bolt but they cannot
break down the door."

Reflection: *The Mystery of Evil and the Kingdom*

We know that the source of evil is never God. God is the source only of good. The fullness of evil - the rejection and death of God - was assumed by Jesus with the utmost love possible on earth.

> God determined to intervene in human history in a way both new and definitive. For He sent His Son, clothed in our flesh, in order that through this Son He might snatch men from the power of darkness and Satan (cf. Col 1:13; Acts 10:38) and that in this Son He might reconcile the world to Himself (cf. 2 Cor 5:19) (Ad Gentes 3)

Jesus saw his liberating mission as a kind of power struggle with Satan, a warfare against the powers of evil in all its possible shapes and forms, and he proved that goodness is ultimately more powerful than evil.

> It was to undo all that the devil has done that the Son of God appeared (1 Jn 3:8).

> Because that is what he has done: he has taken us out of the power of darkness and created a place for us in the kingdom of the Son that he loves, and in him we gain our freedom, the forgiveness of our sins (Col 1:13-14).

The disastrous effect of original sin in us; the innate tendency to dominate, to lord it over, to oppress, will turn into the willingness to serve if we allow Jesus to conquer our hearts and offer us his new freedom from sinful brokenness, if we allow him to be the Lord of our lives.

QUESTION: **We hear it being said, "Within every heart abide angels and devils". Where in my life do I feel the power of evil that keeps me captive and prevents me from loving generously? Who rules my life? Who is my Lord?**

As disciples of Jesus we are called to spread the Good News that God's Kingdom has arrived and is present in our midst today. Jesus did not only send us to proclaim the Kingdom but he also gave us the power to set people free from evil powers and to heal them from the effects of having been under the influence of evil. This we can only do if we ourselves have experienced within ourselves and within our Christian communities this liberating and healing power of God's Kingdom. It is a power that set us free and so helped us to overcome prejudice and discrimination in the way the following story explains it.

> The military commander of the town where I lived lifted the curfew to allow us to go to Midnight Mass. Just before the Eucharist a group of German soldiers marched into the church to celebrate with us. No upright Dutch man or woman would ever associate, let alone eat, with them. As kids we stole from them whatever we could, but when they offered us some candy, remembering their own children at home, we would never accept anything, preferring to spit in their faces. At communion time they came to kneel with us at the communion rail - as we did in those days - and nobody objected to those soldiers being there. *For a moment all was as it one day will be.* We were not enemies. We were interconnected. We were, for a brief moment, at the end of our common journey. The final gathering, the ultimate reconciliation, the definitive shalom were all realized "already." *The future had become real and present* just for a moment, just as it always had been in the life of Jesus (J. G. Donders, *"Charged with the Spirit,"* p.78).

Beatitudes of Reconciliation

Blessed are those who are willing to enter into the process of being
   healed, for they will become healers.
Blessed are they who recognize their own inner violence,
   for they will come to know non-violence.
Blessed are they who can forgive self,
   for they will become forgivers.
Blessed are those who are willing to let go of selfishness and
   self-centeredness, for they will become a healing presence.
Blessed are those who listen with compassion,
   for they will become compassionate.
Blessed are those who are willing to enter into conflict,
   for they will find transformation.
Blessed are those who know their interdependence with all of creation,
   for they will become unifiers.
Blessed are those who live a contemplative life stance,
   for they will find God in all things.
Blessed are those who strive to live these beatitudes,
   for they will be reconcilers.

(Sisters of St. Joseph, Concordia, Kansas.)

QUESTION: How have I experienced the liberating and healing power of God's Kingdom in my life and the lives of others?

There is a POWER FOR GOD in the world, an energy at work in the deepest forces of nature and the human heart. To believe in God, to believe in the resurrection and the Kingdom is to believe that this power for God is stronger than the power for evil - and will prevail! And our faith in Jesus and in the Kingdom will release this power. Once again a true story of a Hutu mother who prepared her children to die in war-torn Rwanda shows that in the midst of evil the Kingdom of God is at work.

Maria Teresa was a Hutu teacher married to a Tutsi. They had four children, three boys and one girl. On Sunday April 10, 1994 the father took his eldest boy and went into hiding. They were killed on April 12. The mother took the remaining children to her parents' place since her house had already been pillaged. On the 13th, four men came to take away her two sons to be killed. Alone with her little daughter she went to the convent and told the sisters how she had prepared the boys for death:

"I am happy because I was able to prepare my two boys for this. I told them: my children, people are bad at this moment. They have killed our father and Oliver. They will probably come and take you away too. But do not be afraid. You will suffer a little, but then you will join our father and Oliver because there is another life with Jesus and Mary, and one day, we will all be together again and we will be very, very happy." The same day, they came for the boys. The men who took them away told me afterwards that the boys were very calm and had been very courageous.

Maria Teresa - as a convinced Christian - said all this with great serenity, strong in her faith, sure of the triumph of love.

Chapter Eight

The Kingdom of God: a gift and a task

The Kingdom as a Gift

There is no difficulty in seeing the Kingdom as a gracious gift from a God who comes with unconditional love to seek out humankind and to offer salvation to all. The Kingdom can neither be brought about by meticulous adherence to the Law as certain rabbis believed, nor can it be forced onto the present by armed violence as the Zealots thought. It is a gift from God which people can only receive in gratitude and awe. God is coming towards us with unconditional love. He seeks communion and intimacy. Since the Kingdom is a gift of love, only symbols and images can offer an appropriate description. Its final coming is totally up to God; it will come as and when he sees fit. It cannot be foretold or calculated. No human initiative can bring about the coming of the Kingdom. It is God's own powerful and sovereign act.

The sayings and parables of Jesus present the gift-character of the Kingdom in clear, unambiguous language. It is God who, by his power and grace, makes the seed grow (cf. Mk 4:26-29). This is the principal teaching of the "growth parables" (cf. Mk 4). It is God who invites us to the eschatological banquet. One may pray *"Thy Kingdom come"* (Mt 6:10), may cry out to God day and night (cf. Lk 18:7), may prepare oneself and hold oneself in readiness like the wise virgins (cf. Mt 25:1-13), may seek the Kingdom (cf. Mt 6:33), but it is God who "gives" it (Lk 12:31). He decides whose it shall be (cf. Mt 5). It does not come through our efforts but through God's overflowing love for us. We can only accept it with gratitude and joy.

Not only does God invest divine love in every nook and cranny of creation; God's ultimate and most precious gift to us is the offer of communion with him, the Triune One. Jesus brought the Kingdom in which love, compassion, justice and all the values of God are concretely and fully realized. This Kingdom can become a reality for us but not through force and human efforts. It only becomes a *life-transforming power* for us if we accept it *as a gratuitous gift*. The Kingdom is ever new, the treasure is always found anew and the most joyful event that can happen to me at any moment is that I let the Kingdom be given to me afresh.

As clear as the New Testament message may be, it was the common belief in the time of Jesus that the Kingdom of God would be given to those who had earned it through faithful adherence to the Law. The value of a person before God was seen as depending on the years one had kept the Torah. The issue was one of "merits" before God. Since children had not yet acquired knowledge of the Torah, they could have no merit before God. The child was therefore considered a person of no importance, deserving neither attention nor favors. A child could not merit the Kingdom of God.

Jesus uses this alleged incapacity of a child to earn the Kingdom as the child's greatest asset. If one wants to earn the Kingdom, one has to stand before God empty-handed like a child with nothing to offer in return for the gift. The Kingdom of God is a free gift of love which a person can only accept with open hands and a thankful heart.

> *Amen, I say to you, whoever does not accept the Kingdom of God like a child will not enter it (Mk 10:15).*

To say that God is gracious means that the relationship with God is not linked to performance or merit. God is gracious to each one of us prior to, or independently of, any achievements on our part.

> Do you know what it means to be struck by grace?...We cannot transform our lives, unless we allow them to be transformed by the stroke of grace. It happens or it does not happen. And certainly it does not happen if we try to force it upon ourselves, just as it shall not happen so long as we think, in our self-complacency, that we have no need of it. Grace strikes us when we are in great pain and restlessness. It strikes us when, year after year, the longed-for perfection of life does not appear, when the old compulsions reign within us as they have for decades, when despair destroys all joy and courage. Sometimes at that moment a shaft of light breaks into our darkness, and it is as though a voice were saying: "You are accepted. You are accepted," accepted by that which is greater than you, and the name of which you do not know. Do not ask for the name now; perhaps you will find it later. Do not try to do anything now; perhaps later you will do much. Do not seek for anything; do not perform anything; do not intend anything. Simply accept the fact that you are accepted. If that happens to us, we experience grace (From a sermon by Paul Tillich entitled "You Are Accepted").

The Kingdom as a Task

Since God's Kingdom is ultimately his unconditional love for each one of us, there is no arguing that the Kingdom is a gift we can never earn or repay. Yet the Kingdom, once accepted, becomes one's task and demands all of one's abilities. The main reason for this is that God needs people through whom he can reach other people as we saw in the election of Moses. Any call means ultimately being sent to engage in God's own mission to bring about his Kingdom for the salvation of all by making anyone our brother or sister despite any difference of race, culture or religion.

There is a priest, a missionary from the 1940s who had been expelled from China. On his way home he got passage to India and from India he was going back to the States. While he was laying over in India he found a huge coastal strip where there were refugees of a community of Jews who had fled the Nazi persecution. There was no effort to help or accept them. They lived in attics and barns throughout the city. It was near Christmas time, so Father Goldry sold his boat ticket and instead brought the Jews pastries so they could celebrate Chanukkah. He then wired for money to get back to the States. When he got back, his superior scolded him, "Why did you do that? These Jews don't believe in Jesus." He replied, "But I do" (W. J. Bausch, *Telling Stories,* p. 137).

We must avoid the danger of viewing the Kingdom as coming completely without human assistance. This is a perennial temptation in many treatises on the Kingdom of God. Lohfink astutely identifies the pitfall in this way:

There is one sentence in modern exegesis that is constantly repeated: The basileia is solely and exclusively God's act. This sentence is then frequently followed by something like this: Human beings must pray for the coming of the basileia, they must prepare and be ready for it, orient themselves towards it and asymptotically draw near to it, but they can do absolutely nothing to cause or hasten its coming, nor can they do anything to stop or hinder it . . . Now obviously we do not deny that the basileia is God's act. However, does that say all that needs saying? (G. Lohfink, *The Exegetical Predicament..*, p.104)

What about human cooperation then? Must we not also say that the coming of the Kingdom is "totally, completely, and entirely" the work of human beings? The gratuitousness of the Kingdom should not lead us to regard ourselves as merely passive objects. Ultimately the Kingdom of God is a personal relationship between God and human beings. Any personal relationship is always a two-way thing. We are challenged to respond, and through this response the Kingdom becomes a reality in our midst.

They tell the story of a woman during World War II who hid Jews. When her friends found out they said, "Don't you realize that if you are discovered you yourself will be imprisoned, perhaps even executed?" The woman said clearly, "Yes, I know that." "Then why in heaven's name," they asked "are you doing it!" And she said simply: **"Because the time is now and I am here"** (J. Chittister, *Winds of Change*, p 71-71).

The woman was concerned about creating human fellowship across racial and religious barriers, and it was the most natural thing for her to do. God's Kingdom had become part of her life. The gift she had received gratuitously was put at the disposal of the one great work of God: to create a community of brothers and sisters here on earth.

Jürgen Moltmann regards a totally passive attitude towards the Kingdom as an invalidation of everything that the New Testament says about Jesus. If Jesus is God and man then we must say, the Kingdom of God is the affair of Jesus. From here he concludes that:

> As the affair of Jesus, the kingdom of God can be readily experienced and can also be readily practiced in his community. "Seek ye first the kingdom and righteousness, and all these things shall be yours as well" (Mt 6:33). The power of God is indeed experienced in the community of Jesus. And through this experience, human beings become "co-workers in the kingdom of God" called to perform the same messianic works as Jesus himself. As you go, preach this message: *"The Kingdom of heaven is at hand. Heal the sick, raise the dead, cleanse lepers, cast out demons"* (Mt 10:7-8). It is the intent of Jesus here to make the kingdom of God our affair as well as his. God is freedom, and to possess authentic freedom means to walk and work in the kingdom (*Jesus Christ for Today's World*, p. 21-22).

Equally as important as working for the Kingdom is the "enjoyment of the Kingdom," i.e., the liturgical celebration. Jesus himself celebrated the Kingdom in the form of meals. He wanted these meals - shared particularly with the marginalized - to be understood and interpreted as the arrival of the Kingdom in the midst of human affairs. They were occasions for the participants to experience the new community God was bringing into the world, where there would be no discrimination any more but where all would be brothers and sisters under the one fatherhood of God.

In celebrating the presence of the Kingdom in the liturgical meal or in sharing God's Word we are participating in the fullness of the Kingdom to come now. Praise, thanksgiving and adoration are the very expressions of the new life and the very means to make it effectively present. We possess the Kingdom when we celebrate it and in celebrating it we find the strength and the power for our mission to work for it. Having "smelled its foretaste" we are empowered to engage anew in making it present in our daily lives. Hildegard of Bingen, the great medieval mystic, scholar and scientist has this to say:

> Be not lax in celebrating,
> Be not lazy in the festive service of God.
>
> Be ablaze with enthusiasm.
> Let us be an alive, burning offering
> before the altar of God!

Jewish tradition tells us that to celebrate the Sabbath is to possess "one sixtieth of the Kingdom of God," and every successful celebration of the Lord's day counts for more. It is good to "work and pray" for the Kingdom but to "rest and celebrate" should be seen as adding a note of completion to the Kingdom (J. Moltmann, *First the Kingdom of God*, p 21).

In 1987 the film *Babette's Feast* won the Academy Award for the best foreign language film. What is so special about this film? The story is very simple. Babette is a superb French chef living an anonymous life among a pious congregation on the desolate coast of Denmark. As housekeeper and cook to two elderly, religious women, she's never called upon to prepare anything more exciting than the traditional boiled codfish and ale-bread soup. Until one day she wins 10,000 francs and decides to spend it all by creating the most memorable, mouth-watering, magnificent meal ever consumed - even though her guests, the simple villagers, have no idea about what they are eating.

In the course of that meal the guests forget past wrongs and hurts, forgive each other for painful misunderstandings and rash judgements, and become once again reconciled. They enjoy the exquisite dishes and have an inkling of what celebrating the presence of the Kingdom is all about, because someone has demonstrated unlimited generosity for the sheer joy of giving.

The Gospels repeatedly show that the Kingdom which Jesus offers becomes our task. We find the most vivid explanation in the Parable of the Talents (cf. Mt 25:14-30). God gives to each one he calls a concrete task for the salvation of all and he will ask for an account for what he has given us. The Parable of the Treasure in the Field offers a similar portrayal. In these parables Jesus not only tells us that the Kingdom is pure gift, but also affirms that it unfolds through our taking risks and giving everything. In the Gospel of John the coming of the *basileia* is totally and completely God's work, and totally and completely the work of human beings.

Jon Sobrino offers a unique way of looking at the Kingdom as gift and task. He sees the Kingdom as establishing first and foremost a filial relationship with God. We are oriented vertically to God, and thus, we are his children. From this vertical orientation follows the horizontal relationship which makes us brothers and sisters. Both are essential and of equal and primary importance. For Sobrino divine sonship is a gift, while the creation of a profound human fellowship is a task. A dynamic unity exists between gift and task. The gift is accepted precisely by carrying out the task entailed in it. Creating a profound human fellowship means accepting the gift of divine sonship. The God of the Kingdom does not allow us to choose between the two aspects. He who lets the Kingdom into his life by becoming a child of God will have to show the presence of the Kingdom by trying to make all human beings his brothers and sisters. Here the gift of the Kingdom is sonship and the task of the Kingdom is the bringing about of this sonship in the horizontal dimension through brotherhood, the creation of a community of brothers and sisters (*Christology at the Crossroads,* pp. 45-46).

Seen from such a perspective, history reveals two aspects. First it is a call to divine filiation by which human persons become God's children. Our vertical vocation, the deepest aspiration of all persons, is complete union with God. Secondly, history is a call to human fellowship by which persons become one another's sisters and brothers. This is our horizontal vocation, the call to attain complete union among ourselves.

These two aspects make it possible to speak of the Kingdom as a GIFT as well as a TASK. In the call to divine filiation, the Kingdom of God is fundamentally God's true gift. But it is a gift that entails by necessity the task of creating an authentic community of brothers and sisters. It is the gift aspect of the Kingdom that demands of us the task as a response. The achievement of true human fellowship in history becomes a historical realization of the promise of total communion with God. But as a historical verification of such a promise, it immediately reveals the partial and incomplete character of the Kingdom now and opens up history towards the complete and total communion of human persons with God (G. Gutierrez, *We Drink From our Own Wells,* p.104).

For Gutierrez the Kingdom of God is the background against which, on the one hand, the situation of oppression and domination is denounced as sinful and incompatible with its coming; and in the light of which, on the other hand, every achievement of brotherhood and justice among human persons is announced as a step towards total communion with God. Seen in the light of the Kingdom of God, the struggle for liberation is no longer solely a response to the economic, social and political situation of poverty and oppression. Neither is it simply an expression of the contemporary awareness of the human person's capacity to transform history. Rather it is fidelity to God's will and fidelity to the practice of Jesus, whose proclamation of the Kingdom reveals God as Father and human persons as one's brothers and sisters ("Finding Our Way," p. 232).

Your Kingdom come

Your Kingdom come;
may it come soon
to the hungry,
to the weeping,
to those who thirst for your justice,
to those who have waited for centuries for a truly human life.
Grant us the patience to smooth the way
    on which your Kingdom comes to us.
Grant us hope, that we may not weary in proclaiming
    and working for it,
      despite so many conflicts,
      threats and shortcomings.
Grant us a clear vision
    that in this hour of our history
    we may see the horizon
    and know the way on which
    your Kingdom comes to us.
               From a Nicaraguan Meditation

However, the final coming of the Kingdom does not depend on our achievements; it still remain as God's work. Our task is faithfully and untiringly to witness to its presence whether we will be successful in our efforts or not. The following anecdote may illustrate the point well:

When Mother Teresa was asked how she could face the overwhelming odds against her work in Calcutta, where the people she cared for were just a tiny fraction of those dying in the streets, she replied, "The good Lord did not sent me into the streets of Calcutta in order to be successful in what I do but to be faithful in witnessing to his love present in the midst of human suffering in the love I show to these people."

Reflection: *Children of God called to create the Kingdom Family*

Since God's Kingdom is ultimately God's infinite love for me, it is always new, always a surprise, always like a treasure I never ever expected to find. This gracious gift of God, the most precious thing God offers, needs to be awaited.

QUESTION: **When did I ever experience God wanting to surprise me with the Kingdom as the most precious gift I can receive? What is my reaction to the invitation of God to adopt the attitude of a child who has nothing to offer in return no merit to put forward to deserve God's gift?**

But discerning God's Kingdom present and active in this world and in us also means that our actions are to be in tune with God's actions. The treasure of the Kingdom which we have discovered is not to be hidden again but to be turned into commitment. He/she who lets God's Kingdom into his/her life has no other choice than to make each person his/her brother or sister.

The great medieval mystic, *St. Catherine of Siena,* was once asked by one of her nuns, "How can I pay God back for his goodness to me? How can I give back to God some glory for all of God's kind compassion, mercy and generosity?" St. Catherine answered, "It won't do you any good to do any more penances. It won't do you much good to build a great church. It won't do you much good to add more quiet time in prayer. But I'll tell you something you can do to really pay God back for the compassion God gives you. Find someone as unlovable as you are and give that person the kind of love that God has given you" (W. J. Bausch, *More Stories,* p 18).

QUESTION: **How conscious am I that if I let God's Kingdom into my life it will become my personal obligation and responsibility to create human fellowship wherever I live and in whatever I do?**

At times this may demand heroic acts, as in the case of the following story, or consist in simple, daily acts of concern and care.

There is a man named Sundar, born in India as a member of the Sikh religion. He became a convert to Christianity and decided to stay in India to be a missionary and bear witness to Jesus. One late afternoon Sundar was traveling on foot high in the Himalaya mountains with a Buddhist monk. It was bitter cold and the night was coming on. The monk warned that they were in danger of freezing to death if they did not reach the monastery before darkness fell.

Well, it happened that as they crossed over a narrow path above a steep cliff, they heard a cry for help. And deep down in the ravine a man had fallen, and he lay wounded. His leg was broken and he couldn't walk. So the monk warned Sundar, "Do not stop. God has brought this man to his fate. He must work it out by himself. That is the tradition. Let us hurry on before we perish." But Sundar replied, "It is my tradition now that God has brought me here to help my brother. I cannot abandon him." So the monk set off through the snow, which had started to fall heavily. But Sundar climbed down to where the wounded man was. Since the man had a broken leg, Sundar took a blanket from his knapsack and made a sling out of it. He got the man into it and hoisted him on his back and began the painful and arduous climb back up the path. After a long time, drenched with perspiration, he finally got back to the path, struggling to make his way through the increasingly heavily falling snow. It was dark now and he had all he could do to find the path. But he persevered and although faint from fatigue and overheated from exertion he finally saw the lights of the monastery.

Then he nearly stumbled and fell. Not from weakness. He stumbled over an object lying in the path. He bent down on one knee and brushed the snow from the body of the monk who had frozen to death within sight of the monastery (W. J. Bausch, *More Telling Stories*, p. 95-96).

Having opted for the 'God of Life,' Sundar risked his life and received it again as a gift while the one who was not willing to lose his life, did indeed lose it. Following the Lord of Life and acting accordingly requires that we share as much as possible in the God-image that Jesus demonstrated to us in his life.

The God-image of Jesus

We could say in brief that Jesus' deeds and words give us the image of:

– A God who is concerned about and involved with the earth and all earthlings, including flowers and birds, and in particular, the human community, its history and destiny, and the quality of life.

– A God who would establish his Reign on this earth, liberating the earth from all oppressive principalities and powers and making it whole and beautiful.

– A God, therefore, who cares for the poor, brings them the Good News and blessings of his Reign, liberating them from anxiety, grief and social exclusion, abolishing conditions of slavery and subverting structures of dominion.

– A God who is in solidarity with the dispossessed of the earth, who makes their cause his own, and who participates in the history of their suffering and struggles.

– A God who acts on behalf of the dispossessed by sending Jesus, anointed with the Holy Spirit, to remove blindness, open prisons and set the down-trodden free.

– A God who thus discloses himself as justice, compassion and love, and who would have us encounter him in people, in the person of the poor and needy brother and sister.

– A God who wants mercy, not sacrifice, who places justice, love and fidelity far above cultic and ascetic practices.

– A God who excludes no one on grounds of race or sex, but offers to all, women and men, gentiles and Jews, the same Gospel and grace, the same call to serve and bear witness; and who, if he has a bias, inclines towards the marginalized and assigns to women crucial roles (in the Incarnation and the Resurrection) in the new history of salvation.

– A God who condemns and rejects mammon, the idol of wealth accumulated and unshared, and the idolatry of greed, as something that dehumanizes and reifies people, causing their power to love -- which defines them as human -- to wither and their selfhood and personhood to shrink and perish.

– A God who leads the way in defying oppressing powers, in resisting forces of death and dethroning the mighty, and in walking alternative paths to those pursued by wealth and weapons, as well as in bidding us stand erect and hold our heads high, for our liberation is at hand.

Such is the Image of God which Jesus traces for us.
(Samuel Rayan)

QUESTION: God the Father called me to carry on the mission of his Son to make His design for the whole of creation come true. Being on that mission, how conscious am I that it is this image of God I have to proclaim and witness to?

Chapter Nine

Salvation and the Kingdom of God

The coming Kingdom of God was seen as consisting of two inseparable elements. It would mean God's judgement of the sinners and the enemies of Israel. Only after this had happened could salvation be offered. The divine judgement on the world had to precede the promised salvation. This had been the view of the prophets but in particular that of the apocalyptic writers. The question is: how did Jesus present his message of the Kingdom? Did he follow the general expectation that judgement as having arrived with him would be the first order of the day concerning the Kingdom he was proclaiming? To understand Jesus' view on this point, it is best to contrast it with that of John the Baptist, the last prophet of the Old Testament.

The contrast between John the Baptist and Jesus

John the Baptist proclaimed the imminence of the Kingdom of God. It was about to be inaugurated by the One who was to come. God was about to visit his people for the purpose of judgement and salvation. But John concentrated mostly on the first aspect: judgement. For him no one could escape from that terrible eschatological judgement and no Jewish privilege would be accepted unless one repented and made him/herself ready to meet the God of the end-time (Lk 3:7-14). Because of this emphasis on judgement, the coming of the Kingdom was seen rather negatively: one acts now, in the present not because salvation is coming but in order to escape the terrible judgement that is imminent. For John, the one absolutely certain event was the impending judgement of God which could neither be avoided nor prevented. To be sure, John's concern was the Kingdom, but it could not come before God had judged Israel and the nations.

Judgement is a genuine aspect of the Kingdom, defined by the demand for justice in the present and anticipation of perfection in the future. It is implicit in the coming of God's Kingdom because what is wicked in the world must be overcome, if God's final power is to penetrate his creation and transcend every boundary that would limit the recognition of his might. There is no other way for God's kingdom to triumph in the world. Those who are antagonistic to it must either be converted or destroyed. As Bruce Chilton puts it:

The conditions of this world, understood as the social order that people construct in any time, are incompatible with the rule of God. That is as evident as the greed and violence that are obvious and ambient within human culture. Some societies may seem more just than others, and a given society might grow or decay in its claim to justice, but the nature of God's justice is radically different from the qualities of human justice; "My ways are not your ways" is a formulation that the book of Isaiah comes to at the climax of an eschatological section (Is 55:8); it expresses a basic principle of Judaic (and therefore Christian) eschatology (*Pure Kingdom,* p.37*)*.

In contrast to John, Jesus puts the coming judgement in brackets, so to speak, and offers the Kingdom as Good News of salvation. He suspends the expected judgement and announces instead God's unconditional love as having come now with him in this precise hour. This offer is absolutely unconditional and has only one aim: the salvation of all, but particularly of those who least expect it: the sinners and the outcasts. The motive for action in the face of the imminent Kingdom now is not the preceding judgement, but this unconditional offer of salvation. Jesus did not do away with the eschatological judgement, but for him the function of this judgement at the moment was to be seen as a warning not to remain deaf and closed to the offer of salvation. Jesus' view of the coming judgement, in contrast to John's view, is dependent on the reaction of human beings to the breaking in of the Kingdom now. In the light of this final offer of salvation, it should be obvious to the hearers of his message that they need to sell all and leave everything in order to gain this great treasure or this costly pearl (Mt 13:44-45). His audience will be judged later on whether or not they have responded to the offer of salvation that Jesus holds out to them now. The final judgement is not canceled but only postponed.

Luke makes this salvational aspect of Jesus' message very clear in the first sermon of Jesus in his home town (Lk 4:16-19). Here Jesus announces the Good News of God's year of favor as it had been foretold by the Prophet Isaiah (61:2 b) as having been fulfilled now in their hearing. He stops just before the phrase of Isaiah *"and a day of revenge for our God."* Jesus deliberately proclaims a year of grace and the coming of God, not as judge but as the one who comes to save, to heal, to forgive, and to create all things new. With this message he steered clear of John's concept of the coming Kingdom.

In prison, John must have heard through his disciples that the one to whom he had given witness, Jesus, was not following his line. It must have upset him greatly. It must have seemed to John that Jesus failed to understand the gravity of the situation. How could he preach a year of grace in the light of the coming wrath of God? John was afraid. One cannot play with God's wrath. Yes, there would be a year of grace, but not before the day of judgement. This Jesus was jeopardizing the whole message John had entrusted to him. In John's distress he sent two of his disciples to Jesus to question him. When they came to Jesus, they said, *"John the Baptist sent us to ask if you are the one he said was going to come, or if we should expect someone else"* (Lk 7:18-20).

In John's vision, what Jesus was preaching was for the *day after* the judgement, not before it. Jesus was offering the Kingdom for too low a price. The difference between both men was not merely one of methodology in teaching. Rather, the difference lay in their God-image and this shaped their message. John stood in line with prophets like Jeremiah and Amos, and sided with the apocalyptic thinkers of his time. They saw Yahweh first as the judge who would come to destroy and judge his enemies in Israel and, in particular, the foreign nations which had oppressed the chosen people. Jesus distanced himself from such a God-image, taking the line which we find well expressed in prophets like Hosea and Isaiah. In the writings of these prophets a different God-image emerges. God is compassionate, tender, and merciful towards his sinful people. He does not desire their destruction nor does he wish to take revenge for their transgressions. Jesus' response to John's inquiry makes it obvious that he embraced the salvific God-image. By weaving together the different texts of Isaiah, Jesus communicated a God who comes to heal, set free and announce the Good News to his people rather than a God of judgement and condemnation. The difference between a God who sets conditions and one who offers salvation gratuitously can be illustrated in the following story:

> "Allow me to explain the Good News my religion proclaims," said the preacher.
> The Master was all attention.
> "God is love. And he loves and rewards us forever if we observe His commandments."
> "IF?" said the Master, "Then the news isn't all that good, is it?" (A. De Mello, *One Minute Nonsense*, p 198)

John needed to make an enormous mental adjustment and a fresh assessment of the Scriptures in order to be able to recognize the eschatological Kingdom in such a man and in such deeds as Jesus was performing. In the spirit of Elijah, John thought of the coming of the eschatological event in terms of earthquakes, wind and fire. But Jesus asked him to contemplate a different kind of coming, in terms of the "sound of a gentle breeze." This, however, he could not do. John failed to recognize the Kingdom when it finally appeared on his horizon, because it did not match his expectations. A new pair of glasses, a new epistemology was needed to recognize the dawn of the Kingdom in the deeds of Jesus. *"Happy is the man who does not find me a stumbling block."*

For Jesus, the Kingdom is a message of peace and joy. It is Good News, not bad news (Mk 1:14). Now is not the time to mourn and fast; this is a time of joy like a wedding feast (Mk 2:18ff.). Satan's reign is collapsing (Lk 10:18). Jesus sees himself as the messenger who brings the Good News as it says in Deutero-Isaiah:

How beautiful on the mountain are the feet of the one who brings happiness, proclaims salvation and tells Zion your God is King.

Jesus separated judgement and salvation which were originally understood as one final event. He offered salvation in the present and left the separation of good from evil to the final judgement (Mt 13:24-30).

It is important to regard the constant breaking in of the Kingdom of God as being *always* Good News and never judgement or condemnation. But Jesus did not abandon judgement (the word appears fifty times in his preaching); he postponed it. Only the one who does not heed the message of the Kingdom *now* will have to face judgement when the fullness of the Kingdom comes. In contrast to the beliefs and expectations of the time, and even of John the Baptist, Jesus stresses that the Kingdom is offering salvation for all now, at this very moment. Therefore, wherever the Kingdom is preached, judgement should not be anticipated by us. The Gospel has to remain Good News always and be preached accordingly.

The Kingdom of God as salvation for whom?

Who were to be the recipients of Jesus' message of salvation? Was the message for the righteous and the Jews only, or also for the sinners and the Gentiles? Jesus understood his mission primarily as a service to Israel and in Israel. He was conscious of the uniqueness of his people, accepted their Scripture as authoritative and restricted his ministry to them. He came to gather and to restore the people of God. Within this community, he saw himself sent first of all as one who was to look after the lost sheep: the poor, the sinners, the outcasts, the marginalized and all those who, in the official theology of the time, had hardly any chance of entering the Kingdom when the Messiah came. But who precisely were these people — called in Scripture — the poor, the sinners, and the outcasts?

a. The poor

To whom did Jesus address his message? To all or only to a particular group of people? How should we understand the phrase: Jesus preached the Kingdom of God as "Good News for the poor." What does this mean? Are the poor the only recipients of the Kingdom and do they provide us with the only key that can unlock for us the secrets of the Kingdom?

Luke, as well as Matthew, sees Jesus addressing his message of the Kingdom not just as Good News but as "Good News for the poor." Jesus did not exclude anyone from the possibility of entering into the Kingdom. He proclaimed God's love to all, but not in the same way. He neither took any antagonistic stance nor manifested any sectarian behavior by offering salvation to a specific group alone. He preached the Good News for all and presented the Kingdom as being within everyone's reach. Jesus' praxis and activity never had an **anti,** but only a **pro** character.

This inclusiveness in the message and in the actions of Jesus is a far cry from the mentality of the rich man in the following story:

> Jesus set up the birds of the air and the flowers of the fields as models for humans to imitate. So did the Master. He often told of the letter he received from an affluent neighbor which read:
> "Dear Sir,
> This concerns the bird-bath that I donated to the monastery garden. I'm writing to inform you that it is not to be used by the sparrows." (A. De Mello, *One Minute Nonsense,* p 196)

Preaching the Good News to all did not prevent Jesus from having a specific addressee in mind when proclaiming the Kingdom of God. And these addressees were the poor. Jesus understood his mission as directed to the poor in line with God's preference for the poor in the Old Testament. The phrase "for the poor" seems to indicate that the recipients of Jesus message will first of all help to clarify its content. Good News is essentially something relational, but not all Good News is equally so for everyone.

Poverty in the Bible

It is not easy to summarize what the Bible says about poverty and the poor. There are stages in the history of God and his Covenant people which reveal different views. We can briefly mention the three most important aspects in the discussions that follow.

The poor are God's privileged people

God is on their side and he is determined to restore their rights. God is not neutral, he is partial, he is on the side of the poor and oppressed. *"I have heard the cry of my people and I am determined to set them free from their slave-masters"* (Ex 3:7-12; see also Ps 72:12-14). Jesus took the same stand (Lk 4:18f). The main reason for this seems to be that poverty is seen as a lack of life, a diminishment of life. Since God is "the lover of life" he - by his very nature - is right there where life is diminished through oppression, injustice and suffering.

Mistrust concerning riches and possessions

The Old Testament is ambiguous: poverty was seen as a punishment and riches were seen as a blessing (Gen 13:14-17; Deut 7:8-10; Ex 23:23-26). Poverty was regarded as a breeding ground for vice, as the fruit of laziness and as a punishment for unfaithfulness (Prov 10:4).

In the Law, poverty was regarded as scandalous and as something that should not exist at all in Israel. As the fruit of injustice, it was directly against the Covenant made with God. No one should ever be the victim of another's gain. The dignity of the individual as a member of the Covenant forbade him to exploit or oppress anyone. The social laws were all based on the Covenant (Ex 20-23). In this context the admonition in Deuteronomy 15:4 has to be understood, *"Let there be no poor among you then."*

The Hebrew word ANAWIM which occurs 92 times in the Old Testament has a double meaning. First, it means a person who is afflicted and bent, that is, dehumanized, reduced by oppression to a condition of diminished capacity or worth. Secondly, in a later understanding, it meant a person who is "wholly dependent on God." He is someone who puts his trust in God alone. But the reason for doing so, most of the time, is because he is sociologically poor (G. Soares-Prabhu, "Class in the Bible...," p. 325).

This second meaning developed particularly during the Exile when the whole of Israel was called the ANAWIM of Yahweh. This refers to all those who remained faithful to Yahweh in Exile. The "poor of Yahweh" soon became a religious term meaning those who lived in total openness to Yahweh, in humility and respect for his commands. In Isaiah 61:1-2 and 66:2 the poor are the small people, the humble, the oppressed, the ignorant, those who have no heritage to rely on, no security, and whose only base on which to stand is their trust in Yahweh and in his coming. Jesus understood himself to be a member of this group and his mission was directed to such people.

The history of Israel, however, proved that riches easily become a source of greed, injustice and unbelief. They create a false security found in possessions rather than in confidence in God alone. In the New Testament, the issue is even clearer: the Kingdom of God is the only security there is, and we cannot serve two masters (Mt 6:24). Possessions are seen to be so fascinating and attractive that we easily take them as our ultimate security.

> Once upon a time the Master said to the disciples, "I put my confidence in God and went through the wilderness with only a small coin in my pocket. I went on a pilgrimage and came back, and the coin is still with me."
> But one of the students stood up and said to the Elder, "If you had a coin in your pocket, how could you say that you relied on anything higher?"

Most of us tend to hold on to something and refuse to share because we are relying on ourselves instead of on God in whose hands our future rests.

Possessions are for sharing

The riches and possessions which one owns are not meant to be possessed egoistically and used for one's own comfort; they are meant to be shared. They are in themselves good and not to be despised, but they exist to be shared with one's fellow human beings. This was the basic view of the early Church (Acts 4:32-35). The fundamental premise for such a view is our shared life in Christ. We are a new creation, a new existence, a new being in Christ. The particulars that separate us have disappeared. Those who have been baptized "into Christ," who have "put on Christ," are all one in him.

> *"As a result, there are no Gentiles and Jews, circumcised and uncircumcised, barbarians, savages, slaves, or free men but Christ is all, Christ is in all" (Col 3:11).*

> *"So there is no difference between Jews and Gentiles, between slave and free man, between men and women; you are all one in union with Jesus Christ" (Gal 3:28).*

The immediate effect of this shared life is that everyone, including the wealthy, now depends on the community for their well-being. The sharing of material goods becomes the expression of that mutual interdependence and sharing at the deeper level of "life in Christ," which is the basis for an authentic Christian existence and the freedom of humanity. However, these texts have been given different interpretations even in our time. While they clearly declare that all privileges and advantages of legal position and opportunity are made null and void because of our unity in Christ, the exegeses given to these texts are not that clear. Many Protestant exegetes have seen the texts in the following way: there is at least one moment in this world where all the differences are annulled and done away with and that is when we are gathered together in worship and listen to the Word of

God. At that very moment, and only then, no difference exists and the texts find their fulfillment. But at the moment we leave the realm of worship and return to our daily lives, this old world with its own structures and classifications reasserts itself.

Such an interpretation is understandable but also dangerous once we take it to mean that we cannot change the world outside of our worship gatherings. All we can do is give some religious signs to what the Kingdom will one day accomplish in the new creation to come. But the present world we have to leave as it is with all its class distinctions and its rules of power struggle and conflicts.

Who are the poor for Jesus?

The Bible does not provide an absolute clear-cut definition of the poor Jesus was thinking of as addressees of the Kingdom. They are the ones on the 'bottom of the heap' in history and those who are oppressed by society and cast out of it. In the Synoptics, the poor are divided into two classes.

First the *economically poor*. They are those who are hungry and thirsty, who are weighed down by burdens, who are sick or in prison. They are those for whom life and survival are a hard task.

Secondly, there are the *sociologically poor*. They are those who are despised by the ruling class in society, who are considered sinners: the publicans and the prostitutes. Then there are the simple-minded, the least, those who carry out despised tasks. They are the marginalized, those whose religious ignorance and moral behavior, in the conviction of the time, closed the gate leading to their salvation.In the words of Soares-Prabhu:

> The poor of the Bible are all those who are in any way, and not just economically, deprived of the means or the dignity they need to lead a fully human existence: or who are in a situation of powerlessness which exposes them to such deprivation. The poor of the Bible are thus the "wretched of the earth," the marginalized, the exploited, all those who are actually or potentially oppressed." ("Class in the Bible", p. 332).

To these poor Jesus showed unwavering partiality, so much so, that what is called the option for the poor can be said to have started with Jesus. Jesus actually resumed the partiality which the great prophets had ascribed to God.

Theologically, it can be said that in the Old Testament the mere presence of poverty laid a heavy responsibility on the non-poor an obligation which was demanded by the Law and not left to the goodwill of the individual (Deut 24:10-15). The prophets especially made it clear that social responsibility for the poor and oppressed belonged to the Covenant and took priority over worship (Is 1:11-17). God had a particular love for the poor and disadvantaged in society and he stood up for them. (J. Dunn, *Jesus and the Spirit*, pp. 33-44). Jesus never did away with the Old Testament view on everyone's responsibility towards the poor in society.

However, Jesus added a dimension to poverty which might be called the **"poverty of spirit."** It means nothing can save us except total reliance on God's infinite love, which actually means now entering the world through Jesus. The things of this world cannot save, and those who rely on their riches and possessions will perish (Mk 10:23-27). The "poor in spirit" are those who have found their security in the knowledge that God loves them and will save them not because of what they have, but because of his love. The spirit of poverty means to live as Jesus himself lived, totally dependent on the Father and his love for us, finding in this love the ultimate security and joy. This poverty of spirit is the most fundamental virtue that Jesus demanded from every disciple: to be free of his or her social status in society. One cannot receive the Kingdom and remain in it unless one lives out of this virtue.

Preferential Option for the Poor

Jesus definitely had a preference for the poor. The general objection against such a preferential option of God for the poor is: how can God have preferences? Does he not love everyone equally? God is free to choose whom he wants for his purpose. God does indeed show preference in the Bible. For example, he chose Abel over Cain, Jacob over Esau, and yet he loved each one in his own way. Preference implies the universality of God's love for everyone which excludes no one. It is only within the framework of this universality that we can understand the preference God has for the poor. The rejection of the preference means failing to grasp that we must combine the universality of God's love with his preference for the poorest. To hold both - God's universality of love and his preference - in balance is not easy.

The poor are not morally better than the rich; they are human beings, which means, they are as sinful as the rest of humanity. We should prefer them not because they are good but because first of all God is good and prefers the forgotten, the oppressed, the poor and the forsaken. It is our following of Jesus who had this preference that compels us to do the same. All of us, poor or rich, have to make this option. The poor, also, have to opt in favor of their brothers and sisters irrespective of race, social class, and culture. The option for the poor is a decision incumbent upon every Christian (cf. G. Gutièrrez, "Option for the poor.. ", pp. 5-10).

In this connection, a question arises about the role of the poor in the history of salvation. God has no favorites but he chooses some to reach others. Every call is a participation in the bringing about of God's design for his creation. God chooses the poor, whom he treats as his favorites, to be his agents of salvation for humankind. The 'mystery of the poor' in the Bible consists precisely in their being the chosen instrument through which God wants to redeem the world (G. Gutierrez, *The Power of the Poor in History*, pp. 9-10). If we read the Bible with the eyes of the poor, we discover aspects which were unrecognized before because we were not situated in history in a way that would have enabled us to understand them.

> *God purposely chose what the world considers nonsense in order to put wise men to shame, and what the world considers weak in order to put powerful men to shame. He chose what the world looks down on, and despises, and thinks is nothing, in order to destroy what the world thinks is important (1 Cor 1:27).*

A text like this suddenly receives a new meaning. Because of the identification of the "nonsense and the weak" with the powerless and exploited of the present world, that is, with concrete people in history, the role of the poor in the history of salvation is newly discovered and all of Scripture is re-read from such a perspective.

The story of Zachaeus, told by Matthew, can be a pattern of what a conversion really means: Zachaeus was rich but at the same time very small, so tiny in fact that he had to climb a tree, for it was only from there that he could see Jesus and hear his message for the poor who were surrounding him. Then Jesus called him down from his perch in the tree and invited him to join the poor so that he might understand that Jesus preached the Good News from the only vantage point which could enable him to see and understand what he was all about.

b. The sinners and outcasts

The second group, after the poor, who are mentioned as the primary recipients of Jesus' Kingdom message are the sinners and the outcasts. A sinner in the Old Testament is not someone who "has committed an offence against God." Rather, to be a sinner means to be someone "who breaks or disregards the Law." The Law is the heart in the Jewish concept of sin and sinner. The Law was intrinsically linked to the Covenant and keeping the Law meant living in the Covenant. Israel's privilege was that God had given his people the Law which made them stand out from the rest of the world. The Law defined the boundaries of the 'People of God', and breaching the

Law meant living outside the boundary marked by the Law, outside the people who, by definition, are those who live within the Law. Sinners were, therefore, first of all Gentiles who lived outside the Covenant; and secondly, all those Jews who did not keep the Law.

The term "sinners" referred to an identifiable social group just as the term "righteous" did, and meant those who did not follow the ways of the fathers as spelled out by the Torah wisdom of the sages. The worst sinners or non-observants were the outcasts. We do not know the exact extent of this class, though it included the notoriously "wicked" (murderers, extortioners, prostitutes and the like), as well as members of certain occupational groups, membership in which made one a "non-Jew"(cf. M.J., Borg, *Jesus A New Vision*, p. 92).

Shepherds and tax collectors, frequently mentioned in the New Testament, belonged to this group. The outcasts had lost all civil and religious rights: they were deprived of the right to sit on local councils and lost their place as children of Abraham in the life of the age to come. They became "Gentiles."

Jesus' example

Against this background we must place Jesus' words: *"I did not come to call the righteous but sinners"* (Mk 2:17). Jesus himself was regarded a sinner since he did not follow the strict observance of the Law which the elite demanded. Jesus accepted the criticism hurled against him. He turned it around and made it a statement of positive intent, forcing his opponents to realize that he had come precisely for these groups whom they had ostracized. There are three areas where Jesus showed himself most at odds with his opponents: his table fellowship with "sinners"; his view regarding the Sabbath; his stance towards women.

Table-Fellowship Movement

There were many movements in the time of Jesus which proclaimed the nearness of God's Kingdom and told people to get ready for its coming. One of the most distinctive marks that set Jesus and his followers apart from other movements was Jesus' habit of expressing the meaning and goal of his mission by sitting at table and having a meal with people, particularly with the outcasts and marginalized. This "sitting at table" became the symbol of what he stood for. Some scholars regard it as the most distinctive feature of Jesus' behavior.

The prophets spoke on behalf of the honest poor, and defended the widows and fatherless, those oppressed and exploited by the wicked, rich and powerful. Jesus went further. In addition to proclaiming these blessed, he actually took his stand among the pariahs of his world, those despised by the respectable. Sinners were his table companions and the ostracized tax-collectors and prostitutes his friends (G. Vermes, *Jesus the Jew*, p. 224).

Others even hold that Jesus' regular table fellowship with the outcast in the name of the Kingdom of God became the decisive factor which led to his violent death.

His enemies criticized him for loving to eat and drink as the friend of tax collectors and sinners (Mk 2:16; Mt 11:19; Lk 7:34). This criticism shows vividly how provocative Jesus' behavior was.

Like the miracles (which are not just works of individual healings but signs of a radical structural change which put Satan's rule to an end, and ushered in a new cosmic social order, God's rule), the table fellowship of Jesus is more than a form of individual pastoral care. It is the expression of a radically new (and therefore thoroughly disturbing) theological vision, rooted in a new experience of God and calling for a new kind of society" (G. Soares-Prabhu, *The Table Fellowship of Jesus*, p. 144).

The Gospels report many scenes where Jesus eats and drinks and enjoys meals in the company of people of dubious backgrounds, but unrestricted table fellowship is the best way to reach out to people who might otherwise stay away from organized religion and from God's offer of salvation. To his opponents' challenging question, *"Why do John's disciples and the disciples of the Pharisees fast, but your disciples do not fast?"* Jesus replies by asking, *"Can the wedding guests fast while the bridegroom is still with them?"* The fact that they called him a "drunkard and a glutton" and that Jesus compared himself to the bridegroom at the wedding demonstrates that the Jesus movement created feasts; in other words, it was a table community movement. Jesus used this gesture to make the reality of the Kingdom visible. It is God calling all people once again into a family of brothers and sisters where there would be no discrimination, but only the one family under the fatherhood of God.

In the words of Joachim Jeremias:

Jesus' meals with the publicans and sinners, too, are not only events on a social level, not only an expression of unusual humanity, and social generosity and his sympathy with those who were despised, but had an even deeper significance. They are an expression of the mission and message of Jesus (Mk 2:17), eschatological meals, anticipatory celebration of the feast in the end time (Mt 8:11) par.), in which the community of saints is already being represented (Mk 2:19). The inclusion of sinners in the community of salvation, achieved in table-fellowship, is the most meaningful expression of the message of the redeeming love of God" (J. Jeremias, *New Testament Theology*, pp. 115-116).

After Easter these meals which Jesus had celebrated so often with his disciples gained a new significance. The Lord's supper became *the* celebration of Jesus' Resurrection which eagerly anticipated his return in glory. It was the risen Christ who gave these meals a definite meaning since he appeared to his disciples during suppers and once again ate with them. The disciples recognized that the Risen Jesus was calling them to return to the celebration of his Kingdom-anticipating meals but this time with a stunning new revelatory clarity. Now the meal with the risen Jesus was definitely an anticipation of the great eschatological banquet Jesus had so often celebrated with them in joy and thanksgiving. The Easter appearance of the risen Lord to the Twelve at a meal should therefore be seen as the primary memory when we celebrate the Eucharist (Lk 20:30-31;42; Acts 10:40-41). The memory of Jesus' Last Supper with his disciples and the theological meaning of this act, which became an integral part of the joyful celebration of the Lord's Supper, remains secondary to the original intent. When the early Christians celebrated the "breaking of the bread with joy and gladness" (Acts 2:46), they experienced, above all, the risen Christ present in their midst as the apostles had experienced him in the meals they shared with him after Easter.

This is also the reason why the Early Church chose Sunday, the first day of the week, to assemble for the celebration of the Lord's Supper, the Eucharist. It was on that day that he had appeared to the Twelve and had eaten with them and the tomb had been discovered empty.

There are therefore two memorials celebrated during the Eucharist: first, the joyful eating and drinking with each other in a meal that the risen Jesus had recommended in memory of his doing so before and after the resurrection; secondly the memorial of his death and suffering for our sake (cf. Michael Perry, *Exploring the Evolution of the Lord's Supper in the New Testament*).

The death of Jesus needs to be understood in the light of the table community. The body of Jesus is food that is shared in community, and his blood is wine that is drunk in community. This does not mean that, upon the death of Jesus, the meaning of the table community is weakened, but rather, that Jesus himself becomes incarnated in the table community movement. Jesus' death must be understood in the light of his life and this movement.

In a way, Jesus died as a result of this movement, and becomes incarnated in this movement through his death. Jesus loved a life of total sharing with others which culminated in his death. He shared himself even to the point of sharing his body and his blood. His death is the perfect realization of the table community movement. The last supper shows that Jesus, even after his death, is resurrected as - and in - the table community (Church).

Scripture makes it clear that the risen Christ can be met again where the material, daily food is shared and eaten. On the way to Emmaus the two disciples recognized him when they finally shared and ate food (Lk 24:13ff). Once again fellowship with the resurrected Jesus is expressed in the fellowship of eating together.

An Emmaus Psalm

How easily, O Christ,
do I long for a firsthand touch
from you, my friend and savior,
risen and glorious, victorious over death,
radiant with luminous life.

Oh, how easily does my yearning arise
to have been one of those in the upper room
when you returned in resurrected form.
I know that my faith would be strong
if, like Mary in the garden,
I had reached out to hug your living presence
on Easter morning.
I do not doubt the quality of my zeal
had I broken bread with you
at the sunset inn on the Emmaus road.

It is not easy to be among the living faithful
fed by second-hand accounts
of your resurrection visits,
even though they have been passed on with loving care
for millenniums mouth-to-mouth.

But I take hope today, in this Easter season,
that I too can taste and feel
your fulfilled promise:
"I am with you always, even to the end."

Every time I break bread with friends or strangers
or encounter kindness on my daily byroads,
when I am visited by you
even though my inner doors are locked in fear,
let my heart be as open as the horizon
for the feast of an Easter visit
from you, my Risen Savior.
(E. Hayes, *Prayers for a Planetary Pilgrim*, p. 144)

Behold, I am standing at the door knocking, if any one hears my voice and opens the door, I will come in to him and eat with him, and he with me (Rev 3:20).

The Eucharist, initiated at the last supper, was a testimony to the table community movement, and it was permanently instituted to support this movement. At the Eucharist, the risen Christ and food are holistically united. This unification is the unity of the Kingdom of God and earthly reality and it symbolizes the revolution against the unjust system that separates heaven and earth (Park Jae Soon, *Jesus' Table Community Movement and the Church*, p. 73).

The Scripture texts that record the initiation of the Eucharist are all closely related to the coming of the Kingdom of God. Accordingly, the bread and wine in the Eucharist are symbols of the Kingdom of God realized now on this earth. Jesus said at the last supper that he would not drink of the fruit of the vine again until he drank it with his disciples in the Kingdom of God.

The Early Church faithfully continued this practice. One of the basic characteristics of the life of the early Christians was the "breaking of bread in their homes and partaking of food with glad and generous hearts." This description is in keeping with the characteristics of the Jesus movement. The Early Church movement is the Jesus movement after Jesus' death.

Soon the table community movement of Jesus became so distorted that Paul had to separate the "love feast" from the Eucharist. The Eucharist remained whereas the love feast was completely dropped in the Church communities. What remained of the table movement of Jesus became formalized in the Eucharist as a religious ritual.

The Gospel of John resisted such formalization of Jesus' table community in a religious ritual only. The last supper in the Gospel of John does not include any words of institution. Immediately before the last supper Jesus demonstrated the perfect practice of love by washing his disciples' feet. After the supper, Jesus gave them a new commandment: to love one another, and said that by this people would recognize them as his disciples (Jn 13:34-35) (Park Jae Soon, *Jesus' Table Community Movement and the Church*, p. 76).

Park Soon argues as follows. Against the tendency to enshrine the Jesus movement exclusively in the Eucharist, the Gospel of John invites the participants at the Eucharist to 'move back' to the concrete life situation of Jesus when he walked this earth and to eat and drink the flesh and blood of Jesus into present reality by bringing the table community movement, started by Jesus, into the life situation of the poor. With regard to the Eucharist and mission, there are therefore two tasks to fulfil. *First* we are asked to create communities of table-fellowship of which the Eucharist is the center. *Second,* in a broader context we are called to promote feasts where people of all races and cultures sit together and enjoy each others' company in life-giving relationships and genuine compassion. It is precisely here that God's Kingdom makes itself felt and can be experienced as present in the midst of human affairs.

This is by no means an easy task, but it is definitely worth an honest effort as the following story illustrates:

Two parishes in Washington, D.C., an Episcopal one and a Catholic one, decided to celebrate Pentecost together one year. Both parishes served a variety of ethnic groups: white and Afro-American English-speaking parishioners; Central American and Latin American Spanish-speaking parishioners; French-speaking Haitians; Portuguese-speaking Brazilians; and Vietnamese-speaking parishioners. They all had their own hymn books, their own symbols, their own music, and their own prayers. Meetings were organized to arrange for the celebration. The interdenominational hurdles were ecumenically overcome without too much difficulty. The cultural arrangements (what languages? Which hymns? What kind of decorations?) were more complicated, but they also were finally arranged. After the liturgical services (identical worship solemnities in both church buildings) a big potluck dinner with traditional food, drinks, music, dancing, and singing would close the celebration. The program promised to be a real treat from all points of view.

In one of the last meetings the group became aware of one final hurdle. Some of the richer people in the parishes employed the poorer ones. The social relationship between those two groups was far from ideal. The workers were underpaid because they were illegal immigrants. Their working conditions were substandard. It would be difficult to sit at the same table after the liturgical ceremony and pick up the unjust working relationships on Monday. In fact, they decided, it wouldbe impossible. The celebration did not take place. The time was not yet ripe to extend what was possible in the church buildings to everyday life of the market square and the labor market. The organizing committee regretfully decided to postpone the festival and to work at making it - politically and socially - possible in the future (J. G. Donders, *Charged with the Spirit,* p. 113).

Sabbath

The Law says: *"To keep the Sabbath is to hold fast to the Covenant"* (Ex 31:12-17). This is the basis for the strict observance of the Sabbath. Breach of the Sabbath was a breach of the Covenant itself. Non-observance of the Sabbath was sufficient to exclude an Israelite from the Covenant people. The keeping of the Sabbath belonged to Israel's self-understanding. Jesus is accused twice of breaking the Sabbath: in Mark 2:23-8 his disciples pluck the ears of corn, while in Mark 3:1-5 Jesus heals the paralyzed man on the Sabbath. Why did he have to heal this person on the Sabbath? Why could the man who had been paralyzed for many years not wait for a few hours more until the sun had set and the Sabbath would be over? The Law permitted the rescue of a person or even an animal on the Sabbath only if life was threatened. But here, in the case of the paralyzed man, there was no such urgency.

Women

The social status of women in the Old Testament is well known. Since blood played such an important role in terms of purity, a normal, healthy woman of childbearing age was prevented from taking part in religious ceremonies for much of her life. There was always the danger that she might render others impure by social contact. Women were not allowed into the inner court of the Temple where the sacrifices were offered.

Jesus overstepped these regulations, disregarding the traditional taboos. Women were among his closest followers and friends (Mk 15:40-41; Lk 8:1-3, 10:38-42). In John 4:27 we find the disciples surprised when Jesus talks with a woman. His teaching on divorce applies to both partners (Mk 10:11-12). He was unconcerned about defilement from the woman with the hemorrhage (Mk 5:25-34) and fearless of contracting infections from those with contagious skin diseases (Mk 1:40-41).

SUMMARY

Borg summarizes well the example Jesus set in all these situations:

> In all these cases Jesus was confronted by boundaries drawn within Israel, by Jews against Jews, boundaries drawn for religious reasons, drawn by those most admirable for the strength of their commitment in religious matters, those most concerned that their religious practice be what God wants. In each case Jesus called these boundaries into question, disregarded them, broke them down. And he did so in the name of God's Kingdom. He came to call sinners, not the righteous. God is for those whom men think to exclude in his name (M. J., Borg, *Jesus A New Vision*, p. 82).

Yet Jesus was not sent only for the Jews, but for the Gentiles as well. None of Jesus' statements about the Kingdom differentiates between the destiny of the Jews and that of the Gentiles. The Gospels, however, clearly show that he did not work for or proclaim his message to the Gentiles but rather restricted himself to the regions of his own people. Even so, the universality of the offer of salvation is implicitly present in his concept of the Kingdom of God. This is shown in the way Jesus foresaw the coming of the nations (Mt 8:11) in the image of the great pilgrimage of Isaiah 2:2-3. For Jesus the coming of the nations is God's work and indicates the end-time. Nonetheless, he does envision the nations' participation in the restoration of Israel. Jesus seems to have personally appropriated the prophetic interpretation of God's history. As the prophets saw it, God selected from the many peoples of the world a single people, Israel, to serve as a visible sign and agent of salvation. But this offer of salvation is not meant for Israel alone. Because God's salvation for all is offered through this people, God's Kingdom in this world will always remain mediated by a visible community. Still God is not necessarily bound to this one people. He can choose other people besides Israel, as Jesus tells us in Matthew 21:43 *"The Kingdom of God will be taken from you and given to a people who will produce its fruits."* Who are these people? Jesus seems to divide the human race into the haves and the have-nots according to Luke's version of the Beatitudes (6:20-26). In the Parable of the Great Banquet (Lk 14:15-24) it is a division between those who decline the invitation and those brought in to take their place. In the Parable of the Sower (Mk 4:3-9) it is a division between those who yield fruit and those who do not.

What matters is that a community remains a sacramental bearer of the Kingdom and that it makes itself available for the realization of God's ultimate plan of salvation for all. Jesus entrusted the mission of spreading the Kingdom of God, previously the role of the people of Israel, to the community of his disciples. With this new election the purpose of the Old Testament people was transferred to this New People. They are now the active carrier of salvation. They are called out of the nations in order to take up a mission for the nations.

Reflection: *There is no Jew, no Gentile, no Male, no Female*

All of us - without exception - **are winners in the Kingdom** of God if we accept its message and its messenger. God's salvation is universal. Although Jesus strongly feels his mission as offering salvation to Israel first and foremost, he does not limit it there. All of us are recipients of God's gift of salvation. Jesus repeatedly sends his disciples to *the other side of the lake* and when he sends out the seventy-two he indicates that they are sent to the whole of humanity. The seventy-two probably referred to the seventy-two grandsons of Noah, who one day were sent out from the homestead of their grandfather to be the beginning of all the nations on earth (Gen 10:32).

There is a story that has been attributed to a Jewish tradition and illustrates the point that God wants ALL to be saved:

> When the army of the Egyptians was destroyed by the Red Sea sweeping over them, all those in heaven cheered and threw a party because the Israelites were saved. But they looked over and saw God weeping. They asked why he was weeping when his people had been saved and the Egyptians destroyed. God replied, "The Egyptians are my people too" (W. A. Barry, *Now Choose Life,* p. 69).

QUESTION: How convinced am I that God's saving will is meant for all, and that God will most probably save all human beings effectively?

Both John and Jesus preached salvation. The *"Repent, for the Kingdom is close at hand"* message of John the Baptist (Mt 3:2a) carries the tone of a stern demand implying dreadful consequences if not heeded, while in the words of Jesus, the call to conversion becomes an invitation to open oneself to the gift of God's merciful love. Judgement is suspended to give room to gratuitous love.

> If Jesus opened our eyes what might we see?
> A vision that is new of self and others, of the world and of God.
> We might look on God's creation with the eyes of God.
> God is inside us looking out rather than outside us looking in;
> and we see ourselves as children of God:
> a son or daughter who is loved
> a sinner forgiven and called
> and we see others the same - a gift not a threat.
> All God's people crying with his cry,
> hungering for food, hungering for a voice to console, a hand
> to comfort and being granted all and even more.

QUESTION: In my life and in my pastoral ministry do I see and proclaim the Kingdom always as Good News or do I revert to John the Baptist who sees God's Kingdom first as judgment before it can become salvation?

For God has never despised
nor scorned the poverty of the poor.
From the poor he has not hidden his face
but he heard the poor when they cried. (Psalm 21)

Jesus had a special love for the poor. In any group he seemed to go straight for those who might otherwise be neglected or excluded. If we want to counter the deadening bad news we hear each day with the Good News that Jesus offers, we need to turn away from our conventional way of seeing this world and the powers that rule it. Jesus' alternative vision and wisdom is quite unsettling when he offers the outcast a head-start position and declares the **poor the blessed** ones (Mt 5:3). They are indeed God's agents of salvation.

QUESTION: If God's favorites are the poor where do I fit in? What does poverty mean to me?

Exclusion and **inclusion** were issues absolutely central to the Law and to holiness. Jesus, however, interprets the Law of Holiness in terms of a God of compassion and mercy. The Kingdom table is, therefore, one where people do not seek status, where social class is not given special attention and where the rules of meritocracy are utterly ignored. No "members only" sign is put up anywhere! The circle drawn by Jesus is always open, there is always a place at his table.

Jesus would certainly agree with the master in the following story:

A visitor, in the course of explaining his religion to the Master, said, "We believe we are God's chosen people."
"What does that mean?" said the Master.
"That God chose us from among all the peoples of the earth."
"I think I can guess who, from among all the peoples of the earth, made that discovery," said the Master drily (A. De Mello, *One Minute Nonsense,* p 197).

During the Eucharist the reality of the Kingdom of God is at the same time promise and fulfilment. During its celebration we are one body, one blood, one spirit - his body, his blood, his spirit.

QUESTION: What does participation in the Eucharist mean to me? Does it go beyond the ritual and open me to a table-fellowship with all people, particularly those at the margins of society who were Jesus' favorite table companions?

Chapter Ten

Definition of the Kingdom

Jesus never defined the Kingdom of God. He described the Kingdom in parables and similes (see Mt 13; Mk 4) and in concepts like life, glory, joy and light. Among theologians we still find a naive helplessness when it comes to defining the Kingdom of God. The best biblical description we can find is given in Paul:

After all, the Kingdom of God is not a matter of whether you get what you like to eat or drink, but the Kingdom of God is a matter of justice, peace and joy in the Holy Spirit (Rom 14:17).

Some authors regard this text as the only definition of the Kingdom ever attempted in the entire New Testament. The constant danger has been to interpret these words exclusively in a spiritual sense and overlook the fact that its basic concepts like "justice, peace and joy" are equally meant to refer to the life of the Christian in the here and now .

Strangely, the closest the Bible ever comes to a definition is found where, by all rights, it should not be found, in Rom 14:17. This verse is usually misunderstood to refer exclusively to private, individual, interior, purely spiritual blessings such as a righteous standing of the individual before God, peace of mind and heart due to forgiveness of sins, the joy of the redeemed child. But, while those blessings are not to be excluded, they do not exhaust or even do full justice to the message of these words. After all, peace means primarily the opposite of war, the tranquillity of order, social order; justice means justice, the virtue proper to social relations; and joy, although it has an individual dimension to it, can mean a rejoicing precisely in the blessings brought by peace and justice (B. Viviano, *The Kingdom of God in History,* p.18).

Albert Schweitzer called Paul's definition "A Creed for all times." In his writings, Paul tends to reserve the phrase *Kingdom of God* for reference to the Kingdom in its future aspect. Only here in Romans 14:17 and 1 Corinthians 4:20 does it refer to the present moment. The three qualities (justice, peace, and joy) he lists are all important concepts for him. The concluding words, "in the Holy Spirit," are to be attached to all three words. With justice, peace and joy, Paul describes the content of the Kingdom of God, which he sees as already concretely present in the eschatological community. We might call these three characteristics the fundamental values of the Kingdom. The phrase could be seen as a rule of faith or of Christian conduct.

The Jewish background is important here. The pious in the Old Testament believed that the Kingdom of God was a reality which did reach this world. This found expression in the phrase: "To take upon oneself the yoke of the Kingdom." It expressed a certain attitude of mind. By reciting the SHEMA (*"Listen, O Israel . . . "* Deut 6:4-5) the pious Rabbi opened his mind and heart unconditionally to God's holy will. This act was seen as the "receiving of the Kingdom of God." Its intention was perfect union with God. Whenever a Jew obeyed a precept of the Law and thus showed himself subject to the author of the Law, there the Kingdom of God was present. What that could mean in the concrete situations of life is related in the death-story of Rabbi Akiba:

> What a typical Rabbi longed for was that sublime moment when the daily profession of a long life might be confirmed by act. When R. Akiba, who died the death of a martyr, was in the hands of his torturers, he joyfully 'received upon himself the yoke of the kingdom of heaven' (by reciting the Shema). When asked why he did so, he answered, 'All my life I have recited this verse ('And thoushalt love,' etc.), and have longed for the hour when I could fulfil it. I loved him with all my heart, I loved him with all my fortunes. Now I have the opportunity to love him with all my soul. Therefore I repeat this verse in joyfulness.' And thus he died. There is no indication of despair in Akiba's death, but also no thought of a crown of martyrdom awaiting him for this glorious act. He simply fulfills a commandment of love, and he rejoices in fulfilling it. It is 'a love unto death,' suffering no separation (S. Schechter, *Aspects of Rabbincal Theology,* p. 71-72).

With this background in mind, it is easy to discover parallels in Jesus' message although expressed in a different vocabulary. Some of these include the following: *"Do not seek what you are to eat or drink, and don't be worried . . . Seek rather your Father's Kingdom"* (cf. Mt 6:25-33 and Lk 12:22-31), and the "yoke" theme as found in Matthew 11:29-30, *"Shoulder my yoke and learn from me. . . . my yoke is easy and my burden is light."* This sentence readily brings to mind the Rabbinical phrase, "to take upon oneself the yoke of the Kingdom of God."

"Seeking the Kingdom of God" or "shouldering the yoke" in the words of Paul means, therefore, nothing else than to commit oneself anew, daily, to the Kingdom. Just as the pious in the Old Testament would commit themselves daily to the great *Shema* and in doing so would "take upon themselves the yoke of the Kingdom" so the disciple of Jesus is asked to commit him/ herself to the same Kingdom by living the values of justice, peace and joy.

The Kingdom, defined in a brief formula, is therefore nothing other than justice, peace, and joy in the Holy Spirit. These are not just feelings or sentiments but realities to be implemented in this world. We might rightly call these three characteristics the fundamental values of the Kingdom.

JUSTICE

Justice in the Old Testament

The literature in recent years on the issue of justice is overwhelming. We are not concerned here with justice in general but how Scripture sees and deals with this reality. Justice as a biblical concept could best be translated as RIGHT RELATIONS or even better as LIFE-GIVING RELATIONSHIPS. According to Christian anthropology, to be a human being means essentially to be in the world (meaning having a body) and to be in relationship.

The essential relations extend in four directions: *to God, to oneself, to neighbor both as individual and as part of society, and to creation as a whole.* To be just means to live in life-giving relationships with my fellow human beings, myself, with nature and ultimately with God. Human identity and authenticity is only achieved when these essentially human relations are "right." Salvation from this point of view means entering into relationships that are God-willed for the fulfillment and happiness of my very being. Eternal life means living in relationships with God, myself, my neighbor and nature that are life-giving and life-receiving. God is a "lover of life" (Wis 11:23ff.) means that where God enters into relationship with human beings there life is fully given. Those whom God has thus enlivened he expects in turn to enter into life-giving relationships with their fellow human beings and with all of creation as well. Therefore it is correct to say:

> In biblical faith, the doing of justice is the primary expectation of God. Everything else by way of ethical norm and Covenantal requirement derives from this, for God is indeed a "lover of justice" (Ps 99:4). Israel is here commanded to attend to the very thing which God most values, namely justice (W. Brueggemann, *To Act Justly, Love Tenderly, Walk Humbly*, p. 5).

Since there are various definitions and conflicting understandings of justice a short interpretation of the words used in the Bible is in place before we continue. We will follow here the presentation by Dean Brackley, in *Divine Revolution*. He explains:

Sedeq, mishpat, sedaqah are the words used for justice in the Hebrew Bible. *Sedeq* is the most comprehensive expression of what is valuable, right and fair in the community. It stands for what is good. In Israel *sedeq* means justice for the oppressed. It is employed as the central concept governing all relationships. It means setting things right between people and living in accordance with what specific social relationships require. That is why justice means vindicating the oppressed.

After *sedeq,* the most important values in the Hebrew Bible are *mishpat* and *sedaqah,* which also have to do with the fulfillment of responsibilities within relationships. Indeed they demand setting right wrong relationships by showing *compassion* to victims. Thus, in contrast to Western justice, there is no tension between biblical justice and compassion (rahamin). *Sedeq mishpat* and *sedaqah* each has its distinctive nuances and can mean uprightness in general, but the important point is that they all have to do with social relationships and share a core meaning, which is well expressed by their being constantly put together in various constellations. The core meaning, they share, is the defense of the weak, the vindication of the victim, the liberation of the oppressed. In conclusion, the God of the Bible is a God who is preoccupied with social relationships and the way they are institutionalized in Israel. The Hebrew concepts *sedeq, mishpat* and *sedaqa*h together with *hesed* and *emeth* are not only central to the ethos of Israel but reflect who Yahweh is: the one who defends the weak and frees them from the oppressor. "This is not a "part-time" concern of Yahweh or a secondary characteristic. This is what distinguishes Yahweh from the other gods (Ps 82)" *(Divine Revolution,* pp. 129-130).

Walter Brueggemann offers this biblical description of justice. "Justice is to sort out what belongs to whom, and to return it to them." Then he comments:

Such an understanding implies that there is a right distribution of goods and access to the sources of life. There are certain elements that cannot be mocked. Yet through the uneven workings of the historical process, some come to have access to or control of what belongs to others. If we control what belongs to others long enough, we come to think of it as rightly ours, and to forget it belonged to someone else. So the work of liberation, redemption, salvation, is the work of giving things back. The Bible knows that when things are alienated from those to whom they belong, there can only be trouble, disorder and death. So God's justice at the outset has a dynamic, transformative quality. It causes things to change, and it expects that things must needs change if there is to be abundant life (*To Act Justly...,* p. 5).

In order to illustrate Brueggemann tells the following story:

A very proper English lady went to a tea shop. She sat at a table for two, ordered a pot of tea, and prepared to eat some cookies which she had in her purse. Because the tea shop was crowded, a man took the other chair and also ordered tea. As it happened, he was a Jamaican black, though that is not essential to the story. The woman was prepared for a leisurely time, so she began to read her paper. As she did so, she took a cookie from the package. As she read, she noticed that the man across also took a cookie from the package. This upset her greatly, but she ignored it and kept reading. After a while she took another cookie. And so did he. This unnerved her and she glared at the man. While she glared, he reached for the fifth and last cookie, smiled and offered her half of it. She was indignant. She paid her money and left in a great hurry, enraged at such a presumptuous man. She hurried to her bus stop just outside. She opened her purse to get a coin for her bus ticket. And then she saw, much to her distress, that in her purse was her package of cookies unopened (*To Act Justly...*, p.6).

We could ask ourselves: what are the things that we might claim as being rightly ours and yet are not? They may not be material possessions but could be our status in society used to lord it over others, titles used for personal advantage, prejudices harbored towards others, self-righteous behavior that makes us feel morally better than others. It is often not easy to discover how canny we can be in putting ourselves in unjustified ways on top of others. Sometimes we claim these privileges, that do not belong really to us, for so long that we come to think they are rightfully ours. We, particularly religious and priests in many parts of the world, can easily fall prey to the illusion that we have a right to privileges on the basis of our profession. Jesus would certainly not justify such behavior although we may claim these privileges in honor of his name.

Then Jesus said to the crowds and to his disciples, "The scribes and the Pharisees sit on Moses' seat; so practice and observe whatever they tell you, but not what they do; for they preach, but do not practice. They bind heavy burdens, hard to bear, and lay them on the shoulders of others; but they themselves will not move them with their finger. They do all their deeds to be seen by others; for they make their phylacteries broad and their fringes long, and they love the place of honor at feasts and the best seats in the synagogues, and salutations in the market places, and being called rabbi.

But you are not to be called rabbi, for you have one teacher, and you are all students. And call no one your father on earth, for you have one Father, who is in heaven. Neither be called masters, for you have one master, the Christ. He who is greatest among you shall be your servant; whoever exalts himself will be humbled, and whoever humbles himself will be exalted (Mt 23:1-12).

It is important to realize that justice is a gift, something we as humans do not know. Only God is just and in the measure we open ourselves to God and get to know him, we become just: *"To know me, means to do Justice"* (Jer 22:16). Only he who opens him/herself to the Kingdom and lets its life-giving power into his/her life will come to realize what right relationships really are.

The Bible is not very interested in justice in the abstract. It gives concrete instances of justice and injustice in the lives of people. In consulting the Scriptures about justice we need to ask: What relationship to particular persons or groups does Scripture characterize as just or unjust? What relationships does Scripture approve or disapprove of so that we may apply them to our modern categories of justice? For what specific reason are these relationships endorsed or condemned?

Justice and worship

The issue of justice in the Old Testament is often linked to the question of true worship. The relationship of justice between the human being and his/her neighbor, on the one hand, and between the human being and God, on the other, easily comes into conflict in the context of worship. Worship of God can conceal deficiencies in relationships with fellow human beings. The prophets, in no way against worship as such, uncovered and attacked the discrepancy between the worshiper's devotion and his or her concrete behavior towards a neighbor in dire need. The only worship that would be pleasing to Yahweh would be one that is integrated into a cohesive whole, consisting of a just relationship with God, and one that would affect social life globally.

The underlying argument runs like this. In worship one turns to a God whom one claims to know. To turn to Yahweh and to express one's devotion to him becomes a lie if this worship is carried out while ignoring the essential connection between knowing Yahweh and doing justice. How can anyone dare to turn to Yahweh in devotion and in search of help while oppressing and exploiting one's neighbor? And what is worse, to believe that such exploitation will go unnoticed? This connection between knowing Yahweh and practicing justice is expressed in the famous text of Jeremiah 22:16, which equates knowledge of Yahweh with doing justice:

"Your Father judged the cause of the poor and the needy; then it was well with him; was not this to know me?," says the Lord.
The critique of the prophets is located here. It is directed precisely against elaborate liturgical feasts, the construction of altars and temples, the practice of fasting and of pilgrimages to traditional shrines. These are no longer seen as expressing true religion. Rather, they are used to avoid the real issues and to soothe the conscience by believing that Yahweh might genuinely be pleased with this kind of relationship. Isaiah writes:

What are your endless sacrifices to me?, says Yahweh. I am sick of holocausts of rams and the fat of calves . . . Bring me your worthless offerings no more, the smoke of them fills me with disgust. New Moons, Sabbaths, assemblies . . . your pilgrimages I hate with all my soul . . . Learn to do good, search for justice, help the oppressed, be just to the orphan, plead for the widow (Is 1:11-17).

In summary, we could say that, according to the prophets, knowledge of Yahweh depends on the practice of justice. God cannot be deceived by sacrifice and worship. Justice towards one's neighbor is the primary human responsibility and, therefore, of utmost importance, even before the duty of worship. It is all too easy at times to substitute some pious prayer or alms for the doing of justice. No prayer, no piety, no sacrifice will be pleasing to God if we use them to escape our primary duty of entering into life-giving relationships with God, with ourselves, with our fellow human beings and with creation.

> In his autobiography, Mahatma Ghandi tells how in his student days in South Africa he became deeply interested in the Bible, especially the Sermon on the Mount. He became convinced that Christianity was the answer to the caste system that had plagued India for centuries, and he seriously considered becoming a Christian. One day he went to a church to attend Mass and get instructions. He was stopped at the entrance and gently told that if he desired to attend Mass he was welcome to do so in a church reserved for blacks. He left and never returned. (de Mello).

Justice in the New Testament

a. The "allergy" of Jesus

In the New Testament the concept of justice is linked to the Kingdom theme insofar as justice refers to life-giving relationships. The whole ministry of Jesus is geared towards re-establishing those relationships on which the Covenant was built. His image of God as the compassionate one concerned with justice, his constant critique of his opponents for having ostracized whole groups and his untiring effort to bring those who had been marginalized back into the Covenant community indicate how Jesus understood his mission in terms of justice. He saw his mission in terms of re-establishing relationships which would give life to those whose life had been "diminished" because injustice had been done to them. He came to heal broken relationships which had led to marginalization, exclusion and a decrease in life, and we are called to do the same.

> There was once a woman who was religious and devout and filled with love for God. Each morning she would go to church. And on her way children would call out to her, beggars would accost her, but so immersed was she in her devotion that she did not even see them.

> Now one day she walked down the street in her customary manner and arrived at the church just in time for service. She pushed the door, but it would not open. She pushed it again harder and found the door was locked.

> Distressed at the thought that she would miss service for the first time in years, and not knowing what to do, she looked up. And there, right before

her face, she found a note pinned on the door. It said, "I'm out there!" (de Mello)

However we may describe Jesus' challenge to his contemporaries, one element of his behavior and actions is most obvious: he was extremely sensitive to any kind of discrimination, be it religious, moral, social, cultural, racial, national or gender related. Since he understood his mission as making human beings children of their common Father and brothers and sisters of each other, he lashed out at anything that would not let this community come about. However, this is often overlooked. It is not so much the individual act of justice which Jesus performed that we must consider here, but rather his whole personality that would not tolerate injustice. Jesus was, so to speak, allergic to any kind of discrimination. He demanded the establishment of God-willed relationships, worthy of the Kingdom that had come with him. Anyone who wants to be a follower of Jesus must catch this "allergy" of Jesus. The disciple's most distinctive mark must be his/her alertness and sensitivity to any kind of discrimination in the way that Jesus' whole life revealed it.

b. The key to unlock the Torah: "life-giving relationships and compassion"

How should a person live his/her mission in terms of basic attitudes? Jesus made it clear that the Pharisaic rulings could never be taken as a pattern for his disciples, although we have to keep in mind that Jesus was not against the Law. It was not the Law that was wrong. But it was the way it was interpreted, and consequently applied by the Pharisees, that Jesus strongly objected to. As James D. G. Dunn observes:

> It was not so much the Law to which Jesus objected, as it was the way in which it was used. Not the Law itself, but the use of the Law as a barrier to exclude others, was what he reacted against; and particularly the overscrupulous interpretation of the Law which resulted in a negative judgement against those who failed to conform, the over-definition of the will of God so that the channels of God's grace became ever more restricted, the attitude which assumed that only what was acceptable to one's own group was acceptable to God (*Jesus, Call to Discipleship*, pp. 83-84).

Israel's faith survived in Exile only insofar as the Israelites separated themselves from the influence of the pagan culture. Separation had become a question of religious survival. The common belief was that the Covenant people had been exiled by Yahweh because they had succumbed to paganism in the first place. Their survival now depended on not doing the same mistake once again. The theological reasoning, however, for this separation was ultimately Israel's Covenant with Yahweh which commanded the people:

"Be holy, for I, the Lord your God, am holy"(Lev 19:2). God was holy and, therefore, Israel had to be holy. Being holy became equated with being faithful and being able to survive. The result was that the Jewish social world after the Exile became increasingly structured around the polarities of holiness and separation: clean and unclean, purity and defilement, sacred and profane, Jew and Gentile, righteous and sinner. Holiness became the paradigm by which the Torah was interpreted. The laws in the Torah which placed emphasis on Israel's uniqueness among all other nations and which stressed separation from everything impure became dominant and particularly important within Israel. In short, the hermeneutical key for understanding and interpreting the Torah had become the concepts of "holiness and purity." The test of who was a faithful Jew, loyal to the Covenant in the circumstances of the time, became a question of how far one lived up to the demands of holiness and purity. All movements in the post-exilic time are deeply concerned with, and formed by, these demands. The major known groups were the revolutionists, the Pharisees and the Essenes.

Jesus' quarrel and controversy with the different groups has its ultimate root here. He refused to accept their key for understanding and interpreting the Torah, namely holiness and purity. He saw his mission precisely as being to call to the Kingdom of God those whom the most zealous of Israel had rejected as having put themselves outside the scope of the Covenant. Jesus vigorously objected to this kind of Torah-interpretation since it was in no way compatible with his own experience of God as an all-compassionate and loving Father. Jesus never opposed the Torah itself; rather, it was his interpretation of the Torah that put him at odds with his opponents. Jesus' key for interpreting and understanding the law was "justice" (life-giving relationship) and "compassionate love."

> A student came to the Master and remarked, "In the past there were people who had seen God face to face. Why do we no longer have such people among us?" And the rabbi replied, "Because nobody wants to bend that low" (Hoffsümmer).

Jesus presented a new understanding of *holiness* in Luke 6:36. He put his definition: *"Be compassionate as your Father in heaven is compassionate"* next to the holiness code of Leviticus: *"Be holy, because I, Yahweh your God, am holy"* (Lev 19:2). The "Yahweh your God" of Leviticus becomes "Father" (*Abba*) in Luke; and so the point of reference shifts from God's 'holiness' in Leviticus to God's "compassion" in Luke. Compassion rather than holiness in the sense of "otherness" or "separation" is now the content of our following the Lord. The "compassion code" of Luke 6:27-36 replaces the "holiness code" of Leviticus as the norm of religious behavior.

Be consecrated to me, for I Yahweh, am holy, and I shall set you apart from all these people, for you to be mine (Lev 20:26).

Holiness is here to be understood not as a moral issue only but as integration into the realm of the *divine*. Therefore, it includes separation from the *profane* world. This idea became all the more stressed after the exile. For the Essences the separation was complete. They formed an isolated commune in the wilderness to keep themselves away from everything that could defile them. The Pharisees who lived in the unclean world of a Roman colony tried to keep themselves uncontaminated by avoiding contact with polluted persons or things and by faithfully performing the required purifying rituals when such contact had taken place.

> In the Pharisaic schools *holiness*, the key word of the Priestly Codes is identified with the word *separation*: separation from the heathens and foreigners in order to preserve the identity of the Jewish people; separation or classification among its own members, segregating the priests and the strict observers of the Code from non-observers, the boorish and the common folk (the so- called *am ha-aretz*) (G Soares-Prabhu, *Table Fellowship of Jesus*, p.147).

Comparable observations can be made concerning the purity laws. Jesus was not in any way opposed to purity. Instead he regarded all Israel as pure. He went against every attempt to restrict purity to a special group of people in Israel which would then use that law to put themselves above others, regarding themselves as the true Jews and the rest as renegades. The discrimination of any Israelite violated the original Covenant, hence, Jesus' allergic reaction to it. The justice of the Covenant demanded that all be treated as pure before Yahweh and no one could claim that law as his/her right much less monopolize it.

Since Jesus understood himself as the one who was sent to restore the Covenant, his stand on this issue of purity categorically granted that privilege to all people once again so that all without exception were equally pure before God. The Kingdom he offered was for all and did not know any barriers; it was accessible for anyone and made everyone once again a fellow human being in the Covenant of Israel. God's Kingdom transcended all barriers and reached out to all by creating relationships that were life-giving and embraced each with compassionate love, the righteous as well as the sinners who in particular needed God's forgiving love. Jesus demonstrated this when he pleaded for understanding from those who accused him of seeking the company of sinners and unclean people. How could he make them understand that he had come first of all to seek out the lost and to offer to them God's love and forgiveness? that he had first come to declare them as pure as the righteous could ever claim to be, because they were God's children once again just like the rest of Israel's pure ones?

If one regards Jesus' mission as being meant first for the house of Israel, such reasoning makes sense. The restoration of Israel existed precisely in making all Israelites once more the ideal Israel, that is, a people pure and holy before God (cf. Chilton, *Pure Kingdom: Jesus' Vision of God*).

It is against such a background that Jesus' provoking behavior concerning holiness and purity must be seen. For Jesus "true holiness is no longer defined by a 'separation' from the world which would reflect the 'otherness' of God, but by the 'compassion' which imitates God's utterly unconditional love. Religion is no longer a matter of ritual purity or cultic competence but of interhuman compassion" (G. Soares-Prabhu, *Table Fellowship of Jesus*, p.148).

The different meaning of holiness is most beautifully demonstrated in the Parable of the Good Samaritan. The priest and the Levite who saw the beaten and wounded man in the ditch were not heartless people who could not care less about their fellow human beings in need. The irony is that they were not allowed to help the wounded man. They had to pass by. They would have put themselves in danger of sinning if they had done what the stranger later did. They actually were doing a good deed in passing him by. In doing so, they remained ritually pure and were fulfilling the Law which demanded this, particularly from the priestly class. Jesus on his part insisted that it was "compassion" that demanded a response if one wanted to please God, and not a holiness that did not know human compassion.

> An old monk prayed many years for a vision from God. One day it came. But then, right in the middle of the vision, the monastery bell rang. It was time to feed the poor who gathered daily at the monastery gate. It was the old monk's turn to fed them. If he failed to show up with food, the unfortunate people would leave quietly, thinking the monastery had nothing to give them that day.
>
> The old monk was torn between his earthly duty and his heavenly vision. But before the bell stopped ringing, the monk made his decision. With a heavy heart, he turned his back on the vision and went off to feed the poor.
>
> Nearly an hour later, the old monk returned to his room. When he opened the door, he could hardly believe his eyes. There in the room was the vision, waiting for him. As the monk dropped to his knees in thanksgiving, the vision said to him, "My son, had you not gone off to feed the poor, I would not have stayed."

Jesus severely questions this kind of interpretation of the Law. For him what comes first is the person in need and no prescription of purity that violates the basic fundamental demand of loving one's neighbor as oneself. Holiness and purity that overlook the person in need are against the primary obligation that God demands from each of us, namely to do justice, which means to enter into life-giving relationships with our fellow human beings.

If one reads the Gospels carefully, it is easy to discover that Jesus was ultimately rejected and put to death because of his way of interpreting the Torah in terms of justice and compassion. His healing on the Sabbath, his eating with unclean hands, his table fellowship with the outcasts and sinners had only one aim: to create a new community in which life-giving relationships would guarantee the fullness of life to everyone and put an end to all discrimination. *"Be compassionate because your Father is compassionate"* becomes the basic rule of conduct.

For Jesus God is not primarily experienced as 'holy', separated from the 'profane' by sharply defined demarcation lines of purity. Jesus experienced God as the one who reaches out in forgiveness and love to all people, across all the lines of separation that we like to draw. His table fellowship with tax collectors and sinners is an acted-out parable through which he brings home to his audience his personal experience of God as "Abba", who wants to draw all people to himself.

In acting like this Jesus, demonstrated what God's Kingdom was all about: the creation of a new community in which all would be brothers and sisters, where there would no longer be any marginalization, but all would be gathered into the one great family of persons created according to the image and likeness of God, the Triune in One.

"Prisoner at the bar," said the Grand Inquisitor. "You are charged with encouraging people to break the laws, traditions and customs of our holy religion. How do you plead?"

"Guilty, your Honor."

"And with frequenting the company of heretics, prostitutes, public sinners, the extortionist tax collectors, the colonial conquerors of our nation - in short, the excommunicated. How do you plead?"

"Guilty, your Honor."

"Finally, you are charged with revising, correcting, calling into question the sacred tenets of our faith. How do you plead?"

"Guilty, your Honor."

"What is your name, prisoner?"

"Jesus Christ, your Honor" (de Mello).

And this was to become the mission of the disciples as well: to go out into the whole world and gather people from all nations, races and cultures into this great new family of God. That this mission consists in establishing God's justice on the earth is expressed in Matthew 19:28 where he outlines the mission of the twelve as that of "judging" the twelve tribes of Israel. The Greek word *krinein* is not correctly translated by "to judge." That is too narrow. Its meaning has to be seen in the light of the prophetic announcements of Yahweh's final coming to "judge" the world. In the prophetic expectation, the phrase "God's coming to judge the nations" means that he will establish justice in the midst of his people and through them among all the nations. He will bring the world to a new state of justice and peace. As described here with the word *krinein*, the mission of the Twelve means, therefore, "to establish God's eschatological justice in Israel and in all the nations." The mission of the disciples (Church) is fundamentally geared to the Kingdom value of establishing the justice of the end time (cf. Horsley, *Jesus and the Spiral of Violence,* pp. 199-208).

Others have drawn the same conclusion, insisting that justice to the poor and the liberation of the oppressed form the heart of the symbol Kingdom of God and belong to its core meaning. We therefore can only affirm the observation made by D. Brackley who writes:

> When Jesus drew from Isaiah's oracles of consolation with their good news to the poor and afflicted, to explain God's coming reign, it would have been impossible for him to use these in a less-than-concrete sense. He would have been proclaiming the coming of another God and starting another religion in radical discontinuity with the Old Testament (*Divine Revolution*, p. 130).

It is obvious that Jesus' whole life and ministry, seen from such a perspective, was a constant struggle to establish God's justice here on earth. He came to lead all into God's life-giving relationships, and he expected those who let themselves be drawn into the Kingdom he preached to live from then on in life-giving relationships with all people. Justice, therefore, was the key concept of Jesus' whole life and ministry. The community that follows the Lord and walks in his footsteps has no other task than that of imitating the pattern of his life, thus continuing the proclamation and enactment of the Kingdom.

> To be a disciple means to put one's feet in the footsteps of Jesus and, in the power of the Spirit, to continue in one's own historical time and place his mission of announcing and signing the coming of the reign of God. Together as church, the community of disciples is in a unique way called to be the instrument of the reign of God in history. Since peace and justice are among the most powerful signs of the reign of God present in the world, it belongs

to the essential mission of the church to make these realities more visible in our time, so marked by oppression, violence, injustice and threat of total destruction (E. Johnson, *Consider Jesus*, p. 77).

Justice and the Integrity of Creation

The issue of justice understood as life-giving relationships includes also our relationship with nature. We can neither become nor remain truly human if we do not develop a relationship with our environment that is according to Kingdom values. The issue of ecology, with its concern for justice for the planet and the species of this earth, calls into question every theological topic dealt with in purely anthropocentric terms. If nature becomes the context of theology, a biblical basis for the issues of ecology can be easily developed. The Kingdom present demands from anyone who claims to be a disciple of Jesus a new life-giving relationship with creation.

The ecological crisis has its origin in the "mechanistic" way we symbolize the world process. This metaphor means viewing the environment simply as a source of raw material and a dumpsite for waste. Nature has value only if it can be forced into our mechanistic imagination. Many regard the "mechanistic metaphor" as the "culprit" of the ecological crisis. It is our inordinate tendency to have, to rule and to possess at all costs that has created the misuse of nature.

> The student asked the Zen Master, "What is the way?" And the Master answered, "Everyday-way is the true way." And the student asked, "Can I study it?" But the Master answered, "The more you study, the further from the way you are." "But if I didn't study it," the student asked, "how can I know it?" And the Master taught, "The way does not belong to things seen nor to things unseen. It does not belong to things known, nor to things unknown. Do not seek it, study or name it. To find yourself in it, simply open yourself as wide as the sky."

Openness to creation is one way to become more whole.

Are there alternative images of the world process? The oldest known is what we might call the "organic metaphor," which sees the whole world in terms of the evolutionary process. Most traditional cultures have lived for ages out of this metaphor. Its strength is in seeing all things as being interrelated. Its drawback is having no concept of development but only the experience of the world as a "cyclic process." Neither our "mechanistic metaphor" nor the "organic metaphor" would suffice dealing with the crisis of the environment in which we find ourselves today. The hope was that the mechanistic metaphor would free us from the domination of nature. But the mechanistic metaphor places a few in control, treating the rest as mere cogs in the machine. The organic metaphor, on the other hand, makes humans the objects of "fate." In other words, while the mechanistic metaphor makes nature the victim of humanity, the organic metaphor tends to make humankind the victim of nature.

How can we strike a balance? Although there have been various responses to this issue, a new cosmology is needed to achieve an integral synthesis. We need a new metaphor, a new symbol, or even a new vision of creation and the world process if all the efforts to save the planet are to get us anywhere. Some have suggested that we must gratefully accept our creative powers in order to comprehend how these powers may be models of cooperation and complementarity with nature rather than models of domination and exploitation.

From the biblical viewpoint, we can say that all human behavior has consequences because of the nature of the physical-spiritual universe in which God has placed us. The universe is subject to a moral order that cannot be disregarded without serious consequences. We will have to bear with the consequences of our actions because of the nature of the physical, spiritual, and moral universe God has created - which reflects, of course, the very character of God. The universe is ordered not just logically, psychologically or sociologically, but also ecologically. The ecological perspective affirms and encompasses all other dimensions. The relationship between humanity and its environment is symbiotic - a mutually supportive, interdependent living with - rather than a parasitic living off.

> According to the Bible, we do not really understand the ecology of the world until we recognize its source, the Lord God and that the space-time physical world is interpreted and held together by a spiritual world and by spiritual energy that comes from God. From this standpoint, we really are not thinking ecologically - even from a scientific point of view — if we do not include the dimension of the Spirit (H. A. Snyder, *Models of the Kingdom*, p. 140).

The Kingdom of God transcends all ecological concerns since it aims at the transformation of the whole of creation. This world is the object of God's ultimate plan, and therefore, the search for an ecological balance of nature is also at the very heart of the Kingdom of God.

> Salvation is about healing and, just as the cosmos itself can be ruptured and torn apart by injustice, so too it can be healed by all human efforts to bring justice, which is balance, back to human relationships to earth, air, fire, water, and one another (Fox quoted in *Earthspirit,* p.49).

PEACE

Peace is a reality that follows wherever justice reigns. Peace cannot exist without justice. It affects our four basic relationships: with God, ourselves, our neighbor and nature. It is a gift from God and not something we can accomplish ourselves. It is the gift of the coming Kingdom.

Peace in the Old Testament

"Shalom" is one of the words in Scripture which cannot be translated literally. This word and its derivatives occur more than 350 times in the Old Testament. The root meaning of shalom in the Old Testament is "to be sound," "to be safe." It means "well-being" with a strong material emphasis.

Fundamentally it refers to wholeness, total health, total welfare. Anything that contributes to wholeness can be expressed in terms of shalom. It covers the sum total of God's blessings on a person who belongs to the Covenant community. In a community where shalom reigns, harmony and opportunity for growth exist for every person.

> We constrict the term shalom if we equate it with "peace." . . . In many instances shalom really signifies bodily health or well-being and the related satisfaction. More commonly shalom is referred to a group, e.g., a nation enjoying prosperity . . . This brings us to the great number of passages in which shalom denotes a relationship rather than a state. The relationship may be that of a people. It may naturally exist between individuals too (G. Von Rad, *"eirene", Theological Dictionary of the New Testament II*, p. 402-403).

In the Greco-Roman world, peace does not primarily denote a relationship among several persons, but rather a state or a condition. It is a "time of peace" or a "state of peace" considered as an interval in a continuous state of war. In Greek thought peace means the absence of war. In Hebrew thought the opposite of shalom is not war but injustice (cf. H. Hendrickx, *Peace, Anyone?*, p. 10).

What the Old Testament means by shalom is best expressed in a text found twice in the Old Testament, in Micah and Isaiah. The passage envisions what will happen when God comes to bring his Kingdom into this world and when people are willing to let this reality into their lives:

> *And they shall beat their swords into plowshares, and their spears into pruning hooks; nation shall not lift up sword against nation, neither shall they learn war anymore; but they shall sit every man under his vine and under his fig tree, and no one shall make them afraid; for the mouth of the Lord of Hosts has spoken (Mi 4:3-4; see Is 2:4).*

Micah presents here a vision of what will be when the nations submit themselves to God's Kingdom. In a nutshell there are two fundamental changes that will take place in the individual and in the nations at large: (1) no war anymore and even no training for war and no war industry; and, (2) the return to a simple and peaceful life-style, concerned not with accumulating more and more, but rather with fostering interpersonal relationships. According to the prophet, when this submission takes place, the whole war machine will be dismantled and a new social order will emerge. He envisions a transformed human consciousness and a new public policy. It is the age-old dream of every Israelite: to settle for a simple standard of living, content with vine and fig trees. The peace envisioned here demands a shift in priorities wherein greed will end, exploitation will cease and an entirely new social order will take over. Brueggemann comments on the radicalness of its vision:

> It anticipates nothing less than the dismantling of the presently-known world for the sake of an alternative world not yet embodied (W. Brueggemann, *To Act Justly...*, p. 11).

The prophet Micah hints at what will be of concern for people when the Kingdom takes hold of them. They will be concerned with their fellow human beings, and they will be contented with a simple life and a peaceful environment around them. We might find this to be utopian and utterly other-worldly. If, however, we look closer at this prophecy, we can easily discover the two great human temptations which have always plagued humanity and our age and time in particular: a war mentality and a consumer mentality. In a rather strong way John Paul II addressed these two mentalities in his 1993 New Year Peace Message. The text is worth quoting:

> Nothing is solved by war; on the contrary, everything is placed in jeopardy by war. The results of this scourge are the suffering and death of innumerable individuals, the disintegration of human relations and the irreparable loss of an immense artistic and environmental patrimony. War worsens the suffering of the poor; indeed, it creates new poor by destroying means of subsistence, homes and property, and by eating away at the very fabric of social environment. Young people see their hopes for the future shattered and too often, as victims, they become irresponsible agents of conflicts. Women, children, the elderly, the sick and the wounded are forced to flee and become refugees who have no possession beyond what they can carry with them. Helpless and defenseless, they seek refuge in other countries or regions often as poor and turbulent as their own. . . . After so many unnecessary massacres, it is in the final analysis of fundamental importance to recognize, once and for all, that **war never helps the human community**, that violence destroys and never builds up, that the wounds it causes remain long unhealed,

and that as a result of conflicts the already grim condition of the poor deteriorates still further, and new forms of poverty appear (4). In today's industrialized countries people are dominated by the frenzied race for possessing material goods. The consumer society makes the gap separating rich from poor even more obvious, and the uncontrolled search for a comfortable life risks blinding people, to the needs of others. In order to promote the social, cultural, spiritual and also economic welfare of all members of society, it is therefore absolutely essential to stem the unrestrained consumption of earthly goods and to control the creation of artificial needs. **Moderation and simplicity ought to become the criteria of our daily lives.** The quantity of goods consumed by a tiny fraction of the world population produces a demand greater than available resources. A reduction of this demand constitutes a first step in alleviating poverty, provided that it is accompanied by effective measures to guarantee a fair distribution of the world's wealth (5).

Isaiah 65:20-23 presents us with another vision of what would happen if the peace of the Kingdom of God were given a chance here on earth. It describes what God wants to see happen in the human community. This has been called the Isaiah Agenda (R. Fung, *The Isaiah Vision*, pp. 5-11). Its objectives are clear and specific:

Children will not die
Old people will live in dignity
Those who build houses will live in them
Those who plant vineyards will eat their fruit.

The vision clearly expresses God's plan and hope for the human community. God desires that children don't die, that old people live in dignity, and that those who work enjoy the fruit of their labor. Most astonishing is its seemingly immediate relevance for today. It is not about paradise or a world to come but about human history, about the here and now. In theological terms, the text does not offer what is most pleasing to God, the fully developed and happy person. Rather it insists on what is minimally acceptable to God concerning human behavior towards our brothers and sisters.

Of course, in this agenda we can find what is included in many manifestos of political parties and secular governments, but this does not make it less a biblical vision. If we believe that God's Kingdom makes itself felt anywhere, then we have here a clear indication - to use a parable of Jesus - that the "leaven of the Kingdom is penetrating the dough of this world." The beauty of the agenda is that we are assured of what God wants of us, what his will for us is now. Here something is offered to which everyone can make a contribution and so make the Kingdom of God felt in our midst.

A story is told about a village on a South Pacific Island where a missionary made his monthly visit to celebrate the Eucharist, baptize children and pray for the recently deceased. In this particular village a unique custom is practiced whenever the missionary arrives in his seaplane.

By tradition, the village chief is the first to greet the padre when he steps on land. The two of them embrace, then the chieftain gives the priest a clump of dune grass. The priest returns the clump of grass to the chief, who then turns and gives it to the person next to him. According to island custom, the clump of earth and grass is a sacred reminder of God's presence to the people who live with the vast ocean about them. The islanders consider it a type of sacramental symbolizing harmony and peace.

This sacred clump of grass passes from one villager to the next, throughout the entire village, until it returns to the chief, who then presents it to the priest, completing the ritual. The custom with the sacred clump of grass symbolizes that the villagers are in harmony with one another and are at peace. It is at this point that the Mass can begin, and not before.

On this particular visit the padre went about his other duties as usual. When the customary time neared for the joyous celebration of the Eucharist, word came to the priest that there was going to be a delay. It seems that there was a bitter disagreement between a father and son, and the clump of grass had not been exchanged between them. There was no celebration of the Mass that month or the next. It took three months before harmony and peace was restored to that family and to the island village (Cavanaugh).

Peace in the New Testament

In the New Testament the word peace is used with at least five different meanings:

(1) as the absence of war or chaos;
(2) as right relationship with God or with Christ;
(3) as good relationship among people;
(4) as an individual state, that is, tranquility or serenity;
(5) as part of a greeting formula.

Two, three and four are of particular importance to our discussion. In the New Testament the word "eirene" (peace) occurs ninety-one times, and means above all, well-being and eschatological salvation. According to the Jesus of the Gospels, peace means wholeness and comprises physical, social, and spiritual elements. When Jesus heals a person he says, *"Go in peace"* (Mk 5:34; Lk 8:48). This peace is not only physical, often it is social as well. When Jesus tells the woman with the hemorrhage, *"Go in peace,"* he indicates that she has been newly reintegrated into society, that she is once again a full member of the community. The same can be observed when he says to the woman with the ointment, *"Go in peace"* (Lk 7:50). At that moment Jesus rebukes those who had ostracized her and restores her to society.

Peace as right relationship with God or with Christ, the vertical dimension of peace, comes close to reconciliation and harmony. It is God's act which restores people to a right relationship with himself (Rom 5:1; Acts 10:36). Peace as good relationships among people is a logical and natural extension of this meaning. The right relationship with God should result in good relationships among people. To live in peace means, positively, to live in harmony, and negatively, to avoid any action that would cause disharmony or contention (Mk 9:50; 2 Cor 13:11; Col 3:15).

The Christian meaning of peace, e.g., "serenity," "tranquility," and "peace of mind," is not part of the meaning of the term in either the Hebrew or Greek secular world. The peace that Jesus leaves with us and gives to us (Jn 14:27) is clearly contrasted with worry and fear. The verse can be restructured in this way:

> Peace of mind (or serenity) is what I leave with you. The peace of mind that comes from me - this is what I am giving you. Do not be afraid, worried or upset.

A person who has entered into a right relationship with God and has good relationship; with people will, as a consequence, experiences peace of mind, serenity and tranquility (D. C. Arichea, *"Peace in the New Testament,"* pp. 201-206).

In short, peace, or the Hebrew word *shalom,* means wholeness, reconciliation, the harmony of having come to full authenticity concerning our four basic relationships: with ourselves, our neighbor, nature and God. Shalom is the ultimate state of fulfillment and the great gift of the end-time. It means not only the absence of war but also the fullness of life.

The Gospel of John sees Jesus' entire mission as related to bringing the eschatological peace announced by the prophets. "Shalom" in John is bound up with Jesus' passion and death. Unlike the Synoptic Gospels, in John it is only after the resurrection that Jesus will greet his disciples with the salutation, *"Peace!"* The Shalom that he has gained for them through his suffering and death is the great gift of the risen Lord to his disciples on Easter morning. *"Peace is my farewell to you. Peace is my gift to you"* *(14:27). "I have told you all this so that you may find peace in me"* *(16:33).* It is the reconciliation of the world with God, the eschatological peace that Jesus was to bring to this world (20:20, 21, 26). Therefore, whatever concerns the Kingdom concerns peace.

JOY

The basic meaning of joy, "chara" (noun) and "charo" (verb), in the Bible is in reference to physical comfort and well-being. The word appears 133 times in the New Testament (20 times in Luke; 11 in Acts; 18 in John; 12 in Matthew; 14 in Philippians; 13 in 2 Corinthians; 7 in Romans; and 6 in 1 Thessalonians). It refers most often to the joy of the eschatological fulfillment of the end-time, in short, to the Kingdom that is experienced as already present now.

Joy is a recurring refrain of the parables. It is used, for example, in relation to finding what was lost (Lk 15), a treasure in the field, and a pearl of great price (Mt 13:44-45). Joy in the biblical sense means LIFE. It is the expression of FULLNESS, LIFE and LOVE. The Kingdom of God is a matter of life and love in abundance. After all, THE image of heaven in the Bible is the WEDDING FEAST where the happiness and joy of all are guaranteed. The basic mood of the company that followed Jesus was joy because with Jesus the Kingdom had arrived. How could they fast and mourn since the Kingdom was breaking into their life? Joy must remain the basic mood of any disciple. It becomes the sign of the presence of the Kingdom now - and sometimes it is most genuine in moments of pain and insecurity.

Once upon a time there was a poor lumber jack. He lived very happily with his family in a small hut on the outskirts of the forest. Although he could hardly make ends meet by chopping wood, there was laughter and singing to be heard coming from his house every night. People in the neighborhood were amazed and puzzled.

The king, who had to pass the house every day on his way to the castle, resented such simple joys. "What reason do these laborers have for their laughter?" he asked with bitter anger in his voice. One day he sent his messenger to the house of the lumber jack with the order, "My Lord and King demands from you fifty bags of wooden chips by tomorrow morning. If you do not fulfill this order, you and your family will die."

"I will certainly not be able to do this," he said to his wife, Buts she consoled him saying, "My dear husband, life has been good to us. We have enjoyed one another's company and that of our children, and we have tried to share our joy with those around us. You are right, we will not be able to fill the bags. Therefore, let us have a feast with our children and friends. Just as we have lived, so we want to die."

And so it happened that the poor people in the small hut celebrated their most beautiful and joyous feast. After midnight the guests left, one after the other. Only the lumber jack and his wife remained.

Sadness filled their hearts as morning dawned. "Now we are finished, the woman wailed." But her husband consoled her, "Let it be. Better to die in peace and joy than to spend our lives in sadness and fear."

At that moment there was a knock on the door. The lumber jack opened it wide to let the King's messenger in. The servant approached hesitantly and after a moment of silence said, "Please, prepare twelve panels of oak for a coffin. The King died during this night" (Hoffsümmer).

In concrete terms, JOY means giving to each person the space to unfold and to become creative according to his/her abilities and gifts. Since it is to be understood in a holistic sense, i.e., including all aspects of human existence, it refers in the present world to what we call "matters of human rights." Every creature has a right to life on this earth which God has given to us as a common heritage to enjoy and to share in all its richness.

In the Holy Spirit

This phrase refers to all three characteristics of the Kingdom: justice, peace and joy. It is the most important aspect of our present discussion. Since the Kingdom on earth is an anticipation of the New Heaven and the New Earth, it can only be a creation of the Holy Spirit, the one who will bring forth the New Creation. Therefore, we can only possess the gifts of the Kingdom as a "foretaste" or a "foreshadowing" of what is to come. Nevertheless, they can be experienced and identified as the Kingdom present and operative now in the midst of our world.

Hildegard of Bingen reflects on the Spirit's action throughout the whole of creation in this way:

O Holy Spirit,
Clear fountain,
in you we perceive God,
how he gathers the perplexed and seeks the lost.
Bulwark of life,
you are the hope of oneness for that which is separate.
You are the girdle of propriety,
you are holy salvation.

Shelter those caught in evil,
free those in bondage,
for the divine power wills it.
You are the mighty way in which
everything that is in the heavens,

on the earth, and under the earth,
is penetrated with connectedness,
is penetrated with relatedness.

Anyone who opens him/herself to the presence of the Kingdom now will receive these gifts. The test of whether and to what extent he\she has let the Kingdom in his/her life will be in the measure to which a person is committed to bringing about justice, peace and joy. Wherever the Kingdom makes itself felt it does so in bringing about justice, peace and joy, because the Kingdom is a matter of these three; justice, peace and joy in the Holy Spirit (Rom 14:17).

How these three fundamental characteristics should determine any theological description of the Kingdom can be seen in the following definitions of the Kingdom by E. Schillebeeckx:

THE KINGDOM OF GOD is the saving presence of God, active and encouraging, as it is affirmed or welcomed among men and women. It is a saving presence offered by God andfreely accepted by men and women which takes concrete form above all in justice and peaceful relationships among individuals and peoples, in the disappearance of sickness, injustice and oppression and in the restoration of life of all that was dead and dying.

THE KINGDOM OF GOD is a new world in which suffering is abolished, a world of completely whole or healed men and women in a society where peace reigns and there are no master-slave relationships - quite a different situation from that of the society of the time. As things are there "it may not be so among you" (Lk 22:24-27).

THE KINGDOM OF GOD is a changed new relationship (metanoia) of men and women with God, the tangible and visible side of which is a new type of liberating relationship among men and women with a reconciling society, in a peaceful natural environment (*Church the Human Story of God*, pp. 116-133).

Reflection: *Act justly, love tenderly, walk humbly*

The healing of a disfigured world can come about if we believe that Christ's message of God's Kingdom is calling us to create and live *"life-giving relationships"* that are intimate and lasting. In this world, which is the creation of God's love, we are not to be only passive recipients of love and grace, but privileged partners bearing a great responsibility. But we do not need mere strategies or weapons to establish a political system worthy of humanity. What we need are men and women who are one in a relationship of respect, above all with the 'other'; who listen and are able to perceive the action of God in the other; who do not play the part of masters but of servants, brothers, sisters. As Hildegard of Bingen says:

> And as human persons view creation with compassion in trust,
> they see the Lord.
> It is God which humankind is then able to recognize in every living thing.
> Does not humanity know that God is the world's creator?
> Just as it occurred to God to create humankind,
> so it occurs to God to save those that trust in him.

QUESTION: What is more important for me: developing authentic relationships or seeking personal achievements?

Meditation

Outside the restaurant,
costly menu
and comfortable smells of food,
a child sits, begging.
The people pass by,
loud laughter, full appetites,
good friendship,
and the child cries,
though no one can hear:
Sons of David, have pity on me.

A homeless girl passes by the bungalows
in view of the sea and the mountains:
All are second houses
and she cries, and with her cries
half the world, though no one can hear:
Daughters of David, have pity on me.

Lord, make sure we can hear,
for it is your voice,
the voice calling for justice.
I know I am not the problem,
There is little I can do,
but I can be part of the solution.
Jesus, Son of God, have pity on me.

QUESTION: **Am I already plagued by 'compassion-fatigue' and do I refuse to see the injustice and the suffering around me?**

As committed Christians today we might be small in number, but we are called to be large in vision and concern. The message of Jesus, as he proclaimed it in Luke 4:18-19, *The Spirit of the Lord has been given to me* .... *He has sent me to bring good news to the poor, to proclaim liberty to captives and to the blind new sight, to set the downtrodden free, to proclaim the Lord's year of favor*, is for today and for all nations.

The basic Christian call to *"love one another as I have loved you"* has a global dimension today. The words of the Indian poet and mystic Rabindranath Tagore apply to all of us, no matter what country or place of birth and ministry:

Leave this chanting and singing and telling of beads! Whom dost thou worship in this lonely dark corner of a temple with all doors shut? Open thine eyes and see thy God is not before thee! He is there where the tiller is tilling the hard ground and where the pathmaker is breaking stones. He is with them in sun and in shower, and his garment is covered with dust. Put off thy holy mantle and even like him come down on the dusty soil! Deliverance? Where is this deliverance to be found? Our master himself has joyfully taken upon him the bonds of creation; he is bound with us all for ever. Come out of thy meditations and leave aside thy flowers and incense! What harm is there if thy clothes become tattered and stained? Meet him and stand by him in toil and in the sweat of thy brow (Rabindranath Tagore).

QUESTION: **Many active members of the Church today consider a commitment to justice, peace and the integrity of creation a significant component of their agenda. What do I fear to lose when I stand up for human rights and justice?**

The Beatitudes

Blessed are the poor in spirit,
those who recognize the sin of injustice in our world, who acknowledge responsibility for it, who admit they are unable to overcome injustice by their own strength, who listen with humble and open hearts to your Word, O God, as you show us new paths towards action in the course of justice. - *Theirs is the Kingdom of Heaven.*

Blessed are the meek,
those who commit themselves to fulfilling God's plan, who deal with power by serving others, who deal with possessions by using them on behalf of the poor, or deal with prestige by avoiding show or titles. - *They shall inherit the land*

Blessed are those who mourn,
those who see the brokenness and alienation within our society, the materialism and consumerism that tear families apart, the ideology that justifies destruction of people and the environment; those who mourn the prejudices, fears, guilt and pain that alienate us from one another; those who know their need of healing. - *They shall be comforted.*

Blessed are those who hunger and thirst for justice,
those who are not satisfied until they experience God's life, his saving power and his care, those who pray for justice, who seek its power in reflection, who knock until the liberating presence of God is made known to them and to the whole world. - *They shall be satisfied.*

Blessed are those who show mercy,
those who forgive failings, hurts and sins, show God's care for those in need, and build up people, groups, the whole world. Who treat all people as the image of God. - *They shall receive mercy.*

Blessed are the pure of heart,
those who show genuine care; those who can be still and know that God is God-with-us and that God cares for us; those who listen to and care about all those voices, all those cares of the universe that are part of God's care. - *They shall see God.*

Blessed are the peacemakers,
those who recognize and affirm the dignity of each person, who consider each person to be precious in the eyes of God, who strive to come to full reconciliation and to live the Gospel in their lifestyles and relationships. - *They shall be called God's children.*

Blessed are those persecuted for justice's sake,
those who suffer rejection because they have experienced God's Word in their hearts and are awakened to God's justice and love; those who are rejected when they share the Good News with their brothers and sisters; those called to be salt of the earth and light of the world. - *The reign of God is theirs.*

QUESTION: How do the Beatitudes affect my life? What makes me feel uneasy when I hear them?

Chapter Eleven

Conversion: Constant Demand of the Kingdom

Jesus joined the statement that the Kingdom of God was a present reality at hand to a declaration that conversion was needed if one was to respond to God's coming in him. This response to the Kingdom "at hand" is described in the words: *repent and believe.*

The word "repentance" is a collective term used by the evangelists primarily to summarize the response Jesus sought from the people. Jesus expressed its meaning in two phrases: "to follow him as a disciple" and "to believe." However, the traditional term "repentance" as used in the New Testament can easily cover a whole range of meanings. Once this term is seen in relation to its Old Testament origins, it can mean becoming poor, giving up everything or following the Lord in absolute obedience.

Since the Kingdom is a dynamic power that constantly breaks into this world, the call for repentance is a permanent one directed at everyone, not only at sinners, but also at the righteous who have committed no grave sins. What then does the phrase "repent," "be converted," mean in the proclamation of Jesus' Kingdom message? Using biblical images, we could picture conversion in the following terms:

Turn around: "Let the Kingdom into your life"

To *convert* does not mean, first of all, to return to the Law and to make amends for one's transgressions of the Law. To repent does not primarily mean to *turn away*, to leave one's way of life, to leave behind everything that is wrong and sin-permeated. No, to convert means first of all: *to turn towards*, to respond to the invitation to let God into my life, a God who loves me, forgives me and is always with me. One is asked to let this new, unheard-of message change one's life, to let oneself be overtaken by this great news and to look at reality in a new way.

> "Why do you never preach repentance?" said the preacher.
> "It's the only thing I teach," said the Master.
> "But I never hear you speak on sorrow for sin."
> "Repentance isn't sorrow for the past.
> The past is dead and isn't worth a moment's grief.
> Repentance is a change of mind: a radically different vision of reality."
> (A. de Mello, *One Minute Nonsense*, p. 241)

Of course, such a *turning around* towards the Kingdom will include a *turning away*. But what makes one turn is the actual breaking in of the Kingdom of God and not some demand to make oneself ready for its future coming. Real conversion is possible only if one can imagine such a God, if one can envision such a love as real and actual now. The question of conversion is: are we willing to let this image of a loving, forgiving, always present God into our lives? Are we ready to let Jesus' vision of reality determine our actions and behavior?

A poet has tried to guess what went on in Peter's mind after he had denied knowing Jesus. He writes:

> In Peter's dreams
> the cock still crowed.
> He returned to Galilee
> to throw nets into the sea
> and watch them sink
> like memories into the darkness.
> He did not curse the sun
> that rolled down his back
> or the wind that drove
> the fish beyond his nets.
> He only waited for the morning
> when the shore mist would lift
> and from his boat he would see him.
> Then after a naked and impetuous swim
> with the sea running from his eyes
> he would find a cook with holes in his hands
> and stooped over dawn coals
> who would offer him the Kingdom of God
> for breakfast.
> (Link, *Journey*)

"Becoming a Child"

The metaphor "becoming a child" (Mk 10:15; Lk 18:17) presents us with another way of understanding conversion:

> Amen, I say to you, whoever does not accept the Kingdom of God like a child will not enter it (Mk 10:15).

At the time of Jesus, children ranked very low on the social scale. Since children did not yet know the Torah they could not claim any merit before God. A child was considered "a person of no significance, deserving neither special attention nor special favors." This makes Jesus' attitude towards children all the more surprising.

There are three groups of sayings in the Gospel that relate children to the Kingdom. The first group insists that the *"Kingdom belongs to them"* (Mt 19:14; Mk 10:13-16; Lk 18:17); the second group states that only *"in becoming like children can we enter the Kingdom"* (Mt 18:3); and, the third group explains that anyone who receives a child receives Christ himself (Mt 10:40; Mk 9:37; Lk 18:17). In addition, there are two occasions where Jesus heals children (Mk 5:35-43; 7:24-30). Finally, he is "indignant" over the disciples' rebuke of those who brought children to him.

By promising the Kingdom to children, Jesus challenged contemporary theological thinking on merit, reward and the entire patriarchal society by declaring that the child's incapacity to earn the Kingdom was its greatest asset. Being "like a child" means one has nothing to give and nothing to show in order to gain the Kingdom. It means a helplessness, a being without any claim of deserving or earning the Kingdom. By no means does Jesus advocate childishness or put forward a naively romanticizing attitude towards children. It is the absolute gratuitousness of the Kingdom that is stressed. To say that God is gracious means that the relationship with God is not dependent on performance or merit. God is gracious to each one of us prior to any achievement on our part.

> Whenever one says that God's love depends upon having met requirements of any kind, one has abandoned grace as the dominant image of reality, no matter how much the language of grace remains (M. J. Borg, *Jesus A New Vision*, p. 102).

The child imagery opens up a vast array of Kingdom qualities; trust, humility, obedience, a forgiving spirit, as well as a helplessness and dependence. The Kingdom "belongs" to the children in the sense that children appreciate a gift as an absolute, something which they know they could not have earned or deserved.

"Becoming a child" is the precondition of entry into the Kingdom. Jesus asks those who want to follow him to take an immediate and all-important step in order to enter the Kingdom. Adults are judged as being out of step with what it means to be human in the eyes of God. We are asked to abandon false values such as status, power and wealth. These values are signs of an inauthentic being, and barriers to entering the Kingdom of God. In the Sermon on the Mount Jesus makes it quite clear that they are the three great barriers we have to overcome to understand Jesus and the Kingdom of God.

Instead of seeking prestige and status, the Kingdom requires that we humble ourselves, get rid of our self-given importance which is measured on the basis of worldly values. Rather we are asked to find our true vocation in obedient service of God. In so doing we become one with Jesus. We become his disciples. "Being a child" indicates more than a change of direction. It implies a new life and a rebirth as expressed explicitly in this Johannine imagery:

> *Jesus answered and said to him, "Amen, Amen, I say to you no one can see the Kingdom of God without being born from above. Nicodemus said to him, "How can a person once grown old be born again? Surely he cannot re-enter his mother's womb and be born again, can he?" Jesus answered, "Amen, Amen, I say to you, no one can enter the Kingdom of God without being born of water and Spirit" (Jn 3:3-5).*

Jesus' demand of "becoming a child" expresses the necessity for adults to make a new beginning, to show a new responsiveness and openness to God and other people. We are asked to learn and re-learn the ways of God. Only then will we rediscover our lost potential and gain integrity and wholeness (B. Chilton and J. I. H. McDonald, *Jesus and the Ethics of the Kingdom,* pp. 87-88).

Well up: "Let it well up from within you"

In the Gospel of John Jesus employs the image of a well to explain what conversion could mean (Jn 4:7-15 the Samaritan woman at the well). The Kingdom here becomes a symbol for the Holy Spirit who dwells in the depth of each human person. The prospect that Jesus holds out to the woman, that he could give her water that would become a spring in her, is first of all an invitation to become a disciple of his. He is saying to her, "Let the water I can give into your life." Jesus was referring here to the Spirit that those who opened themselves to him and his words would receive.

> *"If anyone thirsts, let him come to me and drink. He who believes in me, from within him shall flow rivers of living water." He was referring to the Spirit which those who came to believe in him were to receive. For there was as yet no Spirit, since Jesus had not been glorified (Jn 7:37-39).*

Only Jesus could give the woman the life-giving water for which she was really searching. According to rabbinic teaching: "The disciple who is beginning is like a well that can give only water it has received, but the more advanced disciple becomes like a spring that gives living water." Jesus was telling the woman that if she followed him she would not only be filled with life-giving water but she herself will become a spring that would never run dry.

Conversion here means to let the life-giving waters of the Holy Spirit well up from within us and bring us to life. In Luke 17:20-21 Jesus speaks about the Kingdom not as coming in signs and wonders but as the Kingdom "within us." The early Church Fathers understood this to mean the Kingdom is within our reach; it is so close and intimate that we can take hold of it if we really want to.

There is no need to search for the Kingdom as something still to come. Wherever one lives the Kingdom is always within reach. Whoever cares for his/her brothers and sisters and serves them joyfully, wherever they may be, already lives in the Kingdom; it has already arrived. Here is a little story by Albert Schweitzer to illustrate the point:

There was once a little brother who lived many happy years in a monastery where he did the household chores for the community with joy and contentment. One day while he was just doing the dishes, an angel came and told him, "The Lord sends me personally to tell you your time is up, you are called to God's eternal Kingdom." The little brother joyfully said, "What a surprise, I am really grateful that the Lord does remember me. But, dear angel, as you can see, there are so many dishes left, I cannot just leave now. You'll certainly agree I would be very ungrateful to my brothers here to leave all this work undone and just disappear. Perhaps the Good Lord could postpone my eternity until I am finished with this work." The angel looked understandingly into his eyes and said, "You're right, I'll see what I can do for you and bring your request before the Lord." After that the angel disappeared, and the brother finished his dishes and many other things afterwards.

One day when the brother was in the garden weeding and digging, the angel appeared again. The little brother just pointed with his hoe at all the unfinished patches and said to the angel, "See for yourself how many weeds are growing here. Can't God's eternal Kingdom wait just a little longer?" The angel smiled and quietly disappeared. The brother weeded the whole garden and dug up the patches and planted them anew. And many other things he did too.

One afternoon he was working in the hospital nursing the sick. Just as he was giving a drink to a patient suffering from high fever, the angel once again stood before him. The little brother spread his arms out seeking understanding, trying to catch the angel's attention to make him see all the sick he still had to take care of. The angel disappeared instantly.

When the brother came home that evening, he lay down on his hard bed, exhausted from all the work. Then he thought about the angel and all the time he had bargained for. Suddenly he felt old and dreadfully tired. He knelt down in his cell and started praying, "Lord, could you send your angel once again now! This time he would be welcome." Hardly had he said that when the angel was right at his side. "If you take me now, this time I'm more than ready to go with you to enter God's Kingdom," he said to the angel. The angel looked deep into his eyes — the way only angels can — and with a smile said to the little brother, "Where do you think you have been all this time?" (A. L. Balling, *Sehnsucht nach dem, was bleibt*, pp. 136-137)

To become Christ-like: "Let Christ make his home in you"

The Pauline perspective sees conversion happening when Christ is taking shape in us (Eph 3:14-19). Indwelling is the endpoint towards which all conversion must be directed. Conversion means a turning to Christ and accepting salvation from him. According to Colossians, all human beings are created in the image of Christ. They carry in themselves his image as their true "hidden self." Thus we read: *"The mystery is: Christ lives in you, the glory to come"* (Col 1:27). From this perspective, conversion means letting Christ take shape in us and leading the person from mere image into likeness.

There once was a sculptor working hard with his hammer and chisel on a large block of marble. A little boy who was watching him saw nothing more than large and small pieces of stones falling away left and right. He had no idea what was happening. But when the boy returned to the studio a few weeks later, he saw to his great surprise a large, powerful lion sitting in the place where the marble had stood. With great excitement the boy ran to the sculptor and said, "Sir, tell me, how did you know there was a lion in the marble?" (H. Nouwen, *Clowning in Rome*, p. 87)

Am I able to see the 'lion' in the marble, the image of Christ in the often formless and ugly appearances of people? Am I able to see this image of Christ first of all in myself? And when I have seen it, am I willing to make it visible? Conversion means SEEING the image in which God has created me and the reality into which he wants to transform me, and then MAKING VISIBLE what I see.

Think differently: "To look at reality with the eyes of Jesus"

According to the Greek word *metanoia,* conversion means thinking differently, looking at reality the way Jesus did. It means accepting his perspective and his frame of reference, using his "spectacles" when looking at the world and human reality.

Some years ago NASA sent into space a satellite, programmed to get as close to Mars as possible before sending pictures back to earth. The satellite reached its destination. The command was given to start taking pictures. But then they discovered a magnetic dust storm raging on Mars that made it impossible to photograph the surface of the planet. It was at this point that scientists arranged a combination of lenses and filters for the camera which made it possible to penetrate the obstacles and obtain excellent pictures of the planet and its surface.

Conversion enables us to by-pass the surface glare, to grasp the depth of reality and to see things as they really are. It helps us to discover the real nature and importance of events in the setting of God's final plan for this world and the direction he is assigning to human history.

Being converted means being equipped with the right lenses and filters. With them in place we are able to get beneath the surface of things, to see through any dust or obstacles that hinder a clear view, and to understand and judge reality accordingly.

Conversion means ultimately accepting Jesus' world-view. It means looking at the world through his eyes. He alone had the right view. He demonstrated through his life how God looks at human beings, at the world, at plants, at animals and at creation as a whole. Jesus revealed God as a father who goes after each one of us with loving concern and care (Lk 15), who cares for the birds in the sky and the grass in the field (Mt 6:25-35), who embraces the "little ones" and identifies with them (Mk 10:13-16).

Being converted means, therefore having a different, but ultimately the only correct view of reality. One who looks at the world with the eyes of faith does not see less but more. Faith is not a distortion of reality; it puts things in the right perspective. It lets me see connections and enables me to see the ultimate ground of all reality. It shows me where this turbulent and seemingly directionless world is moving. It enables me to hold on to the claim of the Bible that the jigsaw puzzle which we call history and creation can be put together into a beautiful design even if many pieces do not fit together at all in the present state of things. Just like the poor jeweler in the story, seeing the intricate pattern in the prayer rug that offered him the road to freedom, so we are challenged to look beyond the blurred images that we are often faced with.

A poor but honest jeweler was arrested for a crime he never committed. He was placed in a high and well-protected prison in the center of the city. One day, after he had been imprisoned for months, his wife came to the main gate. She told the guards how her husband, the poor jeweler, was a devout and prayerful man. He would be lost without his simple prayer rug. Would they not allow him to have this single possession? The guards agreed that it would be harmless and gave him his prayer rug. Five times daily he would unroll his rug and pray.

Weeks passed, and one day the jeweler said to his jailers, "I am bored sitting here day after day with nothing to do. I am a good jeweler and, if you will let me have some pieces of metal and some simple tools, I will make you jewelry. You could then sell what I make in the bazaar and add to your low salaries as jailers. I ask for little - just something to fill the idle hours and keep my skill in practice.

The poorly-paid jailers agreed that it would be a good arrangement. Each day they brought the jeweler some bits of silver and metal and some simple tools. Each night they would remove the tools and metal and take home the jewelry that he had made. Days grew into weeks, weeks into months. One bright morning when they came to the jeweler's cell, they found it empty. No sign was found of the prisoner or how he had escaped from this well-protected prison.

Some time later, the real criminal was arrested for the crime the poor jeweler had been falsely accused of. One day in the city's bazaar, long after that, one of the guards saw the ex-prisoner, the jeweler. Quickly explaining that the real criminal had been caught, he asked the jeweler how he had escaped. The jeweler proceeded to tell the amazing story.

His wife had gone to the main architect who had designed the prison. She obtained from him the blueprints of the cell doors and the locks. She then had a design woven into the prayer rug. Each day as he prayed, his head would touch the rug. Slowly, he began to see that there was a design, within a design, within another design, and that it was the design of the lock of his cell door. From the bits of leftover metal and his simple tools, he fashioned a key and escaped! (W. J. Bausch, *Storytelling*, p. 204-205)

These images, like new lenses or new glasses are relative, but they all indicate a profound change in the person who opens himself or herself to the new reality, the breaking-in of the Kingdom of God, allowing it to determine the direction of his or her life. One's whole attitude towards the Kingdom message will be different depending on whether the Kingdom is seen first as something beautiful that calls for our full attention, or whether it is first of all a call to repentance, to leave old ways of doing and living. The continual awareness that Kingdom and conversion belong together is important. The preaching of the Kingdom is always connected with the call to turn towards it, to let its power into our lives. Since the Kingdom of God has become a reality that constantly breaks into this world and radiates into our life, encompassing all creation, the call for conversion will always accompany this message. Conversion is, therefore, not something that happens once and for all, but a demand that asks for a continuous response. We can indeed say that whenever Jesus preaches the Kingdom, conversion is always an essential element of his message.

Sin, too, must be judged in the light of the coming Kingdom of God. Sin means that we refuse to let the power of the Kingdom determine the direction of our lives. The Kingdom wants to free us from the constant temptation to be our own masters and to determine the course of the world according to our own way of thinking. Only when God becomes the Lord of our whole life and the Lord of the whole universe will the fullness of the Kingdom be accomplished.

Commitment to the values of the Kingdom: To love compassionately, to be ready to forgive and to serve

Having let the Kingdom into my life and having received it like a child, what rule of conduct should determine my life as a disciple? Jesus made it clear that the Pharisaic rulings could never be taken as a pattern for the behavior of his disciples. It was not the Law that was wrong, but the way it was interpreted and applied by the Pharisees, as we saw earlier. What must rule a disciple's conduct is justice and compassionate love towards all beings.

Compassionate love

The norm of conduct that Jesus left his disciples and which would forever be the 'Magna Carta' of all their actions, is expressed in these words:

A new commandment I give you; love one another. As I have loved you, so you must love one another. If you have love for one another, then all will know that you are my disciples (Jn 13:34).

This is my commandment: love one another, just as I have loved you (Jn 15:12).

The most important words in this commandment seem to be: "AS I." We are not just asked to love but are told what kind of love we should have. The way we should love is determined by the way Jesus loved us. Christian love must take its measure from Jesus' love, from his "as I have loved you."

What kind of love is this? The love of Jesus for us is characterized by two basic characteristics: it is UNIVERSAL - and it is COMPASSIONATE love. These two characteristics will always have to remain the points of reference for the question of how we are to love each other and all human beings. The first indicates that our love must be inclusive. The second determines the kind of love we should have for each other which Luke describes in these words:

Be compassionate as your Father is compassionate (Lk 6:36).

As we saw earlier, this statement reveals the revolutionary way in which Jesus saw the Law. Jesus puts his definition of holiness: *"Be compassionate as your Father in heaven is compassionate."* next to the holiness code of Leviticus: *"Be holy because I Yahweh your God is holy"* (Lev 20:26) As Marcus Borg sees it:

The challenge is signaled at the outset by the *imitatio dei* of which Jesus speaks. It is striking that "Be compassionate as God is compassionate" so closely echoes "Be holy as God is holy,"even as it makes a radical substitution. The close parallel suggests that Jesus deliberately replaced the core value of purity with compassion. Compassion, not holiness, is the dominant quality of God, and is therefore to be the ethos of the community that mirrors God (*Meeting Jesus*, p. 53-54).

The 'compassion code' of Luke 6:27-36 replaces the 'holiness code' of Leviticus 20:26 as the norm for religious behavior. True holiness is no longer defined by a 'separation' from the world which would reflect the 'otherness' of God, but by the 'compassion' which imitates God's utterly unconditional love, forgiveness and involvement in human affairs. The disciple's concern must not be holiness and separation from the world and fellow human beings but a commitment to suffering humanity which shows no fear of being contaminated nor knows any kind of discrimination because of religion, culture, race or moral behavior.

After the war there was a German prison camp in Latvia. An old woman used to give bread to the starving men there whenever she had a chance. One day she was caught and brought to the Russian camp commander. He confronted her harshly and shouted, "Is it true that you give food to these Germans?" The women said very calmly, "Not food I give but bread I do." "Do you know that is absolutely forbidden?" the commander retorted. The women replied, "I read somewhere it's forbidden. But no one can forbid anyone from helping unfortunate people in dire need." "Does that mean that you're going to keep on giving these prisoners bread?" the commander wanted to know. The old lady responded, "Comrade commander, please pay attention to me for once. When the German armies invaded our land and lorded it over us, Russian prisoners were brought here to work. They suffered severe hunger, and I gave them bread. After them the Jews were brought here. They were starving, and so I gave them bread. Now the German prisoners are here starving, and I will give them bread. And if by some misfortune you, comrade commander, should one day be a prisoner here and suffer starvation, I would also give you bread." With this the woman turned around and left. The commander never took action against her (A. L. Balling, *Sehnsucht nach dem, was bleibt*, p. 55).

This almost impossible command, to be compassionate like God, remains the ethical foundation of all Christian behavior. But what exactly does compassion mean? The word "compassion" belongs to a Hebrew word group that is normally translated in English with the word "mercy" which denotes the quality of care for another person, the willingness to make an effort, even to the extent of great sacrifice, to ease another's pain. The readiness to forgive and the eagerness to help are also connoted by this word. The Hebrew word for the English equivalent word "mercy" is: *Rahamim*. The word "mercy" is broader than compassion, including fidelity and grace in its meaning."

The word *"rahamin"* is related to the word for "womb." It designates "womb-love," the love of a mother or father for a child, the love that brother and sister, who shared the same womb, have for each other (Am 1:11). It implies a physical response. This compassion for another is felt in the center of one's body. This "mercy" also results in action. It is a word frequently ascribed to Yahweh who has mother-love (Is 49:15; Jer 31:20) or father-love (Ps 103:13; Is 63:15-16) for Israel. The "womb-love" of Yahweh leads to forgiveness for his wayward children.

The word defines an essential truth in the Old Testament theology. The God who is covenanted to Israel is defined as merciful: *The Lord, the Lord, a merciful (Rahum) and gracious God, slow to anger and rich in kindness and fidelity (Ex 34:6).*

This is the God of Isaiah who does not want our sacrifices and elaborate liturgies but asks first that we take care of justice for the poor and all those who are in need before we come to bring our offerings of worship and devotion (Is 1:11-17).

An old monk prayed many years for a vision from God. One day it came. But then, right in the middle of the vision, the monastery bell rang. It was time to feed the poor who gathered daily at the monastery gate. It was the old monk's turn to feed them. If he failed to show up with food, the unfortunate people would leave quietly, thinking the monastery had nothing to give them that day.

The old monk was torn between his earthly duty and his heavenly vision. But before the bell stopped ringing, the monk made his decision. With a heavy heart, he turned his back on the vision and went off to feed the poor.

Nearly an hour later, the old monk returned to his room. When he opened the door, he could hardly believe his eyes. There in the room was the vision, waiting for him. As the monk dropped to his knees in thanksgiving, the vision said to him, "My son, had you not gone off to feed the poor, I would not have stayed."

The Greek word that comes closest to the Hebrew word *"rahamin"* in the New Testament is *"splanchnizomai."* This word is used when referring to the attitude of Jesus, and to the actions of the key persons at the turning points of three important parables.

When used to describe Jesus' behavior the word means, "his heart contracted convulsively" at the sight of human needs. It characterizes the messianic compassion of Jesus towards, e.g., a leper with his petitions to be healed (Mk 1:41), a people like sheep without a shepherd (Mk 6:34; Mt 14:14; cf. also Mk 8:2; Mt 15:32: "I have compassion" in direct speech), the harassed and exhausted crowd shortly before sending out the Twelve (Mt 9:36), two blind men who besought him (Mt 20:34) and the widow of Nain mourning her only son (Lk 7:13). In Mark 9:22 it is used in the petition for driving out a demon.

In two parables, the Unforgiving Servant (Mt 18:23-35) and the Prodigal Son (Lk 15:11-32) the word *splanchnizomai* expresses the strong feeling of a merciful (Mt 18:27) or loving (Lk 15:20) reaction which constitutes the turning point of the story. In both parables, *splanchnizomai* makes the unbounded mercy of God visible. In the Parable of the Unforgiving Servant we also see God's deadly and determined anger against the one who, having experienced mercy, denies the experience by being unmerciful himself. In the Parable of the Good Samaritan (Lk 10:30-37) *splanchnizomai* in v. 33 expresses the attitude of complete willingness to use all means, time, strength and life for a saving action at the crucial moment. It contrasts with the passing by on the other side.

The height of God's compassion has been revealed in Christ's life and death. All the miracles Jesus did were done out of compassion. Twelve times in the Gospels we find the word "compassion" used exclusively for Jesus and the Father.

Whenever Jesus saw suffering people he was shaken and moved. He felt the depth of their sorrow. He felt it even more deeply than they did. It seems that he was more sick, hungry or sorrowful than they were. It is here that the real depth of God's love is revealed. As already said in a previous chapter, the true mystery of our God is not that he takes our pain and suffering away, but that he first wants to share it with us. Only when he has tasted and experienced our suffering and pain can it be changed, only then can new life come forth. The God of Jesus is not primarily an all-powerful God but a compassionate God.

Compassion as revealed in Jesus is not a bending down towards the underprivileged from a privileged position. It is not a reaching out from on high for those who are miserable and low. It is not a gesture of sympathy or pity to those who have failed to make it. On the contrary, the compassion of God means that he moves directly to people and places where suffering is visible and most tangible, and pitches his tent there. He does not leave this situation before having personally experienced all the misery, anxiety, loneliness, pain and suffering of the human race. God can always and with certainty be found among the rejects, the outcasts, the marginalized of society. This is the real mystery of the God revealed by Jesus. God's unconditional love for us becomes, in a sin-permeated world, a compassionate love. It is a love that redeems the world by first suffering all the effects of our rebellion against God and then transforming the old world into the new.

In conclusion we can say: Jesus saw this kind of love as the key factor in seeking to live in accordance with the Law. Consequently, he summed up the Law in the twin commandment of love of God and neighbor:

> He set forth love of neighbor as a principle which showed how the law is to be observed in the light of circumstances, rather than a rule to be obeyed whatever the circumstances (J. Dunn, *Jesus' Call To Discipleship*, p. 84).

Yet for Jesus, love of God and neighbor is not something a disciple can do on his/her own; it is a response to God's prior action. It is God's love, his compassion and forgiveness, which he has granted us and which in turn enables us to love and forgive. We can love God and neighbor because we have been forgiven and in this way we can express our gratitude. One follows from the other. This is clearly expressed in the Parable of the Great Sinner (Lk 7:36-50). The love the woman showed towards Jesus was the result of God's forgiving love which she had received and accepted: *I tell you then, the great love she has shown proves that her many sins have been forgiven (Lk 7:47).*Daniel Berrigan formulated this prayer:

> Christ our brother, you welcome the repentant to your side.
> You sit at the table with social outcasts.
> Your healing embraces illness of body and soul;
> you judge the secret sin, even as you forgive.
> Your forgiveness is judgment.
> You bid us forgive our debtors before we offer gifts at the altar.
> Forgiven by you,
> May we win forgiveness of those we cruelly wrong.
> Bid us turn. Bid us return.
> Turn our hearts from coercive blindness, fury of destruction, our mad race to oblivion.
> You know us to the quick. Your glance penetrates the dark declivities of the heart,
> the self-blinded conscience.
> You know us. Hell bent, sowing the earth with dragons' teeth, hapless and misled,

victimized even as we multiply the victims, self deceived amid our spoiled paradise.
Bid us turn. Bid us return.
Disarmed Christ, sole hope of the self damned, light amid blindness, straight way in wilderness;
bid us return (McKenna, *Rites of Justice*, p. 145).

Readiness to forgive

The experience of being loved to the utmost bears fruit in a love of neighbor which itself endures through all disillusionment and setbacks. This love expresses itself in two characteristic ways: forgiveness and service.

Readiness to forgive then becomes the ultimate measure of how far one has truly become a disciple of Jesus (see Mt 18:21-22; Lk 17:3-4; Mt 5:43-45). Yet the disciple cannot forgive unless he or she has first experienced God's forgiving love. It is only in the strength of the forgiveness received that we are able to forgive those who have wronged us. According to Matthew 6:14-15, those who do not forgive demonstrate that they have not received, or have not accepted, God's forgiveness. They refuse to allow God's forgiving love into their lives and therefore they are unable to forgive others. How deeply we can be touched by someone who asks for our forgiveness, especially if it is a person from our immediate family, is portrayed in the following story:

> While distributing communion I noticed that one of the eucharistic ministers walked away. After some time she came back. After the service she asked, "Did you see me walking away?" When I answered that I had noticed, she told me that she and her teenage daughter had had a terrible week. They had offended each other and had not spoken since.
>
> That morning the daughter had stayed in bed when the mother came to church. At least that is what she thought. But when she was distributing holy communion, she saw the daughter lining up in front of her to receive the sacrament. Her daughter could have lined up in front of any of the other eucharistic ministers, but she chose her line. When she gave her daughter the host, she was so moved that she began to cry and had to walk away for a while to regain her composure. The Eucharist brought them together again (J. Donders, *Charged with the Spirit*, pp. 80-81).

In moments like these, the reality of the Kingdom of God is transparent in our world.

Readiness to serve

The second characteristic of Jesus' commandment of love is expressed in "service of neighbor." The disciple is not forbidden to think thoughts of greatness, but the greatness he is directed to is that of service (Mk 10:35-45). Again, the model is Jesus himself who put concern for his neighbor's well-being above everything else, not just social conventions and taboos, but also possibilities of social advancement, prestige and even life itself.

Albert Schweitzer was once asked what advice he could give to those who, as Christians, were looking for a motto in life. His answer was:

> You ask me to give you a motto. Here it is: *SERVICE*. Let this word accompany you throughout your life. Let it be before you as you seek your way and your duty in the world. May it be called to your minds if ever you are tempted to forget it or set it aside. It will not always be a comfortable companion but it will always be a faithful one. And it will be able to lead you to happiness, no matter what the experience of your lives is (in R. J. Furey, *The Joy of Kindness*, p. 125).

A famous Buddhist monk was once asked what he regarded as the most striking and most distinguishing aspect of the Christian religion. His answer was, "It is the attitude that Jesus revealed in washing his disciples' feet. Nowhere can it be found that a god kneels in front of his creature and washes its feet. Such love is unsurpassable and breathtaking."

Forgiveness and service, as the ultimate demands of discipleship, take concrete shape in one's life according to the values of the Kingdom: justice, peace and joy in the Holy Spirit. The phrase "in the Holy Spirit" again makes it clear that living for these values and making them our rule of conduct are a consequence of our having first allowed the Kingdom into our lives. In this context conversion means beginning to live these new relationships of justice, peace and joy, and, in doing so, witnessing concretely to the presence of the Kingdom now. The acid test of true discipleship will always be whether the community of Jesus' disciples lives the "Creed for all times:" justice, peace and joy in the Holy Spirit (Rom 14:17).

The Kingdom as trust and belief

According to Mark, Jesus attaches the phrase, *"and believe the Good News,"* (1:15) to the word "convert." "To believe" does not mean primarily to accept something as being true. "To believe" means, rather TO TRUST, TO ENTRUST ONESELF, TO FIND ONE'S SECURITY IN. Paul and

John rarely use the words "convert" or "repent;" they prefer "believe." In Hebrew, it is AMEN, which originally meant: "I know where my security lies" or "to know, to be secure" (e.g. Is 7:9). What Jesus is asking for is trust in his message. There is no other security to be found than in the Kingdom he now offers. It is God's unconditional love for each one of us that is the rock on which we can stand. It is something never heard before, something most beautiful, something to which we can entrust our whole being. We are asked to accept that God has already accepted us with infinite love and compassion. It is our final salvation.

Conversion is a joyful occasion; it is Good News - not a terrible event of judgement and condemnation. The lost child has come home (Lk 15:25); the dead man has come alive again: *"This son of mine was dead but he is alive; he was lost but now he has been found"* (Lk 15:24,32). Conversion is preceded by God's action to which we are called to respond. Only God's love makes a response possible at all. Conversion is, therefore, a person's reaction to God's prior action.

However, the Kingdom of God is not only a summons to conversion; it is at the same time a summons to "faith." The disciple holds firm to the belief that the messianic future is already operative now. This promise pervades all our relationships and circumstances. The presence of the Kingdom robs the oppressive circumstances in this world of their seemingly ultimate validity. Faith in the Kingdom becomes a kind of resistance movement against fatalism. The world does not have to stay as it is. Our lives and the circumstances in which we live can be changed. Our task is to dismantle patiently the harmful structures and direct our steps towards the coming Kingdom. It makes all the difference if there are communities who pray for God's Kingdom to come, who advocate the cause of the poor and oppressed and who proclaim the acceptable year of the Lord, God's liberating future.

A Benediction

Send us forth now as you sent Mary Magdalen, to announce the good news,
    the only news, the news forever new; your resurrection.
Send us forth as you sent the twelve to confront murderous power,
    to walk peaceably amid the fires of violence.
Send us forth as you sent the first Christians,
    to act as fools for your Christ's sake.
Send us forth; that reviled, we may bless; that persecuted, we may endure;
    that slandered, we may reconcile.
Send us forth, to places likely and unlikely; to the seats of power and strife,

that we may deny their ascendancy with a fearless word;
to the dwellings of the powerless, that we may bring hope, and win hope.
Send us to those who love, to those who fear, to those who are indifferent.
That we may sow love where there is no love and so bring forth love.
Send us forth, as your word goes forth, and returns heavy with a harvest of peace.
Send us forth, bid us return. Knowing that far or near,
our names are written in your heart. Amen (McKenna).

The Kingdom as commitment to the person of Jesus

No matter how we may try to describe or define the content of the symbol "Kingdom of God," it ultimately reveals God's unconditional love for his creatures. This incomprehensible love (Eph 3:18-19) became visible and tangible in the person of Jesus of Nazareth. Therefore, we have to keep in mind that the Kingdom is not just a "grand design," a "utopian dream come true," "God's ultimate plan for creation;" it is in the last analysis a person: JESUS CHRIST. In the words of John Paul II:

> The Kingdom of God is not a concept, a doctrine or a program subject to free interpretation, but before all else a person with the face and name of Jesus of Nazareth, the image of the invisible God. If the Kingdom is separated from Jesus, it is no longer the Kingdom of God which he revealed (*Redemptoris Missio* 18).

The real nature of the Kingdom can only be sensed or envisioned in a personal encounter with the one *"who loved me and who gave his life for me"* (Gal 2:20). At the time when we come to realize this personal aspect of the Kingdom, we will experience the urgency of letting ourselves be grasped and swept away by the unheard of and unbelievable Good News of the Kingdom that is offered to us here at this very moment. Conversion surely means a change of one's life, attitudes and behavior towards God and fellow human beings. But we must keep in mind that conversion does not primarily mean a change of something, or a conversion to something; it means to turn to SOMEONE. It means to welcome, to accept Jesus as the center of one's whole life. To him and his Gospel we subordinate everything else (Mk 10:28), even life itself (Mk 10:32). Prior to the question about the nature of the Kingdom, there is always the question, "Who is Jesus for me?" Consequently conversion is a personal commitment to Jesus, an open declaration for him. The person of Jesus ultimately becomes the decisive factor for salvation which means acceptance or rejection in the Kingdom of God. This personal attachment to him is a new and unparalleled element in the claims of Jesus. It means adopting his way of life and living in close company with him. Only the one who commits himself or herself to close fellowship with the Lord will ultimately come to see what the Kingdom is and who Jesus is, in whom the Kingdom makes itself present.

Reflection: *Conversion as a Way of Life*

True conversion is a life-long process and one we tend to resist very much. While we feel a deep longing for true intimacy with God, yearning to be loved unconditionally, we also notice in us the opposite: we are afraid of getting too close to God, of handing ourselves over completely to him. We prefer to keep him 'at arm's length' instead of surrendering control over our lives to him. But God does not give up on us. He stands at the door and knocks (Rev 3:20), and as in the famous painting of this scene, the door has no knob or handle on the outside. We need to open the door from the inside, and to do so willingly.

QUESTION: **Where do I look for the Kingdom? Is it in holy places, in particular religious practices, or is it deep within me? Is the Kingdom a well-spring of joy and peace for me?**

Until we become fully aware of all that is wrong and false in our world, we will never really appreciate the urgent need for God's Kingdom of justice and peace nor will we 'let it into our lives' as the gratuitous gift the Father is offering us. If we want to discover the seeds of God's Kingdom as they manifest themselves in the midst of all the corruption and sinfulness around us, we need to look at this world with the eyes of Jesus.

QUESTION: **What kind of 'glasses' do I wear when I look into the world? Are they 'glasses' that change my viewpoint? What do I see through the 'eyes of the Kingdom' when looking at myself and all that is around me?**

The stark contrast between the message the media tries to present to us and the message Jesus conveyed could really serve as an eye-opener:

Cultural Gospel	**Gospel of Christ**
Blessed are the rich and comfortable	*Blessed are the poor in spirit*
Blessed are the tough	*Blessed are the meek*

Blessed are those whose every want is satisfied	*Blessed are they who hunger and thirst for righteousness*
Blessed are they who get even	*Blessed are the merciful*
Blessed are you when they accept you and pamper you	*Blessed are you when they insult you and persecute you*
Look out for yourself; nobody else will	*Give, and it shall be given to you in good measure*
Avoid pain and suffering at all costs	*Take up your cross each day and follow me*
Success is the name of the game, you are a loser if you don't achieve it	*What profit would there be for one to gain the whole world and forfeit one's life?*
The only way to peace is to have more and better weapons	*All who take the sword will perish by the sword*
Go to church and keep up appearances, but don't be religion freak	*Love the Lord your God with all your heart....and with all your mind*

QUESTION: When comparing the two gospels where do I find myself? How serious am I in adopting the Gospel of Christ?

The only way to adopt the Gospel of Jesus as a blue-print for our lives is to contemplate his life so that we are not satisfied with just a brief glance at his fascinating personality but come to know him more and more intimately and desire nothing more than to remain in his presence. Because we love Jesus, we admire his values and want to make them our own - even if they go totally against the grain with us. Once I have started to allow Jesus and his values to enter my life I will soon realize that this is the most challenging experience I have ever ventured into.

This Jesus challenges me

I am FURIOUS, and he tells me: *FORGIVE!*
I am AFRAID, and he tells me: *TAKE COURAGE!*
I have DOUBTS, and he says to me: *HAVE CONFIDENCE!*
I feel RESTLESS, and he says to me: *BE CALM!*
I prefer to go MY OWN WAY, and he tells me: *COME AND FOLLOW ME!*
I make MY OWN PLANS, and he says to me: *FORGET ABOUT THEM!*
I aim for MATERIAL GOODS, and he says: *LEAVE THEM BEHIND!*
I want SECURITY, and he says: *I PROMISE YOU ABSOLUTELY NOTHING!*
I like to live MY OWN LIFE, and he says: *LOSE YOUR LIFE!*
I believe I AM GOOD, and he tells me: *GOOD IS NOT ENOUGH!*
I like to BE THE BOSS, and he says: *SERVE!*
I like to COMMAND OTHERS, and he says: *OBEY!*

I like to UNDERSTAND, and he says: *BELIEVE!*
I like CLARITY, and he speaks to me in *PARABLES.*
I like POETRY, and he speaks to me in *REALITIES.*
I like my TRANQUILITY, and he likes me to be *DISTURBED.*

I like VIOLENCE, and he says: *PEACE BE WITH YOU!*
I draw the SWORD, and he says: *PUT THAT AWAY!*
I think of REVENGE, and he says: *OFFER THE OTHER CHEEK!*
I speak of ORDER, and he says: *I HAVE COME TO BRING THE SWORD!*
I choose HATRED, and he says: *LOVE YOUR ENEMIES.*

I try to sow HARMONY, and he says:
I HAVE COME TO CAST FIRE UPON THE EARTH!
I like to be the GREATEST, and he says:
LEARN TO BE AS SMALL AS A CHILD!
I like to remain HIDDEN, and he says:
LET YOUR LIGHT SHINE!
I look at the BEST PLACE, and he says:
SIT IN THE LAST SEAT!
I like to be NOTICED, and he says:
PRAY IN YOUR ROOM BEHIND LOCKED DOORS!

No, I don't understand this Jesus. He provokes me. He confuses me.
Like so many of his disciples, I, too, would like to follow another Master
who would be more certain and less demanding.
But I experienced almost the same as Peter: "I do not know of anyone else,

WHO HAS THE WORDS OF ETERNAL LIFE!" (Pe. Zezinho, SCJ, Brazil)

It is useless to proclaim the Kingdom of God if we are not building it in
our communities, where we try to let God's love, forgiveness and compassion
for us become the wellspring of our lives. Thus we can truly live and find
our identity, joy and enthusiasm knowing that we are loved, forgiven and
constantly cared for.

QUESTIONS: How compassionate a person am I? Can I love people in
    spite of all their inconsistencies, faults and sins? Do I bear
    others' burdens?

The closest you will ever come to God and his Kingdom
while you are here on earth
is when you are helping someone.

Chapter Twelve

The Person of Jesus and the Kingdom he preached

In the New Testament there is a noticeable shift from the pre-Easter Jesus preaching the Kingdom of God to the post-Easter Jesus the Christ, now become the content of the preaching. Is this shift from the Kingdom to Jesus Christ a legitimate transition or is it a distortion?

We must therefore ask what is the connection between the Kingdom of God which Jesus preached as having arrived, and the preacher himself. Did the person of Jesus have anything to do with the message he preached? Is it the Kingdom that interprets the person of Jesus as well as his mission, or is it Jesus who interprets the Kingdom?

Although Jesus' central message was the Kingdom of God, we cannot overlook the fact that in the New Testament it is the picture of Jesus that emerges more clearly than that of the Kingdom. Consequently, the starting point for the ultimate understanding and interpretation of the Kingdom of God seems to be the person of Jesus himself. The Kingdom must be explained and comprehended in the light of Jesus Christ. Only in so doing can we say that Jesus Christ is to be understood in the light of the Kingdom theme. Or in the words of Jürgen Moltmann:

> Whoever becomes involved with Jesus, becomes involved with the kingdom of God. This is unavoidably so, because the concern of Jesus — then and now — was and is the "kingdom of God." Whoever searches for God and asks about the kingdom wherein "righteousness and peace embrace" (Ps 85:11) must look to Jesus and immerse themselves in his story — the narration of events that took place in the past but still occur today through the spirit. This is self-evident and quite in our grasp, because the response to the question of who is Jesus is that he is none other than the kingdom of God in person. Jesus and the Kingdom of God, the Kingdom of God and Jesus, the two are inseparable. . . If then, one wants to learn about the mysteries of the "kingdom of God," one must look to Jesus; and if one wants to understand who this Jesus is, one must first experience the kingdom of God ("First the Kingdom of God," p. 6).

Whatever definition one wants to give to the symbol of the Kingdom, it definitely must center on its dimension as God's ultimate offer of his UNCONDITIONAL LOVE. The concrete form of God's "final visitation" was his becoming man in Jesus of Nazareth. Only in him can we come to understand the real meaning of the Kingdom he preached. This coming of God to redeem his creatures must be considered within the total scheme of creation.

Jesus: God's ultimate offer of salvation

The earthly life of Jesus can be outlined briefly as follows: Jesus was born into the culture and religion of the Jewish people. There he learned about Yahweh, the God of Israel, who had elected his chosen people and had promised them through the prophets a "final visitation" — soon to come — which would complete all prior promises. Jesus, who from early childhood on experienced such an intense love relationship with Yahweh that he came to call him "ABBA," realized at some stage in his life that Yahweh wanted to lead Israel, and ultimately all human beings, into that intimacy and love which he himself experienced. As we saw earlier, this was the fire burning in him, which he could not restrict to himself but had to communicate to others. Jesus perceived this as being the Kingdom of God that was to come through him into the world as God's unconditional love. This love knows no limits in the fulfilment of the age-old promise of salvation for every person and the whole of creation.

A man who lived in the same town as Rabbi Zusya saw that he was very poor. So each day he put twenty coins into the little bag in which Zusya kept his phylacteries, so that he and his family might buy the necessities of life. From that time on, the man grew richer and richer. The more he had, the more he gave Zusya, and the more he gave, the more he had.
But once he recalled that Zusya was the disciple of a great maggid and it occurred to him that if what he gave the disciple was so lavishly rewarded, he might become even more prosperous if he made presents to the master himself. So he traveled to Mezritch and induced Rabbi Baer to accept a substantial gift from him. From this time on, his means shrank until he had lost all the profits he had made during the more fortunate period. He took his trouble to Rabbi Zusya, told him the whole story, and asked him what his present predicament was due to. For had not the rabbi himself told him that his master was immeasurably greater than he?
Zusya replied. "Look! As long as you gave and did not bother to whom, whether to Zusya or another, God gave to you and did not bother to whom. But when you began to seek out especially noble and distinguished recipients, God did exactly the same."

God's unconditional love is accessible only through Jesus. Anyone who comes in contact with him comes in contact with God's unconditional love for his creatures. The demand for conversion consists, then in turning to

Jesus and accepting in him God's salvific love, in order to lead all to their final destiny. This offer is made first to those who know that they have claim neither on God through their religious practices and good works nor on society through prestige, power or wealth. They are asked only to let God's gracious gift enter their lives, to allow themselves to be transformed in the process, and to commit themselves radically to Jesus.

HIS NAME IS JESUS

God has come home, retracting glory.
God has sought permission
of the womb of a little girl
trembling at the decree from Caesar
and has become one of us:
A Palestinian among many
on a street with no address,
a semi-skilled worker doing rough jobs,
who watches Romans
and swallows come and go,
who later on, dies a bad death,
murdered outside the city.

I know
that it's a long time ago that you know about it, that they've told you,
that you know it coldly
because they've told you with cold words...
I want you to know it -
with a jolt, today, perhaps for the first time,
attentive, uneasy, freed from any myth,
freed from so many petty freedoms.

I want the Spirit to tell it to you
like an axe falling on a living trunk!
I want you to feel him
like a rush of blood in the heart of your routine
in the midst of this race of clashing wheels.
I want you to stumble over him
as you might stumble over the doorway
of your house,
coming back from the war, under the gaze and the restless kiss of your Father.

I want you to shout him out
as the victory cry over the lost war,
as the bleeding birth of hope
on the bed of your listlessness,

with night coming on,
and all learning darkened.

I want you to find him, in a total embrace,
Companion, Love, Response.

You will be able to doubt that he's come home
if you expect me
to show you the warrant of his wonders
if you want me to sanction life's untidiness.
But you will not be able to deny
that his name is Jesus,
and he has the stamp of a poor man.
And you will not be able to deny
that you are waiting for him
with the crazy emptiness of your rejected life,
as you wait for breath to relieve asphyxia
when death was wound round your neck
like a questioning serpent.

His name is Jesus,
His name is what ours would be
if we were really ourselves. (Casaldàliga)

Since Jesus himself is God's ultimate gift to us, he is God's Kingdom present in the world. Jesus is the Kingdom in person, the "auto-basileia," or as Origen put it: "Jesus is the Kingdom of God realized in a self." John Paul II speaks in the following terms:

> The proclamation and establishment of God's Kingdom are the purpose of Jesus' mission: "I was sent for this purpose" (Lk 4:43). But that is not all. Jesus himself is the "good news," as he declares at the very beginning of his mission in the synagogue of Nazareth when he applies to himself the words of Isaiah about the Anointed One sent by the Spirit of the Lord (cf. Lk 4:14-21). Since the "good news" is Christ, there is an identification between the message and the messenger, between saying, doing and being. His power, the secret of the effectiveness of his actions, lies in his total identification with the message he announces: He proclaims the "good news" not just by what he says or does, but by what he is *(Redemptoris Missio* 13).

The death of Jesus and the final coming of the Kingdom

To understand the incarnation, God's becoming a human person, two very important concepts need to be considered: *identification* and *representation*. Jesus is God's self-communication to us, he is the *God *with us*, identical with us in everything except sin (Phil 2); he identifies with us, is one of us.

The second equally important aspect is: having identified himself with us, Jesus represents us to God the Father; he is *us* before God. God can no longer look at this Jesus of Nazareth without seeing in him all of us who are not only part of his Son but who have become his Son. We are his body. We are his brothers and sisters and he is the "eldest among brothers and sisters" as the letter to the Hebrews says (Heb 8-10).

But in Jesus, God not only identified himself with us; he also took upon himself our "situation in its state of broken existence." He entered a world of people who had behind them a long history of NO to God, who had no *ground on which to stand*, who were cut off from God and from each other, in short, a world alienated from God. Jesus' brothers and sisters are living in a state apart from God, in dire need of being brought back to the God who desires to come into life-giving contact with them once again.

If we look at the life of Jesus we can see that it was ruled by two principles. First, he was totally dedicated to his Father: *"My food is to do the will of him who sent me"* (Jn 4:34). From the Father Jesus drew his life. The Father's love was the fire that sustained him and the fire he wanted to cast on this earth. This love was the "rock" on which Jesus stood; it was his AMEN.

Secondly, Jesus was totally dedicated to his mission, i.e., to us: *"No one has a greater love than the one who lays down his life for his friends"* (Jn 15:13). *"He always loved those who were his own..now he showed how perfect his love was"* (Jn 13:1ff.). His deepest desire was to draw all of us, his brothers and sisters into this new relationship with God. With great enthusiasm he preached this love hoping that Israel as a whole would respond spontaneously and generously to his offer. But very quickly Jesus came to realize that Israel would not listen to his message. What should he do next? How could he make God's Kingdom come true if people did not want it? If they put him to death what would become of his message? Was his death necessary for the Kingdom to come in its fullness?

Why was Jesus executed?

If we read the Scripture carefully it is easy to answer this question. His image of God as one who loves all human beings unconditionally, forgives all human beings without distinction and is compassionately present in all human affairs, especially with those who are discriminated against, would be too much and too hard to accept. God could not be like this, therefore Jesus had to be wrong. His message was just too dangerous for a well-defined and established religion with its holiness code that asked for separation and distinction from so many people and things. But Jesus was not willing to compromise his Kingdom vision. It was ultimately his interpretation of holiness in terms of compassion.

> The story is told of a young French soldier who deserted Napoleon's army but who, within a matter of hours, was caught by his own troops. To discourage soldiers from abandoning their posts the penalty for desertion was death. The young soldier's mother heard what had happened and went to plead with Napoleon to spare the life of her son. Napoleon heard her plea but pointed out that because of the serious nature of the crime her son had committed he clearly did not deserve compassion. "I know he does not deserve mercy and compassion, " the mother answered. "It wouldn't be compassion if he *deserved* it." (McBride)

Jesus wanted to present God's salvation as including all human beings, thus abrogating all privileges and positions of honor based on "holiness" and purity. All people are God's children and we are all brothers and sisters. There is no room for any kind of discrimination be it cultural, racial, religious or gender related. For Jesus all are equal, and God was coming to bring about the ultimate fulfillment of his creation: union and communion with God, union and communion among all human beings in a transformed world. It was his understanding and experience of God, together with his vision of God's ultimate plan for creation, that caused him to be brought to trial and put to death. It was the impossibility of his vision of the God of the Covenant that his opponents could not take because for them it would mean the end of the Covenant and the people of Israel at that time in history.

Summarizing what was presented in detail in the previous chapters, we could easily say: Jesus was put away because of the "allergy" he showed towards any kind of discrimination. His table-fellowship practice with the *unholy* and the *unclean* and his non-discriminatory behavior towards everyone brought him ultimately to the cross. Both attitudes witness to and demonstrate clearly the core of his vision of the Kingdom expressed in the symbol of the eschatological banquet in which all would partake, regardless of whether or not they were children of Abraham (Lk 3:8; Mt 8:11-12).

On purely historical grounds, scholars agree that Jesus was condemned on two charges. *First*, he was condemned as a political agitator, as being "King of the Jews" according to the inscription on the cross. This was the

Roman version. The Romans at least must have thought him to be dangerous because he excited the hopes and dreams of the Jews. At the same time, however, they must have regarded his movement as harmless since they left his disciples unmolested.

Secondly, Jesus was put to death by the Jewish leaders on charges of being a false prophet and a blasphemer. Was it Jesus' stand towards Judaism that finally brought him the death sentence or was his death the plot of the Temple aristocracy, as some scholars would have it? Each side has its arguments. Whatever they were, in the end all agreed that this man was too dangerous and had to be put away, no matter what doctrinal or personal differences existed among those who made this decision.

When Jesus realized that they would put him to death, he could only weep for his people and the city he loved so much and whose salvation he had sought so earnestly. They had failed to recognize in him the one whom God had sent for the final restoration of the Covenant and the coming of God's Kingdom for the salvation of all.

Jerusalem, Jerusalem, you that kill the prophets and stone those who are sent to you! How often have I longed to gather your children as a hen gathers her brood under her wings, and you refused! So it be! Your house will be left to you. Yes I promise you, you shall not see me till the time comes when you say: Blessings on him who comes in the name of the Lord (Lk 13:34-35)!

As he drew near and came in sight of the city he shed tears over it and said, "If you in your turn had only understood on this day the message of peace! But, alas, it is hidden from your eyes!" (Lk 19:41-42)

However, historically correct a "consequential" interpretation of Jesus' death may be, it does not suffice as a theological explanation. The death of Jesus ultimately has a redemptive meaning and cannot be treated as something that happened to him by accident. The death of Jesus overcomes the causes of sin itself and its ultimate consequences.

You take upon yourself our burdens

O Christ,
you take upon yourself all our burdens
so that,
freed of all that weighs us down,
we can constantly begin anew
to walk, with lightened step,
from worry towards trusting,

from the shadows
towards the clear flowing water,
from our own will
towards the vision of the coming Kingdom.
And then we know,
though we hardly dared hope it,
that you offer to make every human being
a reflection of your face. (*Songs and Prayers from Taizé*)

How did Jesus interpret his death?

To the question whether Jesus knew from the beginning that they would kill him, one answer is certain: very soon in his public ministry he could have had foreseen what would have happened if he had to stick uncompromisingly to his vision. He and his opponents were worlds apart. John the Baptist's death was the ultimate signal that he would most probably have to go the same way. The question therefore is: how did Jesus look at his death, how did he understand it? How could that fit into his vision? Was the Father asking for it, and if so what was its meaning?

Albert Schweitzer proposed a solution which has been accepted by a number of scholars as the most probable one. He argued that the arrival of the eschatological Kingdom of God could never have been proclaimed by Jesus without his knowledge of the trials and sufferings which this apocalyptic phrase evoked. Schweitzer explains:

> The reference to the Passion belonged as a matter of course to the eschatological prediction. A time of unheard of affliction must precede the coming of the Kingdom. Out of these woes the Messiah will be brought to birth. That was a view prevalent far and wide: in no other ways could the events of the last times be imagined. According to this view Jesus' words must be interpreted. It will appear then that in his preaching of the Kingdom he brought into sharp prominence the thought of the Affliction of the last times (*The Mystery of the Kingdom of God,* p. 137).

If Jesus proclaimed the Kingdom of God as imminent, then the thought of suffering had to come to him quite naturally. It was not possible to separate the eschatological Kingdom from the thought of eschatological trials, the coming Messiah from suffering in the age that would immediately precede the arrival of the Kingdom. Suffering had to be proclaimed as necessary for the final coming of the Kingdom of God. Although this teaching of a period of great tribulation marking the transition between the present time and the age to come was widespread in Judaism, we have to admit that most of these sayings occur, however, in later rabbinic sources.

The numerous references to suffering and eschatological trials in the proclamation of Jesus should be seen from this perspective. In particular the Gospel of Mark makes this connection quite obvious. Before the Galilean crisis these references are only implicit but after the crisis the necessity of suffering and its relation to the Kingdom is openly proclaimed. Jesus, who clearly understood his connection with the coming Kingdom, realized that he had to undergo suffering and death as a necessary prerequisite for the Kingdom's finally breaking into this age. W. Kasper, making Schweitzer's view his own, concludes:

> Jesus certainly saw the trials of suffering and persecution as part of the lowly and hidden character of the Kingdom of God, and as such they passed into the mainstream of his preaching. There is, therefore, a more or less straight line from Jesus' eschatological message of the BASILEIA, the Kingdom, to the mystery of his passion (*Jesus the Christ*, p. 116).

The arguments about his person were connected with his message of the passing of the old and the coming of the new. Jesus accepted this conflict as part of his message and interpreted his death accordingly. Ultimately, it was the will of the Father that Jesus felt he had to fulfill at all costs, and in the strength of the Father's love he was able to do it.

> There was once a leper colony in the most heart-breaking and most hateful sense of the term. There were men with nothing to do, and for whom nothing could be done. They were lonely, abandoned men who cold only prowl around their yard.
>
> Yet one of these men kept a gleam in his eye. He could smile, and if you offered him something, could still say, "Thank you." There was this one single man, who was still a man, still human.
>
> The Sister in charge was anxious to know the reason for this miracle. What kept him clinging to life? She watched him for a few days and she saw that there used to appear above the high, forbidding wall, every day, a face. A little tip of a woman's face, no bigger than a hand, but all smiles.
>
> The man would be there, waiting to receive this smile, the food of his strength and support and his hope. He would smile back and then the head would disappear. Then his long wait for the next day would begin afresh.
>
> When the Sister one day took them by surprise, he simply said, "She is my wife," And after a pause, he went on, "Before I came here, she hid me and looked after me with anything she could get. A native doctor had given her some paste to treat my disease. Every day she would smear my face with it - all except one tiny corner ... just enough to put her lips to. But it couldn't last. They picked me up. She followed me here and when she comes to see me every day, I know that it is because of her that I can still go on living" (Arcodia).

The Last Supper and the Kingdom

It is during the final meal with his disciples that Jesus reveals clearly that his death is necessary for his vision of the Kingdom to become true. There is no other way left (Mk 14:17-25 and 1 Cor 11:23-25). All gatherings at table — that had provoked such scandal because Jesus excluded no one, not even public sinners, and which thus expressed the heart of his message — were seen by Jesus as symbols of the feast to come in the time of salvation (Mk 2:18-20). The Last Supper, as all gatherings at table, is now presented as an anticipation or foreshadowing of the consummation of the Kingdom. It is an "already" of the "not yet," the advent of the perfect Kingdom of God, the fulfillment of the great banquet, everything that can only become a full reality after his death. The final gathering presupposes this giving of himself for the many:

> *Amen, I say to you that I will drink no more of the fruit of the vine until that day when I will drink it anew [Mt: with you] in the Kingdom of God (Mk 14:25; Mt 26:29; Lk 22:16).*

The texts have the following meaning: Jesus will no longer sit at table with the disciples on earth but will do so again for a new meal in the coming Kingdom of God. For this to happen, his death which he awaits, is a necessary pre-condition. The disciples can partake of the final eschatological banquet only if Jesus first lays down his life for them (Lk 22:20).

To partake in the Kingdom of God is only possible after Jesus has fulfilled this condition, after he *"has drunk the cup and has been baptized with a baptism"* (Mk 10:35-40). The true nature of the task that Jesus had to undertake in order to bring in the fullness of the Kingdom is expressed in the words regarding the bread and wine. He must surrender his life so that men and women may share the feast of the Kingdom with him:

> His resolution to complete the mission that God had given him in relation to the Kingdom and his confidence that he would soon be participating in its joy sound the keynote of his last meal with his disciples. The Last Supper is framed in affirmation of the death of Jesus in prospect of the Kingdom of God (G. R. Beasley-Murray, *Jesus and the Kingdom of God*, p. 263).

The death of Jesus: God's ultimate Revelation

At some point in his life, Jesus must have come to realize that the only way left to fulfill his mission was to demonstrate the immensity of God's love for us to the very end (Jn 13:1). The cross and his death appear as the only way that remained to prove God's redeeming love in the sin-permeated history of humankind. The "Galilean Crisis" is regarded by many as this turning point in Jesus' life. From then on his attention was focused on his death and suffering in Jerusalem (Mk 8:31, 9:31, 10:33, 10:45).

Even when Jesus came to realize that the "will of the Father" was leading him to the cross in order to prove God's love for humankind, "to the very end," he did not run fanatically towards the cross and his own death. Rather, Jesus was afraid and even horrified when he thought of what was to come:

> *There is a baptism I still must receive and how great is my distress till it is over (Lk 12:50).*

> *Now my soul is troubled. What shall I say: "Father, save me from this hour?" But it was for this very reason that I have come to this world (Jn 12:27).*

> *In the days of his earthly life Jesus made prayers and requests with loud cries and tears to God to save him from death . . . (Heb 5:7).*

> *His sweat was like drops of blood falling to the ground (Lk 22:34).*

> *At three o' clock Jesus cried out with a loud shout: "My God, my God, why have you abandoned me" (Mk 15:34).*

In the darkest hour of his life when the Father abandoned Jesus on the cross and he had to face the *incomprehensible and hidden* God, Jesus never failed to hold on to his faith in a loving and caring God.

What do these passages tell us? Was Jesus afraid of physical death? What horrified him whenever he thought of his coming suffering and death? Did he break down at the end? Did he experience the darkness and distress of death more deeply than any other man or woman? Many solutions from one extreme to the other have been offered. Some see in the cry on the cross a cry of despair; others regard it as a cry of victory. If Jesus consciously took upon himself the "eschatological tribulations and sufferings," the question remains as to the nature of these tribulations that make the final coming of the Kingdom possible.

A solution could be developed along the following lines. In the life of Jesus there is a tension between his intimate life with the Father and his "living our life to the very end." Nevertheless, he remains faithful to his mission of *identification and representation*. Jesus, it seems, felt that the more he identified with us, the more he would experience our sinfulness, our forlorn situation and the insecurity of those who had rejected God's gift of love. He came to realize that if he would carry his mission through to the very end — taking upon himself our hollow existence — he would have to experience the full reality of what it means for a creature to be "cut off" from God. For Jesus it would mean experiencing being cut-off from the Father who meant everything to him, from whom he drew life and whose will he had come to do. The thought that this moment was coming horrified him. The Father would regard him as "humankind in its God-forsaken, abandoned state." Jesus would have to experience his being completely IDENTIFIED with us in our sinfulness and being dealt with as our REPRESENTATIVE before God. What Jesus had to go through is well expressed in this way:

> The Son of God has thus passed through the entire gamut of human anguish. He experienced death in all the tragic religious meaning acquired as a consequence of sin: estrangement from God. He became, as Paul will say, "sin," a "curse" (2 Cor 5:21; Gal 3:13), and that to the extreme consequence of sin: death. The theological dimension of abandonment now comes to light: Jesus, the incarnate Son, has completely assumed the human condition of estrangement from God (G. Rosse, *The Cry of Jesus on the Cross*, p. 67).

The cry on the cross is the moment when Jesus most identified himself with our God-forsakenness (Mk 15:34). In this moment it seemed as if the love of the Father from whom he drew life had stopped flowing. Jesus entered into the abyss of lovelessness and consumed it from within, so that in his dying, death and sin are no more. What appeared to be God-forsakenness thus turns out to be the purest expression of God' love for us and our salvation.

> The three victims mounted together onto the chairs. Their three necks were placed at the same moment within the nooses."Long live liberty!" cried two adults. But the child was silent. "Where is God? Where is He?" someone behind me asked. At a sign from the head of the camp, the three chairs tipped over. Total silence throughout the camp. On the horizon, the sun was setting. "Bare your heads!" yelled the head of the camp. His voice was raucous. We were weeping. "Cover your heads!" Then the march past the dead men began. The two adults were no longer alive. Their tongues hung swollen, blue-tinged. But the third rope was still moving; being so light, the child was still alive.... For more than half an hour he stayed there struggling between life and death, dying in slow agony under our eyes. And we had to look him full in the face. He was still alive when I passed in front of him. His tongue was still red, his eyes not yet glazed. Behind me, I heard the same man asking: "Where is God now?" And I heard a voice within me answering him: "Where is He? Here He is - He is hanging here on these gallows..." (E. Wiesel, *Night*).

The "eschatological tribulations" are precisely this experience of our true state without God, forsaken, condemned and without hope. In this light we have to see the death of Jesus as Mark portrays it (Mk 15:34). On the cross Jesus experienced God as the one who withdrew and left him abandoned. This was the real trial of the coming Kingdom which was to overcome sin, condemnation and death. The cross reveals the tension between God and sinful humanity. On the cross the Father enters into compassionate solidarity with Jesus until human freedom has played itself out and Jesus is destroyed. The resurrection is the conquering of all negativity wrought by human sinfulness. It is Jesus' love and his fidelity, along with God's overcoming the negativity of the cross in the resurrection, that saved us, and not the cross itself. It was love that brought forth the new life.

God's unconditional love for his creature reaches its ultimate climax here. Paul has expressed this in different ways:

God dealt with sin by sending his own son in a body as physical as any sinful body and in that body God condemned sin (Rom 8:3).

Christ redeemed us from the curse of Law by being cursed for our sake (Gal 3:13).

For our sake God made the sinless one into sin, so that in him we might become the goodness of God (2 Cor 5:17).

The cross is not the revelation of a vengeful God, a God who needs a sacrifice, who wants to see blood flowing. It is sad to know there are still many good Christians who hold firmly to the idea that God needed blood to be reconciled, the blood of the best person ever born into this world. They just cannot see how far away this idea is from the God revealed in the Old and New Testaments. The death of Jesus must be seen in connection with the foundational reality of our faith: the God-image that Jesus came to throw like fire into this world. It is the image of God that we outlined in the beginning with the three basic elements: God loves us unconditionally, he forgives us always and he is always compassionately with us. The cry on the cross is the highlight of this love, the culmination of it.

The cross reveals two essential realities. *First,* it manifests the immensity and incomprehensibility of God's love for his creatures as compassionate love. The fullness of God's love for us is laid open here. It means that God did not redeem the world by reaching down from on high and pulling us up to heaven. He *"came down from heaven,"* entering into our human misery by experiencing it to the ultimate. In experiencing the effect of sin as condemnation, God took upon himself in Jesus Christ the destiny of a humankind alienated from its own being. *"He descended into Hell!"* These are the "eschatological tribulations" which had to be endured for the Kingdom to finally come in full glory.

> Christ entered into this humiliation and this forsakenness so that he could become a brother for the humiliated and forsaken, and bring them God's Kingdom. He doesn't help through supernatural miracles. He helps by virtue of his own suffering - through his wounds. 'Only the suffering God can help,' wrote Dietrich Bonhoeffer in his death cell. God always helps first of all by suffering with us. 'Even in hell you are there.' So no suffering can cut us off from this companionship of the God who suffers with us. The God of Jesus Christ is the God who is on the side of the victims and the sufferers, in solidarity with them (J. Moltmann, *Jesus Christ Today*, p. 40).

Secondly, the cross reveals the utter hopelessness of our human condition as sinners who have rejected God's love. The cross tells us what sin really is. God redeemed the world in Jesus by taking upon himself all the consequences of our free decisions against him; he suffered our state. By going to the limit, God went ahead of us and caught us in our fall before we were smashed to pieces. Moltmann observes:

> Only if all destruction, all abandonment by God, absolute death, and immersion into nothingness are found in God himself will union with God be eternal salvation, never ending joy, sure election, and divine life (*The Crucified God, p. 287)*.

Among Catholic theologians H. Urs von Balthasar has dealt most profoundly with Jesus' abandonment by the Father and his descent into "hell." He writes:

> Jesus becomes the true possessor, through his own experience, of what 'Hell' means in the New Testament; he becomes the judge who has measured out all the dimensions of man in his own experience, and now can assign to each his lot eschatologically. And thus it is from this point that we see the emergence of concepts of Hell, Purgatory and Heaven, which for the first time are theologically meaningful (*The Glory of the Lord: A Theological Aesthetics. VII: Theology*, p. 233).

Rosse concludes his findings as follows:

> But in order that salvation may be offered to all, Jesus, in his journey to the dead, in his experience of death, not only bears the pain of the impious — in the loss of all spiritual light of faith, hope and love (Urs von Balthasar) — in order to reach even those who will refuse. He thus runs through all the dimensions of hell so that every man in his estrangement from God will have the possibility of recognizing himself in Christ (*The Cry of Jesus on the Cross*, p. 93).

Mark presents the death of Jesus against the background of three signs which serve to interpret it by means of "visual theology:" the darkness, the torn curtain and the centurion's confession of faith. The first sign is darkness: "At noon darkness came over the whole land until three o'clock" (Mk 15:33). In prophetic and apocalyptic language, darkness is part of the "Day of the Lord," i.e., the day of the great judgement at the end of time. By using this language, Mark expresses the universal and eschatological meaning of the death of Christ which inaugurates the judgement of the world. Thus one reads in the Scriptures:

> *On that day, says the Lord God, I will make the sun set at midday and cover the earth with darkness in broad daylight (Am 8:9).*

The torn curtain and the centurion's confession raise a few perennial questions. Where can God be found? In the Holy of Holies? Mark tells us that the moment Jesus died the huge curtain which hung before the Holy of Holies was torn in two from top to bottom. What is Mark telling us? According to Jewish belief God touched the earth with his foot in the Holy of Holies. Here one could be sure of finding God. From the moment Jesus died, God could no longer be found in the Temple. In the cry of this dying Jesus of Nazareth, God has revealed his very nature, which is unconditional, compassionate love: *"How incomprehensible is God's love for us"* (Eph 3:14-19). The cross becomes the climax of God's self-revelation in the history of humankind.

The second question Mark asks is: who recognized Jesus on the cross as Son of God? The theologians? No! The pagan centurion! The centurion, "looking at the crucified," represents all those who believe in Christ, and especially the gentiles. As Rosse observes: "Before the crucified, and through the mouth of the centurion, the Christian community expresses its faith in the crucified Jesus, the Son of God." Thus, in Scripture we read:

> *No one has ever seen God. It is the only Son who is nearest to the Father's heart, who has made him known (Jn 1:18).*

> *Yes, God loved the world so much that he gave his only Son . . . God sent his Son into the world not to condemn the world, but to save it (Jn 3:16-17).*

The cross remains THE revelation of God's unconditional, compassionate love. It is the revelation of what Jesus really wanted to "throw" into the world (Lk 12:49). Now it is possible to point to a visible, historical fact, located in space and time, and say: Here is God's ultimate self-communication to us. Now we know who he is, now we know what Jesus meant when he said: "Your God is ABBA." Now we know what God's Kingdom is and how it will come about in due time. God can never withdraw again. He said yes to us and to the world. Now, all can and will be well at the end.

> "I can make all things well
> I know how to make all things well,
> I desire to make all things well,
> I will make all things well.
> And you will see with your own eyes
> that every kind of thing will be well."
> (Julian of Norwich)

Conclusion

How is the Kingdom of God connected with the person of Jesus? The Kingdom is not a thing, not just a gift from God to his creatures; it is ultimately God's self-communication to us in love concretely manifested in the person of Jesus of Nazareth. Its meaning has been made visible in sacramental form in Jesus. He is the incomprehensible and compassionate love of God "who did not spare his only Son but gave him up for our sake so that we may have life and have it in abundance" (Rom 8:32; Jn 10:10).

Reflection: *Jesus, the Kingdom of God in Person*

Our Christian life is lived within the Kingdom of God revealed in the person of Jesus Christ. Whoever gets involved with Jesus, gets involved in the Kingdom of God and in so doing becomes increasingly aware of God's unconditional love. The following hymn invites us on a meditative journey along the path of salvation:

DAYENU

Dayenu is a Hebrew word which means "It would have been enough." It is the refrain of a traditional, cumulative Hebrew hymn in which each verse builds on the one before. It is sung at the Passover Seder. The Jewish Dayenu describes all the wonderful things God did for the Israelites and praises God with great gratitude for them. The following is an adaptation for the Christian liturgy, using the same pattern but different events.

It Would Have Been Enough!

If God had created us and not revealed Himself in all his marvelous works...
  It would have been enough!
If God had revealed Himself and not made a Covenant with his people...
  It would have been enough!
If God had made a Covenant with his people and not breathed the Spirit into us...
  It would have been enough!
If God had breathed his Spirit into us and not shared his heart with us...
  It would have been enough!
If God had shared his heart with us and not watched over us when we strayed from his love...
  It would have been enough!
If God had watched over us when we strayed from his love and not delivered us from the bonds of slavery...
  It would have been enough!
If God had delivered us from the bonds of slavery and not led us into a land of freedom...
  It would have been enough!
If God had led us into a land of freedom and not sent us holy men and women to speak to us of his love...
  It would have been enough!
If God had sent us holy men and women to speak to us of his love and not promised us a Savior...
  It would have been enough!
If God had promised us a savior and not sent us his own beloved Son...
  It would have been enough!
If God had sent us Jesus, his own beloved Son, and he had not become our very brother...
  It would have been enough!
If Jesus had become our very brother, and not shared our joys and sorrows, our laughter and tears...
  It would have been enough!
If Jesus had shared our life and not taught us how to forgive each other...
  It would have been enough!
If Jesus had taught us how to forgive each other and not shown us how to love...
  It would have been enough!
If Jesus had taught us how to love and not taught us how to serve each other...

It would have been enough!
If Jesus had shown us how to serve each other and not left us the Eucharist as a reminder of his love...
It would have been enough!
If Jesus had left us the Eucharist as a reminder of his love and not revealed to us the Father's love for us...
It would have been enough!
If Jesus had revealed the Father's love for us, and not called us to carry on his work in the world...
It would have been enough!

But as it is, Father, your Son Jesus has revealed your love for us. His whole life, his death and his resurrection from the dead testify to your deep mercy and compassion. Therefore, Father, we bless and thank you. We praise and worship you with all creation, for you are worthy of our worship and all the praises of our hearts. To you and to your Son, Jesus, and to the Holy Spirit belong all glory, now and forever. Amen.

QUESTION: **To follow the Lord down to Jerusalem demands that I fix my eyes not only on Jesus in Galilee but also on the passion by which he entered the final stage of his life here on earth, so as to reveal to us the immensity of the Father's love to us. How does that translate in my everyday life?**

Jesus did not carry out only half of God's commission to liberate the world, but steadfastly went on to its completion - his death on the cross. Indeed, he went through hell to bring us out of there. Yet Jesus' suffering was not an end in itself but aimed at the liberation of the whole of creation and the establishment of God's Kingdom in this world. People who have witnessed and experienced extreme forms of suffering are very much attuned to the message of salvation that is spoken in the apparent silence of God:

In the pain, misfortune, oppression, and death of the people, God is silent.
God is silent on the cross, in the crucified.
And this silence is God's word, God's cry.
In solidarity, God speaks the language of love.
(J. Sobrino in J. Morley, *Bread For Tomorrow,* p. 93)

QUESTION: If Jesus suffered for all of us what does it mean when Paul writes: *Now I rejoice in my sufferings for your sake, and in my flesh I am filling up what is lacking in the afflictions of Christ on behalf of his body, which is the church, of which I am a minister in accordance with God's stewardship given to me to bring to completion for you the word of God* (Col 1:24-25)? How can I participate in the "filling up what is lacking in the afflictions of Christ" on behalf of my brothers and sisters?

At times, when we hear the phrase: "The cross lies at the heart of Christian life", our spontaneous reaction is to ask, "In what sense is this Good News to any except the masochists?" Jesus himself did not seek or will suffering; he prayed to escape from it. He suffered because he lived the ultimate consequences of the Father's unconditional love for all of us. As a powerless, vulnerable, silent and hidden God, God enters into the pain, weak-nesses, sinfulness and corruption of human life. In Jesus God absorbs into himself the concentrated and venomous onslaught of sin, and transforms it.

On September 2, 1997 the Indian diocesan priest, Fr. Christudas, vice-principal of a school in Bihar, was stripped naked and walked through the streets of the town up to the Bishop's House about 13 kilometers away. On the way he was beaten and his hair was cut off. The crowd that accompanied him and the students who inflicted the humiliation and the abuse remained silent. No one came to his aid. He was refused bail and kept in prison without a proper warrant or a proper trial. While in prison, he wrote the following verses:

The first fatal blow from my foes
Broke open my head
Blood poured out and ran down my body
I appeared all over, red

"Jesus," was the word I uttered loud
They laughed in anger
And mocked and pronounced every curse
I could bear no longer

My heart chanted His Holy Name
And pleaded for grace
Possessed by a 'multitude' they jumped
And spat on my face

And in their frenzy stripped me naked
Clipped off my hair
With chappals old, me they garlanded
Why, a deal so unfair?

No answer did my heart receive
I was in pain.
The administrative forces, too,
joined in the madness
And enjoyed their gain

Looked I for some human help
No heart, no hands
Ah, they kicked, punched and felled me
Down on the sands

"Lord," I cried, "give me thy hands
Help me to rise"
I knew for sure that Jesus my Lord
Me will not despise

He accompanied me in my passion
And kept me strong
My body they tortured but to the spirit
could do no wrong.

Jesus, my Master with His mantle of love
Covered my shame
Shared my agony and bore my pain
Great is His Name!

My tongue shall praise and sing
To Him a new song
And my soul for JESUS alone
For ever will long.

**QUESTION: How does my image of God's love change as I read
about the way Jesus suffered injury, insult, and degra-
dation in order to save all of humanity and redeem the
whole cosmos? How am I affected by the experience
of another human being suffering in the way Jesus
suffered?**

Much of our suffering has nothing to do with the cross of Christ, for it
is not pain incurred through walking in his footsteps, but the pain of our hurt

ego when we see our own little kingdoms threatened. Maybe, rather than trying to enter into the Passion of Christ, we ought to ask him to enter into our suffering so that we can find him present and beckoning in our pain. Only in this way can we become witnesses to hope and the Good News of the Kingdom. Words and prayers that arise from tortured hearts and suffering people who have not given up hope, like the Archbishop of Khartoum who is so deeply aware of his people's pain, speak to us of a hope that is based on the message of Scripture.

A PRAYER

Lord, I like that part of the Gospel:
Those two disciples did not recognize you.
That is when you experienced
what no human being has ever experienced:
hearing people discussing your death and burial,
and signing you off as a hopeless case.
And they were so discouraged!

We continue to discourage one another
in your presence Lord;
to treat you as a stranger,
to our problems and fears,
so we exaggerate them
and console ourselves
that we are sharing your cross.
You did well to die on a cross:
there is place for only one person
and you have taken it.
Risen and alive,
you appear unannounced
wherever there is fear,
doubt, despair, suffering and death,
and what peace, joy and courage
you leave behind - when you disappear!

Lord, keep up these mysterious appearances
when we need you most
and may that 'most' be always.

And be patient with us, Lord,
when we feel and speak more

of your death and ours,
of your pains and ours,
of our sins and failures
instead of the life and the victory
you have won for us all.
(Archbishop Gabriel Wako of Khartoum - Easter 1994)

QUESTION: When in the Gospel of John Mary revealed the stunning
news that Jesus was no longer in the tomb, the disciples
took off running to see for themselves! Does the news
that Jesus is truly alive set my heart racing?

Chapter Thirteen

The Kingdom and the Holy Spirit

How is the Kingdom of God now present in the world since the resurrection of Jesus? The answer is simple: the Kingdom is present in the Holy Spirit. We can therefore say: Where the Spirit is, there is the Kingdom. Where the Kingdom is, there is the Spirit. To understand this response we need to look briefly at the role of the Holy Spirit in the history of salvation.

The Messianic Gift of the End-time

Just as the "true Israel" was expected to emerge only at the end-time, so also was the outpouring of the messianic Spirit anticipated as an eschatological event. This outpouring was regarded as the distinctive mark of the latter days of the final period in history, the "golden age of the Spirit." Tappeiner writes:

> In this final age of God's glory (Is 11:9; Hab 2:14) and the glory of his people the Spirit really comes into His own, because that age is uniquely characterized as the age of the Spirit ("Holy Spirit," p. 732).

The Spirit's Link to Creation and Life

The Old Testament combined the phrase "ruah-elohim" with the notion of a CREATIVE and LIFE-GIVING FORCE. The Spirit is seen as the "divine breath" which guarantees the life of every human being and of everything that exists. To live means to participate in the life of the life-giving Spirit. God the Artist-Potter desired and still desires to form us into beautiful vessels:

> It isn't you who shape God;
> it is God who shapes you.
> If then you are the work of God,
> await the hand of the Artist
> who does all things in due season.
> Offer the Potter your heart, soft and tractable,
> and keep the form in which
> the Artist has fashioned you.
> Let your clay be moist,
> lest you grow hard and lose the imprint of the Potter's fingers. (Saint Irenaeus)

As long as the Spirit is active in a person he or she lives. But when God withdraws the Spirit, life comes to an end. The basic scriptural text for this view is Genesis 1:2. It is the "ruah elohim" that brings forth the world out of the inchoate primeval waste. He creates the world. Nothing comes into existence except through the power of God's creative Spirit. He is the agent of creation as well as of life (Eichrodt, *Theology of the Old Testament II,* pp. 46-68).

Teilhard de Chardin says this:

> Fire, the source of being...In the beginning was Power, intelligent, loving, energizing... In the beginning there were not coldness and darkness: there was the Fire... Blazing Spirit, Fire... be pleased yet once again to come down and breathe a soul into the newly formed, fragile film of matter with which this day the world is to be freshly clothed. (*The Heart of the Matter*, pp. 121-122)

As Genesis 2:7 tells us, life is found in the human person because God *"breathed into his nostrils a breath of life, and thus man became a living being."* The spirit in human beings is God's Spirit in the sense that he is its creator. The Spirit's role in all creatures is most explicitly and beautifully expressed in Psalm 104:29-30:

> *If you hide your face they are dismayed, if you take away their breath, they perish and return to dust. When you send forth your Spirit, they are created and you renew the face of the earth.*

What strikes home most in this passage is the dynamic aspect of this creative power of God. It is God's Spirit who not only creates all things but who holds all things constantly in existence. Anything new that might emerge has its origin in this creative power of God. The Spirit is seen in these passages as the "ground of life," the "power of life," in short, "the origin of life".

THE INDIAN'S PRAYER

O Great Spirit,
Whose voice I hear in the winds,
and whose breath
    gives life to all the world,

Hear me! I am small and weak,
I need your
    strength and wisdom.
Let me walk in beauty
and make my eyes ever behold
    the red and purple sunset.

Make my hands respect the things
you have made
   and my ears sharp to hear your voice.

Make me wise
so that I may understand things
   you have taught my people.

Let me learn the lessons you have hidden
   in every leaf and rock.

I seek strength, not to be greater than
   my brothers and sisters,
   but to fight my greatest enemy - myself.

Make me always ready to come to you
   with clean hands and straight eyes;

So when life fades, as the fading sunset,
   my spirit may come to you without shame.

This realization of God's all-pervasive presence in whatever exists and lives provides us with the theological basis for any discussion concerning the care for nature and life on this planet.

An old monk once was visited in a dream by the risen Christ who suggested they go for a walk together. The monk, of course, excitedly agreed. After a long and contemplative stroll in the woods, the monk turned to Jesus and asked, "When you walked the hills of Palestine, you mentioned that one day you would come again in all your glory. Lord, it's been so long; when will you return for good?" After a few moments of silence the resurrected and living One said, "When my presence in nature and all around you and my presence beneath the surface of your skin is as real to you as my presence right now, when this awareness becomes second-nature to you, *then* will I have returned for good." The monk pondered these words in his heart as they walked back to the hermitage in silence. (Dowd).

Issues of ecology for us Christians should be approached from the biblical insight that God has created everything and sustains everything with the creative power of love. Things are valuable because God created them and declared them as being good. We human beings do not give value to created things. Rather, they have value because of having been created and being loved by God's Spirit of love.

It is God whom human beings know in every creature.
(Hildegard of Bingen)

The human is the being in whom the Earth has become spiritually aware, has awakened consciousness, has become self-aware and self-reflecting. In the human, the Earth begins to reflect on itself, its meaning, who it is. So in our deepest definition and its deepest subjectivity, humans are the Earth-conscious. (*Earthspirit*, pp. 19-20)

When the prophets announced a "new creation" (Is 43:19: *"I am going to do a new thing"*), it is the Spirit who is linked immediately to this innovative activity. He is portrayed as the Spirit of the new creation and the Spirit of life everlasting. The prophet Ezekiel, in particular, sees the final coming of Yahweh linked with the superior activity of the Holy Spirit (Ezk 36:27; 37:1-14). But also Is 44:3; Zc 6:1-8 and Jl 2:23-30; 3:1-3 promise the outpouring of the creative and life-giving Spirit in abundance on "all flesh" at the eschatological time. The end-time will be the "golden age of the Spirit." The Spirit of God is seen as the consummating power of the New Age." Pannenberg describes the situation in the following passage:

For Israel the distinction between the eschatological and the present working of the Spirit consists in the fact that in the eschaton, the Spirit . . . will be completely given to men. Therefore, we can expect that life in the eschaton will be a higher life in comparison to the earthly condition in which men do not really have the Spirit of God but can only be driven by him (*Jesus-God and Man*, p. 171).

The age to come will be distinguished as the age of the Spirit in a threefold way. First, the "one who comes" is characterized "as a man of the Spirit" (Is 11:2; 42:1; 61:1). Secondly, the age to come is inaugurated by the outpouring of the Spirit on all flesh (Is 32:15; 44:3; Ezk 39:29; Joel 2:28). Thirdly, this age of the Spirit is marked by a deeper, inward spirituality; a new Covenant (Is 59:21; Jer 31:31-34; 32:37-40) will emerge and a new heart will be given through the abiding presence of God's Spirit (Ezk 36:27).

COME, HOLY SPIRIT

Come Creator, come Holy Spirit!
Through you this world was created.
Recreate it again and again.
The 'world',
that needs your creative power,
is our heart.
Create anew what you have made.
Unite what is falling apart,
arouse what does not bear fruit,
revitalize what has become old.

Give us eyes
that see your created and uncreated light.
Give us the strength to bear fruit
and to rejoice with body and soul.

Make flexible all that is rigid,
give us new life,
because we have become paralyzed with fear.
Give courage to the disheartened

and hope to the downcast;
give freedom to those bound in guilt
and faith to all who want to believe.

Give a voice to the mute,
a word of gratitude to those with grateful hearts.
A word of truth to those who seek the truth.
Give a word of trust to those who cannot trust,
and to those, who do not know
how to praise you, a word to praise you with.

Bring to life the dead,
so that the weak will rise with strength renewed,
those who cannot stand up, will walk erect,
those who cannot walk,
will stride with confidence,
those who have lost the way,
will find the one you show
and those who see no meaning,
will see their goal.

Come, Creator God, Holy Spirit!

The Spirit of Prophecy and Revelation

Analyzing the action of the Holy Spirit in the Old Testament, Turner comes to this conclusion:

The Spirit was primarily represented in two ways: (1) as the invisible activity of God in power, and (2) his presence in revelation and wisdom (cf. Turner, *The Holy Spirit,* p.3).

Besides the creative and life-giving power promised for the end-time, the Spirit, especially in later Judaism, is seen preeminently as the Spirit of PROPHECY AND REVELATION. The prophets are the bearers of the Spirit of God par excellence. But it is important to notice that God's Spirit was typically related to God's covenantal activities in and on behalf of Israel and so the work of the Spirit was restricted almost exclusively to the people of Israel.

The Spirit was seen to be 'on', 'with' or 'in' the leaders of Israel, enabling them to act with God's power or to reveal his will. The *ruah* of God was regarded as a charismatic endowment on the judges (Judg 3:10; 6:34; 11:29). He was particularly seen and perceived as an endowment on Moses (Num 11:17,29) through whose power he led Israel to freedom. This spirit was shared with the seventy elders (11:25-29) and gave them wisdom. In short, we could say the Spirit of God acted as the *channel of communication between God and a human person.* This "Spirit of prophecy" was perceived to have made God's will and wisdom known to the charismatic leader, to the king giving him divine directions for the religious and political guidance of the people (Ezk 2:2f; 3:24; 11:4-5) His range of inspiration is so broad that it includes even the artisans (cf. Turner, *The Holy Spirit*, p. 4).

The future expectation of the Spirit was that all of Israel would share in the Spirit of prophecy (Joel 2:28; Num 11:29). All would receive immediate knowledge of God. The future was characterized by the lavish outpouring of God's Spirit (Is 32:15 44:3; Ezk 39:29) and the revelation of his glory and power. This was the mission of the future liberator or king endowed with the Spirit of wisdom and power (Is 11:1-9).

In Judaism the activities of the Spirit were more clearly reflected on. There are four activities which are most frequently listed.

The most common is the Spirit of prophecy which bestows charismatic *revelation and guidance* although this has nothing directly to do with the "Spirit of prophecy". Secondly, the Spirit of prophecy grants charismatic *wisdom* (Sir 39:6), that means, the Spirit gives lively enthusiasm and understanding of God's word that is characterized by doxological joy in God and enables the sage to become a charismatic teacher. Thirdly, the Spirit of prophecy affords *invasively inspirited prophetic speech. Invasive* means that the Spirit comes upon the person, who is caught up and inspired to speak. Fourthly, the Spirit of prophecy bestows *invasively inspirited charismatic praise or worship.* This is what the New Testament means by the gifts of tongues. The Targum has this to say referring to 1 Samuel 10 and 19 where the Spirit falls upon the prophets:

> And the spirit of prophecy from before the Lord will reside upon you, and you will sing praise with them, and you will be changed into another man.

In the messianic age this prophetic Spirit will be poured out upon all of Israel and all will receive prophetic insight; not just prophets but even slave girls, the bottom of the social scale in ancient society (Joel 3:1-2). Here the Spirit becomes that divine power that sets us apart, cleanses us and impels us in our innermost being to obedience to the will of Yahweh (Jer 31:31-34). The indwelling Spirit of Yahweh becomes the agent and guarantee of divine human fellowship (Ezk 36:24-28). The Spirit becomes the law itself in us (2 Cor 3:3-6; Rom 8:2) (cf. Schneider, "Kata Pneuma agiosunes", p. 378). This means two things. First, the Spirit will reveal the will of God (the LAW) not only to the prophets but to everyone (Joel 3:1-2). Secondly, the Spirit will create in us the "divine human fellowship" that links us to God's own life and is the final fulfillment of the eschatological expectation - human beings in union with God. In the eschatological time, therefore, the Spirit not only reveals to us what God wants us to do (1 Jn 2:27), but also gives us the power to do it. He enables us to respond to God's offer of divine life. He makes us "sons and daughters in the Son"; he enables us to address God as Father; he draws us into God's own life (Rom 8:15; Gal 4:6).

Although the Spirit as "prophetic Spirit" was dominant in Judaism, the view of the Spirit as "creative and life-giving power" can still be found, especially in Ezekiel where it is written that God will make us into "new creatures" (Ezk 37:19-21). He will fill our new hearts with the power of the Spirit, enabling us to lead holy lives because the Spirit himself will be our law and guide (Ezk 36:26-27) (cf. Koch, "Spirit," p. 876).

SPIRIT OF GOD,

You are the breath of creation,
the wind of change that blows through our lives,
opening us up to new dreams and new hopes,
new life in Jesus Christ.

Forgive us our closed minds
which barricade themselves against new ideas,
preferring the past to what you
might want to do through us tomorrow.
Forgive our closed eyes
which fail to see the needs of your world,
blind to opportunities of service and love.

Forgive our closed hands
which clutch our gifts and our wealth
for our own use alone.

Forgive our closed hearts
which limit our affections to ourselves
and our own.

Spirit of new life,
forgive us and break down the prison walls
of our selfishness,
that we might be open to your love
and open for the service of your world,
through Jesus Christ our Lord. Amen.
(Ellis, - Isaiah 6:9-10)

The Spirit and the Messiah

Although the evidence for the expectation that the Messiah would be equipped with the Spirit of God is not extensive, there are enough passages to support this idea (cf. Barret, *The Holy Spirit*, p. 120). The Messiah is perceived as prophetic (Dt 18:15: *"A prophet like me will the Lord, your God, raise up for you from among your own kinsmen; to him you shall listen"*), as kingly, as a charismatic leader (Is 11:1-10) and as a glorious supernatural person of divine qualities (Dn 7:13ff). Isaiah 11:1ff. presents a masterly portrayal of the future ideal ruler, who is to be endowed permanently with the Spirit of the Lord. On the messianic King "rests" all the fullness of God's Spirit (the sevenfold gifts in which this fullness consists). It is first the Messiah who will receive the Spirit and, through him, all who will join the new community.

There are three texts from Isaiah that attest to one outstanding activity expected from the messianic bearer of the Spirit: the practice of compassion, concern for justice and for the rights of the poor, the lowly, the weak, and the marginalized.

What is at stake is the creation of a community without exploitation of and discrimination against the weakest in its midst. It is the establishment of a true society of Yahweh in which all are respected and possess equal rights:

> *But a shoot shall grow out of the stump of Jesse. A twig shall sprout from this stock. The spirit of the Lord shall alight upon him . . . He shall not judge by what his eyes behold, nor decide by what his ears perceive. Thus he shall judge the poor with equity. And decide with justice for the lowly of the land (Is 11:1ff.).*

The same connection is found in Isaiah 42:1-3:

This is My servant, whom I uphold. My chosen one, in whom I delight. I have put My spirit upon him . . . He shall teach the true way to the nations. He shall not break even a bruised reed, or snuff out even a dim wick. He shall bring forth the true way.

The servant protects the endangered and the vulnerable. His mission is a universal one. He will extend his judgement to the peoples of the whole world.

The third text is Isaiah 61:1-4, which speaks of the Spirit of Yahweh resting upon the one who is sent to bring good news to the poor and to proclaim a year of liberation for those in captivity and slavery. It is this text that Jesus applied to himself in Luke 4:16ff. Matthew 12:18ff. explicitly connects Isaiah 42 to Jesus and his activity. Jesus is the one on whom the Spirit of Yahweh rests and remains. He will bring "justice to victory" for all the nations (cf. Welker, "The Holy Spirit," pp. 5-11).

These three texts of Isaiah affirm the three basic attitudes that God revealed about himself in the history with his people. First, Yahweh is a God who hears the cry of the poor and he comes to liberate them from their oppression (Ex 3:7-9). Second, he is a "lover of justice" (Ps 99), and to "know him means to do justice" (Jer 22:16). Third, the God of Israel is a God who is moved by compassion towards the weak and the downtrodden. The Messiah is portrayed in these texts as the one who will be filled with these divine attitudes and whose mission consists in accomplishing final salvation for all by living according to these attitudes.

There once was a wise and beloved king who cared greatly for his people and wanted only what was the best for them. The people knew the king took a personal interest in their affairs and tried to understand how his decisions affected their lives. Periodically, he would disguise himself and wander through the streets, trying to see life from their perspective.

One day he disguised himself as a poor villager and went to visit the public baths. Many people were there enjoying the fellowship and relaxation. The water for the baths was heated by a furnace in the cellar, where one man was responsible for maintaining the comfort level of the water. The king made his way to the basement to visit with the man who tirelessly tended the fire.

The two men shared a meal together, and the king befriended this lonely man. Day after day, week in and week out, the king went to visit the fire tender. The man in the cellar soon became close to his strange visitor because he came down to the basement where he was. No one else had showed that much caring or concern.

One day the king revealed his true identity to his friend. It was a risky move, for he feared that the man might ask him for special favors or a gift. Instead, the king's new friend looked into his eyes and said, "You left your comfortable palace to sit with me in this hot and dingy cellar. You ate my meager food and genuinely showed you cared about what happens to me. On other people you might bestow rich gifts, but to me you have given the greatest gift of all. You have given me the gift of yourself" (Cavanaugh).

The link between the person of the Messiah and the gift of the Spirit is supported by apocryphal texts, as noted by Barret:

In him dwells the Spirit of wisdom, and the Spirit that gives insight, and the Spirit of understanding and might, and the Spirit of those who have fallen asleep in righteousness [cf. Is 62:2; 11:1ff.] (Henoch 49:3).

The heavens shall be opened and from the temple of glory will come upon him sanctification with the Father's voice as from Abraham to Isaac. And the glory of the Most High shall be uttered over him and the Spirit of understanding and sanctification shall rest upon him in the waters (Lev 18:2-14).

And the heavens shall be opened to him and the blessing of the Most High shall be poured down upon him and he will pour down upon us the Spirit of grace. And you shall be his true children by adoption and you shall walk in his commandments first and last (Judg 24:2ff.) (The Holy Spirit, pp. 42-44).

These apocryphal writings, which influenced Christian literature and helped to form the baptism stories, associate the messianic office with a particular bestowal of the Spirit. The Messiah is regarded as filled with the Holy Spirit. The outpouring of the Holy Spirit upon the eschatological community is intimately linked with the Messiah who receives the Spirit first and then gives it to the messianic community.

Jesus and the Holy Spirit

The New Testament understanding of Spirit generally corresponds to the wide range of the word "ruah" in the Old Testament. In particular, the major aspect of the Spirit in the Old Testament, as the experience of God powerfully present and active in the midst of His people, remains one of the main characteristics of the Spirit in the New Testament. A dramatic shift, however, occurs in the New Testament to the effect that this experience of the Spirit is intrinsically bound up with the historical Jesus (cf. Tappeiner, "Holy Spirit," p. 732).

The Earthly Jesus and the Holy Spirit

The Gospel of Luke reveals a particular interest in the Holy Spirit:

> To Luke must go the title "Historian of the Holy Spirit," even as Paul and John must share the title "Theologians of the Holy Spirit." This is not to say that Luke is not theological in his treatment of the Church's experience of the Holy Spirit. Rather it is because he uses the vehicle of history preeminently to provide an external framework large enough to contain the full significance of the experience of the Holy Spirit . . . Luke focuses on the movement of salvation history, on the leadership of the Holy Spirit in the missionary task of the Church, and on the manifestation of the Holy Spirit in the external frame of history (Tappeiner, "Holy Spirit", p. 732).

Of great interest for us here is the connection that Luke makes between the Spirit, Jesus and the Kingdom of God. The link between Jesus and the Spirit is most clearly seen in Luke's threefold pattern of salvation history as was mentioned earlier: In the first stage, Jesus is the *creation* of the Spirit (Lk 1:35). At the Jordan (second stage) Jesus becomes the uniquely anointed *Man of the Spirit* (3:22). In the third stage, his exaltation, Jesus becomes the *Lord of The Spirit* and Baptizer of the Spirit (Acts 2:23). The same three-epoch pattern is also found in Mark and Matthew. As in Luke, Jesus is the *creation of the Spirit*, the *unique bearer of the Spirit* and the *future dispenser of the Spirit* (Dunn, "Spirit and Kingdom", pp. 38-39).

The Annunciation Story

Luke brings the activity of Spirit into his infancy narratives in association with Jesus' conception, birth and childhood. Elisabeth and Zechariah experience the Spirit of Prophecy in *invasive prophetic speech*. The same happens to Simeon and Anna. They all give recognition, assurance of salvation, revelation and guidance in line with the role assigned to the Spirit in Judaism. Luke seems to portray here the dawn of the eschatological restoration of the Spirit of prophecy of Israel. Accordingly, what is important here is what is said about the Spirit referring to John and Jesus. The Baptist is *filled with the Holy Spirit* from his mother's womb on; this indicates the new age and that John will be under the guidance of this spirit in ever growing measure.

But the new eschatological quality of the Spirit in Israel is most clearly manifest in connection with the role he plays in the conception of the Messiah (Lk 1:32-35; Mt 1:18). The child born to Mary is to be hailed as the "*son of the Most High*", and given the eschatological throne of David because he will be no child of ordinary wedlock (1:35). The semi-miraculous conception of John to his aged parents (1:4-25) and the ascending parallelism of the narrative require that this means a virgin conception of Jesus, by the creative activity of the Holy Spirit. Jesus is not merely filled with the Holy Spirit, like John, but rather his very being is attributed to the Spirit. Here the Spirit is primarily seen as the miraculous power of new creation. Jesus, bestowed with that Spirit, will be the fountainhead of Israel's restoration which is indicated by the "overshadowing" as the cloud of God's presence in the Old Testament. His wisdom and his knowledge of the Father are uniquely the result of being Spirit-filled (2:49-50) and cannot be grasped by his parents (Turner, *The Holy Spirit*, pp. 23-25).

For Luke, the whole life of Jesus is closely related to the Holy Spirit. From the very beginning Jesus is the work of the Spirit. As the Spirit of God was active at the creation of the world, so that same Spirit was to be expected at its renewal. The entry of the redeemer into history was regarded as the work of the Spirit. The activity of the Spirit in the infancy narratives introduces the messianic-eschatological age. The part played by the Holy Spirit in those narratives is the fulfillment of God's promised redemption in a new act of creation, comparable with that of Genesis 1. As the Spirit hovered over the "chaos at the beginning" to bring forth the world of creation, so he hovers now over a virgin to bring forth the NEW creation (Turner, *The Holy Spirit*, p. 24).

Mary and the Holy Spirit

Mary,
who conceived the Incarnate Word
By the power of the Holy Spirit,
and then in the whole of her life
allowed herself to be guided
by that Spirit's interior activity,
is contemplated and imitated
above all as the woman
who surrendered
to the voice of the Spirit,
a woman
of silence and attentiveness,
a woman of hope who,
like Abraham,
accepted God's will
'hoping against hope' (Rom 4:18)
Mary gave full expression

to the longing of the poor of Yahweh
and is a radiant model
for those who entrust themselves
with all their hearts
to the promises of God.

The Baptism of Jesus

The coming down of the Spirit upon Jesus is the initial fulfilment of John's promise that the messianic ministry of Jesus was now coming into effect. In the power of the Spirit (descending visibly upon him and "remaining upon him" indicating that from that time on the Spirit will be with Jesus as the power to exercise the messianic task) Jesus begins now with the restoration of Israel and its cleansing with fire (Lk 12:49).The fullness of this Spirit, however, would be poured out on Pentecost. The mention of fire here and on Pentecost as descending like tongues of fire are linked together not unlike the "already" and the "not yet" of the Spirit.

Turner might be right when he links the Spirit of conception with the Spirit coming down on Jesus after his baptism and empowering him for his mission:

> It would be possible to understand this visionary experience as nothing more than a disclosure to Jesus of the impending significance of the Spirit already upon him: i.e. the Spirit he received in the miraculous conception (Lk 1:35) was about to empower the messianic task through him (p.28).

Here, as in the birth narratives, the Spirit is the creative activity of God that calls into being the messianic era. The Spirit, descending as a dove from heaven, hovers over Jesus to bring forth in him the new creation as he does in the classic Old Testament paradigms. Koch writes:

> Just as on the morning of the first creation, the ruah-elohim flew to and fro like a bird above the primordial waters as a power of fruitfulness and life, or as after the flood the dove bore a fresh olive branch in its beak as a sign of peace for the new humanity embodied in the Messiah (Gn 8:11) ("Spirit," p. 879).

All four Evangelists testify to the Baptism of Jesus as a special bestowal of the Holy Spirit at the beginning of Jesus' public ministry. In addition, John stresses that the Spirit not only comes upon Jesus but remains there; thus characterizing him as *"baptizer with the Holy Spirit"* (Jn 1:32). Although Jesus already possessed the Spirit by virtue of his unique conception, this special bestowal of the Holy Spirit was necessary if Jesus was to fulfill his role as initiator of the age to come. The account of the Baptism of Jesus by John further shows that Jesus experienced a new consciousness of his sonship and of the Spirit. It was the awareness of the Spirit in him that made Jesus realize that the end-time had come and that John's ministry was over. The decisive indication for Jesus that the Kingdom had arrived was the presence of the Spirit working in and through him. Associated with that descent of the Spirit is the realization of "sonship." Jesus is declared to be the "beloved Son" (Dunn, *Jesus and the Spirit,* pp. 64-65).

A new relationship is established between Jesus as the representative of the new messianic community and God. The Spirit provokes the end-time by leading humankind through Jesus into that final relationship that God had promised as the great gift of the last days. In the baptism story, the life of the Trinity is extended into this world since Jesus "as one of us" already lives that "divine-human fellowship" which is promised as THE great gift of the end-time. It is the fulfillment of God's saving plan for humankind. Through the outpouring of the Holy Spirit, new beginnings are made possible.

A journalist writes: After waiting for a long time I was finally granted permission to enter the jail in Tellers. I looked into the tired and expressionless faces of the prisoners as they walked in strict formation through the inner court of the prison. The supervising warden pointed out, "There are quite a few talented people among them. For example, the little man over there paints beautiful pictures!" When we came to his office he showed me one of the paintings which struck me because of the very vivid colors: twelve men gazed up to the sky in utter amazement; their hair disheveled and their faces bathed in brilliant light. Their eyes were wide open and larger than normal. The warden remarked in a rather disparaging tone, "He calls the picture "Pentecost". It was painted for our prison chapel, but it cannot be placed there, because all the people in the picture are inmates and they are the worst criminals in the prison!"

Later I had a chance to talk with the painter. "I find your picture very exciting," I began, "but why did you paint only your inmates, the disciples in the upper room were all converted persons?" He was deeply touched by the question and replied with some agitation, "On Pentecost everything changed. The pious do not need that kind of realization. But those who despair in themselves, you have to show that a new beginning is possible and that the power of the Spirit can defeat and transform sin!" I would not give up so easily, "But why did you pick the worst of the offenders?"

"Pentecost is a miracle," he replied, "the small sinners even your wife change - maybe even time in prison can do that. But the very big sinners - only God can change." I noticed how he was struggling and then, without a word, he pointed at a particular spot in the picture. Then I noticed for the first time that he had painted himself as one of the sinners, "The real big sinners," he repeated once again, "only God can change" (Hoffsümmer).

The Public Ministry of Jesus

To the eschatological Kingdom of God belongs the eschatological activity of the Spirit. They cannot be separated. The final coming of the Kingdom was present for Jesus because the Spirit of the eschatological age was active in and through him. He is so filled with the Holy Spirit that "he was driven into the desert" (Mk 1:12) where the struggle between the Kingdom of God and the anti-kingdom of the evil one is initiated. The exorcisms, the miracles and the forgiveness of sins that Jesus performs are all signs of the "New Age." They are clear signs of the eschatological Spirit in whose power he drove out demons (Mt 12:28), healed the sick and infirm and raised the dead to life (Lk 4:36; 5:17; 6:19; 8:54; 13:32). He prayed in the Holy Spirit (Lk 3:21; 5:16; 6:12; 9:18; 11:1; 22:32; 23:34-46) and he overflowed with joy in the Holy Spirit (cf. Koch, "Spirit," p. 879). Particularly important is Matthew 12:28:

> *"Since it is by the Spirit of God that I cast out demons then the Kingdom of God has come upon you."*

The emphasis should be focused on the two phrases, "Spirit of God" and "Kingdom of God." Both phrases are intimately linked together. The significance of the saying is twofold. First, the Kingdom is present now because of the effective power of the Spirit which shows itself in the work of conquering the demonic powers. Secondly, Jesus claims to have in himself the end-time Spirit in contrast to all others who drove out evil spirits. Their work can be compared with his being empowered by God to begin the final battle with Satan. Jesus' self-understanding and his Kingdom message are deeply linked with his being conscious of having the eschatological Spirit. It was because the Spirit was at work in Jesus that his contemporaries could be sure that the Kingdom had come. The manifestations of the Spirit are the manifestation of the Kingdom.

The link between Jesus and the Spirit is so intimate that it could be said that Jesus did not just have the Spirit, but he was the Spirit in human form (cf. Boff, *Church Charisma and Power,* pp. 147-148). In Jesus the Kingdom and the Spirit are so closely linked that we can say with Dunn: "The Kingdom is present because (and so far as) the Spirit is operative in Jesus and submitted to by Jesus." We can, therefore, also say that where Jesus is, there is the Kingdom and where the Spirit is, there is the Kingdom. Or, in the Word of Jesus as transmitted by the Gospel of Thomas.

Whoever is near me is near the fire, and whoever is far from me is far from the Kingdom. (Thomas, saying 82)

In the light of these words Dunn's comment about the link between Jesus, Spirit and Kingdom might be better understood when he says:

When Jesus says,'*The Kingdom of God is among you*' (Lk 17:21) we must understand Luke to mean that the Kingdom was present not simply because Jesus was present, but rather because Jesus as the unique Spirit-bearer was present ("Spirit and Kingdom", p. 39).

Yet, the Gospel avoids direct emphasis on the Spirit for the following reason:

Jesus acted under the necessity of a divine constraint. Lack of glory and a cup of suffering were the messianic vocation, and part of his poverty was the absence of the signs of the Spirit of God. They would have been inconsistent with the office of a humiliated Messiah (Barret, *The Holy Spirit*, pp. 158-159).

Or, in the words of John's Gospel, "*The Spirit has not yet been given, because Jesus was not yet glorified*" (Jn 7:39). During Jesus' life the Kingdom was present because only Jesus had the Spirit. He alone was the Man of the Spirit; the Reign of God was actualized and demonstrated in and through him by the Spirit. In the time of Jesus the Kingdom was still a matter of the future because on Pentecost other men and women would be baptized into the Kingdom through the Spirit.

The Spirit is particularly important in the *already* and *not yet* tension of the Kingdom. The presence of the Spirit is the "already" of the Kingdom. Although this *present-future* tension as function of the Holy Spirit is clearly seen in the theology of St. Paul, it can already be discovered in the Gospels.

The Glorified Christ and the Holy Spirit

The cross is the climax of God's love for us in the human form of the incarnate Son. From this perspective, Easter should be seen as the "eternalization" of that love. This love becomes the "*dynamis*," i.e., the power, that will ultimately transform this old creation and bring it into the NEW CREATION. Jesus' death was necessary in order that the Kingdom could become a "transforming power" for the whole of creation. The power of the new creation is the Holy Spirit, the principle of life and love itself. The first fruit of Jesus' death out of love for us is the transformation of his earthly body into the New Creation. The resurrection of the crucified Jesus is seen in Scripture as the work of the Holy Spirit, which is the life-giving power of God:

> *It was the Father - in response to Jesus' faithfulness until death - who raised Jesus to glory through the Spirit who gives life (Rom 8:11; Eph 1:19-20; 1 Cor 6:14; 2 Cor 13:4).*

According to Acts 2:33, it is Christ himself who first receives the Spirit from the Father. This causes the raising up of his body and his exaltation at the right hand of the Father. Christ became such a spiritual being in the resurrection that from then on he is pulsating with the overflowing and life-giving power of the *divine breath.* He became life-giving Spirit (2 Cor 3:17). In his humanity, Christ is in solidarity with us in the condition of sinful flesh (Phil 2:7; Rom 8:3; Gal 3:13; 2 Cor 5:21). As such he is first the "recipient" of the Holy Spirit who transforms Jesus' humanity into the New Creation that he might become *"the first born from the dead."* Flesh, i.e., the old sin-permeated world, has been created anew, and in the risen Christ the Kingdom of God in its final form has become a reality. As our representative now, the risen Lord is in himself already the final fulfillment of our future "in advance".

Jesus' resurrection is the fulfillment of the promise that God will pour out his Spirit upon all flesh at the end-time. For John the mission of Jesus is to "release the Spirit." In John 19:30 the last breath of Jesus is seen as the breathing forth of the eschatological Spirit who was present up to them only in Jesus alone. The death of Jesus is necessary for the coming of the great eschatological gift - the Holy Spirit.

> From the wound in his side when he was crucified (Jn 19:34; see also 1 Jn 5:6ff.), from the glorified body of Christ as the messianic temple (see Jn 2:19; Ezk 47), the Spirit was indeed to be poured out over all the earth and to the end of time (Koch, "Spirit," p. 881).

On the evening of the day of his resurrection, the risen Lord imparts to his disciples his great Easter gift, the Holy Spirit: *"He breathed on them and said, 'Receive the Holy Spirit'"* (Jn 20:22). Again the image from the creation story comes to mind. As God created the first Adam into a living creature by "blowing his breath into his nostrils" (Gen 2:7), so the new Adam, the eschatological community, comes into existence through the life-giving Spirit going forth from the mouth of the risen Lord. It is His life-giving Spirit who brings forth the new creation, the end-time community.

Luke presents the same view only in different images. For him, the empowering with the Holy Spirit happens fifty days after the resurrection, on Pentecost. First, he makes sure that the connection between the Jesus who proclaimed the Kingdom and the risen Lord is maintained: *"For forty days after his death he appeared to them . . . and talked with them about the Kingdom of God"* (Acts 1:3). Secondly, they, the disciples of the Lord will soon be empowered by the Holy Spirit whom Jesus will send from the Father. Endowed with that power from on high, they will continue Jesus' mission: proclaiming the Kingdom as present by driving out demons, by healing people and by forgiving sins. In short, they will be enabled to perform the same signs of the Kingdom as Jesus had done in the power of the eschatological Spirit. The Kingdom will remain present because the eschatological Spirit is present: the end-time has arrived.

The Present Kingdom and the Holy Spirit

Christ has gone into the NEW CREATION completely. How then does his saving work continue? Jesus promised: *"I will not leave you orphans; I will come back in the power of the Holy Spirit."* At the juncture between the ministry of Jesus and the life of the Church stands the event of Pentecost, the decisive imparting of the Holy Spirit to believers. The experience of the early Church is the outpouring of the eschatological Spirit who brings to life this "new entity," the new community. In John this happened on Easter Sunday when the risen Lord "breathes over" the community of the disciples. For Luke it is the day of Pentecost when the eschatological Spirit comes down on the disciples in *tongues of fire.* The Spirit who was at work at the beginning of the world, who "hovered over the chaos," to bring forth the world of creation (Gen 1:1), now hovers over the small group of Jesus' disciples (Acts 2:1-4) and brings forth the new creation, the eschatological community. The Church is created by this event. She is the sphere in which Christ makes himself constantly present through the power of his Spirit. To have received the Holy Spirit means to be in contact with the risen Lord, and to be in contact with him means to be living *already* in the sphere of the NEW CREATION: *"Anyone who is in Christ Jesus IS a NEW CREATION"* (2 Cor 5:17).

The Surprises of the Holy Spirit

I am a person of hope because I believe
that God is born anew each morning,
because I believe that God is creating
the world at this very moment.

God did not create it at a distant
and a long-forgotten moment in time,
it is happening now;

we must therefore be ready
to expect the unexpected from God.

The ways of Providence
are by nature surprising.
God is here, near us,
unforeseeable and loving.

I am a person of hope,
not for human reasons
not from any natural optimism,
but because I believe
the Holy Spirit is at work
in the Church and in the world,
even where the name remains unheard.

I am an optimist because I believe
the Holy Spirit is the Spirit of creation.
Those who welcome the Spirit
will receive each day fresh liberty
and renewed joy and thrust.

The long history of the Church is filled
with the wonders of the Holy Spirit.
Think only of the prophets and saints who,
in times of darkness,
have discovered a spring of grace
and shed beams of light on our path.

I believe in the surprises of the Holy Spirit.
To hope is a duty - not a luxury.
To hope is not a dream,
but turns dreams into reality.

Happy are those who dream dreams
and are ready to pay the prices
to make them come true.
(Cardinal Suenens)

The community knows that part of the future hope is already realized
in their midst. But it knows equally well that another part still remains in the
future. It does experience - at least dimly, as a foretaste - the justice, peace

and joy of the Kingdom in the power of the Holy Spirit (Rom 14:17). However, it also still experiences itself and the world as permeated by sin.

The experience of those who allow the power of the Kingdom into their lives has been described in many ways. The Spirit of Jesus the risen one has given us a new way of life: *"We were all as good as slaves (Gal 4:3) but freedom is what we have, for Christ has set us free"* (Gal 5:1). Now we are called to a new life in community where there is no *"difference anymore between men and women; gentile and Jew, rich and poor"* (Gal 3:28). *"We have moved from death to life because we love our brothers and sisters"* (1 Jn 3:14).

The true sign of whether we have been open to the power of the risen Lord is our willingness to create "just relationships" with our fellow human beings. The power of the Kingdom is focused on creating that ultimate community where there will be no more division. Here the ultimate goal of God's intentionality with creation will come to completion: union and communion with the Triune God and with each other in the eternal banquet: *"I will be their God and they shall be my people for ever and ever"* (Rev 21:3). Christ has already drawn us through the Spirit into this new union with the Father and each other. An absolutely new intimacy is now offered which we cannot verbalize, but to which the Spirit himself gives expression:

> *We do not know how to pray, but the Spirit witnesses with our spirit that we are God's children since he cries in us ABBA, FATHER (Gal 4:6; Rom 8:15).*

A profound connection is made between the Spirit and the Kingdom of God, particularly in the theology of St. Paul. First, according to Paul, the Spirit prepares a person for the Kingdom: if anyone is to inherit the Kingdom of God in the future he must experience the work of the Spirit in the present. But secondly, and even more importantly, the Spirit not only prepares a person for the future Kingdom, the Spirit also enables the Christian to experience the future Kingdom in the present. The Spirit is the "first instalment and foretaste" of the Kingdom. The Spirit not only guarantees the full inheritance; he is himself the beginning and first part of the inheritance. Paul solves the problem of the *already* and the *not yet* precisely through the presence of the Spirit now. Christians have already been given life (Rom 6:4,13); but eternal life is still an end to be striven for (Rom 6:22; Gal 6:8). They have already received the status as sons and daughters (Rom 8:15; Gal 4:5), but they still wait for the adoption of sons and daughters. As Dunn sees it, Paul solves the present-future tension through the present-ness of the Spirit:

The present-future tension is a function of the Spirit; the Spirit himself is the part now enjoyed of the whole yet to be realized; the Spirit operates the process leading to perfection, the fulfilled Now which works for the consummated Yet to be... The Spirit we might say is the *present*-ness of the coming Kingdom. Where he is the Kingdom is, so that to have the Spirit is to have part and lot in the Kingdom here and now ("Spirit and Kingdom", p. 37).

The possession of the eschatological Spirit does not lead to a withdrawal from the world. We, who have the "first fruits of the Spirit," did not receive them for our own selfish needs. Like Jesus filled with the power of the Holy Spirit, we are to go out and to proclaim and witness to the Kingdom. Our task is to continue Jesus' own mission in the power of the Spirit we have received from him. This great gift of the risen Christ should open our eyes and hands to the whole of creation that groans and eagerly awaits the final transformation by the Spirit already operative in us. In the words of Edward Schweizer:

The new creation of man and woman by the Spirit is not a flight of faith into heaven or an abandonment of this imperfect world. On the contrary, the new creation means beginning to see the world as it is, suffering with it and taking its suffering to heart. The work of the Spirit is to make us aware of our solidarity with the world (*The Holy Spirit*, pp. 109-10).

In the light of the Kingdom we come to see that creation is one. It is the possession of the Holy Spirit that leads us into solidarity with the whole of creation in its destiny and its hope. This is well expressed by Bonhoeffer:

The hour when the Church today prays for the coming of God's Kingdom drives it for better or for worse into the company of the earthlings and worldlings, into a compact to be faithful to the earth, to its distress, its hunger, and its dying (*Gesammelte Schriften*, vol. 3, p. 274).

Conclusion

The initial question of our previous chapter asked: What is the connection between Jesus the preacher of the Kingdom of God and the message he preached? We answered by saying that, since the Kingdom is God's unconditional love for humankind made visible in the person of Jesus Christ, then Jesus is the Kingdom in person. God's redeeming love made itself visible and thus accessible to us in the life, death and resurrection of his Son. The love of Jesus that reached its climax in his death on the cross became, in the resurrection, the all-pervasive power of the Holy Spirit. That power will transform all human creation and lead it into God's eternal design.

The Kingdom makes itself present now in the power of the Holy Spirit who is the great gift of the risen Lord. Since Jesus is risen and lives as our representative in the New Creation, nothing can prevent the realization of God's final plan for creation - the New Heaven and the New Earth. Indeed, the eschatological struggle will go on. Some battles will be lost; some will be won, but the final outcome of this war is clear. As dark as the world may seem, as hopeless as the times may appear, the Christian should always heed Paul's battle cry:

Keep in Mind that Jesus Christ Is Risen from the Dead (1 Cor 15:20-28).

Reflection: *Spirit of Disturbing Peace*

When we think of, experience or pray to the Holy Spirit, we tend to use a great variety of images and symbols. These symbols are common to all peoples and all eras. Christian art throughout the centuries has been reluctant to portray the Holy Spirit in human forms. Scripture depicts the Spirit with a wide spread of images. John the Baptist *"saw the Spirit descend as a dove" (Jn 1:32); "like a dove"* is the expression Mark (Mk 1:10) and Matthew (Mt 3:16) use. Luke says, *"The Holy Spirit descended in bodily form as a dove"* (Lk 3:22). This explicit mentioning of the Spirit as dove was frequently transferred to passages where dove does not occur in the biblical text. Most notably *"The Spirit of God moving over the face of the waters" (Gen 1:2)* is imagined as a dove.

Some of the cosmic and female images for the Spirit's presence in the world might help us overcome the dualism of spirit and matter that has been plaguing us for so long and has influenced our attitude towards creation in a rather detrimental way.

Cosmic Images

From the birth of the cosmos, when the Spirit moved over the waters (Gen 1:2) to the end, when God will make all things new (Rev 21:5), the Spirit keeps on bringing forth life out of chaos. In this ongoing creation, human beings are invited to become co-creators with God and nature. Together with the Spirit they are to set up bonds of kinship among all creatures, humans and non-humans alike, all of whom are energized by this one source of life. Such life-giving, right relationships provide the basis for the struggle for survival and liberation of the poor and marginalized. They also go against the ruthless exploitation of creation which we witness around us.

God did not "make" the universe as if he had been a manufacturing engineer. The universe was born, nourished and cherished by the Holy Spirit.

QUESTION: What concrete, imaginative expressions can we, therefore, use for the Spirit's powers of indwelling, renewing and moving?

The scriptures liken the Spirit to the **wind** which can be discerned as actively present in dramatic events: blowing back the Reed Sea so that escaping slaves can run free (Ex 14:21), blowing life into the dry bones (Ezk 37:1-14) and shaking the house where Jesus' disciples are praying, impelling them to bear public witness to the good news (Acts 1:13-14; 2:1-4). The symbol of wind for the Holy Spirit helps us to begin transcending the hard dualism of spirit and matter and divine unrelatedness to creation.

Fire is another cosmic symbol of the Spirit. It has no definite shape and is ever-changing. It can be dangerous and can easily escape our control, yet its light and heat are indispensable for our well-being. Fire points to the greater fires in the universe and ultimately to the mysterious presence of God...in the burning bush, the tongues of fire, in the primeval explosion that brought about the universe. The act of creation is already a Pentecost, a first and permanent outpouring of the fiery Spirit of life, the Spirit who creates community.

Water, like fire, is essential for life. It too can kill. As a symbol for the Spirit, it points to the bottomless wellspring of the source of life and the joy that results from the immersion in this mystery. Scripture is full of instances where water symbolizes the Spirit of life. In Isaiah's vision, justice and peace result when the Spirit is poured out. (Is 32:15-18), Jesus promised this Spirit as living water to the Samaritan woman and Paul speaks of God overflowing in us as *"the love of God poured into our hearts" (Rom 5:5)*. Water, just like fire and wind, speaks of the presence of the Creator Spirit in this world moving, breathing, pouring out, blessing and dancing.

QUESTION: How was I taught to think of the Holy Spirit? Have the images remained with me? Or with what have I replaced them?

Female Symbols

In addition to the natural world, **women's reality** is also used to image the Spirit, especially in wisdom literature where the Spirit's functions are depicted as acts of Woman Wisdom.

She is a people-loving spirit: *Wisdom is a kindly spirit (1:6)*
She is the *fashioner of all things (7:22)* and knows the secrets of creation
She guides the world to harmony as *She reaches mightily from one end of the
world to the other, and orders all things well (7:12)*...she does so justly, not
by exploitation or oppression.
She bonds people in a web of kinship: *in every generation she passes into
holy souls and makes them friends of God and prophets (7:27).*

In the Jewish rabbinic tradition of the **shekinah**, the female symbol of
God's indwelling is the one actively present in the midst of a broken world.
She accompanies the people of Israel through the post-slavery wilderness
and through their exile and gives hope in time of suffering.

Women's experience of mothering provide suitable symbols for the
Creator Spirit:

like **a woman with her knitting needles** she knits together new life in a mother's
womb (Ps 139:13)
like **a woman in childbirth** she labors and pants to bring about the birth of
justice (Is 42:14)
like **a midwife** she works with a woman in pain to deliver the new creation (Ps
22:9-10)
like **a washerwoman** she scrubs away till the people are like new (Is 4:4; Ps
51:7)

Jesus uses maternal images that describe the Spirit's work in his
conversation with Nicodemus (Jn 3:4-6): The Spirit as mother or woman
giving birth. Baptism is seen, therefore, not only in terms of rites of initiation
through which the neophyte has to go, but refers to a process by which one
is born and nourished as a new creature. The Spirit is constantly hovering
over creation to bring forth something new.

**QUESTION: How much do I incorporate these cosmic and female
images into my prayers? Am I comfortable with
women's experiences when I pray to the Holy Spirit?**

Using cosmic and female images for the Spirit's presence and action
in the world enables our minds to attend to the patterns of divine relationships
to the world in ways that are **ecologically helpful**. The Holy Spirit is like a
"choreographer of an unfinished dance" improvising steps that require
the creativity of the dancer to complete the piece.

Female images of the Spirit do not speak of a commanding power
over creation, but rather of a reverent and empowering love and thus can

positively shape our attitude towards creation. The Spirit of God dwelling in the world destroys dualism and creates a circle of mutuality and inclusiveness. Because the Spirit creates matter, matter bears the mark of the sacred. Hence the world is holy, nature is holy, bodies are holy, women's bodies are holy. For the Spirit creates what is physical - worlds, bodies, senses, sexuality, passions - and moves in these just as much as in minds and ideas.

The ancient hymn to the Holy Spirit offers many of the rich images in poetic forms:

VENI CREATOR

Holy Spirit by whose breath
Life rises vibrant out of death:
Come to create, renew, inspire;
Come, kindle in our hearts your fire.

You are the seeker's sure resource,
Of burning love the living source,
Protector in the midst of strife,
The giver and the Lord of life.

In you God's energy is shown,
To us your varied gifts made known.
Teach us to speak, teach us to hear;
Yours is the tongue and yours the ear.

Flood our dull senses with your light;
In mutual love our hearts unite.
Your power the whole creation fills;
Confirm our weak, uncertain wills.

From inner strife grant us release
Turn nations to the ways of peace,
To fuller life your people bring
That as one body we may sing:

Praise to the Father, Christ his Word,
And to the Spirit, God the Lord;
To them all honor, glory be
Both now and for eternity. Amen.

Each one of us is called to discern the Spirit's work, to recognize the ongoing history of the Spirit's gifts in us. These gifts are not to be buried, but to be lived in their multiple forms and ways and to bear fruit that will endure.

A PSALM TO THE WIND OF HEAVEN

O wind that blows when and where it will,
  teach me to reverence the Wind of Heaven.
O mover of tree tops and tall grasses,
  you who are the servant of no other forces,
  open me up to the mysterious Breath of God.

O Divine Wind, blowing with the Spirit's sweetness
  through a chant-filled mosque in Arabia,
  or causing a silent heart to dance
  in a hidden hermit's cave high in the Himalayas,
  or caressing with compassion
  an abandoned packing crate in an urban slum,
  let me feel your loving touch.

Lift me up above my selfish interests,
  spreading my concerns wider than myself.
Exhale a gale of your grace into me
  and set me under full sail
  as your servant of life and of love.

Remind me with your every movement
  that history has shown clearly
  how you are the private property of none,
  how great and passionate movements
  have lost touch with your breath of life
  and so have become empty of their youthful zeal.

Wind of Inspiration, Creative Spirit of God,
  teach me not to forget
  that you come always as gift.
Remind me always to be ready
  to receive and romance and dance with joy
  wherever and whenever you visit,
  or risk that you may move on without me.
May I ever be sensitive to your gentle breezes
  and willing to soar with your wild winds.
(Hays, *Prayers for a Planetary Pilgrim*)

**Spirit of truth
whom the world can never grasp,
touch our hearts with the shock of your coming;
fill us with desire for your disturbing peace;
and fire us with longing to speak your uncontainable word
through Jesus Christ. Amen.**

Chapter Fourteen

The Community of Disciples
in the Service of the Kingdom

Jesus entrusted his mission to his disciples: *"As the Father has sent me so I am sending you"* (Jn 20:21). Since he described his mission as *"being sent to proclaim the Kingdom of God to villages and towns"* (Mk 1:38), the disciples are under the same command. The object of their mission is the same: to proclaim that God's Kingdom has arrived with and in the person of Jesus, the Christ.

This Kingdom which Jesus came to bring aims at the transformation of the whole of creation. It is identical with God's saving will. How does the Church fit into such a universal design? So much is clear: she must be considered and defined in the context of this divine intentionality. Her essence and mission make sense only in this setting. Her mission is to reveal through the ages the hidden plan of God to lead all humankind towards its final destiny. She must see herself entirely in the service of this divine plan meant for the salvation of all creation.

Vatican II starts off by describing the Church as the mystery of Christ. In her the "eternal plan of the Father is realized and manifested in Jesus Christ: to bring humanity to its eternal glory." Here the Church is seen in connection with the "bringing about the secret hidden for ages in God" (Col 1:16; see Eph 3:3-9; 1 Cor 2:6-10). Therefore the Church has to be seen in this broad perspective of God's plan of salvation, which includes all human beings and creation as a whole (see 1 Tim 2:4; Rom 8:19-22).

Church and Kingdom are not identical

Jesus' message of the Kingdom is indeed addressed primarily to his disciples.To them the Kingdom belongs, they will celebrate it, and be in it. But this special proximity of the group to the Kingdom does not turn them into a closed society. In the same way, the Church has no monopoly on the Kingdom of God. Citizenship in the Kingdom is not so much a privilege, but rather a summons to solidarity with people, particularly with the excluded and discriminated against.

One of the chief temptations for the Church in history is to claim the Kingdom for herself, to take over the management of the Kingdom, and even to go so far as to present herself as the realized Kingdom of God vis-a-vis the world. The Kingdom of God is not the Kingdom of the Christians (Jan, Milic Lochman, *Church and World in the Light of the Kingdom of God*, p. 69).

When God inaugurated the Kingdom in the world and in history, he did so in two stages. First, the Kingdom was inaugurated through the earthly life of Jesus, his words and works; yet it was only fully inaugurated through the Paschal Mystery of his death and resurrection. This Kingdom, present in history, must now grow through history to reach its eschatological fullness at the end of time. The Council clearly accepted this distinction between the Kingdom present in history now and the eschatological fullness still to come (see LG 5,9). But the question not clearly answered is whether the Council also made a clear distinction between Kingdom and Church.

Did the Council identify the Kingdom of God in history with the pilgrim Church, or did it consider the Kingdom of God in history to be a reality that is broader than the Church?

The majority of theologians today hold that the Catholic Church in Vatican II did distance herself from any identification with the Kingdom in history now. The theological basis for doing so is seen in the Council's definition of the Church as a "Sacrament of the Kingdom" (LG 9). Since God's saving grace can never be bound exclusively to a sacrament, one has to accept that the Kingdom is still broader than the Church. Such a separation is indirectly expressed in article 5 of *Lumen Gentium* and in article 45 of *Gaudium et Spes*. McBrien sees in this separation of Kingdom and Church a major achievement of Vatican II. He comments:

> The nature and mission of the Church are always to be understood in relationship and in subordination to the Kingdom of God. This principle is expressed in article 5 of *Lumen Gentium* and again in article 45 of *Gaudium and Spes*. It replaces what was perhaps the most serious pre-Vatican II ecclesiological misunderstanding, namely, that the Church is identical with the Kingdom of God here on earth. If it is, then it is beyond all need for institutional reform, and its mission is to bring everyone inside lest salvation elude them (R. McBrien, *Catholicism*, p. 686).

Schnackenburg affirms McBrien's view regarding the ecclesiological misunderstanding that resulted from the identification of the Kingdom now present in history with the Church when he writes:

> Let us ask ourselves here immediately about the relationship between the Church and the Kingdom or the Lordship of Christ. Is the Church the Kingdom of God on the earth, admittedly in a provisional form, until the Kingdom is

fulfilled eschatologically? This view, long held within Catholic theology even though with various nuances, but which leads to a dangerous image of the Church, to a triumphalistic understanding of the earthly Church, is definitely to be rejected. True, in the New Testament the Church is seen in strict relation with the Lordship of Christ, for example in Col 1:12f: "God has delivered us from the dominion of darkness and transferred us to the Kingdom of the Son." We are only received into his Kingdom. Christ exercises his Lordship of grace in the Church by means of the Holy Spirit: but the Church remains a community of human beings who are at the same time sinful and weak ("Signoria e regno di Dio nell'annuncio di Gesu e della Chiesa delle Origini", Communio 86 (1986) pp 41-42).

While one can argue as to whether or not Vatican II did really make this distinction, it is clear that in *Redemptoris Missio (RM)* and in the Document *Dialogue and Proclamation (DP)*, a joint statement of the Council for Interreligious Dialogue and the Congregation for the Evangelization of People, this distinction is clearly made. Both documents confess that the Kingdom of God is a broader reality than the Church.

> RM and DP appear to be the first two documents of the recent central doctrinal authority to distinguish the pilgrim Church from the reality of the reign of God in history; both documents profess that the reign of God is a broader reality than the Church which is present and operative beyond her boundaries among the members of other religious traditions" (J. Dupuis *"Dialogue and Proclamation"*, p. 150).

Equally significant is the fact that these documents not only clearly distinguish Church and Kingdom, recognizing that the one larger reality of the Kingdom cannot be encompassed by and contained within the Church, but the documents also unambiguously subordinate the Church to the Kingdom by affirming that the Church is meant to be a servant of the broader and more important Kingdom of God.

> It is true that the Church is not an end unto herself, since she is ordered towards the Kingdom of God of which she is the seed, sign and instrument (RM 18).

> The Church is effectively and concretely at the service of the Kingdom (RM 20).

> The Church's mission is to foster the "Kingdom of the Lord and his Christ" (Rev 11:15) at whose service she is placed (DP 35; see also 59).

With these statements the official Church has passed another milestone. In Vatican II the Christian Church was no longer identified with the Catholic

Church; the Church was seen as embracing other churches as well. Now it is stated that the Kingdom of God is not to be identified with the Christian Church.

The Kingdom present in the Church

Although the Kingdom cannot be identified with the Church that does not mean that the Kingdom is not present in her. The word Church may not appear often in Jesus' teaching but the very concept of the messianic community, intrinsically bound up with the Kingdom, implies the same thing as the concept of Church. It is, therefore, correct to say:

> The Kingdom of God and the Church are two key New Testament concepts, both are crucial for the understanding of God's plan for humanity. They are central to the fulfillment of his redemptive purpose. While the Church cannot be identified with the Kingdom, for the latter is a larger and more comprehensive term, the two are nevertheless in such close correlation that they cannot be separated either (P. Kuzmic, *"Church and Kingdom"*, p. 49).

The Kingdom in 'spatial' and 'dynamic' terms

The following observations should clarify what we mean by saying the Church is not the Kingdom, and yet it is a community chosen by God in which the Kingdom is made present in a special way. In the New Testament, we find two sets of ideas connected with the Kingdom of God which might help towards a better understanding of the tension that exists between the Kingdom and the Church. They are the following:

First, the Kingdom is understood in spatial terms, as a territorial reality. This understanding underlies many images of the Kingdom. One can enter the Kingdom (Mt 5:20, 7:21, 18:3) and one can be thrown out of it (Mt 8:12). There are keys to the Kingdom. The Kingdom is also compared to a house into which people are invited. The spatial terms of the message of Jesus are largely new, but are pervasively present in his Kingdom message.

Secondly, the Kingdom is understood as God's sovereignty or kingly rule. It is a dynamic concept, signifying God's active rule over all reality, particularly at the end of time. It is all-embracing, yet still provisional in the sense that the fullness is still to come (P. Kuzmic, *"Church and the Kingdom"*, pp. 61-63).

These two strands create a tension that is fundamental in the New Testament. While they help us to understand better the relation between the world and the Kingdom, they may help us also to clarify the tension between Church and Kingdom. They indicate that while the Kingdom is a reality that embraces all of creation, God has still situated the Kingdom concretely, i.e., now within a particular group in space and time.

Dulles makes a similar observation: the symbol Kingdom in the New Testament refers to reign and realm:

> The term basileia in the Greek New Testament frequently means kingship (reign) but it sometimes must be translated as kingdom (realm). The two concepts are inseparable. Christ's kingship or lordship implies a community over which he reigns - in other words, a kingdom. Conversely, the concept of the kingdom always implies a king. Several different expressions such as "kingdom of God," "kingdom of heaven," "kingdom of the Son," and "kingdom of Christ" are used almost interchangeably in the New Testament, and the differences of nuance among them need not concern us here ("The Church and the Kingdom" in *A Church for all People*, ed. Eugene LaVerdiere, p.14).

It is the Kingdom now that creates the Church and keeps her constantly in existence. Therefore, we can say that the Kingdom makes itself present in the Church in a particular way. The Church is an "initial realization" or a "proleptic anticipation" of the plan of God for humankind; or in the words of Vatican II, "She becomes on earth the initial budding forth of the Kingdom" *(Lumen Gentium 5)*. Secondly, the Church is a *means or sacrament* through which the plan of God for the world realizes itself in history *(LG 8 and 48)*.

> The Kingdom creates the Church, works through the Church, and is proclaimed in the world by the Church. There can be no Kingdom without the Church - those who have acknowledged God's rule - and there can be no Church without the Kingdom; but they remain two distinguishable concepts: the Rule of God and the fellowship of men (E. Ladd, *The Presence of the Future*, p. 277).

The Petrine ministry as the 'key-holder' to the Kingdom

There is one more line of thought, intrinsically relating Church and Kingdom and arguing that the Church has a particular function to fulfill during the historical period of the Kingdom in the here and now. Jesus entrusted to the Church a *key-function regarding the Kingdom*. Jesus gave to Peter, upon whom he built his Church, the *"keys of the Kingdom of God"* (Mt 16:18-19). This text is the only one in which Kingdom and Church are brought together in the teaching of Jesus. The keys are entrusted to the Petrine ministry in the Church. This ministry carries the responsibility of disclosing to people the conditions for entry or exclusion from the Kingdom of God. In other words, the key lets the Church unlock the secrets of the Kingdom always anew in the changing circumstances of the time until the Kingdom comes in glory. It should, however, never be forgotten that the purpose of this ministry is to _serve_ the Kingdom of God in the here and now.

The Kingdom belongs to God and not to the Church; it is his to give and to withhold. Therefore, the Church has no power to decide to whom the Kingdom will ultimately be granted nor who will ultimately be excluded. In this context the words of Jesus, _"Many will come from east and west and will take their places in the Kingdom of God while the presumed heirs of the Kingdom will be thrown out" (Mt 8:11-12),_ are very significant. Yet we cannot overlook that the Church does have an essential part to play in any consideration of how the Kingdom is to be understood and proclaimed.

Composer Giacomo Puccini wrote a number of famous operas. In 1922 he was suddenly stricken by cancer while working on his last opera, _Turandot_, which many now consider his best. Puccini said to his students, "If I don't finish _Turandot_, I want you to finish it for me." Shortly afterward he died.

Puccini's students studied _Turandot_ carefully and completed the opera. In 1926 the world premiere was performed in Milan with Puccini's favorite student, Arturo Toscanini, directing. Everything went beautifully until the opera reached the point where Puccini was forced to put down his pen. Tears ran down Toscanini's face. He stopped the music, put down his baton, turned to the audience and cried out, "Thus far the Master wrote, but he died."

A vast silence filled the opera house. Then Toscanini picked up the baton again, turned to the audience, smiled through his tears, and cried out, "But the disciples finished his work."

When _Turandot_ ended, the audience broke into a thunderous applause. (Link)

Voiced 'reservations' to a 'Kingdom-centered Church'

Having admitted the distinction, both RM and DP are worried that this view easily leads to two pitfalls. The Kingdom-centered approach seems to stress the Kingdom to such a degree as to leave out the Church almost entirely. Additionally, in so doing it forgets to bind the Kingdom to Jesus Christ. These are clearly the worries the Pope voices in his encyclical _Redemptoris Missio_ 17-18. The same concern is also echoed in the document _Dialogue and Proclamation:_

One may not separate the Kingdom from the Church. It is true that the Church is not an end unto herself, since she is ordered towards the Kingdom of God of which she is the seed, sign and instrument. Yet while remaining distinct from Christ and the Kingdom, the Church is indissolubly united with both (18).

The same concern is also echoed in the document *Dialogue and Proclamation:*

The Kingdom is inseparable from the Church because both are inseparable from the person and work of Jesus himself ... It is therefore not possible to separate the Church from the Kingdom as if the first belonged exclusively to the imperfect reality of history, while the second would be the perfect eschatological fulfillment of the divine plan of salvation (DP 34).

Some theologians worry that, with such strong statements, the magisterium actually annuls what it clearly stated in the beginning, namely, that the Kingdom is broader than the Church. By stating strongly that the Kingdom is intrinsically bound up with Christ, and that the Church is his chosen instrument for the Kingdom, the whole argument seems to go so far as to say that you cannot promote the Kingdom unless you are promoting the Church. If the Kingdom can be found only in Jesus and if the Church is the continuation of Jesus' presence through the ages, then - so the argument goes - the Kingdom can be found only in the Church. They see here a subtle return to an ecclesiocentric approach to the Kingdom which makes it impossible to develop a Kingdom-centered understanding of the Church. The danger is that the universality of the Kingdom is continually reduced to the particularity of the Church once again.

Since certain trends in liberation theology and in the theology of religions seemed to highlight the reality of the Kingdom at the expense of the Church and to distance themselves from the Church, the reaction (of the official Church) has taken the form of barring any access to the Kingdom except through the Church. Or to put it in another way, instead of understanding the Church in relation to the mystery of the Kingdom, this trend wants to understand the Kingdom of God in terms of the Church, and indeed turn the Church itself into the Kingdom (F. Wilfred, "Once again.. Church and Kingdom," p. 10).

As these theologians see it, if such a trend was to gain the upper hand in Catholic theology today, one of the most powerful sources for the renewal of the Church and its theology could be seriously stifled. Only if we maintain the distinction between Church and Kingdom clearly and uncompromisingly can such a symbol once again become THE religious symbol of our time. It provides us, on the one hand, with a way to relate to this world and its destiny productively and, on the other hand, with a way to enter into a more open and creative dialogue with other religious traditions and ideologies. Therefore, we have to be on our guard not to allow such an identification once again, subtle though it may be. The Church is not the Kingdom now since the Kingdom makes itself felt outside the Church as well. Her mission is to serve the Kingdom and not to assume its place.

The many qualifications made by RM and DP to the statement that Kingdom and Church are not identical are true to the firmly held position of the magisterium that whatever "traces of the Kingdom" may be found outside the Church must be seen and related to the Kingdom that Christ proclaimed and brought. There cannot exist any "Kingdom revelation" in the world that is not related to or independent of Christ. Referring to the reality of the Kingdom outside the Church DP adds the following caution, which once again makes clear the strong stand of the official teaching authority.

> Part of the Church's role consists in recognizing that the inchoative reality of his Kingdom can be found also beyond the confines of the Church, for example in the heart of the followers of other religious traditions, insofar as they live evangelical values and are open to the action of the Spirit. It must be remembered nevertheless that this is indeed an inchoate reality, which needs to find completion through being related to the Kingdom of Christ already present in the Church yet realized fully only in the world to come (DP 35).

There remains the unsolved theological problem: *How* to relate a Kingdom outside the Church to the Kingdom that Christ proclaimed and gave to the Church. Should one assume that there are other revelations of the Kingdom not related to Christ? While such views are voiced today by a number of theologians, the official Church has so far steadfastly refused to allow any such propositions to be even considered.

The official response of the Catholic Church to this question of how the Kingdom of God, which Jesus brought irrevocably into this world through his life, death and resurrection, is now also to be found outside the Church is this: God's Kingdom entered this world finally and definitely with the incarnation of Jesus but took on a more comprehensive presence in the resurrection of Jesus, the Christ. In the resurrection the limitations of Jesus' earthly existence are gone. The Kingdom was definitely present in the Jesus who walked this earth but its presence was - so to speak - restricted to the physical body of Jesus. This is to be concluded from the fact that John could speak about the Spirit who *"was not yet because Jesus was not yet glorified"* (Jn 7:39). But in his death and resurrection, the Kingdom he had proclaimed as having arrived with him took on a new dimension; it embraced the whole of creation now. In the risen Christ, matter has been transformed into the state of the New Creation. Christ is, in his risen body, the cosmic Christ, the world to come. He, therefore, assumes a new global relationship with reality as a whole: he is present in creation in a new way.

There was a very wise king who had built for himself a strange and wonderful palace. In the center of the palace was a room in which stood the throne. Only one door led into this room. All through the palace were passageways, halls and corridors that twisted and turned about and led in every direction.

When the palace stood finished, the king sent an order to all his people asking them to come before him. He sat on his throne and waited. The people came to the outside of the palace and stared in wonder at the confusion of corridors. They cried, "There is no way to the king!" But the crown prince, who was standing at the door pointed inside and said, "Here, the king waits for you. All ways lead to him."

As the future of the present world, Christ relates to creation in a new way. The whole world belongs to him not only on the basis of creation (Col 1:1-15; Jn 1:1-14) but now also on the basis of its transformation in the resurrection of his body into the New Creation. We cannot limit the presence of the New Creation to the Church only. This all-pervasive presence of the Kingdom of Christ in the world makes itself visible not only in the Church but also in historical movements outside the Church and in the other religious traditions found anywhere in the world. It is ultimately the identification of the Kingdom with Jesus Christ that makes it impossible for the official teaching of the Church to see any Kingdom presence in the world or in other religious traditions that are not related to Christ.

Dupuis referring to the salvation of all outside the Church, summarizes the position of the Catholic Church as follows:

Salvation must be held possible outside the Church. The Second Vatican Council (1962-65) has reaffirmed this doctrinal stand in unambiguous terms in its Dogmatic Constitution on the Church ("Lumen Gentium", nn. 16-17), as well as in its declaration on the relationship of the Church to non-Christian religions ("Nostra Aetate"), its Decree on the Church's missionary activity ("Ad Gentes"), and its Pastoral Constitution on the Church in the Modern World ("Gaudium et Spes"). A celebrated passage of the latter document, after stating how Christians come in contact with the paschal mystery of the death and Resurrection of Jesus Christ, affirms clearly that the same applies — 'in a way known to God' — for members of the other religious traditions.

It says: 'All this holds true not for Christians only, but also for all men of goodwill in whose hearts grace is active invisibly. For since Christ died for all, and since all men are in fact called to one and the same destiny, which is divine, we must hold that the Holy Spirit offers to all the possibility of being made partners, in a way known to God, in the paschal mystery' ("Gaudium et Spes", n. 22).

Several points need to be noted here. First, the Council looks at God's universal salvific will not as an abstract possibility but as a concrete reality, actually operative among people. Second, the concrete possibility of salvation available to all men and women of good will is salvation through Jesus Christ and his paschal mystery. Third, this salvation reaches out to them through the universal action of the Holy Spirit. Fourth, the manner in which salvation in Jesus Christ is made available outside the Church through the working of the Holy Spirit remains for us mysterious. This last point does not amount to saying that the 'how' of salvation outside the Church lies altogether beyond the scope of theological investigation; however, whatever theological explanation may be given would have to preserve the reference to Christ and his Spirit. God's saving grace or the faith that justifies has, even outside the Church, a Christological and pneumatological dimension.(J. Dupuis, "Religious plurality and the christological debate" *Sedos*: Vol. 15, no. 2-3, 1995).

The Church, the "Universal Sacrament of Salvation" as Mediator of the Kingdom

With regard to the salvation of non-Christians, the following question still arises: if the Kingdom as God's universal will to save all people is active outside of the Church, is this activity still mediated through the Church or in a way that is independent of her? The answer varies according to whether one identifies the Kingdom now with the pilgrim Church or not.

Not "mediated" through the Church

Those who maintain a distinction between Kingdom and Church argue as follows: Pope John Paul in *Redemptoris Missio* (RM 10) asserts that "for those people (non-Christians), salvation in Christ is accessible by virtue of a grace which, while having a mysterious relationship to the Church, does not make them formally part of the Church, but enlightens them in a way which is accommodated to their spiritual and material situation. This grace comes from Christ."

This text is seen as a clear rejection of *ecclesiocentrism*. The necessity of the Church for salvation does not mean that access to the Kingdom is possible only through the Church. One can partake in the Kingdom of God without being a member of the Church and without passing through her mediation (cf. Dupuis, *Jesus Christ and the Encounter of World Religions,* p. 6). Theologians who take this stand in no way deny that the salvation of any human being is based on Christ's death and resurrection. For them all grace is christo-centric.

In the letters of St. Paul, the Kingdom of God is seen present under a new form, that of the Kingship of the Risen Christ in which it is realized. But this kingship is not seen as extending only to the Church but rather to the whole world. In Colossians 2:10 and Ephesians 1:10 the Kingship of Christ extends not only to the Church but to the entire world: Christ is the head of the world and of the Church; but only the Church is his body (Col 1:18; Eph 1:22; 4:15; 5:23). The Kingship of Christ as the presence of the Kingdom in history extends to the whole world, visible and invisible. Christ is the fountain of all salvation but his saving grace is seen as reaching people differently. He reaches non-Christians not directly through the Church, but his saving grace is mediated to them directly through the Holy Spirit and not through the Church "in ways only known to God."

> The Kingdom of Christ is . . . a more comprehensive term than "Church." In the Christian's present existence on earth, his share in Christ's Kingdom and his claim to the eschatological Kingdom . . . find their fulfillment in the Church, the domain in which the grace of the heavenly Christ are operative . . . But Christ's rule extends beyond the Church . . . and one day the Church will have completed her earthly task and will be absorbed in the eschatological Kingdom of Christ or of God (Schnackenburg, *God's Rule and Kingdom, p. 301*).

Theologians who hold to the identification of the Kingdom on earth now with the Pilgrim Church cannot accept this position. Their reasoning is most often placed on a concept of Church that is so universal and inclusive that she embraces all human beings, beginning with Abel the just one.

> "This is the group of the savewhich also has been called the Church *a tempore justi Abel usque adultimum electum, ab initio mundi usque ad finem*" (Henn, "The Church and the Kingdom of God", p. 122).

If one regards the whole of humanity implicitly as Church, then there is no difficulty in seeing all saving grace as "church related".

Mediated through "prayer and intercessions" of the Church

For these authors, all saving grace passes through the Church; otherwise the Church could not be called"the universal sacrament of salvation." They base their view on a careful reading ofthe main Documents of Vatican II and maintain that one cannot deduce from these documents that the Church in Vatican II made a distinction between theKingdom present now in history and the Pilgrim Church here on earth. Their arguments are the following:

The Church is described as being by its very essence the *universal sign of salvation*. The description, which holds a prominent place in the *Dogmatic Constitution on the Church* (LG 48), is quoted both in the *Decree on the Church's Missionary Activity* (AG 1) and in the *Pastoral Constitution on the Church in the Modern World* (GS 45). When speaking of sacrament, the Council means a symbolic reality established by Christ, a sign that contains and confers the grace it signifies. The Church, therefore, is not merely a cognitive sign, making known something that already exists, but an efficacious sign that brings about the redemption to which it points. Since the Church is seen as a universal sacrament, i.e., as *"an instrument for the redemption of all"* (LG 9), we must assume that the salvation of all human beings does in some way depend on the Church. The Church is involved in the salvation of all who are saved (LG 16). Whatever faith or belief people may confess, we must assume that the grace which saves them, is in a *mysterious way* linked to the Church. They are, in the words of the Council, through this grace *ordered* to the Church. That means the saving grace they receive outside the Church gives the recipients a positive inclination towards the Church, so that all who live by God's grace are in a certain sense affiliated with the Church (Dulles, "Vatican II and the Church's purpose", pp.344-345).

The question that now arises is: does the Church simply save by being the reality towards which people are oriented? or does she act deliberately to bring about the salvation of such persons? The perception of the Church as "a universal instrument" of salvation (LG 1) suggests that the Church is actively at work in the salvific process; however, it does not explain by what activities the Church accomplishes this result.

Francis Sullivan puts the question this way: "In what way can the Church be said to exercise an instrumental role in the salvation of all those people who apparently have no contact with the Church?" Referring to the encyclical *Mystici corporis* of Pius XII, the teaching of the Council

(*Constitution on the Liturgy)* (SC 83) and the eucharistic prayers, Sullivan sees the Church mediating salvation to non-Christians through prayer and intercession. Accordingly, the Church - at least by means of intercessions, especially during the Eucharist -, prays and offers Christ's sacrifice for the salvation of all people. Thus her intercessory mediation extends to all who are being saved.

> On the basis of the teaching of the council, and the eucharistic prayers which reflect this teaching, we have sound reason for affirming that because of the church's role as priestly people, offering to the Father with Christ the High Priest the sacrifice from which grace of salvation flows to the whole world, the church is rightly termed the universal sacrament of salvation in the sense that it plays an instrumental role in the salvation of every person who is saved (Sulllivan, *The Church to Believe In*, p.128*)* .

The orientation of the Church towards the Kingdom is most beautifully revealed in the central act of worship, the celebration of the Eucharist. Mark's account of the Last Supper closes with Jesus' words: *"Truly, I say to you I shall not drink again of the fruit of the vine until that day when I drink it new in the Kingdom of God"* (Mk 14:25). Thus the Eucharist is situated within the context of the eschatological Kingdom. In his handing on of the story of the origins of the Lord's supper, Paul also clearly sees its celebration within an eschatological context: *"For as often as you eat this bread and drink this cup, you proclaim the Lord's death until he comes"* (1 Cor 11:26).

But the link between Church and Kingdom in the Eucharist is still more profound. It is with his blood that Jesus establishes the new Covenant (Lk 22:20; 1 Cor 11:25), the divine order of eschatological grace for the whole humanity. Only by virtue of the universal efficacy of the blood of this Covenant (Mk 14:24) is it possible for human beings to be saved. In the celebration of the Lord's Supper, the Church is clearly presented as belonging to his Kingdom; she celebrates this Covenant, established by the blood which, according to the Lucan account, is poured out "for us" (22:20). The eschatological benefits of salvation are intended "for us" - which must be understood as including those believers in Christ who are actually celebrating the Eucharist. But these benefits do not extend to Christians alone; they reach out to all human beings whose salvation is ultimately guaranteed through the death and resurrection of Christ (Henn, "The Church and the Kingdom of God," p. 130*)*.

The threefold mission of the Church

Once the Church is no longer seen as the sole holder of the Kingdom she does not have to define herself anymore as "the Kingdom of God under siege" by the powers of this world. Since Vatican II she sees herself more as *leaven* of the Kingdom or in the *service of* the Kingdom that is broader than herself. In other words, a theology of transcendence gives way to a theology of transformation. Out of such a view of Church and Kingdom the mission of the Church has been outlined as follows:

1. To proclaim in Word and Sacrament that the Kingdom of God has come in the person of Jesus of Nazareth. Sacrament means that in her symbolic order the Church opens up the everyday world to the ultimate, the Kingdom of God. But in doing so the Church is also forced to accept her provisional character. In the words of Schillebeeckx:

    The Church is not the Kingdom of God, but bears symbolic witness to the Kingdom through word and sacrament, and her praxis effectively anticipates that Kingdom. She does so by doing for men and women here and now, in new situations (different from those in Jesus' time), what Jesus did in his time: raising them up for the coming Kingdom of God; opening up communication among them; caring for the poor and outcast; establishing communal ties within the household of faith and serving all men and women in solidarity (*Church: The Human Face of God,* p. 157).

2. To create Church communities anywhere and to offer its own life as a *test-case* which demonstrates that the Kingdom is present and operative in the world today. This should reveal itself in the Church's own life where justice, peace, freedom and respect for human rights are concretized. The Church should offer herself as a "contrast society" to society at large.

Vatican II, being fully aware of the mystery of the Church, shunned definitions and fixed concepts. The Council Fathers, however, were very concerned with correcting a Church image that was generally conceived as being too rigid and in many ways out of touch with the reality of the present world. They wanted to present *a vision of the Church* that could once again inspire and stir up people's imagination.

Knowing how ecclesial documents want to express their main concern and thrust in their first words, we can sense how the Council wanted to "*envision*" the Church for today by just considering the opening phrases of the two main Council documents on the Church.

Lumen Gentium, meaning *"Light for the Nations,"* defines the Church as being light to all nations (although the term "light" refers first and foremost to Christ). Here the Church could be compared with a ship equipped with powerful lights, moving through the ocean of centuries and indicating to other ships the way they should move to reach the shores of salvation. If we compare this picture with the older one, we note a change in how the Church is perceived. The older ecclesiology, taking the scriptural image of the dragnet, which Jesus used in his Kingdom parables, and applying it to the Church, also saw the Church as a ship. But in this case it was moving through the centuries, dragging an enormous net, and trying to catch as much fish as it could—all in the firm belief that only those actually caught in this net could be saved. Today we would say there are as many ships as there are religions that are capable of carrying people to salvation. The Church's mission is perceived here not as necessarily taking the people from their ship into the "barque of Peter" but rather as indicating to them which way to steer their boats.

The document *Gaudium et Spes* (joy and hope) sets out to define the Church's relationship to the world. It basically describes the Church as a community whose mission it is to give joy and hope to a world that often looks so gloomy and desperate, almost totally void of real joy and knowledge of the way to move and the direction to take. In these two images the Council provided us with a vision of the Church for our age and time, something that can inspire enthusiasm and renewed commitment, something one can live for, work for, suffer for and, if necessary, die for.

The Church I Long For

When we pray *Come Holy Spirit*
we open ourselves
to all kinds of new possibilities;
and we confess
that we are a Church of sinners.
The Church I long for
is a Church much more aware
of its sinfulness and of its need to repent.

In the Church I long for,
the Spirit is liberating and transforming,
not bolstering up and justifying systems.
The prayer of longing *Come Holy Spirit*
is a prayer
that the Church becomes a community
where people know each other by name
and share each other's stories.

A life-giving Church,
a Church full of hope and joy,
this is what I long for.
A Church of humility
and longing for justice
that is the Church I long for.

A Church living in the Spirit,
and praying for the Spirit,
is the one I long for.
(Brian Hearne CSSp)

What is proposed in *Gaudium et Spes* is a true vision of the Church. But the question remains: Did the Council succeed with its vision? Did the renewed Church become a "light for the nations" and a community that radiates "hope and joy" into the world today?

The best way to start describing the Church theologically is to conceive her as the community of the end time in the 'here and now', as the fulfilment of the eschatological Kingdom anticipated in space and history. She is the 'already of the not yet', meant to be the concrete realization of God's Kingdom now and sent to witness the Kingdom present and proclaim it to the whole world. Wherever a Christian community emerges, its ultimate mission is to be a "light for the people" and to give "joy and hope" in the midst of an often hopeless situation. It can do this only because right in its midst the community experiences 'already' the presence of the vision for the world that God intended would come true at the proper time.

3. To challenge society as a whole to transform itself along the basic principles of the Kingdom now present: justice, peace, brotherhood/ sisterhood and human rights. To this interreligious dialogue, as the second element of evangelization, must be added. These are "constitutive elements of proclaiming the Gospel" since the ultimate goal of the Kingdom is the transformation of the whole of creation. The Church must, therefore, understand her mission in the service of the imminent Kingdom.

This threefold mission of the Church is also called evangelization. At least among Catholic authors the words "mission," "evangelization" and "witness" are nowadays often used like synonyms. Although each of these words has its own meaning and history they are all used to designate in a comprehensive way the one complex mission of the Church.

This threefold mission found its expression in the document *Redemptoris Missio.*

> The Church is effectively and concretely at the service of the Kingdom. This is seen especially in her preaching, which is a call to conversion. Preaching constitutes the Church's first and fundamental way of serving the coming of the Kingdom in individuals and in human society . . .

> The Church, then, serves the Kingdom by establishing communities and founding new particular Churches and by guiding them to mature faith and charity in openness towards others, in service to individuals and society, and in understanding and esteem for human institutions.

> The Church serves the Kingdom by spreading throughout the world the "Gospel values" which are an expression of the Kingdom and which help people to accept God's plan. It is true that the inchoate reality of the Kingdom can also be found beyond the confines of the Church among peoples everywhere to the extent that they live "Gospel values" and are open to the working of the Spirit, who breathes when and where he wills (cf. Jn 3:8) (RM 20).

RM regards interreligious dialogue as a constitutive element of the Church's evangelizing task as well. It is "part of the Church's evangelizing mission" (RM 55); it is one of its expressions and moreover, "a path toward the Kingdom." (RM 57) *Dialogue and Proclamation* adds:

> Inter-religious dialogue and proclamation, though not on the same level, are both authentic elements of the Church's evangelizing mission. Both are legitimate and necessary. They are related but not interchangeable (DP 77).

Church - world - other religious traditions

The distinction made by the Council between the Kingdom and the Church bore immediate fruits in the development of a post-conciliar theology, at least in two theological fields: in the theology of Liberation and in the theology of Religions. The symbol Kingdom of God provides the horizon for a solution of two theological problems.

First, in the context of *work for justice, liberation and peace* it provides the bridge between the historical achievement of justice and liberation of the oppressed in this world and the eschatological Kingdom still to come in fullness at the end of time. It shows how work for justice and liberation inside and outside the Church is intrinsically linked with the Kingdom present now, since the ultimate goal of the Kingdom of God is the transformation of all reality.

The Kamakura Buddha was lodged in a temple until one day a mighty storm brought the temple down. Then for many years the massive statue stood exposed to sun and rain and wind and the changes of the weather.

When a priest began to raise funds to rebuild the temple, the statue appeared to him in a dream and said, "That temple was a prison, not a home. Leave me exposed to the ravages of life. That's where I belong" (de Mello).

Secondly, in *inter-religious dialogue* the Kingdom symbol furnishes the theologians with a broader perspective for entering into dialogue with other religious traditions. If the Kingdom is the ultimate goal of God's intentionality with all of humanity, then the question is no longer how these other religious traditions are linked to the Church but rather how the Kingdom of God was and is concretely present in these religions.

We are not saying that all religions are equal giving way to a religious pluralism. The issue is, if we accept that in other religions God's Kingdom (his saving will for all) makes itself present now through the power of the Holy Spirit whom Jesus released through his death and resurrection, then God's saving grace for all does remain linked to the one mediator Jesus Christ. The presence of the risen Lord in the world now is a presence mediated through the Holy Spirit.

This view avoids a too narrow an *ecclesiocentrism* which links God's Kingdom so close to the Church that it is hard to see how one can enter into any dialogue with other religious traditions. Strictly speaking *ecclesiocentrism* holds: no Kingdom brought through Jesus Christ can be found in other religions unless it has been mediated through the Church. When one asks how this is possible the answer is usually the quote from Vatican II: this is done "in ways only known to God alone."

The distinction between Kingdom and Church therefore, can help us relate to this world and its destiny more fruitfully, and enter into a more open and creative dialogue with other religious traditions and ideologies.

The Kingdom that Jesus brought has cosmic dimensions going beyond the confines of the Church. It demands the restructuring and transformation of all religious and socio-political structures and institutions. The Christian community has, therefore, no other choice than to engage in dialogue with the world and other religious traditions for the sake of the Kingdom present. The teaching office of the Church in *"Dialogue and Proclamation"* takes up this challenge by stating that dialogue constitutes an integral and essential part of the Church's mission. The Church must dialogue with other religions in order to carry out its mission and realize its identity (DP 2). Some theologians regard this as another milestone in the Catholic Church's view of other religious traditions.

But how is this to be done? Looking at the Jesus who walked this earth, and trusting that we have his Spirit still with us, we might find a clue as to how it could be done in our age and time. There were three possible ways available to Jesus to actualize his Kingdom vision: the *revolutionary*, the *sectarian* and the *worldly*.

The *revolutionists* in the time of Jesus, with their battle cry *"Let us take it,"* wanted to change the present by overthrowing those who ruled, bringing in God's reign by force. This option was open to Jesus but he neither commanded nor accepted it. The *sectarians*, following the motto *"Let us create it,"* insisted on a total withdrawal from society and the creation of a new model of community in which the Covenant would be realized to the full. This was the option of the Qumran community. With this option the world is abandoned as being beyond all repair. Jesus did not choose this option either. He did not join the Qumran community but stayed where the people were and used their marketplaces for his preaching and actions. Jesus chose what Dunn called the *"worldly option,"* with its command *"Live it!"* He showed that the Kingdom is taking place now in the midst of human affairs and that human actions may become the carriers of this Kingdom. To accept the Kingdom means to celebrate its presence now, not away from but within this world. Jesus' option can be called "worldly" since it asks us to live wholly within this world by otherworldly values, challenging this world to allow itself to be transformed by the values of the Kingdom Jesus came to bring (J.D. Dunn, *Call to Discipleship,* pp.44-52). We are called to point out where the Kingdom is already present in this world and in other religious traditions, and to learn from them aspects of the Kingdom we ourselves may not have discovered or seen in our own tradition.

The priest announced that Jesus Christ himself was coming to church the following Sunday. People turned up in large numbers to see him. Everyone expected him to preach, but he only smiled when introduced, and said, "Hello." Everyone offered him hospitality for the night, especially the priest, but he refused politely. He said he would spend the night in the church. How fitting everyone thought.

He slipped away early next morning before the church doors were opened. And, to their horror, the priest and people found their church had been vandalised. Scribbled everywhere on the walls was the single word BEWARE. No part of the church was spared: the doors and windows, the pillars and the pulpit, the altar, even the bible that rested on the lectern. BEWARE. Scratched in large letters and in small, in pencil and pen and paint of every conceivable colour. Wherever the eye rested one could see the words, "BEWARE, beware, Beware, BEWARE, beware, beware.....

Shocking. Irritating. Confusing. Fascinating. Terrifying. What were they to beware of? It did not say. It just said, BEWARE. The first impulse of the people was to wipe out every trace of this defilement, this sacrilege. They were restrained from doing this only by the thought that it was Jesus himself who had done the deed.

Now that mysterious word BEWARE began to sink into the minds of the people each time they came to church. They began to beware of the scriptures, so they were able to profit from the scriptures without falling into bigotry. They began to beware of sacraments, so they were sanctified without becoming superstitious. The priest began to beware of his power over the people, so he was able to help without controlling. And everyone began to beware of religion which leads the unwary to self-righteousness. They began to beware of church law, so they became law-abiding, yet compassionate to the weak. They began to beware of prayer, so it no longer stopped them from becoming self-reliant. They even began to beware of their notions of God, so they were able to recognize him outside the narrow confines of their church.

They have now inscribed the shocking word over the entrance of their church and as you drive past at night you can see it blazing above the church in multi-coloured neon lights (de Mello).

What can we learn from this *worldly option* of Jesus for our own age and time? Scholars who talk today about the future of the Church and of Religious Life in the Church refer constantly to small ecclesial communities which are regarded as the ferment for any renewal in the Church and in Religious Life. Important for such communities is the ability to live as *open communities* in the world. These communities must have flexible borders, willing to let others in and willing to go out to others and learn from them the way of the Kingdom in the world and in other religious traditions. By celebrating the presence of the Kingdom in their midst, they are enabled to see the same Kingdom at work in the world around them, and are able to point it out so that people become aware of its presence. This is not easy. It needs a deep spiritual life at the core of the community which is shared and nourished. Without a burning center they will lose their identity as disciples of Jesus. The fire of Jesus' vision cannot remain burning if they do not remain close to him. Even Liberation theologians like Segundo Galilea and Gutierrez realize that the members of these communities must be quasi-contemplatives, full of the fire and the vision that drove Jesus. The *worldly option* of Jesus, adapted to our age and time, seems to provide us with the openness necessary to be able to enjoy and experience the presence of the Kingdom in the midst of our own Christian community. It enables us to see its presence in the world around us, and respond to it with openness and an embracing attitude.

The following story may illustrate how we can be centered and yet open to the outside.

> Years ago I was out in California visiting that remarkable giant sequoia forest. The guide who was taking us through the forest remarked that actually the roots of the sequoia are very shallow. That was a surprise to me and the others. How in the world could such giant trees stand up with shallow roots? Why, the first wind would knock them over like bowling pins. So I asked the guide about that. He said, "You are right. But, you see, sequoias interconnect their roots and their branches so that when there is a fierce wind they interlock and support each other. That's why they don't fall." (W. J. Bausch, *Telling Stories*, p. 151)

The two ways of mission

From what we have said up to now, it becomes clear that our mission in the service of the Kingdom is basically a twofold one.

First, we are called to make God's Kingdom present by proclaiming its presence in word and sacrament. This happens through the creation of Christian communities in which God's Kingdom shines forth like a symbol, a sign or a parable, where its presence can clearly be discerned and its final goal appears like a foretaste of what is to come in fullness in God's own time. The disciples in such communities are to celebrate the presence of God's Kingdom in their midst and let themselves be set on fire again and again. Especially when they remember the Lord in the table fellowship of the Eucharist, the disciples should make present once again that compassion of God which Jesus showed in such feasts to be the heart of his own God-experience. The Kingdom can therefore never be separated from the Church, which, after all, is God's chosen instrument for his Kingdom here on earth. The following quotation might sound strong but it is certainly correct:

> The Kingdom is, of course, far broader than the Church alone. God's Kingdom is all-embracing in respect of both points of view and purpose; it signifies the consummation of the whole history; it has cosmic proportions and fulfills time and eternity. Meanwhile, the Church, the believing and active community of Christ, is raised up by God among all nations to share in the salvation and suffering service of the Kingdom. The Church consists of those whom God has called to stand at His side to act out with Him the drama

of the revelation of the Kingdom come and coming. The Church constitutes the firstling, the early harvest of the Kingdom. Thus, though not limited to the Church, the Kingdom is unthinkable *without* the Church. Conversely, growth and expansion of the Church should not be viewed as ends but rather as means to be used in the service of the Kingdom. The Church, in other words, is not a goal in and of itself; but neither is it—as some at present would seem to imply—a contemptible entity that should feel ashamed of its calling and seek its redemption in self-destruction. The keys of the Kingdom have been given to the Church. It does not fulfill its mandate by relinquishing those keys but rather by using them to open up the avenues of approach to the Kingdom for all peoples and all population groups at every level of human society. It makes no biblical sense whatever to deny, as many do, that the upbuilding of the Church everywhere in the world is a proper concern of the proclamation of the good news of the Gospel; and it is high time for a forthright repudiation of such nonsense (J. Verkuyl, *The Biblical Notion of Kingdom...*, p. 73).

But in particular, the celebration of the Eucharist which always recalls the memory of Jesus' custom to enjoy a meal with those others had excluded from table-fellowship, should lead the participants beyond the narrow confines of their own Churches and open them up to the ultimate aim of the Kingdom: to lead all human beings into the one family of God, especially those who are so easily excluded from the human family today:

> *To celebrate the Eucharist today*, in this world of crying social injustice, is to resist the compromising role of consuming egoism. It is to learn to always share gifts and goods. It is to cultivate the virtue of solidarity. It is to take up the course of the excluded, an attitude which has its risks, but is coherent with the practice of Jesus and with a sincere discipleship. To celebrate the Eucharist today, in this world of so many divisions, is to undertake the commitment to breaking down barriers, making bridges and building communion within the Church and outside it... To celebrate the Eucharist today is to renew our faith in the lived experience of the Word which impels us to mission, because a faith which doesn't share itself tends to disappear (Dom Silvestre Luiz Scandian).

Secondly, we can see that neither Jesus nor his Spirit have abandoned the world; they continue to be present and active among people. In us, the community of believers and followers of Jesus, his action which is present everywhere, acquires a visibility and symbolic reality. Because of this, we are called and sent into the world to serve and to promote the ongoing action of Jesus and the Spirit. From here follows the second dimension of our mission: to be at the service of, and to promote in a collaborative way, God's own continuing action in the world and among people.

There was a very poor mountain village where the farmers owned only very small fields on very steep slopes. Everything had to be done by hand. There was a lot work but little money.

Once upon a time there was a small wooden church in the village but a candle which had been left burning unattended set fire to the building. Since then the place where the church had been standing was an open space. Mass was being celebrated in one of the class rooms in the school building. Since the village was small there was space for all.

The people would have loved to have a proper church, but first they had to save, because a church building is expensive. Then one old lady in the village dies and wills all her money for the new church.

At that time the people hear about a severe earthquake in a neighbouring country. On their TV screens they see how badly damaged the people's homes are. They realize that the villagers are just as poor as they are and they decide to send the money to them. However, they do not stop saving money for their little church and after some time they have enough to begin the construction.

Just then the papers are full of pictures with boat people from Asia and the villagers ask themselves, "How can we build a church while these refugees have no place to live? Without a moment of hesitation they renovate three old houses for these refugees. And once again they begin to save money for their church.

But every time they have the right amount, they hear about people in need and they generously give from their savings.

"We do not have a church," they say, "but we are happy in our village. We are like a big family. In the square where the church should stand one day, our children are playing" (Hoffsümmer).

If the Church community "feasts" on the presence of God's Kingdom in its midst most intensely in the Eucharistic meal celebration, then there must also be a "feast" aspect in the Church's second missionary task. We are, therefore, called to promote "feasts" where people of all races and cultures are sitting together and enjoy each other's company in life-giving relationships and genuine compassion. It is precisely here that God's Kingdom makes itself felt and can be experienced as present in the midst of human affairs.

The two "feast" aspects are two interrelated ways of pursuing the one goal of mission which is the realization of the 'New Heaven and the

New Earth' that is God's promise to all peoples. One could say that it is in getting actively involved in promoting God's transformative action in the world that the Church-community will build itself up as an authentic symbol of and witness to that action (M. Amaladoss, "New Faces of Mission").

As the community of those chosen to carry on the vision of Jesus, the Church must define herself in relation to the Kingdom, which is meant for humankind and the whole of creation. Her mission is to reveal through the ages the hidden plan of God (Eph 3:3-11; Col 1:26) and to lead humankind towards its final destiny. She must be seen to be entirely at the service of this divine salvific plan for all human beings and all of creation which is operative and present wherever people live, no matter what religion or faith they may confess.

> The Church is not placed at her own service: she is entirely oriented towards the Kingdom of God that is coming. For only the Kingdom, as the fullness of God's manifestation is absolute... The abiding vocation of the Church does not consist in the qualitative increase of her members. In dialogue and collaboration with all the people of good will (who may belong to other religions and spiritual families), she is called to manifest and foster the Reign of God which ... keeps happening through the religious history of humankind, well beyond the visible boundaries of the "People of God." (C. Geffre, as quoted by J. Dupuis, "Dialogue and Proclamation", p. 158).

Kingdom consciousness

The identity of the Church depends ultimately on her Kingdom consciousness based on Scripture. She would reveal this in her sensitivity to the priority of the Kingdom. According to H. A. Snyder such Kingdom consciousness includes the following five aspects:

1. Kingdom consciousness means living and working in the firm hope of the final triumph of God's reign. In the face of contrary evidence Kingdom Christians hold on to the conviction that God will eventually swallow up all evil, hate, and injustice. It is the firm belief that the leaven of the Kingdom is already at work in the dough of creation, to use Jesus' own parable. This gives Christians an unworldly, audacious confidence that enables them to go right on doing what others say is impossible or futile.

2. Understanding God's Kingdom means that the line between "sacred" and "secular" does not exist in concrete reality. God's Kingdom means

that all things are in the sphere of God's sovereignty, and therefore, of God's concern. All spheres of life are Kingdom topics.

3. Kingdom awareness means that ministry is much broader than Church work. Christians who understand the meaning of God's reign know they are in the Kingdom business, not the Church business. They see all activity as ultimately having Kingdom significance.

4. In Kingdom perspective, concern of justice and concrete commitment to the Word of God are necessarily held together. An awareness of God's Kingdom, biblically understood, resolves the tension between these two vital concerns. Those committed to the Kingdom want to win people to personal faith in Jesus Christ, since the Kingdom is the ultimate longing of every human heart. They are also committed to peace, justice, and righteousness at every level of society because the Kingdom includes "all things in heaven and on earth" (Eph 1:10) and the welfare of every person and everything God has made.

5. The reality of the Kingdom of God can be experienced now through the Spirit who gives the believer the first fruits of the fullness of the Kingdom in the here and now. Particularly in their liturgy Kingdom people anticipate the joy of the Kingdom. The different charisms given by the Holy Spirit witness concretely to the Kingdom present and are appreciated by all as clear manifestations of the powerful presence of the Kingdom in the midst of their daily life (H. A. Snyder, *Models of the Kingdom*, pp. 154-155).

Looking at the world of today, there is reason to doubt whether the human species has the requisite capacity to change. Many view the present world situation with despair. Christian faith has been one important way in which people have lived with hope in the midst of apparently hopeless conditions. But those who open themselves to the Kingdom will discover that there is a power at work in us which can transform even our distorted wills. This transformation is not subject to our control but comes as a gift. We call it grace, and we can place no limits on the extent to which grace can make us into new men and new women.

Reflection: *The Church in the Service of the Kingdom*

Just as much as the message of universal salvation is bound to the person of Jesus, so the Church - inseparable from the person of Jesus - has a mission of salvation for the world. The Church exists in the world and for the world as Jesus' chosen agent of salvation, although not the exclusive one, to make present and tangible the Kingdom which Jesus came to initiate.

The Church as the 'sacrament of the Kingdom' is God's project for the whole world, which reaches from within us out beyond this world for all time to come. This vision of God broke through in its fullness in the person of Jesus and is to continue to do so in us. Looking at the all-too-human face of the Church we can easily identify with Pedro Casaldáliga's dream:

> *I dream of a Church wearing only the gospel and sandals;*
> *I believe in the Church despite the Church,*
> *sometimes, in any case I believe in the Kingdom,*
> *journeying in the Church.*

QUESTION: **What does the Church of your dreams look like? How far do you see the Council's vision of the Church as *Light to the Nations* and *Hope and Joy for the World* realized in the Church today?**

Pedro Casaldáliga claims that

> *The Kingdom unites.*
> *The Church divides when it*
> *does not coincide with the Kingdom.*

QUESTION: **What might have brought about such a strong statement? How do you see and experience the relationship between Church and Kingdom?**

Because the Kingdom of God is at work like a leaven within the Church, inserted into and part of the world, the Church is no airtight room where the privileged celebrate salvation and make merry. The Church is the open sign of salvation: the "official" place, where salvation is celebrated in community. And the invitations to this celebration have been personally distributed by Jesus.

Hurry down, Zacchaeus, because I must stay in your house today (Lk 19:5).

Jesus never wanted to be the exclusive agent of salvation. How could he celebrate it alone? When he heard that John the Baptist had been arrested, he left Nazareth for good and moved to Capernaum. There he began to preach about the Kingdom and the need for conversion. But at the same time, he also decided to associate and unite himself with others. He did this by calling his disciples. It seems to be normal that if one wants to change anything in this world, one needs to associate with others, come together, unite and do it as a joint venture.

Jesus, indeed, resisted the devil who invited him to make his life a *one-man show* and instead he picked Simon and Andrew, John and James, Mary Magdalen, Mary and Martha.... you and me. It was in that community that they went out together to preach and to heal ....and together they moved in the direction of the Kingdom. On the way we need to encourage one another and celebrate each time we sense the power of the Kingdom in our midst and experience renewed strength for a commitment that aims at establishing life-giving and just relationships.

QUESTION: **How do you understand your being a member of a disciple-community? Does the Church community in which you live give you strength and sustain your enthusiasm for being a disciple? Do you share with your community the joy you experience in your personal vocation and mission?**

Scholars say now that even when Jesus was still alive, there seemed to have been two traditions of open fellowship: one of bread and wine, the other of bread and fish. The bread and wine finally won out - that meal is what we call the Mass today.

But the bread and fish stories point to an open table fellowship tradition, too. The exciting thing about these stories is that they emphasize surplus and outside guests. At the end of each of them there are seven or twelve baskets of food left over. That surplus seems to be a point of this form of table fellowship. This is a type of meal we'd call a potluck supper today. Apparently Jesus invited everybody to bring their food and there was plenty for all the poor.

It is unfortunate that we lost the bread and fishes ritual meal, because the bread and wine ritual meal didn't emphasize this idea of surplus, real food that actually fed the poor. The bread and wine tradition lent itself more to the cult and ritualization. The bread and fish tradition, if retained, might have contributed to issues of justice, community and social reordering (R. Rohr, *Jesus' Plan*, p. 93).

QUESTION: **If the Kingdom is found outside the Church as well as within, how do you see earthly events and people of other faiths and convictions? How can we find ways of using "bread and fish" to celebrate the presence of the Kingdom outside the Church - with people who are not members of our Church nor share our faith?**

There are two mile-stone-decisions concerning the Kingdom which the official Church has made. They will have great repercussions on our understanding of the Church and her mission today. First, the Kingdom is a broader reality than the Church. Secondly, the Church must see and define herself entirely in the service of the Kingdom of God.

QUESTION: If the Church's identity depends on her Kingdom consciousness which of the five above mentioned aspects of such consciousness are most appealing?

Once upon a time there was a wonderful prince. He lived in a valley where he was loved by all the people. He and his people worked together, ate together and celebrated together. There was great peace and harmony in the land because of the love they all had for one another.

One day the people decided to show their great admiration for the kindly prince.

"Let us build him a castle," they said. "A fine home for him to live in, even better than those of other princes."

"Together we will build the most wonderful castle the world has ever seen," they exclaimed, "for with our prince we are beyond doubt the happiest people on earth."

It did, indeed, turn out to be the most marvellous castle imaginable. The walls were hewn from rare marble, so fine as to be almost transparent. The towers were made from precious stones - one of ruby, one of sapphire, one of emerald, and one of onyx. The floor was inlaid ivory and the roof gold. People everywhere agreed that it rivalled the sun in brilliance and beauty.

Word of the castle began to spread beyond the valley. At first the curious came from nearby. Then travellers began arriving from far and wide. It became necessary for the villagers to set up inns and restaurants to provide for the needs of these tourists. The greater the influx of travellers, the greater became the commerce in the village.

The villagers knew that their good fortune was due to the wonderful castle. In order to assure their continued prosperity, they would regularly polish its stones and clean its towers. The castle continued to sparkle like a jewel, drawing visitors from the world around.

The village grew into a city. There was commerce and industry. But with the trade came rivalry, with rivalry jealousy, with jealousy hate, and with hate contention. There was no longer peace in the valley.

Finally, one day the wonderful prince emerged from the castle. The people had all but forgotten that he lived there. Without saying a word, the prince walked around the castle seven times. When he was done, the castle collapsed.

"Why have you done this?" the angry people shouted.

"I have done nothing," the prince replied. "Seven times I walked its circumference searching for your image in the walls and on its towers. I found none. The castle no longer reflected the hearts of the people. It could stand no longer" (Aurelio).

Chapter Fifteen

The Lord's Prayer:
Summary of Jesus' Kingdom Message

Jesus proclaimed the Kingdom of God as having arrived with him. It had become a present reality, no longer a far distant hope, reachable by everyone who wanted to enter it. To the question of how one could enter it, of how one could make it his/her own, Jesus demanded conversion, a turning toward him and the message he proclaimed. A more concrete question, however, would have to be asked by those who had let the Kingdom into their lives and had heeded the call to conversion: What should be the norm by which we, your disciples, have to live now that we have responded to the Kingdom present? Jesus' answer is found in the Sermon on the Mount (Mt 5-7), the *"Magna Carta"* of all Christian behavior and the norm for all Christian action.

The Sermon on the Mount also gives the answer to a question deeply linked to Christian living, namely: how should we as disciples of Jesus pray? To this Jesus replied: "This is how you should pray: *'Our Father in heaven ...'"* (Mt 6:9). The Lord's prayer is, therefore, THE norm that should guide and direct all our prayers. As we will see, the Lord's Prayer is more than a guide to prayer, it contains, in brief, all that Jesus came to bring and provides a summary of Jesus' whole Kingdom message.

A Jewish Prayer

Whence did Jesus get this prayer? Did he formulate it himself? or did he take it over from his Jewish heritage? Jesus was a Jew of the first century. As a boy and young man, he attended the synagogue every Sabbath, perhaps Monday and Thursday as well, to listen to the Scriptures and to pray. As a faithful Jew, he would have recited the *Shema* upon rising and retiring each day, the heart of which affirmed: *"Hear O Israel: The Lord God is one Lord; and you shall love the Lord your God with all your heart, and with all your soul, and with all your might."* He presumably participated in the Jewish festivals and went on pilgrimages to Jerusalem. The Gospels show his obvious familiarity with the Scriptures, the Hebrew Bible. He may have known it from memory, a feat not uncommon among the learned. More than likely, the Psalms were his "prayer book" (Borg, *Jesus: A New Vision*, pp. 39-40).

We have to expect that Jesus took the basic material for the "Our Father" from Jewish sources as he did for his parables. The structure of the Lord's Prayer corresponds to the ideal structure of Jewish prayer. It begins with praise of God and ends with thanksgiving if we add the doxology found in the *Didache:* "For yours is the Kingdom, the power and the glory for ever and ever. Amen."

An Eschatological Prayer

The Lord's Prayer is the prayer most prayed among all Christians, individually and communally. It has been analyzed and explained in many ways. The literature about it is immense: more than 2500 articles and books have appeared over the years. Most of them present meditations rather than exegetical or theological treatises on the prayer. What is presented in this short treatise on the Lord's Prayer is based on the analysis given by Joachim Jeremias who treats the Lord's Prayer as an ESCHATOLOGICAL PRAYER.

There are, of course, other ways to interpret this prayer. An eschatological interpretation takes the Our Father as a prayer of those who experience the Kingdom of God as a present reality - the "already" - and who wait for and cry out for its final consummation - the "not yet."

Jesus' message centered on the imminent Kingdom of God. What people of this time considered as ONE EVENT - the decisive intervention of God in history - Jesus split into two related but separate events. He did this by bringing the beginning of the eschatological time into the "now" and postponing the consummation as a future event. This creates the classic problem of the "ALREADY" and the "NOT YET which we took up in chapter six."

The Christian community is, therefore, living in a peculiar state of affairs. On the one hand, it experiences the future fulfilment of the Kingdom already, in a "proleptic" or "anticipatory" way. It already possesses the eschatological gift, i.e., the Holy Spirit, who creates that intimate union with God the Father (Rom 8:14; Gal 4:6) and enables us to create communion among ourselves (Gal 3:28; 1 Jn 3:14). This is a reality that belongs to the New Heaven and the New Earth at the end of time. On the other hand, this community is still in this world, circumscribed by all the restrictions of "being in the flesh." Day after day this community experiences sinfulness, its own as well as that of the world around it, and the stunning power of evil at work in this world. This forms the backdrop for praying the Lord's Prayer. It is a prayer for the "in-between time," the time of the Church. We should not forget it is the only prayer Jesus gave us.

Difficulties with the Lord's Prayer

The common ways people use this prayer often create difficulties. It easily becomes a prayer for all kinds of occasions: for good weather, the poor souls, peace in the world, better health, etc. In addition it was often a "penance" in confession and a means for indulgences. In short, it becomes a way out when we do not know what to pray. The effect of such overuse is that we no longer know, experience, and appreciate its real meaning.

A more recent problem is that some find difficulty with the opening address, "OUR FATHER," as the name for God. For them this is either an overly male-chauvinistic approach to God or an impossibility due to negative experiences, e.g. of an abusive father. To address God as "Father" no longer seems to have an experiential correlation in their lives (Strolz, "Fatherhood of God," pp. 191-200).

The only real answer to these problems seems to lie in a continual effort to explain the depth of this prayer. Frequent preaching about it can unlock its treasures and the great concerns Jesus wants us to have. It is an excellent text for meditation. Repeating it should not be a problem for those who feel themselves drawn into exploring its real depth and meaning.

At a time when people are asking, "How should I pray?" and "What should I pray?", it is even more important to go back to what Jesus himself taught as a pattern of how and what his disciples should be concerned with when praying.

The Sermon on the Mount, *Magna Carta* of all Christian behavior and the norm for all Christian action, is understandable only in the setting of Jesus' eschatological message of the Kingdom as a present reality. In other words, this *Magna Carta* of Jesus' ethical requirements presupposes the proclamation and concretization of the Kingdom in the corporal dimension (Lohfink, *Jesus and Community*, p. 33).

The Lord's Prayer in the Ancient Church

In the beginning of the early Church the Lord's Prayer seems to have been mainly a prayer of the individual Christian. The *Didache* 8:2 (written around the year 110) tells us to pray it three times a day. Other sources say the Christian should pray it with the Symbol (creed) after rising in the morning and before going to bed in the evening. Very soon, however, the prayer became the prayer of the community. According to Cyril of Jerusalem (350), the Lord's Prayer was part of the liturgical service before Holy Communion and prayed only by the baptized, i.e., the "full members" of the Christian community. It was an expression of their identity as Christians. Together with the Lord's Supper, it became one of the most holy treasures of the Church, reserved for the full members only, and not disclosed to those who stood outside (*disciplina arcani*). In short, it was a privilege to pray it (cf. Jeremias, *The Prayers of Jesus*, pp. 82-85).

The awe and reverence with which the early Church looked at this prayer can be seen by the way it was introduced:

> Make us worthy, O Lord, that we joyously and without presumption may make bold to invoke Thee, the heavenly God, as Father and to say: OUR FATHER.

In the revised Liturgy of the Hours we find almost twenty different introductions to the Lord's Prayer, which correspond with the ancient Church's view of the Our Father.

The Earliest Texts of the Lord's Prayer

We have two versions of the Lord's Prayer: Luke 11:2-4 and Matthew 6:9-13. We normally use the Matthean version with seven petitions and no doxology. Luke has only five petitions. The *Didache* adds the doxology to the Matthean version. Mark does not have it. Some exegetes conclude that it was the early Christian community that composed this prayer, based on Jesus' own prayer life, as depicted in Mark 14:36; 39. But this theory is generally not accepted. The two forms are normally explained by the different audiences that both evangelists had to address. Matthew presented a catechism on prayer to Jewish-Christians. They had learned to pray in childhood, but their prayer was in danger of becoming routine. The Lucan catechism is addressed to people who "for the first time, learn to pray." These Gentile-Christians had to be encouraged to pray constantly.

What is the Original Form?

There is no agreement among scholars about what the original form of the Lord's Prayer is. A growing number, however, takes Luke's version as the more original. It seems closer to the style of Jesus' own prayer, especially the use of the simple "FATHER" as the opening address. This preference of Luke fits well with his constant attention to and interest in Jesus' life of prayer. Matthew, whose Gospel became the Gospel of the Church, presents the prayer in the form the community had made its own: OUR FATHER WHO ARE IN HEAVEN (Stendahl, "Your Kingdom Come," p. 263). For some scholars, the material added by Matthew has the effect of making the prayer more suitable for use in worship, without adding anything really new to the prayer. Others, who argue for the originality of the Matthean version, point out that Matthew would never have dared to add anything to a prayer of Jesus so treasured in the early community (cf. Harner, *Understanding the Lord's Prayer*, pp. 12-17). Careful analysis of both versions shows that they are really much more alike than may be apparent at first sight. It does not really matter which version one takes to understand the Our Father. After consulting about forty commentaries, I believe Luke's form is probably closer to the form that Jesus gave to the prayer.

Scholars have reconstructed the Our Father in Aramaic. This is what it sounded like in Jesus own words:

> **Abba!**
> Father
> **Yitquaddash shemâk**
> May be sanctified name yours.
> **Têtê Malkûtâk.**
> May come kingdom yours.
> **Lachmân de limchâr**
> Bread ours of tomorrow
> **hab lân yômâ dên**
> give to us day this.
> **u shebôq lân chôbênan.**
> and forgive to us debts ours
> **kedi shebaqnân le chayyâbênan.**
> as herewith forgive we to debtors ours
> **we lâ ta'êlinnan le nisyôn.**
> and not let fall us into trial
> (Wijngaards, *My Galilee...*, p. 90).

After a careful text-critical analysis, Jeremias proposes this wording as the original, based on the above Aramaic version:

Address:	**DEAR FATHER**
First "Thou petition":	**HALLOWED BE THY NAME**
Second "Thou petition":	**THY KINGDOM COME**
First "We petition":	**OUR BREAD OF TOMORROW GIVE US TODAY**
Second "We petition":	**AND FORGIVE US OUR DEBTS AS WE HEREWITH FORGIVE OUR DEBTORS**
Concluding Request:	**AND LET US NOT SUCCUMB TO TEMPTATION**

The Meaning of the Lord's Prayer

In Jesus' time various religious groups, like the Pharisees, Essenes, and Disciples of John, all had their own prayers that distinguished them from other groups. The disciples in Luke 11:1 asked Jesus for an "Identification Prayer," something that would bind them together, identify them and bring to expression their chief concerns. They asked for a prayer that would be their "badge," their distinctive symbol. Jesus answered by giving them a prayer that is "the clearest and, in spite of its terseness, the richest summary of his proclamation we possess"(*The Lord's Prayer...*, p. 12). The Lord's Prayer is, therefore, not just a prayer: it is THE MANIFESTO of our Christian faith.

The Address: "Dear Father" (Abba)

Fatherhood of God in the Old Testament and Judaism

Other ancient religions, as well as the Jews of the Old Testament, knew the word "Father" for God. Homer, for example, calls Zeus "the father of men and gods." In the Old Testament God is called "Father" only fourteen times. Many of these passages, however, are very important. God's fatherhood in the Old Testament is never linked to mythological motifs (as in the ancient world) but always to the events of salvation history. God reveals himself as father by acts of saving power in the history of his people.

Absolute authority and "tenderness" are the two important aspects of "fatherhood" in the Old Testament. Tenderness is a word we normally associate more with a mother. The concept of Father for God in the Old Testament is, therefore, not to be understood in authoritarian categories and definitely not to be construed in male-chauvinistic terms. Attributes that our culture attaches to the concept of "mother" also belong to the biblical image of God as Father. By calling God Father, the Old Testament stresses the tenderness, mercy, care and love of God for his people. Fuerst explains the Old Testament nuances at length:

> The social meaning for "father" in Israel had to do with authority, care, discipline, protection, and dignity. It represented a role in a society that is harshly judged and incompletely understood today. It makes no sense to wish that Israel's God might not have been called father or king. At least when God's work is compared to that of a parent, the language is warm, gentle, affectionate, nurturing, caring, and at the very least and by any account respectful. When God is called father the texts are talking about creation,

leading, and affection. "Father" was a social assumption, part of the social and cultural mold into which the faith of the Old Testament was poured. Like "king," it had a rightful and necessary place in the mold; to remove it is not an editor's job, because it would require an operation with an incision three thousand years old (Fuerst, "How Israel Conceived and Addressed God," p. 73).

The prophets in particular reveal the depth of Yahweh's relationship to his people expressed in his fatherly care which contrasts with their constant ingratitude. The final word about divine fatherhood is God's incomprehensible mercy and forgiveness:

For I am a father to Israel and Ephraim is my first born (Jer 31:9). Is Ephraim not my dear son . . . Is he not my darling child? Therefore, my heart yearns for him; I must have mercy on him (Jer 31:20). And I thought you would call me "My Father" and would not turn from following me (Jer 3:19ff.).

When Israel was young, I loved him; I called my son out of Egypt. It was I who taught him to walk, I who had taken him in my arms. . . . I drew them with strings of love. I was to them like one who lifts a little infant close against the chin. I bent down and gave him to eat (Hos 11:1ff.).Stand not aloof! For you are our Father. Abraham ignores us and Israel does not acknowledge us. You, Yahweh, are our Father; "our redeemer" is your name from of old! (Is 63:15ff.).

However, according to Jeremias, the invocation of God as "my Father" or "our Father" never occurs directly in any prayer in the Old Testament. The language is always indirect as though it implied a promise of what would be fulfilled someday.

In contrast, in the Rabbinic literature the expression "heavenly Father" is used for God. Even the two words "Our Father" are found in Jewish prayers used in their liturgy. It occurs three times in the Eighteen Benedictions (Amidah): "Make us return, Our Father, to your Torah"; or, "Forgive us, Our Father, for we have sinned,"; and again, "Bless us all, Our Father . . ." The same could be said about the services for the New Year and the Day of Atonement. The invocation of God as "Our Father" expresses the trust and confidence, the security and mutual love, between God and God's people (*The Prayers of Jesus in Their Contemporary Setting*, published by The Study Center for Christian-Jewish Relations, 17, pp. 9-10).

Matthew seems to have taken over this Rabbinic tradition, whose meaning is expressed in two convictions: first, one has to obey God, which is equal to following the Torah; secondly, God is the one who helps in time of need, particularly when no one else can or will help. However, in later

Judaism, a development away from the prophets ensues when God is spoken of as the "Father of the individual Israelite," the one who cares for the individual personally:

> Thou art he whose mercy toward us is greater than that of a father toward his son. On whom can we depend? Only on our heavenly Father. My son, if you return, will it not be a return to your Father? (Jeremias, *The Prayers of Jesus*, pp. 29, 52, 96-98).

The Rabbinical teaching always distinguished between paternity and fatherhood. Paternity denotes the person who is responsible for the birth of a child: there is only a physical connection between father and child. Fatherhood, in contrast, describes a relationship of love and intimacy, of confidence and trust between parent and child.

"Father" as a Title for God in the Sayings of Jesus

The New Testament refers 421 times to God. Of these, 183 (43 percent) call him "Father" absolutely or the Father of Jesus or the believer. It is, therefore, the dominant model of God. Sixty-five percent of the texts in John and 56 percent of those in Matthew refer to God as Father (cf. Kreutz, "God in the New Testament," p. 87). In the Gospels we find the word "Father" for God on the lips of Jesus 170 times. "Father" was evidently the designation for God in Jesus' preaching. Mark uses it four times, Luke fifteen, Matthew forty-two and John 108. There is a definite increase in the use of the word, particularly in Matthew in comparison to Luke and Mark. Kreutz explains this development:

> *Matthew's striking and frequent use of "Father" for God marks his most significant departure from Markan and Lukan patterns. He uses the term over forty times in a variety of expression . . . He presents the most vivid interpretation of the father idea among the four Gospels . . . God is a Father who rewards the modest, hears those of a few words and forgives us when we are forgiving towards others ("God in the New Testament," p. 85-86).*

In John it becomes THE title for God where it usually denotes the special relationship of Jesus to God. After a thorough analysis of the Gospel passages closest to the actual words of Jesus, Jeremias concludes:

> The important thing is that we have discovered that all four gospel traditions report unanimously and without any hesitation that Jesus constantly addressed God as "My Father" (except Mk 15:34), and show that in so doing he used the Aramaic form "ABBA." To call God ABBA is one of the most outstanding characteristics of the historical Jesus (*The Prayers of Jesus*, p. 57).

"ABBA" belongs to the language of childhood and the home, a diminutive of endearment, used by adults for their own fathers. For the Jewish mind, ABBA was THE word that could express most adequately the most intimate and personal relationship anyone could think of. It was, therefore, inconceivable for a Jew to address God with the word "ABBA." Such an address would not indicate adequate respect for Yahweh and cause scandal to godly persons.

A Jew would normally begin his/her prayer with a phrase of praise and thanksgiving like, "Blessed are you, Lord, God of the universe." He/ she would be hesitant to address God directly but would first express the distance between them by praising and exalting the greatness and majesty of God. A personal dialogue with God could only take place after such praise. If ever a Jew would address God as "Father," he would qualify the expression by saying "Our Father" or "Father in heaven," but never would he just say "Father." The word "Father" standing on its own, as we find it in the prayer of Jesus, is most unusual and exceptional (Wijngaards, *My Galilee...,* p. 89).

Jesus, in his prayers, leaves us with a different style of praying. He addresses God directly with the word "Father": *"I thank you, Father, Lord of heaven and earth . . ."*(Lk 10:21). *"I give you thanks, Father . . .* "(Jn 11:41). There is only one instance in the Gospels when Jesus does not just use the word "Father." Otherwise he uses the more intimate form "Abba." In the Gethsemane prayer of Mark, Jesus says: "Abba, Father, all things are possible for you, take this cup of suffering away from me" (Mk 14:36). Mark is also the one who conveys to us the only occasion when Jesus addresses God no longer with the word Father but simply with the word "God." That is the moment before he dies (Mk 15:34). It is as if he could no longer say "Father" in that terrible hour when he had to experience the God-forsakenness of sinful humanity. Wijngaards discusses this point:

It is a truism that Jesus called God by the Aramaic term "ABBA." The term occurs three times in the New Testament: Mk 14:36; Rom 8:15; and Gal 4:6. Only the first is on Jesus' lips. In each case the Greek translation "the father," "ho pater," is immediately added . . . In Gethsemane, Jesus expressed the conviction that his actions were the direct outcome of the will of God. Abba expresses closeness to God because it is an intimate familiar term. Jesus lived in the conviction that the Father knew him, that he knew the Father and that through him God as Father is close to the disciples and known by them as God of mercy. This unusual term survived in the church in Aramaic, even though it needed translation (Rom 8:15; Gal 6:4). The force of this tradition indicates that the term expressed something prized by the church . . . The term is inserted into a new and fitting context because of what Jesus himself had done and taught (*My Galilee,* pp. 88-89.).

If we accept the arguments of Joachim Jeremias, there is no parallel in Jewish literature where the pious would have dared to address God with the word "Abba":

> We are thus confronted with a fact of utmost significance. Whereas there is not one instance of God being addressed as "ABBA" in the literature of Jewish prayers, Jesus always addressed him in this way (except for the cry from the cross, Mk 15:34) (*The Prayers of Jesus,* p. 57).

By using this word Jesus reveals the heart of his relationship with God: a simple trust and confidence, with which a little child comes to a father whom he knows, loves and trusts. Jesus, therefore, spoke with God as a child speaks with his father - simply, intimately, securely.

The word ABBA encompasses the whole message and claim of Jesus: He came to lead us into a relationship with God that would be most adequately expressed with the word ABBA. The astonishing point is that Jesus authorized his disciples to repeat the word ABBA after him. We are called to share in this sonship and empowered to speak with our heavenly Father in the familiar and trusting a way as a child would with his father. This is the "new relationship" which opens the door to God's Kingdom. Jesus leads his disciples into an intimacy with God expressed most adequately by being able to address God as "ABBA." What this means in reality is expressed very well in Galatians 4:6 and Romans 8:15. Both remarks show us that the cry of ABBA is beyond all human capabilities and is only possible within the new relationship with God given by his Son. Lochman concludes:

> The simple name "Father", then, carries with it the whole revolution in the concept of God which is linked to the message and especially to the destiny of Jesus Christ: Immanuel, the God of faithful nearness in the deepest, most binding, and truly unconditional sense, in the sense of incarnation, his identification with sons and daughters in life and death and to all eternity, God not merely in the height of his heavenly but also in the depth of his earthly course (*The Lord's Prayer,* p. 20).

It is THE gift of the New Age we are already entering now - a totally new relationship with God - a relationship that only the Holy Spirit can adequately express in us. Jeremias remarks:

> Perhaps at this point we get some inkling why the use of the Lord's Prayer was not commonplace in the early Church and why it was spoken with such reverence and awe (*The Prayers of Jesus,* p. 98).

Barclay, in his commentary on the Lord's Prayer, stresses the importance of the "our" in the exposition of Matthew. The prayer is not an "I" prayer but a "we" prayer. We come before God not as individuals but before the God of us all. The opening address settles once and for all not only our relationship with God but also that with our fellow human beings. If God is our Father, then our fellow human beings are our brothers and sisters. As he sees it, all discrimination, racism, exploitation, etc., stand condemned in the two words that open the Lord's Prayer (cf. Barclay, *Beatitudes and the Lord's Prayer,* pp. 157-173).

Before we take up the individual petitions of the Lord's Prayer, it is important to emphasize that we must see every petition in the light of the opening address. If we direct our prayer to God, how should we address him? Who is he? To whom do we want to speak? The creator of the universe, the omnipotent, ever present, almighty, never changing Lord of Heaven and earth? No, for us the God to whom Jesus directs us to pray is ABBA. The address is, therefore, in no way just an introduction to the prayer but indicates what makes this prayer possible at all. This point is vividly expressed by Lochman:

> One cannot emphasize enough that the very first word of the Lord's Prayer is a decisive one that points the way. It is the word "Father." Whether we follow Luke and take it in all its simplicity, or Matthew with his liturgical expanded form ("our Father, who art in heaven"), the first word is one that we cannot exchange: "Father." It sets the stage for our whole exposition of the individual petitions. In the history of exposition it has rightly been observed repeatedly that one's understanding of the whole prayer depends upon one's understanding of this first word (*The Lord's Prayer*, p. 16).

The Two "Thou Petitions"

As the old Jewish form reveals, the two "Thou Petitions" are eschatological. They ask for the revelation of God's eschatological Kingdom. The oldest form of the "Kaddish" prayer ,which concluded the service of the synagogue, runs like this:

> Exalted and hallowed be His great Name in the World that he created according to His will. May He establish His Kingdom in our lifetime and in your days and in the lifetime of the whole household of Israel, speedily and at a near time. May His great Name be praised forever and unto all eternity.

The two Thou-Petitions of Jesus can be regarded as a powerful shortened version of the Kaddish. Yet in spite of all the similarities between the Kaddish prayer and the two Thou-petitions of the Lord's Prayer, we should not overlook the great difference: With Jesus the Kingdom has come, it is a reality now (Perrin, *Rediscovering the Teaching of Jesus*, pp. 57-59).

Hallowed Be Thy Name

Although the word "hallow" means praise, bless, glorify, this is not just an expression of praise or respect for God but a real petition. The mood in "hallowed be" has the same force as in "come" and "be done"; therefore, petition, not praise, is expressed. What then does it mean to pray that God's name may be hallowed? To know the name means to know the reality behind the name. Name is an expression of innermost being, essential nature and personal identity. To know God's name is to know God as he makes himself known to us and offers us salvation. The name here signifies God himself. It refers to his innermost nature, especially as he reveals himself to us and acts on our behalf. Here, it refers to the address of the prayer, ABBA. It expresses the new relationship with God that the disciples receive as followers of Jesus: "O Righteous Father, I made Thy name known to them" (Jn 17:25-26). In this sense the word ABBA governs all the petitions in the prayer (cf. Harner, *Understanding the Lord's Prayer*, p. 63).

Hallowed has many meanings. It is important, as stated above, to regard it as a petition, a request directed to God, asking him to do something. What is it that he should do? Some scholars translate it negatively: Knowing that we can never adequately "vindicate God's honor," the petition refers to the fact that only God can and will do it. By hallowing his name, God creates Israel anew, and in so doing, the Kingdom of God breaks into the world. That was the eschatological expectation connected with this petition. In this petition we pray: "Father, let the world come to know your name through your final revelation. We know who you are, what you are like, because your Son has revealed your name to us, your being ABBA. Now let us see it in action." It is a petition for God to manifest and realize universally his unconditional love and care for the world as revealed in Jesus Christ. In it we seek the hour in which God's profaned and misused name will be glorified and his reign revealed according to his promise: "I will vindicate the holiness of my great name which has been profaned among them; and the nations will know that I am the Lord, says the Lord, when through you I vindicate my holiness before their eyes (Ezk 36:23) (cf. Jeremias, *The Lord's Prayer*, p. 22).

This petition is a missionary petition as it contains the whole mission of the Church. We are called to make known God's name to the world, to let all people know who God really is: ABBA. We know it, but we also know that most people do not really know who God is. Therefore we cry out in this petition: "Father, may the world get to know who you really are!" The petition contains three different elements: First, "let us come to know more and more who you are and let us celebrate it in praise, thanksgiving and adoration." Secondly, "may the whole human race come to know through our proclamation and witness of community living that you are our Father and we are all brothers and sisters." Thirdly, "let the day come soon, when you will reveal in fullness to all creation your true name and being." It is a petition for the final consummation of the Kingdom, the day of the parousia.

Thy Kingdom Come

The central theme of Jesus' ministry was the proclamation that the Kingdom of God was imminent (Mk 1:15). One might have expected that this would be the FIRST petition. But the first and the second petitions are intimately connected. The name of God refers to God's own innermost nature. The Kingdom of God refers to his activity. Since his innermost nature finds expression in his activity, it is appropriate for the petition concerning God's name to precede the petition concerning the Kingdom. The entreaty is a petition for the final consummation. We are praying to God to establish his Kingdom completely, just as he began to establish it in the life and ministry of Jesus. The petition refers to the future aspect of the Kingdom, but this in turn is grounded in the fact that the Kingdom is already partially present. We find this same phrase expressed in the early Church in the phrase, "Maranatha, Come Lord Jesus!" (1 Cor 16:22; Rev 22:20), which concludes certain liturgical services. Having experienced the "in-breaking of the Kingdom" into the present and celebrated it in the liturgy, the community cries out for the final consummation.

Matthew's third petition, "THY WILL BE DONE ON EARTH AS IT IS IN HEAVEN," says the same thing in another way. Since God's will is identical with his rule, this petition means: your rule should be established here on earth. May God, who reigns in heaven, finally establish his rule here on earth too. This will be the sign that God's Kingdom has already come into this world. These petitions are like a cry from the depth of distress. The "rule of evil", a world enslaved by sin and misery, is experienced. Yet the disciple knows that the "rule of God" is already operative in this world. He knows that the turning point has already come because God has already begun his saving work. He, therefore, asks for the full revelation of what has already been granted.

The Lord's Prayer is a prayer for the "in between time," for the "already" of the "not yet." It is for those who experience two "ages" and stand with one foot already in the New Age and the other still in the Old.

Some may see in this petition a cry to God for those who do not find God's will easy and implore him to help them to fulfil it. Here, too, we can still maintain the above presented interpretation. After all, to do God's will means practice to let his Kingdom, which is already present, rule one's life. The petition would then mean: "Lord, let nothing except the presence of your Kingdom rule and determine all my actions and my life." This petition should be interpreted then in the light of Jesus' own struggle with the will of the Father. Particularly important here is the Gethsemane story (Mt 26:36-46; Mk 14:32-42; Lk 22:40-46). This is an authentic commentary on Jesus' understanding of the petition. At the heart of this prayer we find the same request twice: *"Thy will be done, not as I will, but as you will."* Jesus trembles before the sufferings he must undergo to make the Kingdom come true. There will be no "cup of salvation" without the cup of eschatological suffering (Lochman, *The Lord's Prayer*, pp. 75-77).

The disciples will have to keep in mind that promoting the Kingdom here on earth and placing one's life under God's Kingdom will not spare them at times from struggling with God's will the way their master had to struggle.

The Two "We Petitions"

In the Jewish prayer called the Kaddish, the two "Thou Petitions" but not the "We Petitions", can be found. The "Thou Petitions" lead to the "We Petitions." They form the heart of the Lord's Prayer. If the two "Thou Petitions" seem to cry out for the coming of the Kingdom in its fullness, the two "We Petitions" seem to put the stress on the NOW, the TODAY. They seem to say: "Lord, if we have to stay in this sin-permeated world to carry on your work, please, give us NOW, TODAY, something from the future so that we can go on witnessing to your Kingdom in our time and situations."

Our Bread for Tomorrow Give Us Today

Some scholars regard this petition as the heart and center of the Lord's Prayer. Up to now the center of attention was God's cause: thy name, thy kingdom, thy will. But now our cause enters into the foreground: our bread, our debts, our temptation, our being menaced by evil. Yet most surprising is that the first petition concerns our daily bread. Many have wondered in the history of interpretation of the Lord's prayer what connection there is between the eternal Kingdom and

> this almost petty attention to transitory and unimportant everyday things, and even more surprisingly to the paltry daily ration that we need to eke out life from today to tomorrow (Lochman, *The Lord's Prayer*, p. 52).

The difficulty here is the Greek word *epiousios* which is usually translated as "daily." There are four major meanings for this term: (1) necessary for existence, (2) for today, (3) for the coming day, and (4) for the future.

Since the word *epiousios* is not used elsewhere in the New Testament, it is impossible to say with any certainty which of the four meanings is correct. The word has puzzled translators and interpreters since the early church fathers. References to bread and meals in the Old Testament, Judaism and Jesus' own ministry are most helpful, particularly Jesus' own understanding of food and meals. This alone would suggest that we might begin best with a literal understanding of bread in trying to interpret this petition of the Lord's Prayer. Eating bread together meant always more than a necessity to sustain one's life. It provided, for example, an opportunity as well for creating and refreshing human relationships. There are also enough passages in the Old Testament and Judaism from which we could conclude that *epiousios* in the Lord's Prayer carries an eschatological sense, meaning "for the future." This would mean that, when the disciples pray "give us this day our bread for the future," they would be asking God to grant them, here and now, some gifts of the wonderful time of salvation that is still to come in its fullness. This view is supported by the Church Father Jerome, who writes in his commentary on Matthew 6:11

> In the Hebrew Gospel according to Matthew it is thus: Our bread of the morrow give us this day; that is, the bread which Thou will give us in Thy Kingdom, give us this day.

> In the Gospel called according to the Hebrews for "supersubstantial" bread I found "mahar," which means "of the morrow"; so that the sense is: our bread of the morrow, that is, of the future, give us this day.

Many scholars agree that there is enough proof to conclude with Jerome that the translation should read: "Our bread for tomorrow give us today" (cf. Jeremias, *The Lord's Prayer*, pp. 23-27). "Tomorrow" meant the "great tomorrow," the age of salvation, the final consummation. The "bread of tomorrow" is, therefore, the "bread of the age of salvation," the "heavenly manna." In this way the bread petition is seen as an eschatological petition. But is that not too much spiritualization? Doesn't the petition simply ask for what we need daily to stay alive, bread that fills the stomachs of the hungry? Yet food and meals are not just a means for staying alive, at least not for the Oriental. For him every table fellowship is a guarantee of peace, of trust, of fellowship. Jesus' eating and sitting at table with sinners and outcasts were correctly understood by his opponents: *"This man receives sinners and eats with them"* (Lk 15:2ff; Mk 2:15-17).

Jesus, by having table-fellowship with outcasts, placed sinners on the same level as the righteous. Jesus understood his meals with the outcasts as "God sitting with man at table," a sign of reconciliation and an anticipation of the heavenly banquet in the consummation of the Kingdom. Every meal with Jesus was for his followers a symbol, a pre-representation, indeed, an actual anticipation of the meal of consummation. The continuation of the daily table-fellowship as a sacred rite after Jesus' death must be understood within this context. Whenever the disciples, in the future, would eat their meals, they would recall their meals with Jesus, who had understood meal-sharing as an anticipation of the heavenly banquet. Every meal for a disciple of Jesus would become a sign of the Kingdom present. Whenever they come together to share a meal, they make the Kingdom present in anticipation of the final table-fellowship of humankind with God. In this petition we pray: give us the necessary food today so that we will be able to make the sign of the Kingdom present now. How can we preach and make the Kingdom present if we do not have the means to create table-fellowship, which is for us the sign of Jesus' presence in our midst?

The stress is on "TODAY." We live in a world enslaved by evil, in a world where God seems to be remote, in a world of hunger and thirst. And yet we cry out: Let us experience "today," "now," "here," the great tomorrow - give us the "bread of tomorrow." This petition has, therefore, a definite reference to the bread that we eat day by day. At the same time it places the bread within a broader context that has as its basis Jesus' proclamation of the Kingdom of God.

The Eucharist, where God sits with us at table and gives us the "bread of tomorrow," is, to be sure, THE anticipation of the great tomorrow. But as we have seen, the bread petition is not exclusively a eucharistic petition. The petition for the bread includes material and spiritual needs without making one more important than the other. Jeremias concludes: "We can fetch down the 'great tomorrow,' the Kingdom, believe it down, pray it down, right into our poor lives, even now, even here today" (cf. Jeremias, *The Lord's Prayer*, pp. 23-27). There remain two little words in this fourth petition which we must not overlook. They are the pronouns "us" and "our." In the light of the Kingdom present my bread is never my bread alone. The bread of the fourth petition is bread that must be shared. It is here that the question of "justice" enters the Lord's Prayer. Lochman - referring to Is 58:7, "Share your bread with the hungry," and Psalm 146, where the psalmist praises God as the one "who executes justice for the oppressed, who gives food for the hungry" - comments:

> The impressive reference to hungry and oppressed, and the emphatic word "justice," cannot be excluded from any theologically responsible discussion of the petition for bread, and certainly not in any circumstances today. For the nub of the problem is that there are hungry people in our world, masses of them. This is true at a time when, as noted, in vast areas of the world the question of bread is to a large extent detached from the context of physical hunger (*The Lord's Prayer*, p.96).

Or in the words of St. Basil the Great (fourth century):

> The bread that is spoiling in your house belongs to the hungry. The shoes that are mildewing under your bed belong to those who have none. The clothes stored away in your trunk belong to those who are naked. The money that depreciates in your treasury belongs to the poor! (As quoted by Boff, *The Lord's Prayer*, p. 84).

In such circumstances any extravagance in food and eating becomes a real sin against our needy brothers and sisters and against God. In a consumer society, the petition for bread becomes a demand for conversion not only on the individual level but on the social level as well. We ask for a change in the modern social order. It means: "O God, to those who have hunger give bread; and to those who have bread give the hunger for justice" (cf. Stendahl, "Your Kingdom Come," p. 263).

And Forgive us our Debts as we also herewith Forgive our Debtors

The great gift of the eschatological age is forgiveness. Jesus, to the surprise of his audience (Mk 3:5; Mt 9:2; Lk 5:20), understood forgiveness of sins within the framework of the imminent Kingdom. The new time of salvation was understood as a time of forgiveness. Then human beings would live in the presence of God, knowing that God had forgiven them and created a new communion with them. Jesus is telling his audience that this time of great forgiveness is already beginning and is already reality at this moment. God's forgiving love and mercy, expected to be boundless in the end-time, is already offered now. Since we are living in this end-time, we already pray in this petition: Grant us, dear Father, this great gift of the Messianic time on this day and in this place. Although we know that we live in this great time of forgiveness, we also know full well that we are still imperfect, sin-permeated and in constant need of forgiveness. We can ask for this forgiveness because we know that in Jesus the Kingdom has become a present reality and its power is available to us (cf. Harner, *Understanding the Lord's Prayer*, p. 103).

The problem here is how to interpret the _V kai of Matthew and the kai gar of Luke. In short, how is God's forgiveness related to human forgiveness? Almost all scholars agree that the phrase, "as we forgive," should not be taken as a comparison as if God would forgive us in the measure that we forgive. The parable of the Unmerciful Servant (Mt 18:23-35) suggests quite clearly that God's forgiveness precedes human forgiveness. God first forgives us and then he expects us to forgive one another. The parable implies that human forgiveness is a consequence of God's prior action. We have no excuse for being unforgiving. We can and must forgive one another because we have first been forgiven. The magnitude of God's forgiveness makes it ridiculous for us not to forgive one another.

The parable indicates that God's forgiveness becomes real for us only when we accept this forgiving love as happening to us. It becomes part of our lives to such an extent that we are willing to forgive our fellow human beings wherever and in whatever way they have wronged us. If we do not forgive one another, we are actually showing that we have not really accepted the great forgiveness of God's love that is offered to us in this eschatological time. Our forgiveness of one another, therefore, becomes the sign of how far we have accepted God's great gift of forgiveness and love that is offered to us now.

Matthew 6:14-15, however, seems to be inconsistent with our interpretation:

> For if you forgive others the wrongs they have done you, our Father in heaven will also forgive you. But if you do not forgive the wrongs of others, then your Father in heaven will not forgive the wrongs you have done.

This passage once again looks like a comparison, meaning human forgiveness precedes God's forgiveness; only human forgiveness makes God's forgiveness possible. The passage seems to be totally inconsistent with the parable of the Unmerciful Servant. Can it be reconciled? Yes, if we keep in mind that:

(1) God's forgiveness always precedes human forgiveness.
(2) Human forgiveness is a consequence of God's forgiveness.
(3) God's forgiveness can become real for us only when we are willing to forgive one another.

In vivid, forceful language Matthew 6:14-15 demonstrates the third point, namely that God's forgiveness can become real for me only if I receive it graciously and let it change my life. In that way I can really forgive others in the power of the forgiving love of God that is here and now present in its eschatological fullness.

The address ABBA signifies that God accepts me as his child and brings me into a new relationship with him. This new relationship enables me to practice forgiveness towards others which I could and would never be capable of by relying only on my own human resources. To be able to forgive is not a purely human capacity, for human beings have a tendency to desire revenge and a chance to get even. Being forgiving toward others is a gift from God and a true sign that one has let the power of the Kingdom present into one's life.

Joachim Jeremias gets a correct translation of Luke's words by translating them back into Aramaic. This yields: "AS WE ALSO HEREWITH FORGIVE OUR DEBTORS." The meaning then is: "We are ready to pass on to others the forgiveness which we have received. Grant us, dear Father, the gift of the age of salvation, thy forgiveness, so that, in the strength of received forgiveness, we might forgive those who have wronged us" (*The Lord's Prayer*, pp. 27-28). How God's forgiveness precedes our ability to forgive and to love is most clearly expressed, according to Jeremias, in Luke's Parable of the Great Sinner (Lk 7:36-50): *"I tell you then the great love she has shown proves that her many sins have been forgiven" (7:47)*. The woman's love for Jesus is the result of the forgiveness received that has given her the strength to love in such a way. It is, therefore, not her love that causes the forgiveness Jesus passes on to her, but the other way around (*The Lord's Prayer*, pp. 214-218).

The Conclusion: "And Let us not Succumb to Temptation"

This, the only negatively formulated petition, stands out harshly. God does not tempt anyone, but we know also that "no one can obtain the Kingdom of God who has not passed through testing." We cannot escape testing, but we can ask not to succumb to the test. All we ask is to stand firm in the midst of temptation. What is promised is the overcoming of temptation. The petition is not a request that he or she who prays may be spared temptation but that God will help him or her to overcome it. What does temptation mean here? There are three possible interpretations:

(1) We ask the Father to help us to avoid anything that is wrong or sinful. This is what a Jew would pray for when faced with "temptations."
(2) We ask that we will not deny our faith in times of suffering or persecution. This meaning refers to Matthew 26:41; Mark 14:38; Luke 22:40,46: "Pray that you may not enter temptation."
(3) A more eschatological interpretation: Jesus, using apocalyptic imagery, sees the Kingdom, that enters this world with him, engaged in a battle with evil forces.

The synoptic Gospels portray the mission of Jesus as "overthrowing the demonic power structure." *"Have you come to destroy us?"* (Mk 1:24). Since the "evil one" is not going to let his kingdom be plundered without resistance, the end-time is regarded as "the time of Satan's final assault" (Rev 3:10). The disciple, who lives in the end-time and who has sided with Jesus in the great eschatological battle, will have to experience the force of the "final assault." THE temptation for the apostle is apostasy or falling away. More precisely, it is the constant temptation to lose faith that the Kingdom is already in the world; it is the temptation to regard the experience of the Kingdom present in our world as an illusion, to give in to despair. It means to give up believing that the Kingdom, which is present only in the form of a tiny seed (Mt 13:31ff.), will ultimately grow into a large tree. It is the ever present temptation to lose hope that God can bring about a glorious end from a tiny beginning as we experience it in the present. This "apostasy" does not have to be a dramatic event. It is a temptation to which we can all easily succumb without even realizing it. It is often a gradual process. It is the temptation to give in to doubts and finally to despair, frustration and bitterness. In short, it is to lose our faith that God's Kingdom is already in this world and will lead this world to its final destiny in the fullness of the Kingdom.

Jesus tells his disciples to ask God for the consummation of the Kingdom. He encourages them in their petitions to "pray down" the gift of the age of salvation into their own poor lives even here and now. But in this last petition he warns them against any false enthusiasm. Remember, you are engaged in the eschatological battle, watch out! We pray: "Dear Father, this one request grant us: preserve us from falling away from Thee." Matthew also understood this petition in this way when he added the petition: "And deliver us from the evil (One)."

The Lucan and Matthean versions of the Lord's Prayer do not conclude with a doxology. Only the Didache has a doxology, which we use today in the liturgy. Such a doxology is proper, for there is no biblical prayer that ends without some words of praise to God (cf. Harner, *Understanding the Lord's Prayer*, pp. 114-119).

Conclusion

The Lord's Prayer·must be seen in the context of Jesus' proclamation of the imminent Kingdom of God. The hallowing of God's name, the coming of the Kingdom, and the petitions of the bread of tomorrow and forgiveness, are all petitions that sound quite different when prayed in this context - which the Old Testament could not provide at all. It is the prayer of those who already experience the Kingdom of God becoming actualized in their present lives and who, in the power of the Kingdom present, cry out for its final consummation. They pray that what they now experience dimly may soon be theirs in all its fullness. Teresa of Avila commenting on the Lord's Prayer had this thought to offer:

> The sublimity and the perfection of this evangelical prayer is something for which we should give great praise to the Lord. So well composed by the good master was it, daughters, that each of us may use it in her own way. I am astonished when I consider that, in its few words, are enshrined all contemplation and perfection, so that if we study it, no other book seems necessary. For thus far in the Lord's Prayer, the Lord has taught us the whole method of prayer and of high contemplation from the very beginning of mental prayer to Quiet and Union (Basset, *Let's Start Praying Again*, pp. 51-52).

Clement of Alexandria has preserved a saying of Jesus which is not written in the Gospels. It says:

> Ask ye for the great things, so will God add to you the little things. You are praying falsely, says the Lord. Your prayers are always moving in a circle around your own small "I," your own needs and troubles and desires. Ask for the great things - for God's almighty glory and kingdom, and that God's great gifts, the bread of life and the endless mercy of God, may be granted to you -

even here, even now, already today. That does not mean that you may not bring your small personal needs before God, but they must not govern your prayer, for you are praying to your Father. He knows all. He knows what things his children have need of before they ask him, and he adds them to his great gifts. Jesus says: Ask ye for the great things, so God will grant you all the little things. The Lord's Prayer teaches us how to ask for the great things (Jeremias, *The Lord's Prayer*, p. 33).

OUR FATHER...

Our Father who are in heaven
   we are your people, the work of your hands,
   we praise your greatness,
   we celebrate your goodness,
   we remember the story of your love.

We pray that your Kingdom may come
   so that it may free us from fear and darkness.

We pray that your Kingdom may come
   so that it may heal our brokenness,
   and bring peace in your creation.

Give us wisdom to understand your will and your presence
   especially when we are hurt by the unexpected,
   when we are confused by what's happening to us,
   when we search for meaning in the midst of our losses,
   when we are trapped by our emotions.

Give us confidence to thank you for your daily gifts
   we so often take for granted:
   the gift of food that provides nourishment for our bodies,
   the gift of beauty that provides nourishment for our minds,
   the gift of love that provides nourishment for our spirits,
   the gift of faith that sustains us,
   the gift of friends that comforts us,
   the gift of every color in your creation that brightens our day.

Help us to forgive each other as you forgive us:
   you cleanse away our resistance
   and bring your light into our sleepy soul.

Help us to reach out to others,
   to become healing instruments in your world,
   to build bridges rather than walls in your creation. Amen.

Epilogue

After many years of labor, an inventor discovered the art of making fire. He took his tools to the snow-clad northern regions and initiated a tribe into the art and the advantage of making fire. The people became so absorbed in this novelty that it did not occur to them to thank the inventor who one day quietly slipped away. Being one of those rare human beings endowed with greatness, he had no desire to be remembered or revered; all he sought was the satisfaction of knowing that someone had benefitted from his discovery.

The next tribe he went to was just as eager to learn as the first. But the local priests, jealous of the stranger's hold on the people, had him assassinated. To ally any suspicion of the crime, they had a portrait of the **GREAT INVENTOR** enthroned upon the main altar of the temple and a liturgy designed so that his name would be revered and his memory kept alive. The greatest care was taken that not a single rubric of the liturgy was altered or omitted. The tools for making fire were enshrined within a casket and were said to bring healing to all who laid their hands on them with faith. The High Priest himself undertook the task of compiling a 'Life of the Inventor.' This became the **HOLY BOOK** in which his loving kindness was offered as an example for all to emulate; his glorious deeds were eulogized; his super-human nature was made an article of faith. The priests saw to it that the **BOOK** was handed down to future generations, while they authoritatively interpreted the meaning of his words and the significance of his holy life and death. And they ruthlessly punished with death or excommunication anyone who deviated from their doctrine. Caught up as they were in these religious tasks, the people completely forgot the art of making **FIRE**.

Selected Bibliography

Amaladoss, M.,   "New Faces of Mission", *UISG Bulletin,* 99 (1995), pp. 21-33

Arcodia, C.   *Stories for Sharing* (Australia: E. J. Dwyer, 1991)

Arnold, Fritz,   "Through Darkness to Light - Towards Mastering the Process of Secularization in the Spirit of Christian Mysticism", *UISG Bulletin* 103 (1997), pp. 17-32

Aurelio, John R.   *Fables for God's People* (New York: Crossroad, 1993)

Balling, Adalbert,   *Sehnsucht nach dem, was bleibt* (Freiburg: Herder, 1992)

Barclay, William,   *Beatitudes and the Lord's Prayer for Everyone* (New York: Harper & Row, 1963)

Barret, C. K.,   *The Holy Spirit and the Gospel Tradition* (London: SPCK, 1947; reprint 1958)

Barron, Frank,   *Short and Sweet* (Mount Merrion, Co. Dublin: The Columba Press, 1991)

Barry, William,   *God's Passionate Desire and our Response* (Notre Dame, Indiana: Ave Maria Press, 1993)

————————,   *Now Choose Life* (New York: Paulist Press, 1990)

————————,   *Paying Attention to God,* (Notre Dame, Indiana: Ave Maria Press, 1990)

Basset, *B.,*   *Let's Start Praying Again* (New York: Herder & Herder, 1972)

Bausch, William,   *Storytelling: Imagination and Faith (*Mystic, Connecticut: Twenty Third Publications, 1991)

————————,   *More Telling Stories* (Mystic, Connecticut: Twenty Third Publications, 1993)

Boff, Leonardo,   *Church Charism and Power*: *Liberation Theology and the Institutional Church* (London: SCM Press, 1985)

————————,   *Jesus Christ Liberator: A Critical Christology for our Time* (New York: Orbis Books, 1978)

———————-,   *The Lord's Prayer: The Prayer of Integral Liberation* (New York: Orbis Books, 1979)

Bonhoeffer, D.,   *Gesammelte Schriften*, vol. 3 (München: Kaiser Verlag, 1958)

Borg, Marcus. J.,   *Jesus: A Vision Spirit, Culture, and Life of Discipleship* (San Francisco: Harper & Row, 1987)

———————-,   *Meeting Jesus Again for the First Time* (San Francisco: Harper & Row, 1995)

Bours, Johannes,   "Die wehrlose Liebe," in *Wir leben, um zu lieben* (Freiburg: Herder Verlag, 1981)

Brackley, Dean   *Divine Revolution. Salvation & Liberation in Catholic Thought* (New York: Orbis Books, 1996)

Breemen, P. van,   *Let All God's Glory Through* (New York: Paulist Press, 1995)

Brueggemann, W.,   *Praying the Psalms*, (Winona, Minnesota: Saint Mary's Press 1982)

Brueggemann, W., Sharon Parks, & Thomas Groome,   *To Act Justly, Love Tenderly, Walk Humbly: An Agenda for Ministers* (New York: Paulist Press, 1986)

Bruners, Wilhelm,   *Schattenhymnus - Biblische Meditationen* (Düsseldorf: Patmos Verlag, 1989)

Casaldáliga, P. & Vigil, J. Maria,   *Political Holiness* (New York: Orbis Books, 1994)

Cavanaugh, Brian,   *Fresh Packet of Sower's Seeds - Third Planting* (New York: Paulist Press, 1994)

Chardin, Teilhard,   *The Heart of the Matter*, translated by René Hague (New York: Harcourt Brace Javanovich, 1978)

Chilton, Bruce & McDonald J. I. H.,   *Jesus and the Ethics of the Kingdom* (Cambridge: University Press, 1987)

Chilton, Bruce,   *Pure Kingdom: Jesus' Vision of God* (Grand Rapids Michigan: Eerdmans Publication Company, 1996)

Chittister, Joan,   *Winds of Change* (Kansas City: Sheed and Ward, 1986)

Cobb, John B. Jr.,   *Sustainability: Economics Ecology & Justice* (New York: Orbis Books, 1992

Congar, Yves,   *Lay People in the Church* (London: Bloomsbury Publishing, London, 1957)

Dines, Jenny   "Not to be served, but to serve: women as disciples in Mark's Gospel", *The Month,* (1993) pp. 438-442

Donders, Joseph   *Charged with the Spirit* (New York: Orbis Books, 1993)

——————,   *Beyond Jesus* (New York: Orbis Books, 1984)

Dowd, Michael,   *Earthspirit* (Mystic, Connecticut: Twenty-Third Publications, 1991)

Dulles, Avery,   *A Church to Believe In: Discipleship and the Dynamics of Freedom (*New York: Crossroads, 1982)

——————,   "The Church and the Kingdom" in A Church for all People, ed. Eugene LaVerdiere (Collegeville, Minnesota: The Liturgical Press, 1993) p.14.

——————,   "Vatican II and the Church's purpose", *Theology Digest* 32(1985) pp.344-345..

Dunn, James, D.   *Jesus' Call To Discipleship* (Cambridge: University Press, 1992)

——————,   "Spirit", *The New International Dictionary of New Testament Theology,* vol 3, edited by Colin Brown (Exeter: Paternoster Press, 1978), 693-707

——————,   *Jesus and the Spirit* (Philadelphia: Westminster Press, 1975)

——————,   "Spirit and Kingdom", *The Expository Times* 32 (1970-71), pp. 38-39

Dupont, Jaques,   "Blind Bartimaeus*"*, *Theological Digest,* 33 (1986), p. 224

Dupuis, Jaques,   "Religious plurality and the Christological debate" *Sedos* 15 (1995), pp. 2-3.

——————,   "Evangelization and Kingdom Values: The Church and the 'Others'," *Indian Missiological Review* 14 (1992), pp. 4-21

—————————, *"A Theological Commentary: Dialogue and Proclamation,"* in Burrows, William R., Redemption and Dialogue, Reading *Redemptoris Missio and Dialogue and Proclamation* (New York: Orbis Book, 1994)

Eichrodt, Walter,   *Theology of the Old Testament II* (Philadelphia: Westminster Press, 1967)

Elliott, Charles,   *Praying the Kingdom: Towards a Political Spirituality* (London: Darton, Longman and Todd, 1985)

Fuellenbach, John,   *Proclaiming His Kingdom* (Manila: Divine Word Publication, 1994)

—————————,   *The Kingdom of God* (New York: Orbis Books, 1995)

Fuerst, Wesley J.   "How Israel Conceived and Addressed God," *Our Naming of God*, edited by Carl E. Braaten (Minneapolis: Fortress Press, 1989)

Fung, Raymond,   *The Isaiah Vision (*Geneva: Risk Books Series, WCC Publications, 1992)

Furey, Robert,   *The Joy of Kindness* (New York: Crossroad, 1993)

Gaden, Janet & John,   "Women and Disipleship in the New Testament", *The Way* 26 (1986), pp. 113-123

Gallagher, Michael,   *Free To Believe* (London: Darton, Longman and Todd, 1987)

—————————,   *Where is Your God?* (London: Darton, Longman and Todd, 1991)

Gubler, Marie-L.,   "Luke's portrait of Mary", *Theology Digest* 36 (1989), pp. 19-24

Gutièrrez, Gustavo,   "Option for the Poor: Review and Challenges", *The Month* (January 1995), pp. 5-10.

—————————,   *We Drink from our Own Wells* (New York: Orbis Books, 1984)

—————————,   *The Power of the Poor in History* (London: SCM Press, 1983)

—————————,   "Finding our Way to talk about God," in *Interruption of the Third World,* ed. by F. Fabella & S. Torres (New York: Orbis Books, 1981)

Harner, Philip B.,   *Understanding the Lord's Prayer* (Philadelphia: Fortress Press, 1975)

Henn, William,   "The Church and the Kingdom of God" in *Studia missionalia 46* (1997) pp.119-147

Hendrickx, H.,   *A Key to the Gospel of Matthew* (Manila: Claretian Publications, 1992)

——————,   *Peace, Anyone? Biblical Reflection on Peace and Violence* (Manila: Claretian Publications, 1986)

Hillesum, Etty,   *An Interrupted Life* (New York: Washington Square Press, 1985)

Hoffsümmer, Willi,   *Geschichten sind wie kostbare Perlen* (Mainz: Matthias Grünewald Verlag, 1984)

——————,   *Kurzgeschichten Volume 1-5* (Mainz: Grünewald Verlag, 1995)

Horseley, Richard A.,   *Jesus and the Spiral of Violence: Popular Jewish Resistance in Roman Palestine* (San Francisco: Harper & Row, 1987)

Jacobi, Paul,   *Damit Unser Leben Gelingen Kann* (Mainz: Matthias Grünewald Verlag, 1990)

Jaschke, Helmut,   *Gott Vater? Wiederentdeckung eines zerstörten Symbols*, (Mainz: Grünewald Verlag, 1997)

Jeremias, Joachim,   *The Prayers of Jesus* (London: SCM Press, 1977)

——————,   *The Lord's Prayer in the Light of Recent Research* (London: SCM Press, 1977)

——————,   *New Testament Theology* (London: SCM Press, 1971)

John Paul II,   *Redemptoris Missio*: On the Permanent Validity of the Church's Missionary Mandate (Vatican City: Libreria Editrice Vaticana, 1991)

Johnson, Elizabeth,   *Consider Jesus* (New York: Crossroad, 1990)

——————,   *She Who Is* (New York: Crossroad, 1993)

Keating, Thomas,   *The Kingdom of God is Like...* (Middlegreen: St. Paul's Publications, 1993)

Knippenkötter, A.,   *Zum Leben Befreien* (Düsseldorf: Klens-Verlag, 1984)

Koch, R., "Spirit," *Encyclopedia of Biblical Theology: The complete Sacramentum Verbi*, edited by Johannes Bauer (New York: Crossroad, 1981)

Kreutz, Edgar M., "God in the New Testament," *Our Naming of God*, ed. by Carl E. Braaten

Kuzmic, Peter, "The Church and the Kingdom of God: A Theological Reflection," in *The Church: God's Agent for Change*, ed. Bruce J. Nicholls (Australia: Paternoster Press, 1986, pp. 49-81)

Ladd, George, *The Presence of the Future: A Revised and Updated Version of Jesus and the Kingdom* (Grand Rapids Michigan: Eerdmans Publication Company, 1974)

LaVerdiere, Eugene, ed., "The Church and the Kingdom" in *A Church for all People*, (Collegeville, Minnesota: The Liturgical Press, 1993)

Link, Mark, *Journey* (Valencia California: Tabor Publishing, 1988)

Lochman, Jan, *The Lord's Prayer*, William B. (Grand Rapids, Michigan: Eerdmans Publishing Company, 1990)

————, "Church and World in the Light of the Kingdom of God," in *Church Kingdom World: The Church as Mystery and Prophetic Sign*, ed. Limouris, Gennadios, Geneva: WCC Publications, Faith and Order Paper No. 130, 1986, pp. 58-72.

Lohfink, Gerhard, "The Exegetical Predicament concerning Jesus' Kingdom of God Proclamation," *Theology Digest* 36, 1989, pp.103-110

————, *Jesus and Community* (London: SPCK Fortress Press, 1985)

Maloney, George, *Broken But Loved* (New York, St. Paul's Publications, 1981)

McBrien, Richard, *Catholicism* (London: Geoffrey Chapman, 1981)

McKenna, Megan, *Parables* (New York: Orbis Books, 1994)

————, *Rites of Justice* (New York: Orbis Books, 1997)

Mello, Anthony de *One Minute Wisdom* (Gujarat Sahitya Prakas ANAND, 1985)

———————————, *One Minute Nonsense* (Gujarat Sahitya Prakas ANAND, 1992)

———————————, *The Prayer of the Frog*, vol 1, (Gujarat Sahitya Prakas ANAND, 1988)

———————————, *The Prayer of the Frog*, vol 2, (Gujarat Sahitya Prakas ANAND, 1989)

———————————, *The Song of the Bird,* (Gujarat Sahitya Prakas ANAND, 1982)

Mette, Norbert, "The Difficult Jesus, Problems of Discipleship", *Concilium* 1 (1997), pp.15-24

Metz, John, B., "For a Renewed Church before a New Council: A Concept in Four Theses," in *Towards Vatican III: The Work that Needs to Be Done,* ed. David Tracy, (New York: Seabury, 1978, p. 139)

———————————, *Followers of Christ* (London: Burns and Oates, 1978)

Moltmann, Jürgen, *Jesus Christ for Today's World,* (London: SCM Press, 1994)

———————————, "First the Kingdom of God," *Tripod* 11, May - June 1991, pp. 6-27

———————————, *The Crucified God: The Cross of Christ as the Foundation and Criticism of Christian Theology* (New York: Harper & Row, 1974)

Morley, Janet, *All Desires Known* (London: Morehouse Publishing, 1992)

———————————, *Bread of Tomorrow* (New York: Orbis Books, 1992)

Nolan, Albert, *Jesus Before Christianity* (New York: Orbis Books, 1988)

Nouwen, Henri, *Here and Now* (New York: Crossroad, 1994)

———————————, *Clowning in Rome* (Garden City, New York: Image Books, 1979)

Pable, Martin, *A Man and His God* (Notre Dame, Indiana: Ave Maria Press, 1988)

Pannenberg, W., "The Kingdom of God and the Church" in *Theology and the Kingdom of God* (Philadelphia: Westminster Press, Fifth printing, 1977)

Perrin, Norman,   *Rediscovering the Teaching of Jesus* (London: SCM Press, 1967)

Perry, Michael,   *Exploring the Evolution of the Lord's Supper in the New Testament* (Kansas City: Sheed & Ward, 1994)

Rad, G. von,   "Eirene," *Theological Dictionary of the New Testament,* vol, 2, ed. G. Kittel (Grand Rapids, Mich.: Eerdmans Publishing Company, 1964, pp. 402-403)

Rahner, Karl,   "Church and World" in K. Rahner et al. (eds.) *Sacramentum Mundi,* Vol.I, (London: Burns & Oates 1968, pp. 346-357)

Raja, R. J.,   "Follow me - Discipleship in the Synoptic Gospels", *Vidyajyoti* 56, 1992, pp. 513-533

Ricci, Carla,   *Mary Magdalene and Many Others, Women who followed Jesus,* (Burns & Oats and Fortress Press, Minneapolis 1994)

Rohr, Richard,   *Jesus' Plan for a New World* (Cincinatti, Ohio: St. Anthony Messenger Press, 1996)

Rupp, Joyce,   *May I have this Dance?* (Notre Dame, Indiana: Ave Maria Press, 1992)

Schechter, S.,   *Aspects of Rabbinic Theology* (New York: Schocken Books, 1961)

Schillebeeckx, E.   *Church: The Human Face of God* (New York: Crossroad, 1990)

Schnackenburg, R.,   *God's Rule and Kingdom* (New York: Herder and Herder, 1963)

Schneider, B.,   "Kata Pneuma agiosunes," *Biblica* 48 (1967) 359-387

Schoelles, Patricia,   "Liberation Theology and Discipleship: The Critical and Reforming Tendencies of Basic Christian Identity", *Louvain Studies* 19, 1994, pp. 46-64

Schweizer, E.,   *The Holy Spirit* (Philadelphia: Fortress Press, 1980)

Shea, John,   *The Hour of the Unexpected,* quoted in Mark Link, *Journey* (Valencia California: Tabor Publishing, 1988)

Sheldon R. I.	"Ideal, Pseudo-ideal, and the Evolution of Consciousness", p. 6 , *Dialogue & Alliance* 10 (1996) pp.3-25
Senior, Donald,	*The Passion of Jesus in the Gospel of John* (Collegeville: Liturgical Press, 1991), p.16
Snyder, Howard,	*Models of the Kingdom* (Nashville TN: Abigdom Press, 1991)
Soares-Prabhu, G.,	"Class in the Bible: The Biblical "Poor" A Social Class?" *Vidyajyoti* 49, (1985), pp. 322-346
——————,	"The Table Fellowship of Jesus. Its Significance for Dalit Christians in India today", *Jeevadhara* 22 (1992), pp. 140-159
Sobrino, Jon,	*Jesus Liberator* (New York: Orbis Books, 1993)
——————,	*Christology at the Crossroads* (New York: Orbis Books, 1978)
Song, C.S.,	*Jesus and the Reign of God* (Minneapolis: Fortress Press, 1993)
Soon Park Jae,	"Jesus' Table Community Movement in the Church" , *Asia Journal of Theology,* 7 (1993), pp. 60-83
Stendahl, Krister,	"Your Kingdom Come," *Cross Current* 32 (1982), pp. 257-262
Strolz, Walter,	"Fatherhood of God in Modern Interpretation," *The Lord's Prayer and Jewish Liturgy,* ed. by J. Petuchoswski and M. Brocke (London: Burns & Oates, 1978)
Sullivan, Francis	*The Church to Believe in (* New York: Paulist Press 1988) p.128 .
Swartley, W. S.,	"The Role of Women in Mark's Gospel", *Bibilcal Theological Bulletin* 27 (1997) pp.16-22)
Tappeiner, D. A.,	"Holy Spirit," *The International Standard Bible Encyclopedia*, vol. II, G. B. Bromiley, General Editor, fully revised (Grand Rapids, Michigan: W.B. Eerdmans Publishing Company, 1982)

The Prayers of Jesus in Their Contemporary Setting, published by The Study Center for Christian-Jewish Relations, 17, London: Chepstow Villas

Thich Nhat Hanh,   *Peace is Every Step* (New York: Bantam Books, 1991)

Turner, Max,   *The Holy Spirit and Spiritual Gifts Then and Now* (London: Paternoster Press, 1996)

Verkuyl, Johannes,   "The Biblical Notion of Kingdom: Test of Validity for Theology of Religion", in *The Good News of the Kingdom: Mission Theology for the Third Millennium,* Chr. Van Engen, Dean S. Gilliland, Paul Pierson, Editors (New York: Orbis Books, 1993, pp.71-81

Vermes, G.   *Jesus the Jew* (London: SCM Press, 1983)

Viviano B. T.,   *The Kingdom of God in History* (Wilmington, Delaware: Michael Glazier, 1988)

Wharton, P. J.,   *Stories and Parables for Preachers and Teachers* (New York: Paulist Press, 1986)

White, W. R   *Speaking in Stories* (Minneapolis: Augsburg Publ. House, 1982)

Wijngaards, John,   *My Galilee: My People Walking on Water* (London: Housetop Publication, 1990)

——————————,   Experiencing Jesus (Manila: Divine Word Publications, 1987)

Wilfred, Felix,   "Once again.. Church and Kingdom," *Vidyajyoti* 57 (1993), pp.6-24.